The Secularization of the Academy

RELIGION IN AMERICA SERIES
Harry S. Stout, General Editor

A PERFECT BABEL OF CONFUSION
Dutch Religion and English Culture in the Middle Colonies
Randall Balmer

THE PRESBYTERIAN CONTROVERSY
Fundamentalists, Modernists, and Moderates
Bradley J. Longfield

MORMONS AND THE BIBLE
The Place of the Latter-day Saints in American Religion
Philip L. Barlow

THE RUDE HAND OF INNOVATION
Religion and Social Order in Albany, New York 1652–1836
David G. Hackett

SEASONS OF GRACE
Colonial New England's Revival Tradition in Its British Context
Michael J. Crawford

THE MUSLIMS OF AMERICA
edited by Yvonne Yazbeck Haddad

THE PRISM OF PIETY
Catholick Congregational Clergy at the Beginning of the Enlightenment
John Corrigan

FEMALE PIETY IN PURITAN NEW ENGLAND
The Emergence of Religious Humanism
Amanda Porterfield

THE SECULARIZATION OF THE ACADEMY
edited by George M. Marsden and Bradley J. Longfield

The Secularization of the Academy

Edited by

GEORGE M. MARSDEN

BRADLEY J. LONGFIELD

New York   Oxford

OXFORD UNIVERSITY PRESS

1992

Oxford University Press

Oxford   New York   Toronto
Delhi   Bombay   Calcutta   Madras   Karachi
Petaling Jaya   Singapore   Hong Kong   Tokyo
Nairobi   Dar es Salaam   Cape Town
Melbourne   Auckland

and associated companies in
Berlin   Ibadan

Copyright © 1992 by Oxford University Press, Inc.

Published by Oxford University Press, Inc.
200 Madison Avenue, New York, NY 10016

Oxford is a registered trademark of Oxford University Press.

Library of Congress Cataloging-in-Publication Data
The Secularization of the academy
edited by George M. Marsden, Bradley J. Longfield.
p. cm.   (Religion in America series)
Includes bibliographical references.
ISBN 0-19-507351-7
ISBN 0-19-507352-5 (pbk)
1. Church and college—United States—History—Congresses.
2. Church colleges—United States—History—Congresses.
I. Marsden, George M., 1939-   .   II. Longfield, Bradley J.
III. Series: Religion in America series (Oxford University Press)
LC383.S43   1992   377′.8—dc20   91-18937

Chapter 1 was published in an earlier version in *First Things* 9 (January 1991) and is published
with the permission of the editors.

Chapter 7 was published earlier under the title "The Troubled Soul of the Academy: American
Learning and the Problem of Religious Studies," in *Religion and American Culture: A Journal
of Interpretation*, vol. 2, no. 1. It is reprinted with the permission of Indiana University Press.

Chapter 10 was originally presented in May 1990 at the Conference for Church-Related Colleges
in English-Speaking Canada at the University of Waterloo, Waterloo, Ontario, and is published
with the permission of the organizers of the conference.

1 3 5 7 9 8 6 4 2

Printed in the United States of America
on acid-free paper

Preface

The volume explores the history of the remarkable revolution from a little over a century ago, when Christianity was a leading force in higher education, to today, when at most it is tolerated as a peripheral enterprise and often is simply excluded. The essays arise from a coordinated effort to map some of the major contours of this largely unexplored topic. The focus of this study is on leading American universities since the late nineteenth century. The presumption is that such institutions, largely Protestant in origin, set the standards that other universities and colleges typically imitate. Both for comparative purposes and out of interest in the subjects in their own right, this analysis includes overviews of American Catholic, British, and Canadian universities. Obviously there are many other dimensions of the topic and other comparisons that remain to be explored. Nonetheless, the contributors to this volume offer what we hope will be an accessible overview of some of the most influential developments in Anglo-American culture.

We are deeply indebted to the Pew Charitable Trusts for their generous funding over the past several years, which has made this study possible. During that time the editors, joined by D. G. Hart for one year, have been the principal investigators in a larger project of which this book is one part. We then supplemented our own efforts by commissioning essays on additional topics, which were presented at a conference held at Duke University in June 1990.

Among our major debts are those to the remarkable group of scholars who participated in that conference. Their insights have expanded and refined the discussion. We are particularly grateful for the responses or other presentations of Michael Cavanaugh, Gerald Fogarty, S. J., Richard Wightman Fox, William R. Hutchison, Peter Kreeft, Bruce Kuklick, David Martin, Richard Mouw, Mark Noll, Mark Schwehn, Winton Solberg, and John F. Wilson. Lucie Marsden provided invaluable help in coordinating that conference and in preparing the index for this volume. We are also in debt to a corps of graduate students who have contributed significantly to the research on this project. These include Diana Butler, Philip Goff, Tony Jenkins, Paul Kemeny, Kathryn Long, Roger Robins, and Jeffrey Trexler. We wish also sincerely to thank the Divinity School of Duke University, especially Dean Dennis Campbell and Mrs. Clara Godwin, the chief financial officer, for their generous support throughout this project.

Durham, North Carolina   G. M. M.
November 1991   B. J. L.

Contents

Contributors

DAVID BEBBINGTON, Reader, Department of History, University of Stirling, Scotland, is the author of *Evangelicalism in Modern Britain: A History from the 1730s to the 1980s.*

PHILIP GLEASON, Professor of History, University of Notre Dame, is the author of *Keeping the Faith: American Catholicism Past and Present.*

D. G. HART, Director of the Institute for the Study of American Evangelicals at Wheaton College (IL), is the author of several articles on American Protestantism and is completing an intellectual biography of J. Gresham Machen.

BRADLEY J. LONGFIELD, Visiting Assistant Professor of American Christianity, The Divinity School, Duke University, is the author of *The Presbyterian Controversy: Fundamentalists, Modernists, and Moderates.*

ROBERT WOOD LYNN, former Senior Vice President for the Lilly Endowment, is Scholar-in-Residence at Bangor Theological Seminary.

FEORGE M. MARSDEN, Professor of the History of Christianity in America, The Divinity School, Duke University, is the author of

Fundamentalism and American Culture: The Shaping of Twentieth-Century Evangelicalism, 1870–1925.

G. A. RAWLYK, Professor of History, Queen's University, Canada, is the author of *Champions of the Truth: Fundamentalism, Modernism, and the Maritime Baptists.*

JAMES TURNER, Professor of History, University of Michigan, is the author of *Without God, Without Creed: The Origins of Unbelief in America.*

The Secularization of the Academy

Introduction

GEORGE M. MARSDEN

When Duke University was established in 1924, its founding bylaws stated: "The aims of Duke University are to assert a faith in the eternal union of knowledge and religion set forth in the teachings and character of Jesus Christ, the Son of God." The founders built a massive Gothic chapel at the center of the campus and next to it a well-endowed school of religion, which suggested the medieval pattern that placed theology alongside medicine and law as a preeminent professional faculty. Not until the 1960s did the new university give up required religion courses for undergraduates.

Duke was not unusual among American institutions of higher education of the era in any of these respects. In 1924 chapel attendance was still required for undergraduates at the nearby University of North Carolina in Chapel Hill, as it was at Yale and Princeton, and administrators spoke of the "Christian" character of their work. In 1939 nearly one-fourth of *state* universities and colleges still held at least voluntary chapel services, and most routinely subsidized campus religious activities.[1] A number of state schools gave credit for course work offered by denominational campus ministries.[2] Most of the leading private universities included divinity schools. New cathedral-like towers were the architectural centerpieces at the University of Chicago, Yale, and Princeton. Wellesley College, founded in the 1870s by friends of Dwight L. Moody, gave up its religion requirements at about the same time as did Duke.

3

Nationally, as late as the 1950s college-educated persons were somewhat more likely than other Americans to be active in religious groups (a trend that has since been dramatically reversed).[3]

Such positive relationships between Christianity and higher education in the twentieth century were residues of a much stronger connection that had lasted for the better part of a millennium. In the United States, for instance, until about 1870 the great majority of colleges had as their presidents clergymen who taught senior courses on Moral Philosophy that involved Christian apologetics and applications of Christian principles to many areas of life and thought. Protestant church colleges often served as virtual public institutions, and state colleges were dedicated to "non-sectarian" Protestantism. Although much about these colleges, including most of their classicist curricula, was secular, they also provided guarantees, through the presence of Christian faculty and by means of considerable coercion, of a strong Christian presence as well. Almost all had at least one required daily chapel service, and many required Sunday church attendance as well. Catholic and frankly sectarian schools typically had even more rigorous religious ties. In Western society higher education had long been under the aegis of the church, and the two domains had not yet been clearly differentiated.

That many educated people today are unaware that until so recently leading American schools promoted Christianity is one index of how secular the current scene has become. Winners get to write the histories first, so the histories of higher education generally have been as secular as the academy itself. Histories that deal with American colleges before 1870, of course, have to take religion into account, since its presence was so pervasive (although a few institutional histories have almost succeeded in ignoring its influence). While with respect to the rise of universities since 1870, as D. G. Hart's bibliographical essay in Chapter 11 shows, a few general works recognize the place of religion, many more in the vast literature of higher education ignore it. Strikingly few published studies provide a sustained focus on what has become of the religious dimensions of the modern university. Until now, no general history has been published on this subject.

Using the term *secularization* in the title of this volume is a risky business, since it is a word that, once mentioned, can easily lead to a morass of sociological debate. It is here meant to refer to something quite specific and descriptive. Our subject is the transformation from an era when organized Christianity and explicitly Christian ideals had a major role in the leading institutions of higher education to an era when they have almost none. As Chapter 1 indicates, this transformation was not a straightforward movement from the religious to the non-religious. Even though in the Protestant culture of the United States the rise of universities was associated with the lifting of church controls, it also involved a shift from a relatively narrowly defined Christianity to a broadly defined liberal Christianity that could be equated with civilization itself. This shift to liberal Protestantism can be seen not primarily as a secularization, strictly speaking, but as a sacralization of the entire enterprise of higher education. Only when the resulting Christian-liberal consensus was challenged by the realities of twentieth-century pluralism did the religious dimensions fade. With the 1960s attacks on liberalism itself, organized religious liberalism virtually abandoned the field of higher education.

Perhaps the greatest danger in using the term *secularization* is that people are likely to confuse its descriptive and its normative senses. Particularly if an author is at all critical of some of the results of secularization, readers are likely to jump to the conclusion that all secularization is being represented as a decline. Such a conclusion, if applied to the present volume, would be highly misleading. Rather, the authors recognize (if I may presume to speak for all of them) that in some respects the secularization of the academy has been a gain. So describing the processes by which that secularization took place does not imply a jeremiad. The Christian higher education of the era preceding our study had a great many faults that deserved to be corrected. If we had called the volume "The Disestablishment of Religion in the Academy," as we might just as well have done, the point would be more clear. None of us is for the re-establishment of religion in the public sector of the academy, although some would favor strengthening its role in church-controlled institutions.

Once this point is made—that we are not using *secularization* naively as equivalent to *decline*—it can be added that most of us see the change in the role of religion in modern higher education as *in some ways* a loss. The authors have differing views on the details. Nonetheless, we are addressing this topic in part because it describes processes that seem to have taken place without much plan or reflection so far as their impact on religion is concerned. Thus by calling attention to these developments, and implicitly or explicitly suggesting that they may not always have moved in optimal directions, we are inviting further discussion of these themes.

Recent debates about the fundamental nature of American universities may be particularly relevant to a reconsideration of the role of religion in higher education. For approximately the first century of the rise of American universities after the Civil War, most academics saw the disestablishment of religion in higher education as simply a liberation and hence a step toward the laudable triumph of science, free inquiry, and liberalism. Since about the 1960s, however, these ideals, inherited from the Enlightenment and nineteenth-century romanticism, have been under massive attack and often put to rout. But the pretenders who have claimed the field have been far more successful in criticism than in construction. They have thus left a moral vacuum that can be filled only by rhetoric and politics. So the modern university, which liberated itself from religious dogmas in order to become a haven for free inquiry, is in danger of becoming largely an arena for political debate based on appeals to dogmatic authority. At the same time, no authority is widely recognized.

The many critics of the resulting moral incoherence, particularly those following in the wake of Allan Bloom's book *The Closing of the American Mind*, have recognized the problem but have not offered realistic solutions. Typically the critics have proposed some version of a return to the Western tradition. While such a return has a prima facie case in its favor—since the universities are in fact located in the West and, like it or not, have to transmit selected dimensions of that heritage—wide acceptance even of this point is not likely as long as the defenders of the West do not take into account the force of the critics' attacks. In fact the critics have shown that the old Western liberalism, with its twin ideals of value-free scientific inquiry and the promotion of individual freedom, was based on a myth. In other words, the very principles that provided the moral rationale for shaping modern higher education have proved untenable. Inquiry is not generally value free, and there is no reason to continue to insist on supposedly value-free scientific methods as the model for all inquiry. Moreover, liberal universities were never as free from political, commercial, class, and gender interests as their rhetoric implied. Perhaps some of the liberal ideals can be salvaged on a pragmatic basis, as simply what might work best in this civilization; but if so, they will have to survive in chastened form.

The question this discussion raises with respect to religion is whether, given the wide recognition of the demise of the old Enlightenment-liberal ideals of value-free learning, there might not be room to reconstruct a place for religious perspectives as one option in higher education. Since the reasons for excluding religious perspectives in the first place have proven faulty, is there any way now to allow them? Certainly with respect to public or quasi-public institutions, it is fanciful to think about going back to Christianity, even of the most liberal sort, as providing the basis for a general moral consensus. The demands of justice in a pluralistic society preclude that. Yet, perhaps the recognition of the collapse of the old liberalism opens the way for the recognition that religious perspectives, if responsibly held and civilly presented, are as academically respectable as any other perspectives.

Such observations may be particularly meaningful for institutions that still have substantial religious connections. If it is true that religiously held perspectives are on the face of it no less responsible intellectually than are non-religious ones,[4] then it should no longer be true that religiously oriented institutions should be expected to abandon their religious perspectives in order to gain academic respectability.[5] Rather, one might expect that a truly pluralistic society would encourage faith-oriented higher learning as well as the various secular alternatives.

Notes

1. Merrimon Cuninggim, *The College Seeks Religion* (New Haven: Yale University Press, 1947), 167–82, 293–302.

2. Winton U. Solberg, "The Catholic Presence at the University of Illinois," *Catholic Historical Review* 76 (October 1990), 765–812, tells the remarkable story of how this practice survived to the present at the Newman Foundation at the University of Illinois, despite faculty opposition that had led Protestants to give it up twenty years earlier.

3. Robert Wuthnow, *The Restructuring of American Religion: Society and Faith since World War II* (Princeton: Princeton University Press, 1988), 158–64, 168–72.

4. See, for instance, Alvin Plantinga and Nicholas Wolterstorff, eds., *Faith and Rationality* (Notre Dame: University of Notre Dame Press, 1984), which discusses the theoretical basis for this claim.

5. On this theme, see Bradley J. Longfield and George M. Marsden, "Presbyterian Colleges in Twentieth-Century America," in *The Pluralistic Vision: Presbyterians and Mainstream Protestant Education and Leadership*, ed. Milton J Coalter, John M. Mulder, and Louis B. Weeks (Louisville: Westminster/John Knox Press, 1992).

1

The Soul of the American University:
A Historical Overview

GEORGE M. MARSDEN

> The secularization of the College is no violation of its motto,
> *"Christo et Ecclesiae."* For, as I interpret those sacred ideas,
> the cause of Christ and the Church is advanced by whatever
> liberalizes and enriches and enlarges the mind.[1]
>
> Frederic Henry Hedge, "University Reform:
> An address to the Alumni of Harvard, at Their
> Triennial Festival" (1866)

Our subject is one of those peculiar phenomena that are taken for granted in the contemporary world but that, from a historical perspective, are curious anomalies. The phenomenon is that the huge numbers of Protestants in the United States support almost no distinctively Christian program in higher education other than in the theological seminaries. Even though over 60 percent of Americans are church members and more than half of them are Protestants, and over 55 percent of the population generally say that religion is "very important" in their lives,[2] almost no one seems to think that religion is "very important" for higher education. Protestants in America are divided about evenly between evangelicals and moderate-liberals. Yet neither group supports any major universities that are Protestant in any interesting sense. Protestants do control a fair number of small liberal arts colleges. Those schools that are connected to mainline denominations tend to be influenced only vaguely by Christianity.[3] The evangelical colleges, more than a hundred of them, are more strongly Protestant, and some of these

9

are fairly good schools. But their total number of students is about the same as that of two state universities. There is almost no Protestant graduate education outside of seminaries.

From the point of view of the churches, it is especially puzzling that both the Protestant leadership and its constituencies have become so little interested in Christian higher education. When the clergy lament that the laity are uninformed, why do they not encourage Christian collegiate education? When the laity complain that the clergy are often poorly educated, why do they not support colleges and universities that would send some of their best men and women to divinity schools? When religious leaders deplore the spread of alien philosophies, why do they not take any serious interest in graduate education?

This situation is particularly striking in light of the long tradition of Protestant higher education. The Reformation began at a university with a scholar's insight,[4] and educational institutions long played a major role in Protestant success. Educated clergy, trained in interpreting authoritative texts, were essential to challenge Catholic authority and to forestall spiritual anarchy. For centuries in Protestant countries, including the Protestant colonies in America, the clergy typically were the best-educated persons in a town or village. In this country, until well into the nineteenth century higher education remained primarily a function of the church, as it always had been in Western civilization. Most educators were clergymen, and the profession of professor was not clearly differentiated from that of minister. The history of American higher education is not, of course, strictly Protestant. The Catholic experience in particular presents a significant alternative. Nonetheless, until recently Protestants and their heirs were overwhelmingly dominant in setting the standards for American universities. If these schools had a soul, in the sense of a prevailing vision or spirit, its lineage was Protestant.

Until the Civil War, the vast majority of American colleges were founded by churches, often with state or community tax support. Since higher education was usually thought of as a religious enterprise as well as a public service, it seemed natural for church and state to work hand in hand, even after the formal disestablishment of the churches. Protestant colleges were not only church colleges but also public institutions. Even the state colleges or universities that were founded after the American Revolution, sometimes with Jeffersonian disestablishmentarian intentions, had to assure their constituents that they would care for the religious welfare of their students. Almost all were or became broadly Protestant institutions, replete with required chapel and often with required church attendance on Sunday. As late as 1890 President James B. Angell of the University of Michigan, an enthusiastic promoter of Christianity on campus, reported that twenty-two of twenty-four state schools conducted chapel services, at twelve of which attendance was compulsory, and four still required church attendance as well. Most faculty were church members and were free to express their Christian perspectives in the classroom as long as they did so in "a reasonable and courteous way" and avoided "sectarian proselyting"[5] Angell spoke only of *state* schools. Church-related colleges and universities, which still typically had clergymen as presidents in 1890, could assume an even more explicitly Christian stance.

The peculiarity of the contemporary situation, then, is all the more striking, not only because Protestants have forsaken a long tradition of leadership in higher education but also because they have forsaken it so recently and forgotten it so completely. Vestiges of the old informal religious establishment persisted throughout the era following the Second World War, though typically in increasingly vague and peripheral ways. Then, in the heat of new cultural pressures since the 1960s, most of what was substantial in such religion quickly evaporated, often almost without a trace, and seldom with so much as a protest.

So the question is why a Protestant educational enterprise that had still been formidable until a century ago, and which until then had been a major component of the Protestant tradition, has been not just largely abandoned but abandoned voluntarily.

Or from the point of view of the universities, why has Christianity, which played a leading role in Western education until a century ago, now become not only entirely peripheral to higher education but has also often come to be considered absolutely alien to whatever is important to the enterprise?

Although if placed in a longer historical perspective such features of the current situation might seem puzzling, to most educated people today, including many religious people, they do not seem puzzling at all. Rather, it just seems obvious that university education must be secular, that it *ought* to be free from religiously informed influences. Academics themselves are often particularly zealous on this point, since they see it as a matter of academic freedom. When it comes to discussion of religious perspectives, they will still typically allude to an ideal of detached impartiality, despite many intellectual trends that question that ideal. University education and the intellectual inquiry associated with it, they typically believe, by its very nature excludes religiously informed points of view. To suggest anything else is academic heresy.

The question then has to do primarily with the definition of the modern university itself: Why has the university been constructed as a thoroughly secular enterprise?

To ask this question suggests a point of view critical of the thoroughgoing secularity of the modern university. Indeed, my own point of view is that of a more or less traditional Protestant who is convinced that Christian perspectives are academically viable, that they have in fact shown themselves to be intellectually responsible both throughout Christian history and in some Christian subcommunities today,[6] and that they deserve a place in the wider academic world as much as do other intellectually responsible perspectives. Just what that place might be is a question that can be reserved until the end of this essay, after I have surveyed how the modern university came to be defined in relation to religious perspectives.

It is important to underscore that criticizing American higher education as it is typically defined today is far different from arguing that there was a lost golden age to which we should return. The contrast with former eras does highlight some features of the situation today; but that does not imply that one should return to former practices. Those practices themselves were often faulty and in need of correction and have thus led to over-corrections that helped set the current patterns. For instance, the old colleges and their predecessors were part of a Christian establishment that provided Christianity with an unjustly privileged social and political position and attempted to promote the faith by associating it with power and coercion. Although these institutions had many good features as well, they needed to be disestablished. Moreover, the nineteenth-century American colleges also simply needed to be improved academically. Typically they were meager enterprises of at most a few hundred students, hardly comparable to the great universities they often fostered.[7] Whatever their virtues, they needed to be changed in substantial ways if they were to survive and serve in twentieth-century settings. Many of the Christian dimensions of the older institutions that were lost were part of trade-offs that seemed necessary to meet the demands of modernity.

So the story is not simply that of some bad or naive or foolish people who decided to abandon one of the most valuable aspects of the Protestant heritage. Rather, it is more a tale of some people who recognized serious problems in relating their heritage to the modern world. Whether the results were an improvement, or even coherent, is another question. Nonetheless, they were responding to some extraordinarily difficult dilemmas, and their choices often were confronted with unintended results.

What I propose in the present analysis is to emphasize three major categories of forces to which the leadership of emerging universities and their constituencies were responding: first, those having to do with the demands of a technological society; second, those having to do with ideological conflicts; and third, those having to do with pluralism and related cultural change. Our understanding of how the current soul of the American universities has been shaped by these forces can then provide a foundation for a consideration of where Christians and other religious people should go from here with regard to mainstream American higher education.

A Technological World

The old-time American colleges, which dominated the educational scene until after the Civil War, retained the outlines of the system of higher education that had prevailed in the Western world for seven centuries. Higher education simply meant expertise in the classics. Students had to show proficiency in Latin and Greek for admission, and they spent much of their time reciting classical authors. Some students might be only in their mid-teens, and their conduct was strictly regulated on the principle of in loco parentis. Much of their work and daily activities was supervised by a number of tutors, recent graduates usually preparing for the ministry. Professors, many of whom were also clergymen, taught a variety of subjects, although they might cultivate a specialty as well. Some natural science had been worked into the curriculum, as had small doses of modern subjects such as political economy. The capstone of the program was a senior course in Moral Philosophy, taught by the clergyman president. This course applied Christian principles to a wide variety of practical subjects and also was an apology for Christianity, typically based on Scottish common sense philosophy. It was also preparation for citizenship—a major goal of these colleges. They required twice-daily chapel, Bible study, and often church attendance, sometimes used to expose students to regular lectures in theology. These colleges had no real place for scholarship. Theological seminaries, new to America in the nineteenth century, provided the closest thing to any graduate or professional education. Theological reviews were the leading scholarly journals of mid-nineteenth-century America.

Two major forces combined to bring the collapse of this clerically controlled classicist education by the end of the nineteenth century. One was the demand for more practical and scientific subjects in the curriculum. This American ideal for education was institutionalized in the Morrill Land Grant Act of 1862, encouraging state schools oriented toward agricultural and technical education, which developed as alternatives to the liberal arts colleges.

The greater force bringing to an end the old classicist colleges was the demand that led to the establishment of universities and graduate education in the decades following the Civil War. Reformers correctly pointed out that for American civilization to compete in the modern world, it would have to produce scholars, and that the amateurism of clerically controlled classicism provided little room for scholarly specialization.

Clerical control of the colleges was thus identified with classicism and amateurism by modern standards. Inevitably the old-guard clergy defended the old system, which had helped secure their status as guardians of the classicist key to higher learning. Also this defense was inevitably intertwined with defending the Christian character of the old curriculum and of the tightly disciplined collegiate life.

The traditional Christianity of the old guard thus typically came to be cast as the opponent of educational openness, professional progress, and specialized scientific inquiry. Some of the opponents of traditional Christianity made the most of this sudden embarrassment of the old establishment. Andrew Dickson White, founding president of Cornell, for instance, published *A History of the Warfare of Science with Theology in Christendom* (1896), in which he projected into the past a supposed opposition of dogmatic Christianity to scientific progress. The enemy for White was not Christianity per se but theology, or traditional Christian dogmatism associated with clerical authority.

To reformers it seemed that colleges had to be freed from clerical control, and hence usually from traditional Christianity, in order to achieve something that we now take for granted—the emergence of higher education as a separate profession, distinct from the clergy. Until this time, although many educators were not clergy, the two roles were not clearly differentiated. Now collegiate education became a distinct profession. And, as was happening with other professions at this time, such as among doctors and lawyers, educators set standards that would control membership in the profession. Hence graduate education leading to the Ph.D. was instituted in the decades following the Civil War, and eventually the Ph.D. became the requirement for full membership in the profession.

Graduate education and accompanying research, which some reformers meant to be the real business of the universities, were free of the old collegiate structures and associated Christian controls. In an immensely important development that was almost uncontested, undergraduate education became the only part of the enterprise (other than divinity schools) in regard to which the question of specifically Christian influences was even being debated. Graduate and professional students were older and were thus exempted from forms of discipline such as mandatory chapel and church attendance. Moreover, the natural scientific model for research which dominated the new academic profession proclaimed, as we shall see, the irrelevance of religious belief.

Along with professionalization went specialization. By the 1890s higher educators had established professional societies in many of the basic fields, such as history, economics, sociology, psychology, and the natural sciences. Prestige in the profession now became dependent on narrowly specialized studies.

It is important to note that this professionalization itself was not inherently anti-Christian. It certainly was a significant step toward the secularization of American schools, but it did not necessarily grow out of ideological antagonism toward Christianity. That is, while it *happened* to be associated with some antagonism to more traditional Protestantism, which *happened* often to be associated with the old order, it was neither necessarily nor usually associated with antagonism toward Christianity per se. In fact, it often was promoted in the name of a broader, more open Christianity that was taking its cultural responsibilities more seriously.

This illustrates a key point regarding secularization in the United States. Much of it appeared in a form benign toward Christianity. Secularization in the modern world can be advanced in two major ways—methodologically and ideologically. (By secularization I simply mean the removal of some activity of life from substantive influences of traditional or organized religion.) I will consider ideological secularism later; but methodological secularization takes place when, in order to obtain greater scientific objectivity or to perform a technical task, one decides it is better to suspend religious beliefs. Courts of law generally follow this methodology. So do most persons engaged in scientific and technological activities. Most people, whether strongly religious or not, approve of such secularization in many cases. We do not want the pious mechanic of our car to tell us that there may be a devil in the carburetor. In the increasingly vast areas of our lives that are defined by technical activities, we expect religion to play, at most, an indirect role.[8]

Christians could therefore readily support many sorts of methodological secularization. Indeed, in the late nineteenth century the champions of professionalization and specialization in American higher education were overwhelmingly Christians—usually somewhat liberal but serious practicing Christians nonetheless.[9] For example, as D. G. Hart shows in Chapter 4, Daniel Coit Gilman, the founder of America's first research university, Johns Hopkins, in 1876, was not antagonistic to Christianity as is sometimes supposed. He was, in fact, a serious liberal Christian. So were the presidents who built the midwestern universities, as Bradley Longfield shows in Chapter 2.

Typically the liberal Protestants who constructed the new universities justified the scientific and technological definitions of many university activities on the grounds that such activities simply *were*

Christian. Thus, in 1887 Gilman explained to the Evangelical Alliance that churches in the modern era must recognize "that Science is the handmaid of Religion, that every effort made to extend the domain of human thought, and to interpret the plan of creation, is an effort to extend the reign of righteousness and truth."[10] Such sentiments were expressed by virtually every university administration of the era, as well as by many faculty. In their view what was going on was not a secularization except in the sense of gaining freedom from the control of the church. In other respects it was a christianization. At Harvard, where liberal Protestantism had a head start on the rest of the country, this sentiment was expressed with wonderful clarity by Professor Frederic Henry Hedge as early as 1866 in the quotation that serves as the epigraph for this chapter. Essentially, he declared, whatever Harvard does *is* Christian.

The generation of reformers who soon adopted this same wonderfully useful principle for schools around the country were predominantly New Englanders and Republicans who had come of age during the era of the Civil War and evangelical post-millennialism. They continued to hold liberal Christian versions of essentially post-millennialist ideals. That is, they believed in the divinely sanctioned progress of Christian civilization. This progress, as preeminently illustrated in the Civil War itself, would employ technological means to achieve moral ends. The new universities were engines designed to serve comparable goals. They would advance Christian civilization both materially and morally. They could help bring a unified higher civilization to the nation and eventually to the world. As Gilman said to the Evangelical Alliance," [T]he end in view—the ultimate end of all educational and scientific effort, as well as of all legislation and statesmanship—is identical with that at which Christianity aims . . . 'Peace on earth, good-will to men.'"[11]

One implication of this view was that science and the scientific method could be treated as sacred. As David Hollinger and others have shown, the proponents of the ideal frequently employed metaphors such as "the temple of science" with its "priests" and "worshipers."[12] "Freedom" served as the ideal that unified the moral ideals of civilization with the scientific. Among the most sacred principles was that science must be freed from dogma. Hence scientific institutions had to be freed from the churches just in order to better promote Christianity.

These ideals provided the perfect justification for what I call methodological secularization. Scientific activity, however narrow or technical, was a contribution to the kingdom. While proclaiming the unity of all truth, the evangelists for these ideals in fact justified a sharp division of labor. Specifically theological claims would have their own domain, which might supplement truths discovered by other means. Universities might even have divinity schools. The modern world, however, would be specialized, and theology would be just one specialty.[13]

Looking at the early developments of the Ph.D. program at Michigan, James Turner concludes that in America the scholar was *defined* as a specialist and hence as not having responsibility to address a broad public.[14] It is important to add that such a narrow definition implicit in the Ph.D. was initially palatable because it came during a transitional stage, lasting until around the First World War, in which scholars typically also had substantial religious affiliations and loyalties, or at least a strong religious background, which ensured that even the most technical activity served a higher ideal. Moreover, such scholars were usually ready to agree that science and scientific method, however sacred within the professions, was not *all* there was.

This two-storied division of labor between scientific technique and substantive religious perspectives, promoted in the name of the unity of all knowledge, helped foster the development of vast academic territories in which the ideal of free scientific inquiry would be the major operative standard.

One proof of how sweeping was this establishment of independent territories was that the ideal of academic freedom now emerged as the most sacred of all principles within the new academic professions. As the historian Richard Hofstadter has documented, the principle of academic freedom had relatively little place in American higher education prior to this century. Rather, as a matter of course American colleges were responsible to their boards of trustees, who typically represented outside interests, including religious interests.

Early in this century such outside control of academics was sharply challenged. The American Association of University Professors, founded in 1915, articulated this challenge. In its first statement of principles the AAUP declared that schools run by churches or by businesses as agencies for propagandizing a particular philosophy were free to do so, but that they should not pretend to be public institutions. Moreover, in addressing "the nature of the academic calling" (as, significantly, they still put it), they argued, "If education is the corner stone of the structure of society and if progressing in scientific knowledge is essential to civilization, few things can be more important than to enhance the dignity of the scholar's profession."[15] The sacred status of scientific knowledge and free inquiry was thus confirmed and to a large extent institutionalized.

The moral justification for professionalization and specialization also involved a service ideal which, after about 1890, often blended with the rising Social Gospel.[16] Woodrow Wilson, for example, well summarized the service ideal in his much-noted speech in 1896, "Princeton in the Nation's Service,"[17] which set the agenda when he became Princeton's first lay president in 1902. Wilson is an interesting case, because in the same speech he questioned the over-extension of the scientific ideal to all disciplines. His antidote, however, was more humane studies and more practical moral activity. So, while as president of Princeton Wilson avoided explicit statements about Christian theology that would appear in any way sectarian, he fervently preached morality and service. Again, as the university moved toward increasing professionalization under Wilson, the transition could be justified by additional and higher Christian moral ideals.

The economist Richard T. Ely is perhaps the outstanding example of the relationship between the Social Gospel of public service and the professionalization of academia. Ely was one of the principal organizers of the American Economics Association in 1886 and served as its first secretary. In the first report of the AEA Ely declared that "our work looks in the direction of practical Christianity," and he appealed to the churches as natural allies of the social scientists.[18] Such ideals brought pressures from another front for the more complete secularization of the social sciences. Business supporters of the University of Wisconsin, where Ely taught, brought him under fire in 1894 for his social Christianity and his pro-labor stance. Ely was exonerated and became a champion of academic freedom.

It was natural, then, that when the AAUP was founded in 1915, Ely should be one of the authors of its "General Declaration of Principles." In that declaration we also find a combination of a faith in independent scientific inquiry and the service ideal. In the organization's description of three major functions of the university, one is to "develop experts for various branches of the public service."[19] Even as the explicitly Christian ideals were perhaps beginning to fade for many Protestant scholars, scientific professionalism still could be justified by its ability to provide "experts" in "the public service." In this view there was nothing to worry about in the advance of independent scientific knowledge. It would still produce virtue.

The theme that ties together all the foregoing developments is that of the insatiable demands of an emerging industrialized technological society. More than anything else, what transformed the small colleges of the 1870s into the research universities of the 1920s[20] and then into the multiversities of the late twentieth century was money from industry and government for technical research and development. Universities became important in American life, as earlier colleges had not been, because they served the technological economy, training its experts and its supporting professionals, and conducting much of its research. At least as early as the Morrill Act of 1862, the demand for practicality had been re-shaping American higher education. Schools have continued to offer as an option a version of the liberal arts education they traditionally provided; but such concerns and the faculties supporting them have played steadily decreasing roles among the financial forces that drive the institutions. Ironically, while twentieth-century universities have prided themselves on becoming free of outside religious control, they have often replaced it with outside financial control from business and government, which buy technical benefits from universities and hence shape their agendas.[21] Any such technological and practical pressures can usually be justified, of course, by the higher cause of service to society, or at least by its profitability. So practical-minded Christians, especially those who rather uncritically regarded American government and business as more or less Christian enterprises, have readily supported such trends. For instance, they typically want their children to gain the economic and social benefits of such education. Nonetheless, the dominance of these technological forces have expanded the areas of higher education where Christianity would have no substantive impact and where many Americans see it as having almost no relevance.

Ideological

Although the pressures toward technical specialization helped push traditional Christian educational concerns to the periphery at the university, support for such methodological secularization came as often from Christians as non-Christians. Such methodological secularization, however, inevitably proved an important ally of ideological secularism. Christians who for methodological reasons thought that technical disciplines were best pursued without reference to religious faith promoted the same standards for those disciplines as secularists who believed that all of life was best lived without reference to religious faith.

For our immediate purposes it may be helpful to over-simplify a great deal by reducing to just three broad categories the ideological contenders for the soul of the American university over the past century and a quarter. First, there was traditionalist Protestantism, which was dominant at the beginning of the era but was easily routed by liberal Protestantism, sometimes aided by secularist ideology. Then, from about the 1870s until the 1960s came the dominance of a broadly liberal Protestantism, which allied itself with a growing ideological secularism to form a dominant cultural consensus. Since the 1960s we have seen the growth of a more aggressive pluralistic secularism that provides no check at all on the tendencies of the university to fragment into technical specialties.

From the 1870s to about the First World War, American college and university faculties included relatively few out-and-out secularists or religious skeptics. A few, however, were frankly proponents of an essentially Comtean positivism.[22] Comtean positivism proposed an evolutionary view of the development of human society in three stages. First there was an era of superstition or religious dominance. Then came an era of metaphysical ideals (which was something like the liberal Protestant era). Finally there was the promise of the triumph of enlightened science, which would free humanity from superstition and metaphysics and enable society to follow a higher, scientifically derived morality.[23]

By the 1920s such views were being more openly and widely expressed by academics, as is indicated by the influence during that era of John Dewey, who endorsed almost exactly the Comtean view. Such ideas could blend with those of liberal Protestantism because they too promised to liberate American society through science. Arthur J. Vidich and Stanford M. Lyman in their study *American Sociology* summarize this point in that field: "By the third decade of the twentieth century an antimetaphysical Comteanism was combined with statistical technique to shape a specifically American positivism which, activated as social technocracy, promised to deliver America from the problems that had been addressed by the old Social Gospel."[24]

Liberal Protestants and such post-Protestants were on the whole allied during this period. Both agreed that traditional Protestantism was intellectually reactionary, and within about only fifty years they effected a remarkable revolution that eliminated most traditional views from respectable academia. Both liberal Protestants and secularists used the prestige of evolutionary biology to discredit biblicism and to promote the virtues of a scientifically dominated worldview. Liberal Protestants and secularists furthermore agreed that the scientific age had brought with it higher-level moral principles that could form the basis for a consensus of values that would benefit all humanity.

Typically, they hoped to find a base for such values in the evolution of Western culture itself. The curricular expressions of this goal were English literature courses, which emerged by the turn of the century, and the invention of the Western Civilization and humanities courses. The Western Civilization course, which dated from the First World War era, was eventually adopted widely throughout the nation.[25] One might wonder why secularist positivists would be among those promoting the humanities. Yet we must remember that positivism always included the promise of a higher morality. Since in its historicist world view civilization itself was the only source of values, the study of the evolution of Western humanities was an important avenue toward this humane objective. Liberal Protestantism promoted a similar outlook, seeing God progressively revealed in the best in civilization.

Such curricular measures can also be seen as major efforts to stem the tide of technological and professional pressures on higher education. With classical requirements collapsing rapidly and formal religion having been pushed to the periphery, the high human achievement of the humanities could still provide coherence to the curriculum.[26]

The Second World War underscored the sense of the importance that education would pass on the best of Western values. The attacks on broadly Christian and liberal culture from Nazism and fascism on the right and Marxism on the left presented a major moral crisis. With traditional Christianity gone as a source for coherence, what else was there? The academic elite typically found the answer in the humane tradition of the West. This view is eloquently stated in *General Education in a Free Society*, the influential Harvard report of 1945. The Harvard committee members clearly recognized that "a supreme need of American education is for a unifying purpose and idea." Furthermore, they indicated frankly that "education in the great books can be looked at as a secular continuation of the spirit of Protestantism." As the Bible was to Protestantism, so were the great books the canon of the Western heritage that education should pass on. Such a heritage, they added (in a nice reiteration of the Whig tradition) is education for democracy, since it teaches the "dignity of man" and "the recognition of his duty to his fellow men." Scientific education is part of that heritage, fostering the "spiritual values of humanism" by teaching the habit of questioning arbitrary authority. These ideals may be seen as the last flowering of the Whig-Protestant ideal, which, as in the Harvard report, celebrated the harmonies of broadly Protestant and democratic culture.[27]

That the days were numbered when such elite educational values might set the standard is suggested by the strikingly different tone of the even more influential 1947 report of the President's Commission on Higher Education for Democracy. This report was a sort of manifesto for the era of mass education that began with the return of the war veterans, and it is much more indicative of the direction that higher education would take once it became essentially a consumer product, largely controlled by governments. In the next decades the vast expansion of higher education would take place overwhelmingly at state or municipal schools. Not only did this trend accelerate secularization, but it also strengthened the practical emphases in American education. So while the President's Commission, like the Harvard report, seeks coherence in a Western consensus, it finds it not in a great tradition but in a pragmatist stance that assumes current democratic values to be a norm. So the report has a thoroughly Deweyan ring to it. "A schooling better aware of its aims" can find "common objectives" in education. The consensus that will emerge embraces both practical education and general education; the goals of the latter are to "give the student the values, attitudes, and skills that will equip him to live rightly and well in a free society." These will be "means to a more abundant personal life and a stronger, freer social order."[28]

Whatever the substance of such ideals, the rise of mass education after the Second World War made it almost inevitable that the pragmatic approach would triumph over appeals to an elite heritage in the establishment of a secular consensus.[29] Nonetheless, through the Kennedy years the two approaches were able to grow side by side, sometimes within the same institutions. Humane liberal arts and practical approaches might be in competition, with the pragmatic gaining ground, yet most American educators at least agreed that there ought to be an integrative consensus of democratic values. By now the consensus was largely secular and most often defined by persons who were themselves secularists. Nonetheless, this was also an era of mainstream religious revival, and Christians, who were still numerically well represented on campuses,[30] seldom provided serious dissent from the search for democratic ideals. Since public consensus was the ideal, however, it was best to be low-key, entirely civil, and inclusive about one's faith. Although explicit Christians could play supporting or even mildly dissenting roles (Reinhold Niebuhr comes to mind), the essential ideals of society that higher education would promote were defined in secular terms and largely by secularists or by Christians who in academic settings thought they must speak as secularists.

Secularism as an ideology also received support from those who had less lofty reasons to abandon Christian standards. The revolution in sexual mores had an incalculable but certainly immense impact on weakening religious ideology and control. Established religion was associated with sexual repression. Changing national mores and opportunities presented by coeducation provided immediately compelling motives for one to ignore religious issues during one's college years. Of course, the more spiritually minded often circumvented these pressures with a species of methodological secularization. In any case, a history of changes in higher education no doubt could be written from the perspective of questions of sexuality alone. Probably a major chapter would have to be devoted to the role of sororities and fraternities, which sometimes have been powerful centers for secular lifestyles.

Cultural Pluralism

The chief factor that forced Christianity into such a minor role in responding to all of these challenges was that they coincided with the vexing problem of dealing with pluralism in modern society.

The Catch-22 of Christianity and public policy in a society that is ethnically and religiously diverse is that if Christianity is to have a voice in shaping public philosophy, it seems that equity demands that it do so in a way that gives its voice no special weight. Public justice appears to demand of Christians that they receive no special privilege but rather provide equal opportunity for all views. In a land where Christians have been culturally dominant and are still the majority, achieving such public equity seems almost to require that Christianity be discriminated against, which amounts to eliminating altogether its voice in shaping public policy. Liberal Christians in particular, who defined their mission largely in public terms and made equity a pre-eminent concern, could get caught in stances that would put themselves out of business.[31]

This dilemma is well illustrated in Protestant institutions of higher learning, which, as we have seen, typically aspired to be public institutions as well as church institutions, pursuing the laudable goal of serving the general public as well as their own people.

The dilemma was not apparent, however, as long as Protestant cultural dominance was presumed. Provided it could be taken for granted that Protestantism was culturally dominant or that it ought to be dominant, the goal of church-related institutions was to shape the whole society according to Protestant standards. This did not just mean that ideally Catholics and others ought to be converted to Protestantism; it also came to mean that all Americans should adopt the set of cultural ideals that Protestants claimed. These ideals were classically expressed, for instance, in the Whig tradition of the mid-nineteenth century. Perpetuating some American revolutionary rhetoric that had its roots in the Puritan revolution in England, Protestants associated political and intellectual freedom with dissenting Protestantism and monarchism, tyranny, and superstition with Catholicism. The Protestant-Whig ideals included affirmations of scientific free inquiry, political freedom, and individualistic moral standards such as hard work. Nineteenth-century college courses in Moral Philosophy were part of the effort to set such non-sectarian Protestant standards for the nation.

By the end of the nineteenth century, however, non-sectarianism was beginning to have to be defined to include more than just varieties of Protestantism. Exclusivist Protestant aspects of the outlook were becoming an embarrassment in a more diverse society. State schools felt the pressures first, but very soon so did any schools, especially prestigious schools, that hoped to serve the whole society. In the decades from the 1880s until the First World War, such schools rapidly moved away from most of their substantive connections with their church or religious heritages, dropping courses with explicit theological or biblical reference and laicizing their boards, faculties, and administrations.

At the beginning of the period one way of demonstrating that a nationally oriented school was non-sectarian was to have no formal creedal test for faculty. Major older schools, however, were still often hiring their own alumni, and old-boy networks could informally ensure some sympathy for religious traditions. Old-time college presidents also had substantial discretionary powers in hiring and could select persons of "good character." By about the end of the century, however, such informal faculty screening for religious views was breaking down, although there was still some discrimination against Catholics and especially against Jews. Any man of Protestant heritage, however, could gain a position regardless of his religious views or lack thereof. Once this happened, it was only a matter of time before religious connections were dismantled.

How rapidly or how thoroughly this disestablishment took place depended, as I have been suggesting, on how public the institution was. Catholic schools and smaller sectarian colleges could retain exclusivist aspects of their heritage much longer. Everyone knew that if they went to Notre Dame or Concordia College, they were going to a church school with church standards. Some mainline colleges, such as Westminster, Bucknell, or Davidson (if southerners could be considered mainline), were able to maintain a primarily church-related identity during the first half of the twentieth century, as long as they were willing to remain small and somewhat modest. But what of Chicago, Yale, or Princeton, which aspired to be major culture-shaping institutions? Was there any way they could remain substantially Christian?

Again, liberal Protestantism, which dominated most major American colleges and universities in this era, offered a solution. Essentially this solution amounted to a broadening of the old Whig heritage. The white Protestant cultural establishment could retain its hegemony if the religious heritage were so broadly defined as to be open to all opinions, at least all liberal opinions. As we have already seen, liberal Protestantism's two-level approach to truth allowed the sciences and the professions to define what was actually taught at universities, to which higher religious and moral truths could be added as an option.

To respond to pluralism and to retain hegemony, the specifically religious dimensions of Protestantism had to be redefined. By the early decades of the century, exclusivist elements of the heritage had been abandoned, and Christianity was defined more or less as a moral outlook. It promoted good character and democratic principles, aspects of the old Whig ideals that were potentially palatable to all Americans. So prestigious universities, virtually all administered by men of Protestant heritage, could continue to promote the melting-pot ideal of assimilation of all Americans in a broad moral and political consensus.

Even this solution presented some problems. The best example is the acceptance of Jewish students and faculty. Jewish immigration increased dramatically in the decades around the turn of the century, and the number of university applications from Jews increased even more. By the 1920s, despite some protests, most of America's prestigious schools had set up quotas for Jewish students, often of around 15 percent. Sometimes they still cited the "Christian" ethos that they were preserving, even though Christian teaching as such had disappeared. In many leading American schools Jewish faculty were discriminated against or excluded outright, especially in the humanities, until after the Second World War.[32]

This example points out the problem. If one is heading up a culturally leading institution, can one legitimately discriminate in any way against people of other religions? Especially after the war and the Holocaust, such dilemmas became acute for American educators of Protestant heritage. The Whig-democratic ideals they had long proclaimed after all included the principles of equity and integration of all peoples which cultural outsiders were now claiming.

By this point the solution to the puzzle with which I began should be becoming apparent. Why is it that Protestants have voluntarily abandoned their vast educational enterprise and are even embarrassed to acknowledge that they ever ran such a thing? The answer is that, on the one hand, they were confronted with vast cultural trends, such as technological advance, professionalization, and secularism, which they could not control; but, on the other hand, the combination of the pressures of cultural pluralism and Christian ethical principles made it awkward if not impossible to take any decisive stand against the secularizing trends.

Although recognition of principles of equity were involved, perhaps I should not make the decisions involved sound so exclusively high-minded. Another way of describing what happened was that eventually the constituencies of the schools, whether faculty, students, alumni, or other financial supporters, would not stand for any Protestant exclusivism. Such groups combined principles of tolerance with the self-interest of those in broadening constituencies who were not seriously Protestant. The most formidable such direct outside pressure came, for instance, from the Carnegie Foundation early in this century when it was setting up a college retirement fund, which eventually became TIAA/CREF. Initially the foundation made it a condition that colleges participating in the program be non-sectarian. Other business contributors, as well as state legislatures, made similar demands. Administrators, who have been said to be able to resist any temptation but money,[33] therefore also had a good deal of self-interest in recognizing the values of pluralism and total disestablishment. Nonetheless, even if self-interest served mightily to clarify principle, disestablishment seemed from almost any Christian perspective the right thing to do.

One important encouragement to such disestablishment was that it could be justified on the grounds that voluntary religion was more healthy than coerced religion anyway. This was a strong argument that could be raised against required chapel, and almost invariably schools went through a transitional era of voluntary chapel, which would flourish for a time. Moreover, during the decades around the turn of the century, when formal disestablishment was taking place at the fastest rate, voluntary Christianity on campuses was probably at its most vigorous ever. College administrations often encouraged YMCAs and YWCAs, which were then somewhat like the Inter-Varsity Christian Fellowship is today. Students of the era helped organize the Student Volunteer Movement, under the initial sponsorship of Dwight L. Moody, and spearheaded the massive American foreign missionary efforts that reached their peak around the First World War. Administrations also often encouraged Protestant denominational, Catholic, and Jewish campus religious groups, which also supported the voluntary exercise of religion. As long as such activities, however peripheral to the main business of universities, were available to the minority of students who might be interested, and as long as the religious programs were modestly flourishing, as they were through the 1950s, disestablishment could be seen as a plausible trade-off, in which the locus of religious activity had moved from the center to the voluntary periphery.

This solution also fit the widely held view that science, which provided the ultimate guidelines for intellectual inquiry, and theology could operate in separate but complementary spheres. The division of labor between universities and theological seminaries, where professional religious training was still available, institutionalized the same principle. At some private universities this differentiation was instantiated by the continuance of divinity schools, which made other disestablishment of Christianity at those institutions seem less threatening.

Despite all the good and compelling reasons for not resisting disestablishment, something seems wrong with the result, if viewed from a Christian perspective or in terms of the interests of Protestant churches and their constituencies. The result that today Christianity has only a vestigial voice at the periphery of these vast culture-shaping institutions, together with its implications for the future of the churches described at the beginning of this chapter, seems a curious and unfortunate one from such perspectives.

One must ask, then, how it is that if Protestant leaders in higher education generally made the right or at least virtually inevitable decisions, what has gone so wrong that the outcome should be so adverse to the apparent interests of Protestant Christianity?

I think the answer lies in some assumptions deeply embedded in the dominant American national culture which Protestantism had so much to do with shaping. These are simply the assumptions, already alluded to, that there should be a unified national culture in which Protestant religion ought to play a major supportive part. At the time of the original British settlements in the seventeenth century, Christianity was presumed to provide the major basis for cultural unity. In the eighteenth century, when the colonies formed into a nation, Enlightenment ideals offered a less controversial scientific basis for a common culture, but Protestantism played a significant supporting role, especially when it could be non-sectarian.

Given so attractive a goal as a unified national culture, it was natural that the way in which dominant American Protestants would deal with cultural diversity was to attempt to absorb it. This was, in a sense, what the Civil War was about—a painful episode that illustrates both the virtues and the dilemmas of seeking nationally unified moral standards. In the next century, as ethnic and religious diversity became massive and impossible to ignore, the ideal became more vaguely Christian or Judeo-Christian and simply was referred to as "democratic." Through the Kennedy era, however, the ideal remained consensus and integration. The civil rights campaign and efforts to integrate blacks into the mainstream seemed to underscore the moral correctness of this strategy.

The intellectual counterpart to this strategy was the belief, supported by the assumptions of the Enlightenment, that science provides a basis for all right-thinking people to think alike. This view was especially influential in the United States, since Enlightenment thought had so much to do with defining national identity. While there might be disagreement as to whether Christianity was integrative or divisive, scientific method was supposed to find objective moral principles valid for the whole race. Dominant Christian groups joined in partnership with science in underwriting this integrative cultural outlook. By the twentieth century, as traditional Christianity appeared too divisive to be an acceptable public religion and liberal Christianity began to drift into a dotage of moralism, scientific method emerged as the senior partner in the integrative project of establishing a unified national culture.

For American education this meant that it continued to be assumed that a proper educational institution ought to be based on an integrative philosophy. There was, of course, some internal debate as to what that philosophy should be or how it should be arrived at, but as long as proponents could claim something of the sanction of the scientific heritage, they could present their outlooks not as one ideology among many but as ones that were fair to everyone, since they were objective, or a least more or less so.

As attractive as all this might have been, and as necessary as it might be to cultivate some common culture, there were several things wrong with the universalist assumptions on which these integrative ideals were based. First, they were socially illusory, since America was not just one culture but a federation of many. Second, the universalist views were intellectually problematic. Not all right-thinking people thought the way white Protestants did, and there was also no universal objective science that all people shared. Rather, science itself took place within frameworks of pre-theoretical assumptions, including religiously based assumptions. Finally, as attractive and plausible as pursuit of this integrative cultural enterprise was, it was not an enterprise to which Christians could forever fully commit themselves if they wanted to retain their identity as Christians. Christianity, whatever else it is, is not the same as American culture, and hence it cannot be co-extensive with its public institutions. As we have seen, liberal Protestants during the first half of the twentieth century dealt with this problem not by sharpening their identity over against the culture, as did fundamentalist and Catholic intellectuals, but rather by blurring their identities so that there was little to distinguish them from other respectable Americans. Hence, until the 1960s they could continue to control America's most distinguished academic institutions. Only if there had been a strong sense of tension between Christianity and the integrative American culture—a tension that was only embryonically suggested by neo-orthodoxy, and never substantially applied to challenge the idea of a culturally integrative science—

might there have been a search for radical alternatives. But a strong sense of such tensions was not a part of liberal Protestantism.

Collapse and Confusion

This analysis of the problematic assumptions of dominant American culture and religion should help us understand and evaluate what has happened to universities since the 1960s and the demise of the old liberal Protestant establishment. Especially intriguing is the paradoxical character of the major contenders to fill its place.

By the mid-1960s two things were happening to destroy the secularized liberal Protestant (or now secularized Judeo-Christian) Enlightenment consensus through a sort of pincers action. First, there was the triumph of mass education with its ideal of practicality. I need not detail this; but it clearly tended to destroy any real consensus in the universities, substituting for it a host of competing practical objectives. Such trends were reinforced by the ever-increasing percentages of university budgets drawn from government and business research grants, which kept the center of gravity away from the humanities. The more universities promote technical skills, the more they fragment into sub-disciplines. Such tendencies are reinforced by the ongoing impetus of professionalism. For faculty, loyalty to one's profession overwhelms any loyalty to one's current institution. The research necessary for professional advancement often subverts interest in teaching. Many observers have commented on these trends.

Second, at the very same time came an attack on the other flank from the counter-culture questioning the whole ideal of a democratic consensus and of the moral superiority of the now secularized American way of life. Part and parcel of this attack was the critique of "the myth of objective consciousness," which pointed out the links among the establishment's claims to authority, its susceptibility to give in to de-personalizing technological forces, and its Enlightenment heritage of scientific authority.

By this time, the old establishment had very little basis for answering such challenges. It had long since given up any theological justification for its views, and the claims to scientific authority were already weakened by the many internal critiques of the myth of objectivity. Moreover, in practical terms scientific authority pointed in too many mutually exclusive directions to be of much use. The establishment's most plausible defense seemed to be its appeal to self-evident moral principles shared throughout the culture. Now, however, the high moral ground of liberty, justice, and openness had been stolen by those who interpreted the terms in a decidedly more radical way.

The result was that the old liberal (and vestigially liberal Protestant) consensus ideal collapsed.[34] Although it persists especially among the older generation, its leadership has been largely displaced by the two forces that challenged it. On the one hand, there is the increasing growth of practical disciplines and sub-disciplines that do not concern themselves with the big questions but rather engage in technical research or teach technical skills. This may be seen as the triumph of methodological secularization, a force that has long threatened to take over the universities and the culture and now is largely unchecked by a competing humanities ideology.

And on the other hand, attempting to fill the ideological vacuum left by the decline of the old liberal-Protestant consensus is an aggressive pluralistic secularism, growing out of the 1960s and flourishing as the students of the 1960s have become the tenured scholars of the 1980s and 1990s. In the name of equality and the rights of women and minorities, this faction questions all beliefs as mere social constructions, challenges what is left of the old consensus ideology, attacks the Western-oriented canon, and repudiates many conventional ethical assumptions.

Religion in the Universities

In the context of all these forces, we can understand the formal role left for religion in universities. Despite the presence of many religion departments and a few university divinity schools, religion has moved from near the center a century or so ago to the incidental periphery. Apart from voluntary student religious groups, religion in most universities is about as important as the baseball team.

Not only has religion become peripheral, but also there is a definite bias against any perceptible religiously informed perspectives getting a hearing in the university classroom. Despite the claims of the contemporary universities to stand above all for openness, tolerance, academic freedom, and equal rights, viewpoints that are based on discernibly religious concepts (for instance, that there is a created moral order or that divine truths might be revealed in a sacred Scripture) are often informally or explicitly excluded from classrooms. Especially offensive, it seems, would be any traditional Christian versions of such teachings, other than some Christian ethical teachings, such as a special concern for the poor, which are already widely shared in the academic culture.

Conservative Christians often blame this state of affairs on a secular humanist conspiracy; but the foregoing analysis suggests that such an explanation is simplistic. Although self-conscious secularism is a significant force in academic communities, its strength has been vastly amplified by the convergence of all the other forces I have mentioned. Liberal Protestantism opposed traditional Christian exclusivism and helped rule it out of bounds. Methodological secularization provided a non-controversial rationale for such a move, reinforced by beliefs concerning the universal dictates of science. Concerns about pluralism and justice supplied a moral rationale. Moreover, to all these forces can be added one I have not discussed separately (though it may deserve a section of its own), the widely held popular belief, sometimes suggested in the courts but not yet consistently applied, that government funding excludes any religious teaching. With an estimated 80 percent of students today attending government-sponsored schools,[35] this force alone is formidable.

We can see more specifically how religiously informed perspectives have fared in the university if we look briefly at the development of the actual teaching of religion in twentieth-century university curricula.[36] During the era of liberal Protestant hegemony it became apparent that the forces of secularization had left a gap in which religion was not represented in the curriculum at all. To counter this, a movement was successfully launched between the world wars to add courses in religion, some Bible chairs, some religion departments, and a few schools of religion even at state institutions. These were originally designed not only to teach about religion but also to train religious leaders and, at least implicitly, to promote religious faith. At state schools, at least, efforts were made to represent Catholicism and Judaism as well as liberal Protestantism.

Such efforts were not always academically strong and did not have a major impact on university education. Nonetheless, they were substantial enough for Merrimon Cuninggim to conclude in a study conducted on the eve of the Second World War, "Religion is moving once more into a central place in higher education."[37] Moreover, the war brought religious revival and widespread concern about the moral and religious basis of Western civilization and so enhanced the role of religion in the undergraduate curriculum. The revival and the prominence especially of some broadly neo-orthodox scholars also increased the prestige of university divinity schools, which had long been educating ministers and now were beginning to be seen as significant centers for graduate education in religion. Religion during this era was considered largely an ethical concern, and hence one of the humanities. Its place in the university was justified by its contribution to helping define the moral mission of the university in modern civilization.

By the end of the 1960s, however, the character of religious studies in the universities had begun to change rapidly.[38] The number of religion departments was increasing so dramatically that by the 1970s almost every university had one. The rationale for them now, however, had largely shifted from the view of religion as one of the humanities with a moral purpose to its being considered one of the social sciences. Correspondingly, religion departments were hiring fewer persons with clerical training and larger numbers with scientific credentials. Practitioners of religious studies who flooded sessions of the American Academy of Religion now often had their own technical language, which served to legitimate its status as a science. Ironically such developments came just as claims to any universal science were going out of style, once again giving religion a problematic character as a discipline.

Nonetheless, the new studies of the history of religions fit in well with the growing enthusiasm for pluralism in the universities. Religion departments increasingly could gain legitimacy by being oriented toward the non-Western, the non-conventional, and the (descriptively) non-Christian.

Such developments also provided an impetus for the growing popularity of a normatively non-Christian stance among teachers of religious studies. Here I have to rely on impressionistic evidence and do not want to attribute larger trends simply to a secularist conspiracy. Nevertheless, my impression is that considerable numbers of instructors in religious studies programs were once traditionally religious themselves but have since lost that faith. Like most teachers, they hope that their students will come to think as they do, so a goal in their teaching becomes, in effect, to undermine the traditional religious faith of their students. In this pursuit they are aided by methodological secularization, which demands a detachment from all beliefs except belief in the validity of the scientific method itself. So a history-of-religions approach that suggests that the only valid way to view religions is as social constructs intentionally or unintentionally undermines belief in any particular religion as having divine origins. Of course, such a negative impact of religious studies on religious faith is mitigated by the fact that many persons in religious studies have entered the field as an extension of their religious calling, and their more positive perspectives are apparent despite pressures not to reveal any explicit religious commitment.

Those who oppose any visible commitment, however, hold the upper hand, whether because of lingering beliefs in scientific objectivity, concerns over pluralism, or alleged legal restrictions. I have even heard the suggestion that no person who believes a particular religion should be allowed to teach about it. Although this proposal is not, I think, anyone's actual policy, one cannot imagine its even being suggested about women's studies or African-American studies. It is almost like saying that no musicians should teach at a music school. And I doubt whether this rule would be proposed regarding a Hindu or a Buddhist. The more common rule, of course, is that in a classroom all evidence of belief must be suppressed, which in effect means that operative interpretive perspectives of believers must be kept hidden from students. Again, this rule is most consistently applied regarding traditional Protestant or traditional Catholic belief. Liberal Protestants may still be advocates if their religious expressions are largely confined to an ethic of political progressivism. Non-theists may openly express their views concerning theism.

Part of the problem, of course, is that in the field of religion we are still dealing with the vestiges of a cultural establishment. Hence it is to some extent understandable that any Christianity that implies some exclusivism should come in for special attack, since it has so long been used to support special privilege.

In any case the presence of religion programs in universities is, on balance, not a countervailing force to the secularization of universities that I have described. It is especially ironic that their presence is sometimes used to assure pious legislators or trustees that religion is not being neglected at their universities. It is not neglected, but its unique perspectives, especially those of traditional Christianity, are often excluded and even ridiculed.

Prescription

So what attitude should those of us who are seriously Christian in academically unpopular ways take toward contemporary university education? Should we attempt to have our distinct intellectual perspectives heard, or must we simply concede to overwhelming trends, perhaps living off the residual capital of the old establishment at university divinity schools? (These too, I might add, especially those that try in some way to be distinctly Christian, are looking increasingly anomalous in this overall picture.)

It seems apparent to me that we could not go back to the days of a Christian consensus, liberal or conservative, even if we wanted to. Realistically there is no way to re-establish in public and prestigious private universities anything like a broad Judeo-Christian moral consensus. At least we could not call it that. Reactions against its identification with Western culture are too strong. Moreover, religious conservatives and liberals have insurmountable disagreements as to what that consensus is.

So what alternative is there other than to continue going about doing our jobs and allowing the trends that have been building for the past century to run their course? How long will it take for distinctive Christian perspectives, other than those provided by voluntary campus organizations, to disappear entirely from America's leading universities?

It would take another major essay to propose adequate alternatives. Nonetheless, it is worth pointing out that two major strategies are available. These may be complementary rather than mutually exclusive.

The first is for seriously religious people to begin to campaign actively for universities to apply their professions of pluralism more consistently.

We can clarify this proposal if we first note a revealing feature of some of the post-1960s university pluralism. On the one hand, one of the most conventional ideas that leading campus pluralists proclaim is that all moral judgments are relative to particular groups, while on the other hand, many of these same people insist that within the university their own moral judgments should be normative for all.[39] In a sense, what is happening is that the post-1960s, post-modernist generation that is so influential in contemporary academia is falling into the same roles that were played by the old white Protestant male establishment. Despite their rhetoric of pluralism and their de-constructionist ideologies, many in practice act as though they held Englightenment-like self-evident universal moral principles. Just like the old champions of liberal consensus, they want to eliminate from academia those who do not broadly share their outlook. In fact, their fundamental premise that all truth claims are socially constructed is not far from that of old-style liberal pragmatists. Like the pragmatists, who also thought they were attacking the Enlightenment, they in practice need to presume a more universal moral standard in order to operate. For old-style pragmatist liberals such often unacknowledged standards were the principles of modern Western democracy. The post-moderns substitute a more broadly inclusivist world-oriented moral absolutism.

This first proposal would be to try to eliminate this anomaly. It seems to me that, as far as public policy is concerned, some version of pragmatic pluralism is indeed the only live option. It is deeply ingrained in the American tradition, and it is difficult to envision a viable alternative. My only proviso is that it ought to be challenged to be more consistently pragmatic and pluralistic. If public places such as our major universities are going to operate on the premise that moral judgments are relative to communities, then we should follow the implications of that premise as consistently as we can and not absolutize one or perhaps a few sets of opinions and exclude all others. In other words, our pluralism should attempt to be more consistently inclusive, embracing even traditional Christian views.

This suggestion for a broader pluralism does not mean that it was a mistake for those who have managed our universities, whether Christians, advocates of the Enlightenment, old liberals, or post-1960s pluralists, to seek some working consensus of shared values. Even de-constructionists cannot do without a presumption of some common values and beliefs. Rather, without illusions that our worldview will be held by all others, we can nonetheless look for commonalities in traditions that can be shared. In fact, there are more such commonalities than we might imagine,[40] since persons living in the same era share many of the same experiences. For instance, a common consensus has developed across most American communities that women and minorities should not be discriminated against in higher education. It makes sense to build university policy on such widely shared principles.

Once we get this far, however, the question is what *do* we exclude? It is clear that not all views are permissible, and certainly some practices, such as sexual or racial harassment, are appropriately excluded. If, however, we are serious about recognizing that we should not expect all communities to share our own moral judgments, then we will not absolutize the views of the majority. Rather, we would permit expressions of a wide variety of responsibly presented minority opinions, including some very unpopular ones.

Advocating such a broader pluralism does not imply that Christians should be moral relativists. In fact, we can believe, as the Jewish and Christian traditions have always held, that true moral laws ultimately are creations of God, whatever approximations or rejections of them human communities may construct. Nonetheless, we may also hold that, as far as public policy is concerned in a pluralistic society, justice is best served by a Madisonian approach that thwarts the tyranny of the majority.[41]

Especially in the universities, which, of all the institutions in a society, should be open to the widest-ranging free inquiry, such a broad pluralism would involve allowing all sorts of Christian and other religiously based intellectual traditions back into the discussion.[42] If I interpret the foregoing history correctly, almost all the rationales for why such viewpoints were excluded (those having to do with disestablishment and beliefs in universal science) are passé.

The only major ongoing factor is concern for justice in a pluralistic society; but that concern would seem now to *favor* admission of religious perspectives.

Regaining a place for religiously informed perspectives will require some consciousness raising comparable to that which has come from other groups who have been largely excluded. Nonetheless, I think it is fair to ask whether it is consistent with the vision of contemporary universities to discriminate against religiously informed views when all other sorts of advocacy and intellectual inquiry are tolerated.

Of course there would have to be some rules of the game that would require intellectual responsibility, civility, and fairness to traditions with which one disagrees.

Nonetheless, it would seem to me to be both more fair and more consistent with the pluralistic intellectual tenor of our times that, instead of having a rule that religious perspectives must be suppressed in university teaching, we *encourage* professors to reveal their perspectives so that they can be taken into account. For instance, if a Mormon, a Unificationist, a Falwell fundamentalist, or a Harvey Cox liberal were teaching my children, it would seem to me that truth in marketing should demand that they state their perspective openly. The same should apply to all sorts of secularists. No doubt one can think of problems with such arrangements, but the current situation presents the serious problem of how to justify discrimination against religiously informed intellectual perspectives.

Perhaps what post-Enlightenment universities, which presumably recognize that there is no universal scientific or moral vision that will unite the race, need to do, in addition to making a pragmatic search for some functional common ground, is to conceive of themselves as federations for competing intellectual communities of faith or commitment. This might be more difficult for American universities than for British or some Canadian universities, which have always seen themselves as federations of colleges among which there was sometimes diversity. American schools, by contrast, were shaped first by sectarian Christian and then by Enlightenment and liberal Protestant ideals that assumed that everyone ought to think alike. Nonetheless, if American schools were willing to recognize diversity and perhaps even to incorporate colleges with diverse commitments, whether religious, feminist, gay, politically conservative, humanist, liberationist, or whatever, pluralism might have a better chance. The alternative seems to be to continue the cycle of replacing one set of correct views with a new consensus that is to be imposed on everyone—which is not pluralism at all.

The second strategy, which may be more realistic, is for serious Christians to concentrate on building distinctly Christian institutions that will provide alternatives to secular colleges and universities. Perhaps the situation in the universities and in the academic professions that staff them is hopeless and irreversible. If so, Christians and other religious people should view the situation realistically and give up on the cultural illusion that serious religion will simply fit in with common culture.

Here I am thinking most immediately of building research and graduate study centers in key fields at the best institutions in various Christian sub-cultures. Such efforts would require some sacrifice of academic prestige, at least temporarily, and hence some sacrifice of possible influence in the wider culture. Nonetheless, if churches do their jobs well in higher education, they are likely to produce communities that are intellectually, spiritually, and morally admirable. They may not be widely liked in the broader culture; but being well liked by the culture has never been one of the Gospel's promises. Perhaps, given the historical developments I have described, it is time for Christians in the post-modern age to recognize that they are part of an unpopular sect.

Notes

1. From *Atlantic Monthly* 18 (July 1866), 299–307, reprinted in Richard Hofstadter and Wilson Smith, *American Higher Education: A Documentary History,* vol. 2 (Chicago: University of Chicago Press, 1961), 561–67, quotation from 562–63.

2. From Gallup surveys of 1980–1984, appendix, *Unsecular America,* ed. Richard J. Neuhaus (Grand Rapids: Eerdmans, 1986), 131.

3. Cf. Richard G. Hutcheson, Jr., "Are Church-Related Colleges also Christian Colleges?" *Christian Century,* September 28, 1988, 838–41.

4. E. Harris Harbison, *The Christian Scholar in the Age of Reformation* (New York: Scribners, 1956), 121.

5. James B. Angell, "Religious Life in Our State Universities," *Andover Review* 13 (April 1890), 365–72. See also Bradley J. Longfield, "From Evangelicalism to Liberalism: Public Midwestern Universities in Nineteenth-Century America," Chapter 2 in this volume.

6. I have discussed the strengths and weaknesses of one sub-community in "The State of Evangelical Scholarship," *Christian Scholar's Review* 17 (June 1988), 347–60.

7. I am grateful to John F. Wilson for making this point and some others reflected herein in his comment on an earlier version of this essay at a conference on religion and the university at Duke University, June 1 and 2, 1990. I am also grateful to other participants in that conference, and in the conference held on this topic in October 1990 at the Center for Religion and Public Life in New York, for their helpful comments, particularly the written comments of Michael J. Baxter, C. S. C., Michael A. Cavanaugh, Richard T. Hughes, William Hutchison, Kathryn Long, David Martin, Richard J. Mouw, Mark R. Schwehn, and James Turner. I am also grateful to Bradley Longfield, Diana Butler, and Roger Robins for their comments on an earlier version, and to David Hollinger and Henry F. May for remarks on a later version.

8. An indirect role, however, could still be of major significance. Because of religious beliefs a mechanic may determine to do the best work possible, cheerfully and honestly, even if she does not allege direct spiritual causes for mechanical problems.

9. I will be using "liberal Christian" rather broadly to refer to people whose theological views were not traditionally conservative or who were at least broadly tolerant of wide diversities of theological opinion within churches.

10. Address by President D. C. Gilman, *National Perils and Opportunities: The Discussions of the . . . Evangelical Alliance for the United States* (New York, 1887), 283.

11. Ibid., 281.

12. David Hollinger, "Inquiry and Uplift: Late Nineteenth-Century American Academics and the Moral Efficiency of Scientific Practice," in *The Authority of Experts: Studies in History and Theory*, ed. Thomas L. Haskell (Bloomington: Indiana University Press, 1984), 147. The way for this was prepared by the reverence for science of pre–Civil War evangelicals; see, for instance, George M. Marsden, "Evangelicals and the Scientific Culture: An Overview," in *Religion and Twentieth-Century American Intellectual Life*, ed. Michael J. Lacey (Cambridge: Woodrow Wilson Center and Cambridge University Press, 1989), 23–48.

13. In a sense this was only an accentuation of a long-standing arrangement. Theology, though traditionally the "queen of the sciences," was seldom very well integrated with the rest of Western higher education.

14. James Turner and Paul Bernard, "The Prussian Road to University? German Models and the University of Michigan, 1837–c.1895," in *Rackham Reports* (1988–1989), 6–52.

15. "The AAUP's 'General Declaration of Principles,' 1915," in Hofstadter and Smith, *American Higher Education*, vol. 2, 862, 864.

16. See, for instance, chapter 2 on midwestern universities.

17. Mark Noll in *Princeton and the Republic, 1768–1822: The Search for a Christian Enlightenment in the Era of Samuel Stanhope Smith* (Princeton: Princeton University Press, 1989), provides important background on this concept.

18. "Statement of Dr. Richard T. Ely," *Report of the Organization of the American Economics Association*, Vol. 1, No. 1 (Baltimore, 1886), 18. Even at this point, some of the early organizers were not happy with such a direct connection between science and service, although such connections persisted, especially in the field of sociology, until the First World War. See, e.g., Arthur J. Vidich and Stanford M. Lyman, *American Sociology: Worldly Rejections of Religion and Their Directions* (New Haven: Yale University Press, 1985).

19. "The AAUP's 'General Declaration of Principles,' 1915," in Hofstadter and Smith, *American Higher Education*, vol. 2, 866.

20. See, e.g., Roger L. Geiger, *To Advance Knowledge: The Growth of American Research Universities, 1900–1940* (New York: Oxford University Press, 1986).

21. Thorstein Veblen, *The Higher Learning in America: A Memorandum on the Conduct of Universities by Business Men* (New York: B. W. Huebsch, 1918), long ago made such points. More recently, Page Smith, *Killing the Spirit: Higher Education in America* (New York: Viking, 1990), identifies this as one of the major problems, e.g. 10–12.

22. Charles D. Cashdollar, *The Transformation of Theology: Positivism and Protestant Thought in Britain and America* (Princeton: Princeton University Press, 1989), provides abundant documentation of this influence.

23. These three stages happen to correspond roughly to the stages of the development of the American university, just described.

24. Vidich and Lyman, *American Sociology*, 5.

25. Laurence Veysey, "Stability and Experiment in the American Undergraduate Curriculum," in *Content and Contest: Essays on College Education*, ed. Carl Kaysen (New York: McGraw-Hill, 1973), 51–52. Veysey shows that the University of California already had a Western Civilization course prior to the war, when the model was supposedly inaugurated at Columbia.

26. See James Turner, "Secularization and Sacralization: Speculations on Some Religious Origins of the Secular Humanities Curriculum, 1850–1900," Chapter 3 of this volume.

27. "The Harvard Report on General Education, 1945," in Hofstadter and Smith, *Higher Education*, vol. 2, 956–69.

28. "The President's Commission on Higher Education for Democracy," in Ibid, 970–90.

29. Edward A. Purcell, Jr., *The Crisis of Democratic Theory: Scientific Naturalism and the Problem of Value* (Lexington: University of Kentucky Press, 1973), provides a valuable account of the debates over how to find a democratic consensus.

30. Robert Wuthnow, *The Restructuring of American Religion: Society and Faith since World War II* (Princeton: Princeton University Press, 1988), 167–72, documents major shifts from the 1950s to the 1980s in the likelihood of college-educated people being church attenders. He also documents vast increases in higher education and in the role of government during the same era.

31. A telling, though trivial, example is that *Christian Century*, May 7, 1990, 484–86, published Elliott Welsh, "Why I Am Suing the Boy Scouts," in which the complaint of the secularist author is that the Scouts discriminate by promoting religious values as a basis for good citizenship. Although the *Century* does not necessarily endorse the author's views, it is a wonderful irony that ten years before the end of the expected "Christian century," the journal with that name should publish an attack on one of the early twentieth-century organizations that most closely reflected its original ideals.

32. David O. Levine, *The American College and the Culture of Aspiration, 1915–1940* (Ithaca: Cornell University Press, 1986), 136–61; Dan A. Oren, *Joining the Club: A History of Jews and Yale* (New Haven: Yale University Press, 1985); Marcia G. Synnott, *The Half-Opened Door: Discrimination and Admissions at Harvard, Yale, and Princeton, 1900–1970* (Westport, CT: Greenwood Press, 1979).

33. Smith, *Killing the Spirit*, 12.

34. The second sexual revolution, unleashed in the 1960s, also had something to do with the displacement of the old liberal Protestant establishment, which (with some notable exceptions) had trouble keeping pace with the youth culture. Liberal Protestants usually endorsed the latest trends, whether political or sexual, but increasingly could be seen as tagging along.

35. John M. Mulder, "Presbyterians and Higher Education: The Demise of a Tradition?" Unpublished address to the Presidents of the Association of Presbyterian Colleges and Universities, March 1990.

36. See Chapter 7 in this volume for more detail on this topic.

37. Merrimon Cuninggim, *The College Seeks Religion* (New Haven: Yale University Press, 1947), 29.

38. For an astute and positive reading of where these trends were leading at the time, see John F. Wilson, "Introduction: The Background and Present Context of the Study of Religion in Colleges and Universities," in *The Study of Religion in Colleges and Universities*, ed. Paul Ramsey and John F. Wilson (Princeton: Princeton University Press, 1970), 3–22.

39. Roger Kimball, *Tenured Radicals: How Politics has Corrupted Our Higher Education* (New York: Harper and Row, 1990), although somewhat tendentious itself, provides striking documentation of these trends.

40. As a Christian, who believes that God created an ordered universe, I think we have a stronger basis for belief in some innate, though limited, human commonalities and abilities to communicate across cultures. For building a public consensus, however, it seems to me that we have to argue from more minimal grounds of common assumptions or practices.

41. I hold what I consider an Augustinian view, in which the city of the world should not be mistaken for the City of God and hence will not run by exactly the same principles.

42. Mark R. Schwehn suggests that "Christians are now treated in a manner rather like women were treated in the pre-feminist era. Women could be hired, promoted, and retained, *so long as their feminism did not figure prominently in their research interests, their scholarly perspectives, and their manner of life generally.*" Letter to author, June 4, 1990.

2

From Evangelicalism to Liberalism: Public Midwestern Universities in Nineteenth-Century America

BRADLEY J. LONGFIELD

> Michigan is a Christian State, and her University can be true to her only by cherishing a broad unsectarian but earnest Christian spirit. I think that her sister universities in the Northwest are pervaded by the same spirit, and that they are contributing their full share to the dissemination of a Christian culture.[1]
>
> James B. Angell, 1877

The public midwestern universities are renowned for fine academics and superior athletics. They are not usually portrayed as the custodians of Christian faith and values. But such has not always been the case. Many of the public midwestern schools—such as the universities of Michigan, Wisconsin, Indiana, and Illinois—were founded as non-sectarian but distinctly Protestant institutions. Clergy presidents and faculty were the norm; daily chapel attendance was required; and courses such as Evidences of Christianity and Natural Theology were frequently mandatory fare. During the Gilded Age many of these traditional religious customs and requirements, under various pressures, were abandoned. But the state schools did not become secular universities overnight.[2] Rather, in the late nineteenth century the broad evangelical tradition of these schools gave way to a more liberal Christianity and to the disestablishment of religion on campus. Until at least the turn of the century, state schools still functioned, in various ways, as propagators of Christian faith and ideals. Defenders of a broad, non-sectarian evangelicalism at mid-century, many state universities became, by the 1890s, unofficial nurseries of liberal Christianity and the Social Gospel.[3]

In 1841 the regents of the University of Michigan expressed their concern that the university, though public and non-sectarian, was to be broadly Christian:

> The establishment of a collegiate institution in a free state . . . should ever be upon liberal principles, and irrespective of all sectarian predilections and prejudices. Whatever varieties of sect exist in these United States, the great mass of the population profess an attachment to CHRISTIANITY, and as a people, avow themselves to be CHRISTIAN. There is common ground occupied by them all, sufficient for co-operation in an institution of learning, and for the presence of a religious influence . . . so essential . . . for the development and formation of the most valuable traits of youthful character, and of qualifications for future usefulness.[4]

Similar concern for the preservation and propagation of a broad evangelical Christianity undergirded Indiana University and the University of Missouri and would be central to the mission of schools such as Wisconsin and Illinois, founded later in the century.[5]

The religious concerns of the schools were manifested in their staff, curriculum, and religious exercises. The presidents of state universities at mid-century were, in many cases, either clergymen or theologically trained laymen. For example, Andrew Wylie (1829–1851), Alfred Ryors (1852–1853), and William Daily (1853–1859) at Indiana, Henry Tappan (1852–1863) and Erastus Haven (1863–1869) at Michigan, and James Shannon at Missouri (1850–1856) were ordained.[6] Moreover, these men were supported in their mission by faculty who were, as Merle Curti said of the professors at Wisconsin, "better trained in theology than in other disciplines."[7] Indeed, the staffing pattern at Indiana University, where five of the first six presidents and a "majority of the professors" were ministers, was fairly typical for the day.[8]

Although the non-sectarian character of these institutions prohibited the teaching of theology unique to any one denomination, distinctively Christian issues were addressed in the curriculum. In the 1850s the first class on Monday morning for all students at the University of Michigan was Greek New Testament. This was intended not only to teach the Scriptures but also "to keep the students from violating the Sabbath by pursuing secular studies."[9] In a similar manner, Minnesota did not hold classes on Monday for fear the students would violate the Sabbath.[10] At mid-century Wisconsin, Michigan, and Indiana required such courses as Natural Theology, Moral Philosophy, and Evidences of Christianity, and prayer before class—no matter what the subject—was not uncommon.[11] One student, in a letter to the college paper at Michigan, thus thanked President Tappan for his "faithful labors to instil correct and religious sentiments, not only in usual daily prayer and Sabbath lectures, but also in the classroom."[12]

Mandatory daily chapel and voluntary religious organizations were another means by which these schools inculcated their charges with Christian ideals prior to the Civil War. At Michigan chapel was required twice daily; at Indiana the students gathered for prayer and Scripture every day before classes; and at Wisconsin worship was an integral part of daily university routine.[13] The University of Illinois, which opened its doors in 1868, followed the lead of its sister schools in requiring chapel every day.[14] Reflecting on the influence of compulsory worship, one Wisconsin graduate noted: "I shall never forget my first evening in South Hall and the sweet, impressive voice of the Preceptress as she led the kneeling girls in prayer. Sunday afternoons we learned a Bible lesson which we recited in the evening."[15] In addition to these mandatory exercises, voluntary religious organizations such as the Students' Christian Organization and the Christian Library Association at Michigan were encouraged by university administrators as worthy endeavors.[16]

Despite the clear Christian tenor of these public schools, institutional jealousy often led denominational representatives to attack the public schools as "godless" institutions that failed to cultivate the Christian faith of the students. In 1855, for example, rumors were circulating that Wisconsin was an "infidel concern" in which the Bible and prayer were ignored.[17] President Haven, responding to similar charges about the University of Michigan in the 1860s, realized the true nature of many of these concerns when he maintained, "It is not a godless education that they fear, but a Christian education not communicated through the forms and channels over which they preside."[18]

The presidents, faculty, curriculum, and religious exercises combined to make the midwestern public universities at mid-century broadly evangelical Christian schools. William Ringenberg's comment that "by all standards of measurement the University of Michigan before 1865 was a Protestant college" could well be made about most of the public midwestern universities in this era.[19] Although these schools were emphatically non-sectarian, religion pervaded the lives of these institutions.

The closing decades of the nineteenth century are generally portrayed as a period of increasing secularization at America's colleges and universities, but in numerous ways state schools remained a powerful force for the propagation of Christian faith and values.[20] Undeniably a growing stress on research, vocationalism, and specialization, and the increasing pluralization of society, encouraged the universities to drift away from many aspects of their evangelical roots. Moreover, by the end of the century mandatory chapel was largely an abandoned tradition. Nevertheless, Christian influences did not simply evaporate from these campuses. Rather, in the waning years of the nineteenth century the broad evangelicalism of the mid-nineteenth century gave way to a liberal Christian ethos, as many professors used their positions to advocate liberal Christian beliefs. Indeed, the broad, non-doctrinal, and public character of these universities provided a perfect environment for the growth of liberal Christianity, which melded a concern for Christianity and American civilization.[21]

The continuing influence of Christianity on the state universities is manifested in the strong religious inclinations of the presidents of these schools in the late nineteenth century. Although universities in general were moving away from clergymen presidents, many state schools continued to look to the church for their leadership. Most notably, President William H. Scott of Ohio State (1883–1895) and chancellors James Marvin (1874–1883) and Joshua Lippincott (1883–1889) of the University of Kansas were Methodist ministers, and presidents Lemuel Moss (1875–1884) of Indiana University and John M. Gregory (1867–1880) of the University of Illinois were Baptist clergymen.[22] Perhaps most indicative of the religious atmosphere of these schools in the late nineteenth century is the fact that the renowned Social Gospel preacher Washington Gladden was a leading candidate for the presidencies of Wisconsin, Ohio State, and Illinois in the early 1890s.[23]

Just as significant as the continuation of the legacy of clergy presidents, however, was the strong religious concern of many of the laymen who came to run these institutions in the latter years of the nineteenth century. John Bascom, president of Wisconsin from 1874 to 1887, was educated at Auburn and Andover theological seminaries but eschewed the pastorate for an academic life. In addition, James Burrill Angell, president of the University of Michigan from 1871 to 1909, and Francis Snow, chancellor of the University of Kansas from 1890 to 1901, had considered ministerial careers.[24] If schools were moving away from clerical domination, they were certainly not abandoning a concern for the Christian commitment of their leadership.

In the face of continuing criticism of public universities from denominational representatives, the presidents of state universities in the late nineteenth century were no less insistent than their earlier counterparts about the Christian character of their schools. Thus, in the 1880s William Henry Scott maintained of Ohio State: "It is Christian, but undenominational. This is the true position, not only for a state university, but for any university. . . . Nothing could more depreciate the value of a higher education than that it should be given and received under the malign influence of a sordid utilitarianism or a dead materialism."[25] And James B. Angell at Michigan argued: "The State as the great patron and protector of the University has a right to ask that . . . the Christian spirit, which pervades the laws, the customs, and the life of the State, shall shape and color the life of the University, that a lofty, earnest, but catholic and unsectarian Christian tone shall characterize the culture which is here [the University of Michigan] imparted."[26] In a similar vein, John Bascom refused to "concede that the state university was necessarily less truly religious than the sectarian college," and Joshua Lippincott insisted that Kansas was a "Christian institution, founded by a Christian State."[27] These schools were, as Professor Henry Frieze said of the University of Michigan in 1887, "at once Christian and liberal."[28]

Given such views, chapel requirements remained in place at a number of state universities for many years after Appomattox.

Although Wisconsin abolished compulsory chapel in 1868, and Michigan followed suit in the 1870s, Indiana preserved the practice at least through the late 1880s, and Missouri held to compulsory worship until 1893.[29] Even after the abolition of required chapel, university-sponsored worship frequently continued and flourished, as at the University of Michigan, where Angell led vesper services into the early twentieth century.[30] Indeed, when James Angell surveyed twenty-four state schools in 1890, he discovered that twenty-two held chapel services in university buildings and four required church attendance.[31] As late as 1906 one survey found that chapel services were still held in seventeen out of nineteen state schools, with worship mandatory in nine of these institutions. At that time the University of Minnesota held a voluntary assembly "for daily worship, conducted by the President and professors, the exercises consisting of the singing of a hymn, the reading of the Scriptures, and prayer."[32]

Required chapel as an institution did not die easily; at two schools, Ohio State and Illinois, devotion to this symbol of Christian hegemony caused major uproars. In both cases supporters of compulsory worship successfully defended their position only to witness the demise of mandatory chapel a few years later.

At Ohio State a conflict over required chapel was at least a contributing factor to the removal of President Walter Q. Scott in 1883. Scott, a Presbyterian minister educated at Union Seminary in New York, was appointed to the presidency of Ohio State in June 1881, five months after the university trustees had adopted a resolution calling for daily chapel. In November 1881 they reaffirmed their commitment to daily chapel, recommending "the reading of the Scriptures (without comment) and prayers, at the discretion of the President of the University," and in March 1883 made their desire still clearer by passing a motion requiring attendance at such worship.[33] Scott, in his 1882 commencement address, declared his dedication to maintaining a university in which "the morality and religion of the Christian civilization shall be recognized and cherished as the most precious elements in the education of the young." Yet for some reason he delayed implementation of daily chapel until the winter of 1883. This resistance to the will of the trustees, combined with Scott's public declarations of his liberal economic values, led to his forced resignation in June of that year.[34] Mandatory chapel, with some allowable exemptions at the discretion of the president, continued at Ohio State until the turn of the century.[35]

At the University of Illinois, chapel requirements resulted in a different sort of conflict. Attendance at daily chapel had been mandatory since Illinois had opened in 1868.[36] In 1885 Foster North, an agnostic, though only a few weeks shy of graduating, decided that he could no longer stand attending worship services. North had gradually grown more and more annoyed by daily chapel until, he later wrote, he "used to mentally dam—yes, god dam—old [President] Peabody and his damned old prayers," and finally refused to attend altogether.[37] Although students could be excused from chapel if they signed a statement claiming that attendance at worship was "repugnant" to their religious convictions, North contended that he could not subscribe to such a statement because he had no religious convictions to which chapel could be repugnant. President Peabody and the faculty, faced with a recalcitrant student, suspended him indefinitely on April 30, 1885.[38]

In June, North petitioned the trustees for re-admission, claiming that the university's chapel requirement violated the constitution of the state of Illinois. But the trustees refused, and the attorney general of Illinois sided with the school, claiming that inasmuch as attendance at the university was purely voluntary, and inasmuch as the school provided exemption from chapel upon request, none of North's constitutional rights had been transgressed.[39] In response to North's petition, President Peabody summed up the view of most of the university's leadership when he claimed: "That the people of the State of Illinois ever dreamed that as the outcome of a misinterpreted constitutional provision, Christianity, the God of Heaven and Earth, and the Bible as His written word could be ruled out of its State University, so that it should be unlawful to read the Scriptures, or to pray to Him, within its walls, is a conclusion too monstrous to be entertained."[40] Mandatory chapel would be abolished at Illinois in 1894, but North had picked a fight he could not win in the mid-1880s.[41]

The reasons for the abolition of compulsory chapel were many and various, ranging from an increasingly diverse and recalcitrant student body, to lack of sufficiently large meeting areas, to scheduling difficulties caused by expanding curricula. In addition to logistical problems and increasing student opposition, however, was the belief among many devout administrators and faculty that compulsory worship was not beneficial and was in many cases detrimental to the cultivation of Christianity. In 1890, for example, James B. Angell, who worked fervently to promote Christianity on the Michigan campus, questioned the advantages of mandatory chapel for undergraduates, writing:

> The attendance of students on religious exercises is not so generally made compulsory as in the colleges under denominational control. But I think I am not mistaken in saying that many religious men in the state universities, and some in other colleges, are persuaded that the voluntary system is best for the students so mature as those in our Western colleges. That is a point on which good men may differ. But where, as at the University of Michigan, the average age of the freshman on entering college is nineteen and a half years, it is at least open to discussion whether the spiritual welfare of undergraduates will be promoted by their being driven to religious service under fear of a monitor's mark.[42]

Angell, in fact, had abolished mandatory worship at Michigan in the early 1870s but continued to lead voluntary worship.[43] While compulsory worship was largely abandoned in the course of the late nineteenth century, this move was not simply, or even primarily, a capitulation to secular ideology. Frequently, as with President Angell, devout Christians believed that voluntary worship would better serve the spiritual mission of the university than mandatory chapel. Thus the demise of compulsory worship could be seen at least as much as an attempt to preserve the influence of Christianity as it was a move away from traditional Christian influences.[44]

Student Christian associations, led by some of the most able students on campus, also maintained a healthy presence, and even increased in vitality at state schools throughout this period.[45] As Francis Kelsey reported in 1897, "Associations for religious work flourish in the state universities, directed and supported in large measure by the members of the faculties."[46] The Christian association at the University of Michigan, for example, which had the official endorsement of the university administration, was the "most active student organization on the campus" in the 1880s, and, at the turn of the century, claimed over one-quarter of the student body as members.[47] Likewise, at the University of Minnesota the Young Men's Christian Association (YMCA) was the "leading student organization" on campus in 1900.[48] Similar groups nurtured the faith of students at Wisconsin, Indiana, Ohio State, Illinois, and Missouri in the last decades of the century.[49]

The activities of these organizations varied, but would typically include worship, hospital visitation, Bible classes, prayer meetings, and orientation events.[50] At the University of Michigan, encouraged by Angell, the Students' Christian Association (SCA) also sponsored faculty lectures by individuals such as John Dewey and Henry Carter Adams addressing "religious dimensions in various fields."[51]

The tenor of these associations can be gleaned from the SCA at Michigan, which in the 1880s required that members of the YMCA be affiliated with one of the evangelical churches that believed in the infallibility of the Scriptures and in Jesus Christ as Lord and Savior.[52] By the 1890s the winds of change were affecting the Michigan association, and in 1895 the Students' Christian Association adopted a more liberal membership policy, dropping the requirement that members belong to an evangelical church.[53] Nonetheless, in 1898 the SCA still insisted that part of its mission was to lead individuals "to a knowledge of Jesus Christ as their Divine Lord and Savior."[54]

By the 1890s denominations were also mobilizing to address religious issues on state campuses. As Clarence Shedd noted in his work *The Church Follows Its Students*, the University of Michigan was one of the earliest arenas for the formation of denominational guilds such as the Episcopalians' Hobart Guild and the Methodists' Wesleyan Guild.[55] The organization created by the Presbyterians, baptized the Tappan Guild, set its purposes as: "1) to draw university students into the Presbyterian ministry, 2) to confirm the faith of students in the denomination, and 3) to influence unbelieving students." The guilds at the University of Michigan offered lectures on religious topics and, in time, led to the formation of the university pastorate movement.[56]

These organizations were supported by student bodies that were largely Christian and members of churches. A survey of sixteen state universities conducted by James Angell in 1896 discovered that over 70 percent of the student bodies of these schools were "church members or adherents," about half of all students being affiliated with the Protestant evangelical denominations. These figures are even more striking in comparison with those for the prestigious private institutions. At Princeton, for example, while almost everyone claimed to adhere to some religious tradition, only 55 percent of the students claimed to be church members, a figure roughly equal to that found at the University of Michigan.[57] By at least one indicator, therefore, the state schools were every bit as "religious" as their private, traditionally Christian counterparts back east.

The Christian faith of faculty at state schools also aided in the persistence of Christian influences at these institutions. John Bascom at the University of Wisconsin, James Angell at Michigan, and Joshua Lippincott at Kansas oversaw faculty that belonged, in large part, to orthodox churches.[58] Likewise, in 1878 the Methodist *Northwestern Christian Advocate* could point to the University of Illinois as evidence "that state schools are successful and trusted by the people in proportion as they are guided by teachers cultured by the church." And in 1885 the *Indiana Student* could claim that Indiana's faculty was "composed largely of men identified with religious organizations & entirely of men of religious lives."[59] In 1890 James B. Angell summed up his findings on the religious ties of professors at state universities in general, arguing that "it appears that seventy-one per cent. of the teachers are members of churches, and not a few of the others are earnestly and even actively religious men who have not formally joined any communion." Moreover, he continued, "if you go to the cities where those universities are planted, you will find a good proportion of these teachers superintending Sunday-schools, conducting Bible classes, sometimes supplying pulpits, engaged in every kind of Christian work, and by example and word stimulating their pupils to a Christian life."[60]

Angell, as head of the leading state university in the nation during the closing decades of the nineteenth century, was in fact greatly concerned with the religious views of faculty. He devoutly believed that

> in choosing members of the Faculty the greatest care should be taken to secure gifted, earnest, reverent men, whose mental and moral qualities will fit them to prepare their pupils for manly and womanly work in promoting our Christian civilization. But never

insist on their pronouncing the shibboleths of sect or party. So
only can we train a generation of students to catholic, candid,
truth-loving habits of mind and tempers of heart.[61]

In 1885 he applied these general guidelines to a specific appointment he was making in the history department. About the position
he wrote, "In the Chair of History the work may lie and often does
lie so close to Ethics, that I should not wish a pessimist or an
agnostic or a man disposed to obtrude criticisms of Christian views
of humanity or of Christian principles. I should not want a man
who would not make his historical judgments and interpretations
from a Christian standpoint."[62] Further south, at Illinois, John M.
Gregory (1867–1880) similarly "assumed that faculty members
should be Christian and Protestant."[63] As late as 1915 Warner Fite
reported that "it has been customary in State universities, no less
than in denominational colleges, to question a candidate for appointment concerning his church connections. Any church connection will do."[64] Although an increasing emphasis on specialization
and research moved much teaching in a more secular direction
during these years, Christian commitment remained a lively concern in the hiring of faculty.[65]

The Christianity that influenced the campuses of the 1880s and
1890s was gradually evolving from that which had pervaded the
campuses of the 1850s and 1860s, however. In the intervening years
intellectual trends such as Darwinism and historical criticism of the
Bible and social changes, including increasing urbanization and
rapid industrialization, had worked to alter the tenor of American
Protestantism. In response to these trends, liberal Christianity,
which stressed the immanence of God, ethics, religious feeling, and
the need to accommodate Christianity to the intellectual currents of
the day, found increasing acceptance among some segments of
American Protestants, not the least of whom taught at midwestern
schools.

While the old required courses in Moral and Mental Philosophy
tended to disappear in the later years of the nineteenth century,
many of the broad religious and moral concerns that these courses
encompassed were picked up in various ways in new philosophy
courses and in the social sciences, which developed from moral
philosophy.[66] By the late nineteenth century the discipline of moral

philosophy, which had been a means of teaching non-sectarian religion in the public forum, spawned such fields as economics, sociology, and psychology. Under the guise of philosophy and the social sciences, many professors at the public midwestern schools, which envisioned themselves as the custodians of democracy and Christian civilization, advocated the values and beliefs of liberal Christianity and the Social Gospel. As L. L. and J. S. Bernard have noted, this reformist impulse in the social sciences was especially at home in the midwestern schools. They wrote:

> Only in the large privately endowed universities did the subject [political economy] remain classical and conservative or become primarily training in the theory of business. In the western state universities, it was liberal and institutional in character, and with the multiplication of courses within the rapidly growing depart-ments, courses on labor problems, socialism, and social reform became frequent and prominent.[67]

Some of these scholars, especially those who advocated the principles of the Social Gospel movement, were seriously challenged for their economic views, but notably not for their religious perspectives. John Bascom, Richard T. Ely, John Commons, and John Dewey provide key examples of the way in which Christian ideals and values were advanced at these schools.

John Bascom was president and professor of Moral Philosophy at Wisconsin from 1874 to 1887 and, as such, set the tone of the university.[68] The descendant of "a long line of New England Congregational ministers," he had inherited a strong Puritan drive for the creation of a Christian commonwealth and became an ardent defender of trade unions, women's rights, and temperance. He accepted the post at Wisconsin in large part because it offered the opportunity to teach philosophy, which, to his mind, lay at the base of social ethics.[69]

A prolific author, Bascom wrote works on ethics, religion, philosophy, and education and was a major theorist of the "New Theology" and the Social Gospel.[70] True to the tenets of late nineteenth-century liberal theology, Bascom stressed God's immanence, ethics, and the importance of adjusting theology to advances in science.[71] He thus discounted the importance of doctrine, telling the 1874 graduating class of Wisconsin: "The dogmas of our time do

not differ from those of previous ages, in being partial, unconces-
sive, restrictive. Conscientiously, in behalf of truth, in our own
behalf, in behalf of religious growth and social development, we
still need to stand for the freedom of faith. . . . We have only to
understand that there are no invariable, exact, exhaustive, final
statements of spiritual truths."[72]

Although Bascom tended toward laissez-faire economic principles early in his career, he adopted more progressive views while in
Madison.[73] In an 1876 baccalaureate sermon he declared that the
love of wealth, power, and station in America were nothing short of
sinful and that the culture was in need of conversion to Christian
principles. "Society," he argued, "must be converted, as distinctly
and fully converted as the individual; and the conversion of the
individual will be very partial till this conversion of the community."[74] In 1887 Bascom expounded on the role of the university in
fulfilling this mission: "The University of Wisconsin will be perma-
nently great in the degree in which it understands the conditions of
the prosperity and peace of the people, and helps to provide them;
in the degree in which it enters into the revelation of truth, the law
of righteousness, and the love of man, all gathered up and held firm
in the constitution of the human soul and the counsel of God
concerning it."[75] The developing social sciences, not surprisingly,
were at the center of this mission of the university. He argued in
New Theology:

> The moral forces which rule the world are the forces which
> religious truth and social science are both dealing with. The
> two—social science and theology—have precisely the same prob-
> lem, expressed on this side as the perfection of society, and on
> that side as the Kingdom of Heaven. Not only must there be a
> mutual understanding between these two forms of effort, there
> must be an extended, yes, a complete interlock of labor.[76]

The university could not teach theology in any traditional sense;
but it could teach sociology, economics, and philosophy, all of
which addressed the same central issue as the New Theology: the
problem of building the Kingdom of Heaven.[77]

No one was more ardent in this application of Christian principles to the budding social sciences than Richard T. Ely, who came
to Wisconsin five years after Bascom left in 1887. As the national

leader of the "new school" of economics, which attempted to promote social reform by creating a "sound Christian political economy," Ely was a leading light in the development of the Social Gospel.[78] Born in New York State of New England stock, Ely could never accept the stern Calvinism of his father and eventually joined the Episcopal church for its "fuller and richer life."[79] He subscribed to a this-worldly Christianity whose mission was to build a "kingdom of righteousness" on earth.[80] Indeed, in his immensely popular *Social Aspects of Christianity*, published in 1889, he proclaimed that "Christianity is primarily concerned with this world, and it is the mission of Christianity to bring to pass here a kingdom of righteousness and to rescue from the evil one and redeem all our social relations."[81]

These convictions about the essence of Christianity pervaded Ely's work in the social sciences. He claimed that sociology was only the "elaboration" of the command of Christ "to love thy neighbor as thyself," and he therefore helped form the American Economic Association "to bring science to the aid of Christianity."[82] For Ely, sociology and theology were but two sides of the same coin. "Love to God is piety," he wrote, "and the science which deals with this part of the gospel is called theology. Love to man is philanthropy, and the science which deals with this part of the gospel is called sociology. The two are inseparable."[83] As such sociology was as Christian a discipline as theology. Ely argued, "It is as truly a religious work to pass good laws, as it is to preach sermons; as holy a work to lead a crusade against filth, vice, and disease in slums of cities, and to seek the abolition of the disgraceful tenement-houses of American cities, as it is to send missionaries to the heathen."[84] He insisted that childrens' and womens' labor, Sunday work, public playgrounds, parenthood, public corruption, and distribution of wealth were all "religious subjects" that merited the church's attention.[85] Christianity was, in fact, essential to social reform. He did not, he wrote in 1885, "believe it possible to accomplish anything of lasting value without the aid of true Christianity."[86]

In line with the accomplishment of social reform, Ely called for "a profound revival of religion, not in any narrow or technical sense . . . but a great religious awakening which shall shake things, going down into the depths of men's life and modifying their character."[87]

If all would receive the "simple Gospel of Christ," Ely believed, "then we shall attain civic reform; then our commonweal will be regenerated; then shall we see our nation a new nation, exalted by righteousness."[88]

Ely largely withdrew from active promotion of the Social Gospel in the years after his celebrated trial at the university over his economic views in 1894, but Christian concerns continued to pervade his writings.[89] In *The Social Law of Service*, published in 1896, Ely claimed, "There is one law, and only one, taught by the Christian religion and on its manward side; that is, the law of love, which finds expression in the social law of service." He demanded: "Let all Christians see to it that they put as much as possible, not of doctrine or creed into the State constitution, but of Christian life and practice into the activity of the State, working, to be sure, to change the constitution in so far as this may stand in the way of righteousness. The nation must be recognized fully as a Christian nation."[90] While John Everett may have overstated the case when he claimed that "Ely worked out his whole social theory from religious assumptions," Ely's work at Wisconsin implicitly and explicitly reflected values derived from his understanding of the Christian faith.[91]

At Indiana University, John R. Commons, a former student of Ely's, proclaimed a similar gospel of liberal Christianity and social reform from 1892 to 1895. Commons, like Bascom and Ely, was a product of a devout Calvinist upbringing. Having graduated from Oberlin College in 1888, he studied under Ely at Johns Hopkins and taught at Wesleyan and Oberlin before arriving at Indiana University in 1892. As Commons noted in his autobiography, his interest in the "'new' political economy" was, in large part, a response to his religious upbringing. His choice of profession, Commons wrote, was "a tribute to [his mother's] longing that I should become a minister of the Gospel." Commons, a practicing Congregationalist, aided Ely in the formation of the short-lived American Institute of Christian Sociology in 1893, which sought "to present Christ as the living Master and King and Christian law as the ultimate rule for human society to be realized on earth."[92]

In 1894 Commons published a series of essays under the title *Social Reform and the Church*, in which he defended Christianity as "the only solution for social problems." Echoing his teacher, he held that sociology was "one half of religion," which addressed humanity's "relations to his fellow-men." Sociology and Christianity thereby went hand in hand. "The main object of Christianity," he held, was "to bring the extremes of society together in brotherly love," and concluded, "We must all come around to the simple gospel of Christ, and we must apply this gospel in its right proportions, realizing that religion is love to God, and sociology love to man, and on these two hang all the law and all preaching."[93]

In an article in the *Indiana Student* Commons argued that Christianity did not necessarily entail acceptance of a creed but did mean that one must "accept the ethical teachings of Christianity." "The Christian," he held, "is here to benefit his fellows in every possible way,—physically, mentally, spiritually." To Commons, Christianity and sociology were partners in the salvation of the world. "Christianity means a purpose, an enthusiasm, a devotion, a faith, a love for humanity," he argued. "Love and knowledge, Christianity and science, theology and sociology, must unite to save the world."[94]

Commons was therefore a strident advocate of the "institutional church." He insisted:

> The Church ought to take on a popular, week-day character. It should be a centre for amusements, athletics, debating clubs, and reading circles. It should be a people's church in the fullest sense. . . . [The preacher] needs to make his church a recognized centre for social and helpful activities. . . . Many other features of Church work will readily be suggested to the preacher who attempts to introduce thoughtful sermons on sociology and to inspire his people with the social missionary spirit.[95]

Such a church would combat the "antichrist of to-day," the "involuntary idleness and irregular employment" that compels men and women to live lives of "crime, intemperance, and shame."[96] By taking the lead in sociology and social amelioration, the church would succeed not simply in "saving individuals out of the world," Commons asserted, but in saving society itself.[97]

Just as Ely's economic views led to conflict at Wisconsin, Commons's convictions did not go unchallenged at Indiana. He came under the attack of certain newspapers which claimed that he "favored socialism, single tax, free trade, Populism." Although there is no clear evidence that opposition to his views ushered him out, when he was offered a position at Syracuse University in 1895 the president of Indiana recommended he accept it.[98] Nevertheless, while Commons was at Indiana he was one of the most prominent members of the faculty and significantly influenced the tenor of the university.[99]

Further north, at the University of Michigan, John Dewey was a chief proponent of liberal Christianity of a different sort. Dewey, who taught philosophy at Ann Arbor for all but one year between 1884 and 1894, was born in Vermont in 1859 and was influenced as a boy by his mother's Calvinist faith and the "liberal evangelicalism" preached at his hometown Congregationalist church. Converted in his early twenties, Dewey regularly worshiped and taught Sunday school with the Congregationalists.[100] Having studied at the University of Vermont and at Johns Hopkins, he arrived at Michigan in 1884 to join the philosophy department.[101]

During Dewey's first stay at Michigan he and his senior colleague, George Morris, combined their Hegelianism with Christian views to give "the department [of philosophy] a distinctly religious atmosphere."[102] Hegelianism, Dewey insisted, "in its broad and essential features is identical with the theological teaching of Christianity."[103] He found a forum for his views not only in the classroom but also as a frequent speaker at the Students' Christian Association of the university and as a teacher at the First Congregational Church in Ann Arbor.[104]

The significance of religion to Dewey at this stage of his career is suggested in his addresses to the SCA. In an 1884 talk he insisted that "there is an obligation to know God, and to fail to meet this obligation is not to err intellectually, but to sin morally." This was so, he argued, because knowledge lays a moral obligation on one. "Science or philosophy is worthless," he claimed, "which does not ultimately bring every fact into guiding relation with the living activity of man, and the end of all his striving—approach to God."[105] Likewise, in an 1886 address, "The Place of Religious Emotion," he maintained that "an outgoing and constant renewing of religious emotion is the only motive force which will awaken us from drowsy torpor, from listless dreaming, from an empty and purposeless life. It alone can call us out of the kingdom of drudgery and routine, and introduce us to the joy of the kingdom of God."[106]

In 1888 Dewey was lured to the University of Minnesota but one year later returned to Michigan to fill the chair of philosophy left vacant by the death of George Morris. In addition to teaching courses in Kant, Hegel, and Logic, Dewey assumed responsibility for courses in Advanced Psychology, Ethics, Political Philosophy, and Early Christian Philosophy. Moreover, upon his return to Michigan he resumed his activity in the Students' Christian Association, winning plaudits as one of its "strongest supporters," and he renewed his ties with the Congregational church.[107]

During this later period at Michigan, Dewey delivered a sermon to the association that manifests his liberal (and continually liberalizing) religion and his move toward instrumentalism.[108] In "Christianity and Democracy," delivered in 1892, Dewey argued that Christianity could not be identified with "any special theory, historical or ethical," or with "some special act, ecclesiastic or ceremonial." Jesus set up no rite or creed, Dewey argued, but instead taught "that Truth, however named and however divided by man, is one as God is one; that getting hold of truth and living by it is religion." Christianity was thus "the continuously unfolding, never ceasing discovery of the meaning of life." But because, for Dewey, individuals could perceive truth only in social relationships, the truth of Christianity was realized in the action of individuals in democracy. "It is in democracy," he proclaimed, "that the incarnation of God in man . . . becomes a living, present thing." Indeed, the freedom of truth in democracy would allow for the "spiritual unification of humanity, the realization of the brotherhood of man, all that Christ called the Kingdom of God."[109] Although Dewey felt comfortable using biblical language and was committed to building the "Kingdom of God" on earth, he was clearly moving away from any traditional understanding of the faith.[110]

In a letter of recommendation to President William Rainey Harper of the University of Chicago, James H. Tufts said that Dewey "[is] a man of religious nature, is a church member, and believes in working with the church. He is, moreover, actively interested in practical ethical activity, and is a valued friend at the Hull House of this city."[111] In 1894 Dewey accepted an offer from Harper to come to Chicago. Although he retained his concern for religion and ethics, broadly conceived, he dropped his church membership, thereby formally breaking his ties with traditional Christianity.[112] Nevertheless, in his years at Michigan, as a rising star in the academic world, he was a prominent advocate of liberal Christianity and a significant influence on students and faculty.

A final sign of the religious tone of the midwestern state universities in the Gilded Age can be found in the person of Washington Gladden. Gladden never formally entered the academic world, but he was, for all intents and purposes, the chaplain of Ohio State University and an unofficial adjunct member of the faculty. The baccalaureate services of the university in the 1880s were regularly held at Gladden's church, and in 1902 Gladden could claim about one-fourth of the faculty as his parishioners.[113] Indeed, one professor at Ohio State doubted whether anyone "ever exerted a greater or more far-reaching influence upon our student body than did Dr. Gladden in his day."[114]

Gladden, born in 1836, was also a product of the New England Puritan tradition. Converted by a "mild Calvinist," Jedediah Burchard, in 1853, he decided to pursue the ministry and entered Williams College, where he studied under John Bascom. Ordained in the Congregational church in 1860, he served in New York and Massachusetts before taking the pastorate of the First Congregational Church in Columbus, Ohio. During his ministry in Columbus he became a key spokesman for the New Theology and social Christianity.[115]

In 1886, in response to President William Scott's conviction that "direct instruction should be given [to the Ohio State students] 'on the great themes of religious thought,'" Gladden was invited to deliver a series of talks "on the relation of religion . . . to modern thought."[116] Gladden's lectures, published under the title *Burning Questions*, were an effort to show that although "criticism has demolished some of the cumbrous and obstructive outworks of our theology," the "central truths" of Christianity remained unharmed. Thus, in answer to the challenge Darwinism posed to Christianity, Gladden argued:

> This modern science which has been supposed by some persons to have banished God from the universe, has not, then, banished order from the universe; it has given us revelations of the order and system which pervades the whole far more impressive than

our fathers ever saw. . . . Nature as Paley saw it exhibited intelligence, order, purpose. . . . Nature as Darwin saw it, exhibits a grander order, a more far-reaching and comprehensive purpose. Why, then, should we cease to believe in an intelligent Creator?[117]

Although Christianity would need to adjust its "theories," to rework its understanding of revelation, redemption, or retribution in light of modern knowledge, he assured the students at Ohio State that the "central facts of Christianity" would not be discredited.[118]

Gladden, whose theology emphasized the fatherhood of God and the brotherhood of humanity, looked for the fulfillment of the Kingdom of God in this world.[119] In the last of his lectures to the Ohio State students he addressed the topic of the Kingdom, surveying the evidence for its swift advent: "Religion is steadily becoming more spiritual and more ethical, less formal, less dogmatic, less crudely emotional; . . . liberty and toleration are taking the place of bigotry and tyranny; character and conduct are exalted above opinion and theory; and love as compassion, and love as good-will is slowly but steadily gaining upon cruelty and strife."[120]

The growth of liberal and social Christianity, in which spirit triumphed over doctrine and love superseded competition, gave Gladden grounds for hope in the future of a Christian America. Implicit in this message, of course, was a challenge to the students of Ohio State to become, as products of a liberal Christian education, the future architects and engineers of God's Kingdom. Students at the other midwestern universities received a similar challenge in various ways in the course of their college careers. As heirs to the twin traditions of Christianity and American culture, the students of the midwestern public schools were to further the advances of a Christian civilization.

During the nineteenth century the religious tenor of the public midwestern universities changed perceptibly. Required courses in Natural Theology and Evidences of Christianity, required chapel, and prayer before class were largely phased out by 1900. But the universities in this era did not simply abandon their religious concerns and become secular institutions. Rather, by means of voluntary religious organizations and worship, denominational guilds, extracurricular lectures, informal religious requirements for faculty, and classes in the social sciences and philosophy that promoted liberal Christianity, administrators, faculty, and students continued to cultivate broad Christian ideals in public schools.

The informal means by which liberal Protestants continued to influence public higher education in the United States, however, could only delay—not arrest—the steady secularizing pressures that were beginning to influence higher education in the late nineteenth century. Since most Americans still saw their country as a Christian nation, public schools, by virtue of their mission of service to the nation, could also serve as nurseries of a liberal Christianity that merged service to God and to country. But as America became more pluralistic and secular, and as an increased stress on research, specialization, and vocationalism and an expanded curriculum worked to further the secularization of higher education in general, state schools found it more and more difficult to favor a particular religious tradition. And so, in the course of the twentieth century these universities, in response to the changing realities around them, would abandon their earlier efforts to serve God and simply pursue a mission of service to the nation.

Notes

I gratefully acknowledge the criticism of an earlier version of this essay by George M. Marsden, Winton U. Solberg, D. G. Hart, Diana Butler, Tony Jenkins, Paul Kemeny, Kathryn Long, and Jeffrey Trexler.

1. James Angell, "The Relation of American Colleges to Christianity," *Providence Journal*, December 1, 1877.

2. The secularization of university education in this era is a major theme among historians of higher education. Key among those who focus on the secularization of higher education in general in this period is Richard Hofstadter, in Richard Hofstadter and C. DeWitt Hardy, *The Development and Scope of Higher Education in the United States* (New York: Columbia University Press, 1952), esp. 33–38. Others who echo this theme to a greater or lesser degree are Earl H. Brill, "Religion and the Rise of the University: A Study of the Secularization of American Higher Education, 1870–1910," (Ph.D. diss., American University, 1969); Winton U. Solberg, "The Conflict between Religion and Secularism at the University of Illinois, 1867–1894," *American Quarterly* 18 (1966), 183–99; William C. Ringenberg, *The Christian College: A History of Protestant Higher Education in America* (Grand Rapids. Christian University Press, 1984); Victor R.

Wilbee, "The Religious Dimensions of Three Presidencies in a State University: Presidents Tappan, Haven, and Angell at the University of Michigan" (Ph.D. diss., University of Michigan, 1967). Ringenberg does note that many state schools "remained considerably religious" into the twentieth century but titles his chapter addressing this period "The Movement toward Secularization." Ringenberg, *Christian College*, 129.

3. Earl D. Ross comments on this, noting, "In the social gospel crusade . . . social scientists in the leading state universities were in the vanguard." Earl D. Ross, "Religious Influences in the Development of State Colleges and Universities," *Indiana Magazine of History* 46 (December 1950), 356.

4. *Proceedings of the Board of Regents, 1837–1863* (Ann Arbor: University of Michigan, 1915), 211, quoted in Wilbee, "Three Presidencies," 23. See also William C. Ringenberg, "Church Colleges vs. State University," *Michigan History* 55 (Winter 1971), 318–19.

5. See Thomas D. Clark, *Indiana University: Midwestern Pioneer*, vol. 1, *The Early Years* (Bloomington: Indiana University Press, 1970), 9, 28, 88; Jonas Viles, *The University of Missouri: A Centennial History* (Columbia: University of Missouri, 1939), 30, 41, 54, 134, 139, 181; Solberg, "Religion and Secularism," 185; Merle Curti and Vernon Carstensen, *The University of Wisconsin, A History: 1848–1925*, vol. 1 (Madison: University of Wisconsin Press, 1949), 407–8.

6. Clark, *Indiana*, I, 37–41, 85–86, 87; Wilbee, "Three Presidencies," 27, 43, 140; Viles, *Missouri*, 52–53, 59.

7. Curti, *Wisconsin*, I, 184.

8. Clark, *Indiana*, I, 150. Clark claims that the first six presidents of Indiana University were ministers, but I can find no evidence that John Lathrop, who left the presidency of Wisconsin in 1859 to become the fourth president of Indiana, was ordained. Lathrop was also the president of the University of Missouri from 1841 to 1849 and 1865 to 1866 and chancellor of the University of Wisconsin from 1849 to 1859. See Viles, *Missouri*; and Curti, *Wisconsin*, I, 57, 111.

9. Charles M. Perry, *Henry Philip Tappan, Philosopher and University President* (Ann Arbor: University of Michigan Press, 1933), 182–83.

10. James Gray, *The University of Minnesota: 1851–1951* (Minneapolis: University of Minnesota Press, 1951), 47.

11. Curti, *Wisconsin*, I, 407, 412; Clark, *Indiana*, I, 150, 165; Wilbee, "Three Presidencies," 95, 107; Ringenberg, "Church Colleges vs. State University," 307; Ross, "Religious Influences," 351, 354; James A. Woodburn, *History of Indiana University*, vol. 1. *1820–1902* (Bloomington: Indiana University Press, 1940), 59. See also Winton U. Solberg, *The University of Illinois, 1867–1894: An Intellectual and Cultural History* (Urbana: University of Illinois Press, 1968), 109.

12. *Michigan Argus*, May 11, 1858, quoted in Wilbee, "Three Presidencies," 115.

13. Ringenberg, "Church Colleges vs. State University," 307; Clark, *Indiana*, I, 158; Curti, *Wisconsin*, I, 190.

14. Solberg, "Religion and Secularism," 189. See also Viles, *Missouri*, 139.

15. "Girls at the University in the Early Days," *Aegis* (February 1896), quoted in Curti, *Wisconsin*, I, 407.

16. Ringenberg, *Christian College*, 81

17. John McMynn to O. M. Conover, July 30, 1855, Conover Papers, State Historical Society of Wisconsin, quoted in Curti, *Wisconsin*, I, 89. See also Ringenberg, *Christian College*, 82.

18. Quoted in Ringenberg, *Christian College*, 83.

19. Ringenberg, "Church Colleges vs. State University," 307.

20. See note 2 on the emphasis on secularization in literature concerning this period. See also Laurence R. Veysey, *The Emergence of the American University* (Chicago: University of Chicago Press, 1965), 112; and Ringenberg, *Christian College*, 129, who note in passing the persistence of religious concerns.

21. See Robert T. Handy, *A Christian America: Protestant Hopes and Historical Realities*, 2d ed. (New York: Oxford University Press, 1984), esp. 82–158.

22. James E. Pollard, *History of the Ohio State University: The Story of Its First Seventy-Five Years, 1873–1948* (Columbus: Ohio State University Press, 1952), 90; Clifford S. Griffin, *The University of Kansas: A History* (Lawrence: University Press of Kansas, 1974), 66, 78; Clark, *Indiana*, I, 130; Solberg, *Illinois*, 88.

23. Curti, *Wisconsin*, I, 562; Pollard, *Ohio*, 134; Solberg, *Illinois*, 330.

24. J. David Hoeveler, Jr., "The University and the Social Gospel: The Intellectual Origins of the 'Wisconsin Idea,'" *Wisconsin Magazine of History* (Summer 1976), 285; Laurence R. Veysey, "The Emergence of the American University, 1865–1910: A Study in the Relations between Ideals and Institutions" (Ph.D. diss., University of California, 1961), 448; Ross, "Religious Influences," 350; Wilbee, "Three Presidencies," 157; Griffin, *Kansas*, 82.

25. Quoted in Pollard, *Ohio*, 51.

26. James B. Angell, *The Old and the New Ideals of Scholars* (Ann Arbor: University of Michigan Press, 1905), 28–29, quoted in Wilbee, "Three Presidencies," 165.

27. Curti, *Wisconsin*, I, 293; Joshua A. Lippincott to D. A. Finley, July 11, 1887 (copy), University Archives, Spencer Research Library, University of Kansas, quoted in Griffin, *Kansas*, 82.

28. William H. Frieze, *The Relations of the State University to Religion* (Ann Arbor: University of Michigan, 1888), 23. Likewise, John M. Coulter, in his inaugural address at Indiana University in 1891, manifested the tolerant but Christian tone of the era, claiming: "Therefore, while all the varying beliefs and disbeliefs must meet here on perfect equality, as is befitting an intellectual community seeking for truth in every direction, we must all unite in *one* belief, that the only kind of life worth living is that one which is governed by the highest moral principles. As for myself, I find the best statement of these principles in the utterances of the great Nazarene." John M. Coulter, "The University Spirit," *Indiana Student* (June 1891), quoted in Woodburn, *Indiana*, 402. See also Richard T. Ely, *The Universities and the Churches* (Albany: University of the State of New York, 1893), 360, for similar comments of President Cyrus Northrop of the University of Minnesota and President Richard Jesse of the University of Missouri.

29. Curti, *Wisconsin*, I, 409–10; Wilbee, "Three Presidencies," 179; Clark, *Indiana*, I, 162–63; Viles, *Missouri*, 242.

30. Wilbee, "Three Presidencies," 179–80; Clark, *Indiana*, I, 271.

31. Wilbee, "Three Presidencies," 138.

32. Clarence P. Shedd, *The Church Follows Its Students* (New Haven: Yale University Press, 1938), 9.

33. Pollard, *Ohio*, 74–75, 77; Alexis Cope, *History of the Ohio State University*, vol. 1, *1870–1910*, ed. Thomas C. Mendenhall (Columbus: Ohio State University Press, 1920), 78.

34. Pollard, *Ohio*, 78, 81–86; Cope, *Ohio*, 76–84.

35. Pollard, *Ohio*, 86–89.

36. Solberg, *Illinois*, 178.

37. Foster North, *The Struggle for Religious Liberty in the University of Illinois* (Los Angeles: Wetzel Publishing, 1942), 30, quoted in Solberg, *Illinois*, 304.

38. North, *Struggle*, 11; Solberg, *Illinois*, 304.

39. Solberg, *Illinois*, 305–6.

40. University of Illinois, Board of Trustees, *Thirteenth Annual Report* (Springfield, 1886), 69, quoted in Solberg, "Religion and Secularism," 196.

41. Solberg, "Religion and Secularism," 198. North eventually took this struggle to the Illinois Supreme Court and lost there, too. In 1914 the Board of Trustees of the University of Illinois voted North a degree, but after receiving his degree at a commencement where a priest read Scripture and prayed, North returned it. See Solberg, "Religion and Secularism," 196–97.

42. James B. Angell, "Religious Life in Our State Universities," *Andover Review* 13 (April 1890), 366. See also Wilbee, "Three Presidencies," 171–72.

43. Wilbee, "Three Presidencies," 179–80.

44. In 1900, at Ohio State University, President William Oxley Thompson, a Presbyterian minister, recommended that a weekly convocation be substituted for daily chapel. No doubt a history of logistical problems surrounding limited seating and taking attendance argued in favor of this decision, but Thompson may well have agreed with Angell that mandatory worship was detrimental to the religious life of the campus. His recommendation certainly would not have been based on a secular ideology. Cope, *Ohio State*, 298–99; Pollard, *Ohio*, 86–89.

45. See Wilbee, "Three Presidencies," 180.

46. Francis W. Kelsey, "State Universities and Church Colleges," *Atlantic Monthly* 80 (December 1897), 830.

47. C. Grey Austin, "The Students' Christian Association," in *The University of Michigan: An Encyclopedic Survey*, vol. 9, ed. Walter A. Donnelly (Ann Arbor: University of Michigan Press, 1958), 1888–1889; C. Grey Austin, *A Century of Religion at the University of Michigan* (n.p.: University of Michigan, 1957), 11.

48. L. T. Savage, "Religious Life in a Typical State University of the West," *Intercollegian* 22 (February 1900), 104.

49. Curti, *Wisconsin*, I, 411–12; Clark, *Indiana*, I, 271; Pollard, *Ohio State*, 100; Solberg, *Illinois*, 180, 302, 376; Frank F. Stephens, *A History of the University of Missouri* (Columbia: University of Missouri Press, 1962), 445.

50. Austin, "Students' Christian Association," 1888–1889; Austin, *Century of Religion*, 12.

51. Wilbee, "Three Presidencies," 183. See Martin D'Ooge, ed., *Religious Thought at the University of Michigan* (Ann Arbor: Register Publishing Co., 1893), for these talks.

52. C. Howard Hopkins, *History of the Y.M.C.A. in North America* (New York: Association Press, 1951), 364–66; Clarence P. Shedd, *Two Centuries of Student Christian Movements* (New York: Association Press, 1934), 114.

53. Edwin H. Humphrey, *The Michigan Book* (Ann Arbor: Inland Press, 1898), 88–89; Wilbee, "Three Presidencies," 194.

54. Wilbee, "Three Presidencies," 194 n.1.

55. Shedd, *Church Follows*, 11.

56. Wilbee, "Three Presidencies," 185–89; Shedd, *Church Follows*.

57. Kelsey, "State Universities and Church Colleges," 827–29.

58. Veysey, "Emergence of American University," 159 n.301; Griffin, *Kansas*, 82.

59. "Education by the State," *Northwestern Christian Advocate*, April 3, 1878, quoted in Solberg, *Illinois*, 181; *Indiana Student* (January 1885), quoted in Clark, *Indiana*, I, 203.

60. Angell, "Religious Life," 367.

61. James B. Angell, "Inaugural Address," in *Selected Addresses* (New York: Longmans, Green, 1912), 30–31, quoted in Veysey, "Emergence of American University," 330.

62. J. B. Angell to D. C. Gilman, October 23, 1885, Daniel Coit Gilman Collection, Sidney Lanier Room, Johns Hopkins University, Baltimore, quoted in Veysey, "Emergence of American University," 330.

63. Solberg, *Illinois*, 103.

64. Warner Fite, "The State-University Idea," *Nation* 101 (September 9, 1915): 323.

65. Wilbee, for example, notes that "Angell frequently expressed concern for the need for a Christian philosophy of knowledge, but as the university grew, the faculty became primarily interested in applied science, in the pursuit of objective research after the spirit of positivism, or in the adoption of 'scientific' methods." Wilbee, "Three Presidencies," 184

66. See Gladys Bryson, "The Emergence of the Social Sciences from Moral Philosophy," *International Journal of Ethics* 42 (April 1932), 304–23; and Ross, "Religious Influences," 356; Solberg, *Illinois*, 8; Wilbee, "Three Presidencies," 182; Dorothy Ross, "The Development of the Social Sciences," in *The Organization of Knowledge in Modern America: 1860–1920*, ed. Alexandra Oleson and John Voss (Baltimore: Johns Hopkins University Press, 1979), 107–38; and Dorothy Ross, *The Origins of American Social Science* (Cambridge: Cambridge University Press, 1991), 36–38, 42, 94.

67. L. L. and J. S. Bernard, "A Century of Progress in the Social Sciences," *Social Forces* 11 (May 1933), 496–97.

68. Curti, *Wisconsin*, I, 246–48.

69. Sanford Robinson, *John Bascom: Prophet* (New York: G. P. Putnam's Sons, 1922), 2–3; Hoeveler, "University and Social Gospel," 285–86; Curti, *Wisconsin*, I, 247.

70. Richard T. Ely, *Ground under Our Feet: An Autobiography* (New York: Macmillan, 1938), 198; Hoeveler, "University and Social Gospel," 286.

71. John Bascom, *The New Theology* (New York: Knickerbocker Press, 1891), 64, 118, 215; Curti, *Wisconsin*, I, 276–80. John Bascom, *Social Theory: A Grouping of Social Facts and Principles* (New York: T. Y. Crowell, 1895), 507, 510, 521, 525.

72. John Bascom, *The Freedom of Faith* (Madison: Atwood and Culver, 1874), 12.

73. Curti, *Wisconsin*, I, 283, 286.

74. John Bascom, *The Seat of Sin* (n.p., n.d.), 14, quoted ibid., 287.

75. John Bascom, *A Christian State* (Milwaukee, 1887), 31, quoted in Curti, *Wisconsin*, I, 287.

76. Bascom, *New Theology*, 118.

77. Hoeveler makes a similar point in "University and Social Gospel," 293.

78. Benjamin G. Rader, *The Academic Mind and Reform: The Influence of Richard T. Ely in American Life* (n.p.: University of Kentucky Press, 1966), 28–29, 36; Ely to Daniel C. Gilman, July 11, 1885, Gilman MSS, Johns Hopkins University Library, Baltimore, quoted in Rader, *Academic Mind*, 36.

79. John R. Everett, *Religion in Economics: A Study of John Bates Clark, Richard T. Ely, Simon N. Patten* (Morningside Heights: King's Crown Press, 1946), 76; Ely, *Ground*, 14–16.

80. Ely, *Ground*, 77.

81. Richard T. Ely, *Social Aspects of Christianity and Other Essays* (London: Wm. Reeves, n.d.), 53; Rader, *Academic Mind*, 61.

82. Ely, *Social Aspects*, 9, quoted in Everett, *Religion in Economics*, 81; Ely, *Social Aspects*, 25.

83. Ely, *Social Aspects*, 86; see also p. 8.

84. Ibid., 73.

85. Ely, *Ground*, 88–91.

86. Quoted in Robert M. Crunden, *Ministers of Reform: The Progressives' Achievement in American Civilization, 1889–1920* (n.p.: Basic Books, 1982; reprint, Urbana: University of Illinois Press, 1984), 69.

87. Ely, *Social Aspects*, 147–48, quoted in Hoeveler, "University and Social Gospel," 295.

88. Richart T. Ely, *The Social Law of Service* (New York, 1896), 276, quoted in Everett, *Religion in Economics*, 81.

89. Robert T. Handy, ed. *The Social Gospel in America, 1870–1920: Gladden, Ely, Rauschenbusch* (New York: Oxford University Press, 1966), 181–82.

90. Ely, *The Social Law of Service*, quoted in Handy, *Social Gospel*, 224, 249.

91. Everett, *Religion in Economics*, 97.

92. John R. Commons, *Myself* (New York: Macmillan, 1934), 50–53, 8–9, 43–45, 48; Joseph Dorfman, *The Economic Mind in American Civilization: 1865–1918*, vol. 3 (New York: Augustus M. Kelley, 1969), 276–77.

93. John R. Commons, *Social Reform and the Church* (New York: Thomas Y. Crowell and Co., 1894), 13, 19, 20, 22, 26.

94. Ibid., 52, 75.

95. Ibid., 25–26.

96. Ibid., 38.

97. Ibid., 71.

98. Commons to H. C. Adams, April 16, 1895, Adams Papers, in possession of Mrs. Henry Carter Adams, Ann Arbor, Michigan, quoted in

Dorfman, *Economic Mind*, 285. See also Woodburn, *Indiana*, 440; Commons, *Myself*, 52.

99. Clark, *Indiana*, I, 287, 331, 342.

100. Bruce Kuklick, *Churchmen and Philosophers from Jonathan Edwards to John Dewey* (New Haven: Yale University Press, 1985), 230–31.

101. George Dykhuizen, *The Life and Mind of John Dewey* (Carbondale: Southern Illinois University Press, 1973), 10–18, 28–43.

102. Ibid., 47.

103. John Dewey, "Ethics and Physical Science," *Andover Review* 7 (1887), 577, quoted ibid., 47.

104. Dykhuizen, *Dewey*, 50.

105. John Dewey, *The Early Works: 1882–1898*, vol. 1, *1882–1888: Early Essays and Leibniz's New Essays Concerning the Human Understanding* (Carbondale: Southern Illinois University Press, 1969), 61–62.

106. Ibid., 90.

107. Dykhuizen, *Dewey*, 57–58, 61–63, 64–65, 72–73. Nevertheless, Dewey's liberal Christianity led him to refuse a position on the board of directors of the Students' Christian Association in 1893 because the association mandated subscription to "the tenets of evangelical Christianity" as a condition of membership. Dykhuizen, *Dewey*, 342 n.6.

108. See Crunden, *Ministers of Reform*, 56–57; Dykhuizen, *Dewey*, 70.

109. John Dewey, "Christianity and Democracy," in D'Ooge, *Religious Thought at the University of Michigan*, 62, 61, 68, 67. See also John Dewey, *The Early Works of John Dewey: 1882–1898*, vol. 4, *1893–1894* (Carbondale: Southern Illinois University Press, 1971), 367.

110. See also Dewey's address, "Reconstruction," in Dewey, *Early Works*, vol. 4, 103–5, for Dewey's liberal religious views in this period.

111. Quoted in Crunden, *Ministers of Reform*, 58.

112. Dykhuizen, *Dewey*, 73–74.

113. Jacob H. Dorn, *Washington Gladden: Prophet of the Social Gospel* (n.p.: Ohio State University Press, 1966), 92, 90.

114. William McPherson, "An Appreciation of Dr. Washington Gladden," *First Church News* 6 (February 1936), 7, quoted in Dorn, *Gladden*, 442.

115. Handy, *Social Gospel*, 19–23.

116. Pollard, *Ohio State*, 100.

117. Washington Gladden, *Burning Questions of the Life that Now Is, and of That Which is to Come* (New York: Century Co., 1890), 247, 28–29; Dorn, *Gladden*, 169.

118. Gladden, *Burning Questions*, 248.

119. Handy, *Social Gospel*, 26–27.

120. Gladden, *Burning Questions*, 242.

3

Secularization and Sacralization: Speculations on Some Religious Origins of the Secular Humanities Curriculum, 1850–1900

JAMES TURNER

Fair Harvard! thy sons to thy jubilee throng,
And with blessings surrender thee o'er;
By these festival rites, from the age that is past,
To the age that is waiting before.[1]

"Fair Harvard!"

American college teachers are familiar with a curious puzzle. Step outside a college, and you cannot fail to see that scientific and technical knowledge orders our lives and shapes our futures. Yet talk to the professors on a college curriculum committee, and you generally find the humanities vaguely regarded as less dispensable, more primordial, than the natural sciences. Even chemists incline to concede that literature and philosophy somehow lie closer to the heart of liberal education than what goes on in laboratories.

Why should this be so? No single answer will suffice. But some of the answers may be found in the transition from old religious conceptions of higher education to new, apparently secular ones. This movement had already begun, spare and sluggish, in the seventeenth century, when American collegiate learning still meant only Harvard. The pace quickened after 1850: by 1900 it was a grand march. Sketching a few of the moves in that dance of secularization may help to resolve the riddle with which this chapter begins. In doing so, this venture in intellectual choreography may perhaps clarify an obscure meaning of the modern liberal arts—one widely sensed, I believe, but not clearly seen. More modestly, it should at least shed a little light on the complex relation between religion and secularization in American higher learning.

Historians of higher education broadly agree when and how curriculum changed as the old classical college evolved into the modern undergraduate college.[2] Before the Civil War, colleges shared virtually a single curriculum, with local variations. The American colonies had inherited the basis of this course of study from the English Renaissance and Reformation. Learning centered on ancient languages, but instruction took place in English. Colonial colleges also taught rhetoric and elocution, mathematics, logic, divinity, and, eventually, natural philosophy.[3] This curriculum cohered around nothing but tradition. But it did assume, almost subliminally, the unity of knowledge: that all truth flowed, it was supposed, from God.[4] We may assume that the fifteen-year-old boys who infested William and Mary or Harvard rarely questioned the axiom.

In the later eighteenth century, Scottish common sense philosophy cast a new light into American intellectual life, an illumination extending even into its feebler penumbras, such as the colleges. The invading Scots brought with them a cogent doctrine in support of this hitherto fuzzy epistemological faith.[5] In colleges the chief curricular fallout from the Scottish assault was a senior course in Moral Philosophy.[6]

Between the Revolution and the Civil War, this course became the capstone of the curriculum almost everywhere. It gave students an explicit, articulated explanation of the unity of God's truth—and hence of the unity of the curriculum.[7] Indeed, like a black hole pulling in all the inter-stellar debris in its neighborhood, the Moral Philosophy course sucked in a hodgepodge of intellectual flotsam and jetsam that would boggle a modern professor: topics ranging from political economy to the origin of language to animals' rights.[8] The lecturer, generally the college president, posed large questions and gave large answers. He showed how solutions to problems in ethics, political theory, law, psychology, religion all flowed from the divine constitution of nature. All this fitted together in a grand schema derived loosely from Protestant theological doctrine, more tightly from Scottish philosophical teaching.[9]

This is not to say that actual course work formed an interconnected whole. Far from it. For one thing, elementary drill in languages and mathematics blighted vast stretches of the day. A virtuoso of moral philosophy could not have persuaded a bunch of eighteen-year-olds swotting Greek verbs that these conjugations led inexorably to Newtonian celestial mechanics and thence to the perfections of the Deity.

Anyway, that was not the point. When knowledge seemed in principle tied together—in the study of a single unified divine creation—a professor scarcely needed to explain *how* particular bits of learning were connected in order to convince himself and his students that somehow they all *did*.[10] But, in fact, the college president actually did just that. He not only exemplified to the senior class that particular bits of learning linked up—that the ethical principle of chastity followed from the sociological facts of demography—but also provided the philosophical framework within which knowledge formed a seamless whole.[11] It was not some palpable connection between individual courses that unified antebellum college curricula. It was the conviction, felt and taught, of coherence ultimately stemming from the Creator.

Yet in the decades after 1860 this sense of coherence grew thinner and thinner, finally vanishing like smoke.[12] Increasing specialization and fragmentation of knowledge contributed to its disappearance: the *pedagogical* map of knowledge, implicit in the curriculum, gradually converged with the ever more detailed *general* map of knowledge, implicit in intellectual work outside the colleges.[13] Another disintegrative force was the weakening of consensus on the existence of God, a belief that was especially fragile in academic circles: when the existence of the Creator began to appear dubious, the unity of creation no longer seemed axiomatic.[14] But the centrifugal forces—and there were others—are not to the point here.

The outcome is. Particularly in the emerging universities, a jumble of new undergraduate curricula hived off from the old unitary course of study. Most of these were aimed at vocational training, loosely defined: architecture, engineering, agriculture, pedagogy, pharmacy, business, science, music, and more.[15] To be sure, amid this collegiate Babel the traditional classical curriculum retained pride of place. Yet the confusion of tongues infected even it. Within the liberal arts course subjects of study multiplied, and the tide flowing toward the elective system pulled them apart from one another. Students shared less and less of a common education. Most tellingly, the old Moral Philosophy course itself disintegrated, giving birth in its death to several of our present academic specialties: economics, philosophy, sociology, political science, and, less directly, anthropology.

The pace of fragmentation varied. The emerging universities moved fastest. Many smaller colleges kept their old curriculum, or at least its religious framework, well into the twentieth century. Yet by 1900, at the institutions recognized even then as leading the change, any claim to an integrated curriculum—much less unified knowledge—appeared dubious, if not downright fraudulent.[16] The firmament, however, did not ring with lamentation. In bald fact, the undergraduate's experience had taken a sharp turn for the better. Teaching methods were less boring, professors less ignorant, students themselves less childish. Even college food improved.

At the same time, faculty members in the colleges moving into this brighter future had good reason to worry about the larger meaning of their curriculum. Not that many of them wasted hours fretting. Cheering the innovations that, incidentally, undermined coherence was understandably the order of the day. Indeed, the abolition of compulsory chapel provoked louder howls, inside academia and out, than the demise of Moral Philosophy. But the implicit secularization of the curriculum struck much closer to the heart of the college. And some professors did grow anxious about the larger meaning of their work. Yet the coincident secularization of academic knowledge made absurd any thought of restoring curricular coherence on the old basis of shared religious beliefs. Where Moral Philosophy had once stood, a great void now gaped.

And, if nature no longer abhorred a vacuum, professors did. Attempts to fill it account for many of the innovations in general education in the twentieth century. Columbia's Contemporary Civilization course in 1919; Robert Maynard Hutchins's reorganization of the Chicago curriculum around the "Great Books" in the 1930s; the General Education program outlined in Harvard's "Redbook" in 1945; the Great Awakening in core curricula that began around 1980—the intellectual history of the modern American college could be written as the Quest for Coherence. But this search to replace the senior course in Moral Philosophy goes on in a secularized academy that cannot admit the God who made the Moral Philosophy course work.

For readers acquainted with the history of American higher education, the foregoing narrative holds no surprises, as far as it goes. But it does not go very far in one direction. In brief, we know that in many schools (and in the long run all) the putatively coherent antebellum curriculum fell apart; and we know in general the sorts of courses and requirements that replaced it. But we do not know how, or even whether, the new curriculum was meant to remedy the intellectual incoherence resulting from the breakup of the old one. This neglected question needs answering: How did these changing colleges, in reconstructing the liberal arts, respond to their crisis of coherence in the decades after 1860?

Answering it is not easy. Historians of higher education in this period, fascinated by the emergence of universities and graduate schools, have neglected undergraduate curricula, still more undergraduate *teaching*.[17] Even histories of expressly liberal arts colleges slight the development, ideologies, and justifications of curriculum in favor of institutional growth and student life. And the content of course work, in particular, is rarely examined. Everyone knows that colleges introduced many new subjects in the last half of the nineteenth century. What professors actually taught under these rubrics is almost terra incognita. To guess at the substance of courses, even their rationales, usually requires inference from anecdotes, from textbooks, or still more remotely from monographs about scholarship in the discipline. What professors actually told students, what students heard professors say (rarely the same thing!), what purposes professors believed their courses served, what methods they used to achieve these goals—the data bearing on such questions remain as pristine as if the archives were in Albania.[18]

A foray into this territory is the aim of this chapter. The particular terrain is the undergraduate arts-and-sciences colleges of universities, with a special eye to perhaps the two most influential instances of the type: Harvard and the University of Michigan.[19] This selection stems partly from the fact that the emerging universities led the transformation of curriculum, partly from idiosyncratic practical reasons.[20] Yet, whatever its justification, the fact remains that this discussion of liberal-arts education never scrutinizes a traditional liberal-arts college such as Amherst or Grinnell. Hugh Hawkins has aptly noted the perverseness of looking mainly at the two largest nineteenth-century American universities: "One can argue that universities set the pattern, but I rather suspect a collegiate ethos developed in smaller colleges which universities came to envy and to imitate."[21] There is much truth in this view. Yet necessity dictates that choices be made; and Michigan and Harvard serve here chiefly to highlight patterns detectable elsewhere in the historiography of higher education. Moreover, the collegiate ethos to which Hawkins properly calls attention perhaps had more to do in the long run with pedagogical method than intellectual content.

Intellectually the most visibile change in the liberal arts curriculum was diversification. This multiplication of subjects itself had multiple causes. Modern foreign languages, along with serious instruction in English composition and rhetoric, began to invade the classical curriculum shortly after 1800, advancing under the banner of utility. The division of the natural sciences into more specialized disciplines required the old Natural Philosophy and Natural History courses to subdivide likewise into physics, chemistry, geology, zoology, and so forth. The old Moral Philosophy course gave birth to economics, sociology, psychology, and other courses in the "social sciences." History, although spinning off from the study of classical languages, commonly took its ideology from the social sciences as well.[22] So various did subjects of study become that the curriculum began to spin out of control. For half a century colleges experimented with versions of the elective system before finally settling, most of them, on the present method of concentration and distribution to bring order to the welter of entries in their course catalogues.[23]

The catalogue entries most relevant here were those in philosophy, literature, and the fine arts. For the new buzzword of undergraduate general education was "liberal culture"; and these three subjects, especially the last two, were most often invoked to exemplify it.[24] (This is by no means to deny the centrality in curricular thinking of the social sciences, which often carried more prestige than the humanities. But, as their label suggests, the social sciences expressed the scientistic more than the cultural aspirations of higher education.) The old shibboleths of the classical curriculum—

that it ensured the "discipline" and provided the "furniture" of "the mind"—had by no means vanished. Indeed, as secularization advanced, "mental discipline" (learning *how* to think rather than *what* to think) possibly "became an even stronger justification for liberal education" than in antebellum curricular rationales.[25] Nor, for that matter, did this liberal culture itself thrive only where education had lost its religious foundation; for instance, a specifically Christian version of it flourished at Yale.[26] Liberal education has never suffered from lack of variety in its rationales.[27]

Yet when a new one shoots into prominence, it merits a close look. By 1880 college presidents intoned the words "liberal culture" like the ritual incantation of some new cult. And rightly so. To be sure, liberal culture was far from the only ideal percolating through undergraduate curricula in the late nineteenth century: scientistic claims probably had vastly greater intellectual appeal to most faculty, and perhaps to most students as well. Nor should it be confused with the liberal arts *tout court*. Psychology, economics, and history, for instance—not to mention the natural sciences—did not mesh well with liberal culture. Yet, insofar as the secular liberal-arts curriculum had any substantive *unifying* principle to replace the divine order outlined in moral philosophy, the protean notion of liberal culture was it.

And protean it was. Defining *liberal culture* would drive a lexicographer to despair. It certainly involved enthusiasm for breadth of learning, as opposed to narrow specialization. It favored the cultivation of imagination over the sharpening of intellect or the acquisition of information. Cynicism further suggests that it produced the kind of social polish later requisite at cocktail parties. Beyond this, the fog sets in. Whatever liberal culture was, students seem to have caught it by exposure to the "best" works of literature and art, famously Homer, Dante, and Shakespeare, Raphael and Rembrandt. Music seldom figured largely, probably because the phonograph did not come along quickly enough.

Like most large ideals, liberal culture wrapped up in a single package a complicated bundle of desires. These ranged from craving for social cachet to yearning for spiritual enlightenment. A week at Harvard circa 1890 would certainly have impressed one with the former, but it is the latter, the "spiritual" face of liberal culture, that now requires attention. For this aspect proved most salient in the specific roles that philosophy, literature, and the fine arts came to play in the emerging liberal-arts curriculum in secular-minded universities.

Of this triumvirate, philosophy had by far the oldest career in American education. Colleges had insisted on it, in some form or another, from colonial days. But the throne from which philosophy reigned over the antebellum college, the senior Moral Philosophy course, had crumbled. Once the monarch governing the hierarchy of knowledge, philosophy was demoted to ordinary citizen in the democracy of the elective system. Stripped of the great melange of knowledge integrated into the Moral Philosophy course, philosophy now meant the remnants left behind when economics, sociology, psychology, and even theology departed.[28]

This remainder fragmented into a collection of technical sub-specialties, ranging from logic to metaphysics.[29] Michigan in 1886–87 provides an example of the change. It had then an exceptionally strong department, comprising G. S. Morris and John Dewey. This polymathic pair offered an astonishing range of courses on the history of philosophy, logic, political philosophy, aesthetics, ethics, and metaphysics, as well as on individual philosophers from Plato to Herbert Spencer.[30] Students had vastly more philosophical training available than in any antebellum college. But it now lay chopped up into scattered pieces, the consumption of any of them left to individual discretion. Philosophy no longer exercised even the shadow of an integrative force.

Yet this observation, while strictly correct, probably does not accurately represent philosophy's place in the new liberal-arts curriculum around 1880 or 1900. Apparently many philosophy professors came to their discipline in search of answers to religious doubts, not a few of them being ministers or ministers manqué.[31] It seems a fair inference that these concerns shaped their teaching. Certainly the premier philosophical work written by college professors in this era—that of James, Royce, and Dewey—had much to do with epistemological and moral problems inherited from the wreckage of traditional Christian beliefs.[32]

Probably few college philosophers were trying literally to rebuild the old Moral Philosophy course. And, in general, they seem to have taught their subject in the late nineteenth century more as analysis, and less as inspiration, than in earlier decades. But it does not take a sharp eye to ferret out thinly disguised religious concerns in the philosophy classroom. These may explain the prominence of idealist metaphysics in philosophy departments around the turn of the century: as a bulwark against the threat of materialist scientism.[33] In any case, it was philosophy teachers of an ethical, even explicitly religious, stripe to whom students flocked, men such as Charles E. Garman at Amherst and George Herbert Palmer at Harvard. Garman's legendary course sought deliberately to shore up the Christian beliefs of his students, so it seems apt that they spoke of him "with perfect reverence."[34] This suspiciously religious phrase provides a clue worth following in other areas of the curriculum.

The teaching of literature lacked philosophy's long pedigree. True, students had always read classical literature as part of learning Greek and Latin. And, more recently, English poetry and oratory had entered college teaching as an aid to the study of rhetoric. Michigan in 1854–55 offered a "cursory" survey of English literature "designed chiefly to establish fundamental principles of [stylistic] criticism, and to cultivate correctness and propriety of style."[35] But such uses were purely ancillary. Apparently no American college taught English literature as an independent subject before 1857, when Francis A. March introduced it at Lafayette College.[36] Despite its late start, literature rose rapidly to curricular stardom. For example, Yale had no truck with the stuff until 1870, when Thomas R. Lounsbury, a professor at Yale's Sheffield Scientific School, sneaked English literature in (as it were) through the back door. Yet by 1900 English had "replaced classics as the backbone of the humanities at Yale."[37]

Both Harvard and Michigan had a long head start on Yale. They introduced English literature in 1858–59, the year after March introduced the course. James Russell Lowell taught the first course at Harvard (a senior elective), Andrew Dickson White at Michigan.[38] During the 1870s the subject sank deep into the curriculum at both schools. The men chiefly responsible stand among the giants of American scholarship. At Harvard the key figure was Francis J. Child, known to generations of undergraduates as "Stubby," and still known to scholars and folksingers for the massive collation of traditional British songs universally called "Child's Ballads"—the towering monument of nineteenth-century American philology.[39]

His counterpart at Michigan was Moses Coit Tyler, whose background as popular lecturer and health reformer gave no clue that his achievements would almost rival Child's.[40] With his two great works on early American writing—*The History of American Literature, 1607–1765* and *The Literary History of the American Revolution*—Tyler founded practically single-handedly two academic sub-disciplines: American literature and American intellectual history.

Both Child and Tyler began their professorial careers as instructors of rhetoric—Child in 1851, Tyler in 1867. Both chafed under the burden of correcting student compositions, and both from the beginning eased the pain with small doses of teaching literature.[41] In the early 1870s both struck out more boldly to fix a large and permanent place for English literature. Child began to offer a course covering Chaucer, Shakespeare, Bacon, Milton, and Dryden, in 1876 splitting Shakespeare off into a separate course. Child himself added a few more courses during the next several years; and in the 1880s Harvard's English department began to add more members, and with them more literature.[42] Meanwhile, Tyler at Michigan in 1874–75 introduced a senior elective in English literature and in the following year, startlingly, one in American literature.[43] The latter proved episodic, but by the end of the decade Michigan students could choose annually from a range of English literature courses open not just to seniors but to all undergraduates.[44]

Yet simply to say that Child and Tyler "taught literature" can mislead. For they approached their subject from a direction now alien to undergraduates and distasteful to most of their professors: by way of philology. Cultivated in Germany from the eighteenth century, transplanted to the English-speaking world in the early nineteenth, philology provided a powerful paradigm of knowledge well into the second half of the century.[45] Only when a very different model of knowledge, one drawn from the nomothetic natural sciences, elbowed philology onto the sidelines in the late nineteenth century did it acquire the seedy air of pedantic fact grubbing that has ever since made the discipline seem as dreary as November in Michigan. In its cheerful youth, philology produced a distinctive mode of college teaching, belonging to neither the antebellum classical curriculum nor the twentieth-century liberal arts.

Philological teachers aimed not to interpret a text but to supply the lost general lore from an author's culture needed to read it comprehendingly. At Lafayette College, Francis March's students approached *Paradise Lost* "as if it were Homer," with March supplying grammatical, etymological, mythological, biographical, "and other illustrative matter" to help students understand what they were reading.[46] Likewise, Child's Shakespeare class entailed close reading of eight or ten plays, with "much thumbing of Schmidt's *Shakespeare Lexicon.*"[47] Direct evidence of Tyler's teaching is hard to come by, but the occasional knowing allusion to *Quellen* suggests no less philological an approach than Child's.[48]

Given these principles, it made no sense to teach recent literature.[49] To concentrate on Spenser and Chaucer was ordinary, to go beyond the seventeenth century striking. The Ur-course in literature, March's at Lafayette, apparently halted at the seventeenth century. Johns Hopkins's first regular instructor in English, appointed in 1879, "touch[ed] nothing later than Shakespeare."[50] Until the 1880s Dryden was the latest author taught at Harvard. (And one wonders whether the course would have stretched to include him, were Dryden not chock-full of obscure allusions to the political and literary life of his epoch.) Common knowledge gave students the information needed to understand a novel or poem of the last century or two. What was there to teach?

At times the philological teachers can sound stultifyingly narrow, especially when described by the professors who pushed them aside.[51] But the relevant distinction was not between generalist and specialist, humanist and Gradgrind.[52] To cover the span of English literature from Chaucer to Dryden in one semester, as Child did, does not imply obsession with minutiae. And James Russell Lowell's casual, not to say lackadaisical, teaching style hardly suggests a nit-picking fussbudget:

> A student would trudge blunderingly along some passage [of Dante], and Lowell would break in, taking up the translation himself very likely, and quickly find some suggestion for criticism, for elaboration or incidental and remote comment. Toward the close of the hour, question and answer, or free discussion yielded to the stream of personal reminiscence or abundant reflection upon which Lowell would by this time be launched. Especially would he recall scenes in Florence, sketch in words the

effects of the Arno, Giotto's Tower, the church in which Dante was baptized, where he himself had seen children held at the same font; and so Lowell gave out of his treasures.[53]

This is the genial man of letters lounging on Parnassus; but it is also the philologist laboring in the classroom, providing students with a detailed commentary to explain individual references in the text, giving them the sort of information that (Lowell assumed) Dante's original readers would have had.[54]

Yet Lowell was more than a philologist. He was a moralist. He believed that imaginative writers were in essence moral teachers, that therefore immersion in great literature made readers more ethical.[55] Lowell had experienced as a Harvard student the moral didacticism of the antebellum college; it was second nature for him to carry it into the classroom when he himself became a professor. But his moralism had a special sheen. He had imbibed something of the Emersonian idea of the poet as seer and of the Carlylean idea of the poet as prophet. So Lowell translated the poetic function of moral illumination onto an almost transcendental, quasi-religious plane. He spoke as readily of the "mysterious and pervasive essence always in itself beautiful" as he did of the etymology of a Provençal noun.[56]

This strain in Lowell—the note of mysticism and reverence sounding amid his hardheaded common sense—echoed in more and more literature classes as the century neared its end. George Woodberry at Columbia was said to have infused a spirit of "natural piety" into the teaching of literature, while at Yale "words of enchantment" issued from the lips of Charlton Miner Lewis.[57] Arthur Marsh, America's first professor of comparative literature, wrote in 1888 that he wished his work to subserve "the imaginative and spiritual life of man."[58] Cornell's Hiram Corson tried to specify these elusive "aims of literary study." The "acquisition of knowledge" was, he conceded, "a good thing." So was "sharpening of the intellect" and "the cultivation of science and philosophy." *But* "there is something of infinitely more importance than all these—it is, the rectification, the adjustment, through that mysterious operation we call sympathy, of the unconscious personality, the hidden soul, which coöperates with the active powers, with the conscious intellect, for righteousness or unrighteousness."[59] This sounds like a melange of Matthew Arnold and Rosicrucianism.[60]

The belief shared by Rosicrucians with the new breed of English professors was that human beings worked out their salvation by establishing relations with spiritual truths embodied in sacred texts. Philology was pushed aside. Mere elucidation of phrases and contexts no longer illuminated a poem, for its significance lay deeper than its signification. The professor's task became one of inspiration, not information. Antebellum teachers had also often sought to inspire their students: at Harvard, Longfellow seems to have approached literature in that mood.[61] Moral Philosophy courses commonly sought to improve the seniors as well as inform them. Yet for inspiration to become the central aim of literary study was a new thing.

And any great work of literature, not just the archaic ones philologists favored, could uplift the properly disposed student. Hence, as the teaching of literature took the inspirational turn in secular universities in the 1880s and 1890s, modern poetry and novels appeared in courses. The goal of literary education became to saturate students with the deep truths revealed in great literature. And to do so the teacher needed to induce in the student a receptive mood of due reverence. In the new version of liberal education, a whiff of incense perfumed not only literature courses but all treatment of the high-cultural heritage.

Indeed, the third key subject in liberal culture, art history, entered the college curriculum only when secular universities began to feel the need to inject a dose of the vaguely spiritual, as distinct from the specifically Christian. Art was not entirely a curricular novelty. Antebellum colleges had occasionally offered drawing courses; and Michigan had made inconclusive gestures in the direction of something larger in the early 1850s. Yale in 1869 created a School of Fine Arts, independent of the college, to teach painting and drawing. Syracuse in 1872 introduced courses in "drawing and the history of art," leading to the establishment in the following year of an art school, as at Yale, separate from the college and focused on practice.[62] None of this touched the liberal arts curriculum except glancingly.

Art history, or "art appreciation," went far deeper. The founder of college teaching in that subject was Charles Eliot Norton. Hired at Harvard in 1874 (by his cousin Charles W. Eliot) for one year on a frankly experimental basis as "Lecturer on the History of the Fine

Arts as connected with Literature," Norton was the next year promoted to "Professor of the History of Art," the position he adorned until his retirement in 1898 at the age of seventy.[63] By 1895 William Dean Howells could write that Norton "stand[s] for Harvard in the humanities." Howells perhaps went overboard in asserting that *no* "fact of our higher civilization" was "more signal, more interesting" than Norton's influence.[64] But in fact it would be hard to over-estimate his resonance in the 1890s as spokesman for, and icon of, liberal culture and liberal-arts education.[65]

Undergraduates being undergraduates, not all took Norton so seriously. In the old man's last years flight from his undeniably sententious lectures via fire escape was apparently not unknown to dapper youth.[66] But many spoke of his courses in—metaphorically at least—hushed tones. Students kept recurring to the word *inspiration*.[67] Norton was supposed to have led young men "to a truer conception of beauty, and a higher ideal of character and purpose."[68]

This note—that the study of beauty benefited character and purpose—sounded again and again in assessments of his teaching. William Lloyd Garrison, Jr. thanked Norton for offering his sons "high ideals, noble ambitions, and the indescribable qualities that constitute character."[69] Another student recalled that in Norton's courses, "Beauty became not aesthetic satisfaction merely but took her place high among Moralities."[70] We are back with James Russell Lowell or Hiram Corson, with art somehow giving birth to the ideal, which somehow builds character, infuses ethics. Norton's son used to joke that his father taught modern morals as illustrated by the art of the ancients.

Such notions hovered in the near vicinity of religion, at least as conceived by liberal moralists. George Woodberry, himself an influential teacher of literature at Columbia around the turn of the century, said expressly that Norton's teaching had given him "a perception of spirituality."[71] Another Norton student, the Harvard English professor Charles T. Copeland, described Norton as "a preacher to his students"—albeit, Copeland added, an "urbane" one (an agnostic Phillips Brooks?).[72] Albert Bushnell Hart, yet another Norton student who ended as a Harvard professor, wrote to him on his retirement, "Yours has been the chapel which students have loved to frequent."[73]

Norton himself had struggled hard enough to legitimate his agnosticism that he was in no danger of confusing his classroom with a chapel.[74] But he did believe that "every generation of youth needs inspirers among the elders," and he intended his teaching to meet this need.[75] Literature served as well as art history for inspiration. Indeed, "the true conception of the Department of Fine Arts," he wrote, "might be expressed by giving to it the name of the Department of Poetry,—using the word 'poetry' in its widest sense as including all works of the creative or poetic imagination."[76] Thus the study of Dante (which Norton taught after Lowell's retirement) became, in Norton's hands, "a study of literature, of poetry, of religion, of morals."[77]

But why did the study of poems and paintings entail "religion" and "morals"? Norton impressed on his students that "there cannot be good poetry, or good painting or sculpture, or architecture, unless men have something to express which is the result of long training of soul & sense in the ways of high living & true thought."[78] Art was more than paintings and buildings. It was "an instrument of expression of the higher faculties & emotions of man."[79] "The study of the history of the Fine Arts," therefore, became "the study of the attempts to realize in form the ideals of the mind."[80] Acquainting students with the greatest works of literature and art brought them into contact with the highest human ideals, with "the noblest men the world has known."[81]

In this way systematic exposure to "poetry in its widest sense" cultivated and disciplined the imagination. And for Norton the imagination was central to the moral life. It brought students into sympathetic relations at once with their fellow human beings and with the highest ideals of the race.[82] It was this profound moral, almost spiritual, effect—this stretching up to the ideal and out to other persons—that made education in the fine arts "a mode of culture without which all other education but imperfectly develops human character."[83]

It followed that Norton treated "art for art's sake" as "folly" and delusion. He recognized that the artist could (and often did: Norton was no naif) pervert his talent and skills to create "what is not beautiful." After all, "expression" depended on "character"; and the artist was no more immune to moral infections than anyone else.[84] But truly great works of art were by definition beautiful and, ipso facto, constituted a course in ideal morality; for "the beautiful is the good made perfect."[85] If beauty was the "good made perfect," it was the highest purely human ideal. And, for an agnostic such as Norton, any ideals transcending the human were illusions. Hence, beauty became for Norton "the highest aim of life."[86] Insofar as he had a religion, beauty was it:

> The poets, clearing our vision, help us to see the fair ideals which they create, veiled by the mists of common life, beckon us onward to the heights that lie in the light above the exhalations of the earth. We follow, and tho' we never overtake, the pursuit is not in vain. With each upward step our imaginations breathe a purer eye, and see with clearer vision.[87]

This fluff was not up to the standard of Thomas Aquinas, but it was the best Norton had to give.

And it worked. Students flocked to the "preaching" in Norton's "chapel" (as Copeland and Hart had it) at the historical moment when attendance at Harvard's real chapel became voluntary, and it drew a much smaller congregation than Norton's secular substitute. For the infusion of moral or spiritual meaning into poems and paintings became necessary only at that symbolic divide: when the secularization of Harvard's curriculum deprived learning of the coherence previously given it by shared religious beliefs. The problem was not to find a replacement for belief—Norton remained exceptional in giving it up—but to replace its lost unifying expression in the curriculum of secularizing universities and colleges. Norton had invented a partial but compelling substitute for the Moral Philosophy course that had once spelled out these shared convictions. Inheriting the moral didacticism of the old college curriculum, Norton grafted it onto the new subjects that lay at the core of liberal culture and somewhere near the core of liberal education. When education lost the *intellectual unity* certified by moral philosophy, Norton replaced it by infusing liberal culture with a common *moral purpose.* Having secularized the sacred, he proceeded to sacralize the secular.

The thinness of this surrogate for religiously founded instruction was not chance. The extreme vagueness of its "spiritual" claims was key to its success. Only so attenuated a religiosity could creep back into Harvard's now secular curriculum, appealing to both traditional Christians and newfangled agnostics.[88] Norton's agnosticism, common knowledge around Boston, had got him into hot water at the outset of his teaching career. His unbelief was still atypical of professors at its end. But by the 1890s he and his teaching had come to be seen as essentially religious. Wrote one former student, himself a minister, "He had no use for the outward forms of religion but he understood and emphasized and illustrated the spiritual values, and he revealed to us"—a revealing word—"that there may be as much true religion in the spirit in which one doubts as in the most exact formulas of belief."[89] Some of the professed guardians of the exact formulas agreed. An orthodox Protestant magazine published its obituary of Norton under the headline "A Christian Gentleman": despite belonging to no church, he was "none the less a follower of Christ."[90]

In retrospect, Norton's doctrine seems feeble, nothing more than idealistic moralism puffed up with a vague spirituality. But his reputation as educator among his contemporaries strongly suggests that he was not alone in promoting it as quintessential to the liberal arts. And recall the shift from philology to inspiration in the study of literature. By the turn of the century, a lot of English professors no longer regarded teaching as a value-neutral form of explication, as philologists had. They aimed instead to reveal to the student those meanings in a work of art that (in Hiram Corson's critical vocabulary) would "adjust" the student's "hidden soul" to "righteousness." No wonder that professors expected students to react with "reverence" to Homer, Dante, Shakespeare, and Milton. It seemed fitting and just to call such works the "canon" of great literature, exactly as one spoke of the books of the Bible.[91]

Was the new liberal culture the old moral philosophy retuned in an inspirational rather than an analytic key? Did philosophy, literature, and art history come to be taught as a way of re-infusing purpose into a college curriculum that had lost its intellectual meaning?[92] Did the humanities provide a unifying goal for education, which the social and natural sciences (despite their greater methodological coherence, their more apparent utility, and their superior contemporary élan) could not? And are the humanities still seen as central in liberal-arts education because they filled the moral vacuum left when explicitly theistic instruction departed the college? Does, then, a form of religion lie at the buried foundations of the humanities, even constituting a hidden agenda? And is their affinity to religion one reason for the curricular primacy, still presumed, of the humanities over the sciences?

If Charles Eliot Norton stood for Harvard, as Howells claimed, and if Harvard stood for all liberal-arts colleges, the answer would seem to be yes. But Harvard is not the world—though the contrary dogma is held in some quarters—so these questions remain questions.

Notes

Criticisms by a number of colleagues improved this essay. I particularly thank, for thoughtful written comments, Hugh Hawkins, David Hollinger, George M. Marsden, and Louise Stevenson, although none of them should be implicated in my conclusions.

1. "Fair Harvard!" in William A. Hayes, *Selected Songs Sung at Harvard College from 1862 to 1866* (Cambridge: John Wilson and Son, 1867), 1.

2. The standard history, despite ever more apparent deficiencies, is still Frederick Rudolph, *The American College and University: A History* (New York, 1962), which, on the specific subject at hand, Rudolph amplified in *Curriculum: A History of the American Undergraduate Course of Study since 1636* (San Francisco, 1977). For a review of the literature that appeared in the fifteen years after Rudolph's *American College*, see James McLachlan, "The American College in the Nineteenth Century: Toward a Reappraisal," *Teachers College Record* 80 (1978), 287–306. My own assessment of the historiography is in James Turner and Paul Bernard, "The Prussian Road to University? German Models and the University of Michigan, 1837–c. 1895," *Rackham Reports* (1988–89), esp. 7–12 and 35–36. Historians of higher education post-Rudolph have tended to follow Laurence R. Veysey, *The Emergence of the American University* (Chicago, 1965), in concentrating on graduate training, research, and the exfoliation of "university" structures around the undergraduate college—understandably, since the most significant changes *seemed* to lie in such developments. The exceptions to this generalization (aside from ever-blooming histories of individual institutions) have mostly explored the social functions of the college, though not very convincingly: see, e.g., Burton Bledstein, *The Culture of Professionalism: The Middle Class and the Development of Higher Education in America* (New York, 1976), and Ronald Story, *The Forging of an Aristocracy: Harvard and the Boston Upper Class, 1800–*

1870 (Middletown, CT, 1980). It is high time for a new general history of American higher education.

3. Rudolph, *Curriculum*, ch. 2, briefly discusses the curriculum of the early American colleges; but the best study of the curriculum transported to the colonies remains Samuel Eliot Morison, *The Founding of Harvard College* (Cambridge, MA, 1935), chs. 1–10. Much light is cast on the origins and ends of this curriculum in Anthony Grafton and Lisa Jardine, *From Humanism to the Humanities: Education and the Liberal Arts in Fifteenth- and Sixteenth-Century Europe* (Cambridge, MA, 1986).

4. The most important force in giving some shape to this apperception was probably the pedagogical logic of the enormously influential Petrus Ramus. The classic study is Walter J. Ong, S. J., *Ramus, Method, and the Decay of Dialogue: From the Art of Discourse to the Art of Reason* (Cambridge, MA, 1958).

5. Invasion came not only in the form of the works of Thomas Reid et al. but also more literally in the persons of Scotch and Scotch-Irish academic parsons such as Francis Alison (College of Philadelphia) and John Witherspoon (College of New Jersey). Henry F. May, *The Enlightenment in America* (New York, 1976), is the most effective general study of this invasion. Some reasons for the Scots' triumph are cogently suggested in John Clive and Bernard Bailyn, "England's Cultural Provinces: Scotland and America," *William and Mary Quarterly*, 3d ser., 11 (1954), 200–213.

6. When first introduced, Moral Philosophy was not necessarily taught to seniors; but it quickly assumed this place. On the origins of the Moral Philosophy course, see Lawrence A. Cremin, *American Education: The Colonial Experience, 1607–1783* (New York, 1970), 400–466.

7. D. H. Meyer, *The Instructed Conscience: The Shaping of the American National Ethic* (Philadelphia, 1972), is an acute and comprehensive analysis of moral philosophy textbooks. The most thorough and illuminating study of instruction in moral philosophy in any antebellum American college, though ranging far beyond the course itself and even the college, is Daniel Walker Howe, *The Unitarian Conscience: Harvard Moral Philosophy, 1805–1861* (Cambridge, MA, 1970). Of all the comprehensive histories of individual institutions, the most sensitive to the role of Scottish philosophy in the curriculum—and one that in general sets a high standard for the genre—is Mark A. Noll, *Princeton and the Republic, 1768–1822* (Princeton, 1989). The only general study of common sense philosophy in American educational thinking, and a very helpful book, is Douglas Sloan, *The Scottish Enlightenment and the American College Ideal* (New York, 1971).

Although this chapter focuses on college curricula, I do not wish to leave the impression that the influence of common sense philosophy on academic life was limited to the instruction of undergraduates. For an example of its resonance in one of the most sophisticated American academic discourses, see John W. Stewart, "The Tethered Theology: Biblical Criticism, Common Sense Philosophy, and the Princeton Theologians, 1812–1860" (Ph.D. diss., University of Michigan, 1990).

8. See, for instance, the best-selling American textbook of moral philosophy, by the president of Brown University, conveniently available in a modern edition: Francis Wayland, *The Elements of Moral Science* (1837), ed. Joseph L. Blau (Cambridge, MA, 1963), as well as the late version (1850s) by President Henry P. Tappan of Michigan, whose Moral Philosophy lecture notes are in the Tappan Papers, Bentley Historical Library, University of Michigan.

9. Nor should one ignore, more remotely, the enormous pedagogical influence of Ramist logic, with its integrative, hierarchical organization of knowledge.

10. There is no such thing as a general study of epistemological assumptions in antebellum American academic discourse, but see Theodore Dwight Bozeman, *Protestants in an Age of Science: The Baconian Ideal and Antebellum American Religious Thought* (Chapel Hill, 1977), and Meyer, *Instructed Conscience.*

11. The example is from Wayland, *Elements,* 272.

12. I know of no study that focuses explicitly on this unraveling of the curricular rationale. But the fact is patent in almost every history of postbellum American higher education. See, notably, Veysey, *American University,* and Hugh Hawkins, *Between Harvard and America: The Educational Leadership of Charles W. Eliot* (New York, 1972). My own interpretation of the internal tensions within the curriculum that propelled its fissioning parts in particular directions is in Turner and Bernard, "Prussian Road," 10–12.

By giving the date of 1850, I do not mean to suggest that no harbingers of change appeared before that date, but only to locate the approximate start of a period of substantial and pervasive remodeling.

13. Thomas Trautmann (personal communication) has suggested this remarkably exact metaphor.

14. I have addressed this development and its relationship to the fragmentation of knowledge in James Turner, *Without God, Without Creed: The Origins of Unbelief in America* (Baltimore, 1985). Most professors—including natural scientists, the group reputedly most riddled with doubters—seem to have remained believers, even Christians, well into this century. (Possibly most still are, in at least some plausible sense.) The point is that, absent a consensus on the existence of God, it became increasingly difficult to construct the framework of knowledge around theistic assumptions.

15. Some of these programs, and the novel degrees awarded at their

completion, are noted in Rudolph, *Curriculum*, 138; but many others can be discovered in the histories of particular institutions, including a number in subjects that later returned to the ordinary liberal arts curriculum (such as the School of Political Science at Michigan, discussed in Turner and Bernard, "Prussian Road," 25–26).

16. I should guess that those colleges which retained a more explicitly and specifically religious identity, particularly a denominational function, suffered this problem less intensively. Systematic analysis of the existing college histories would provide a tentative confirmation or rejection of this hypothesis. Philip Gleason's forthcoming study of Catholic higher education should provide a more useful test case.

17. To cite specific examples of a generic inclination would be invidious; but I do want to stress that the landscape is not utterly waste and barren and to acknowledge the great help I have found in the exceptions to this generalization, such as the work of Hugh Hawkins.

18. There is, for instance, nothing comparable to the works cited above in note 7 on Moral Philosophy courses and the role of Scottish common sense philosophy in the antebellum curriculum. Yet, at least in the college and university archives that I have visited, evidence of classroom instruction, in the form of lectures and syllabuses by professors and lecture notes by students, is more voluminous for the period after 1860 than for the decades before.

The pioneering study by Thomas Le Duc, *Piety and Intellect at Amherst College, 1865–1912* (New York, 1946), did try seriously to examine teaching, notably in the chapter on Charles E. Garman; but Le Duc made surprisingly little use of material revealing what actually occurred in the classroom. More generally, courses in English literature (added to traditional instruction in rhetoric from around 1860) are also now a partial exception to this rule with the publication of Gerald Graff, *Professing Literature: An Institutional History* (Chicago, 1987), which contains some acute comments on the early teaching of English literature in American colleges and universities, as well as fascinating illustrations of it. Graff's book is, unfortunately for present purposes, constructed around aims tangential to those of this chapter. Moreover, in some instances where I know the material independently (all before 1900), Graff's evidence seems to me shaky, his categories anachronistic. But, especially because I question Graff's interpretation of early college teaching, I do wish to acknowledge, in general, that his willingness to pioneer deserves applause and, in particular, that his work led me to several of the cases I cite.

In contrast to Graff's work, other studies of the academic discipline of English have little to say about teaching: see Kermit Vanderbilt, *American Literature and the Academy: The Roots, Growth, and Maturity of a*

Profession (Philadelphia, 1986), and Jo McMurtry, *English Language, English Literature: The Creation of an Academic Discipline* (Hamden, CT, 1985). An older book, Arthur N. Applebee, *Tradition and Reform in the Teaching of English: A History* (Urbana, IL, 1974), devotes two chapters to the teaching of English before 1900 but stays resolutely away from what actually happened in the classroom.

It is typical of the state of the historiography of American higher education that we know more about the teaching of rhetoric and composition before the Civil War than we do about the teaching of literature after it. See, e.g., Wallace Douglas's chapter on Harvard, "Rhetoric for the Meritocracy," in Richard Ohmann, *English in America: A Radical View of the Profession* (New York, 1976), 97–132. It is, by the way, also typical of the historiography of American higher education that we know more about the teaching of rhetoric (and almost everything else) at Harvard than anywhere else—Yale coming in a close second. I cannot claim to be much help in this respect in this chapter. Mea culpa.

19. One can make a case for focusing on these two schools on grounds of size, influence, even diversity of type (at least among universities). Harvard was a private university self-consciously striving to educate an elite, Michigan a public university with democratic aspirations. Harvard under Charles W. Eliot was a standard setter for late nineteenth-century higher education, Michigan under Henry P. Tappan and James B. Angell the foremost model for the great midwestern state universities. Finally, both Michigan and Harvard, being among the largest universities in the period when modern American higher education took shape, as well as among the more innovative, faced more rapidly and more urgently the breakup of the old classical course of study than did small colleges, some of which kept the old curriculum, and the old convictions associated with it, virtually intact into the twentieth century.

The key works on undergraduate education at Harvard in this period are Hawkins, *Between Harvard and America*, and Samuel Eliot Morison, ed., *The Development of Harvard University since the Inauguration of President Eliot, 1869–1929* (Cambridge, MA, 1930). Given the volume of writing about Harvard's history and the quality and accessibility of the sources available for it (in this period notably the Charles W. Eliot Papers), it is more than a little surprising that there is neither a full scholarly history of Harvard nor a modern biography of Eliot himself, although Hawkins's book goes a long way toward remedying the latter defect.

In his inaugural address President Eliot declared that the "poverty of scholars is of inestimable worth." The historiography of the University of Michigan richly illustrates another dictum: that poverty of scholarship falls at the opposite end of the scale of value. Inquirers must resort primarily to

Wilfred B. Shaw, ed., *The University of Michigan: An Encyclopedic Survey*, 4 vols. (Ann Arbor, 1942), which has been supplemented by later volumes covering later years, and Burke A. Hinsdale, *History of the University of Michigan*, ed. Isaac N. Demmon (Ann Arbor, 1906), both of which are encyclopedic in nature and erratic in coverage. Further bibliographic information, as well as a discussion of curricular change at Michigan before 1900 (though one oblique to the concerns of this chapter), can be found in Turner and Bernard, "Prussian Road," 6–52.

20. Harvard and Michigan happen to be the two institutions on which I have done extensive primary research. I have written about German influences on the curriculum at Michigan between 1837 and 1895 and am writing the biography of a professor who taught at Harvard between 1874 and 1898. Readers will note that the evidence from the two schools is skewed in predictable directions: I tend to treat Michigan rather generally and personify Harvard quite particularly.

21. Personal communication, February 26, 1990.

22. I rely here for information on the leading secondary works cited earlier, although I have confirmed this picture through browsing in a large number of histories of individual institutions. Often the introduction of new subjects, or demand for greater attention to old ones, produced fission in the curriculum, such as Eliphalet Nott's "scientific" (i.e., non-classical) course at Union in the 1820s or the founding in the 1840s of the Sheffield School (not actually acquiring that name until 1860) of science at Yale. I am restricting attention only to courses of study regarded by contemporaries as providing (in our terms) a liberal arts education (i.e., a non-professional, non-vocational, un-specialized undergraduate general education). This standard would probably include Nott's "scientific course," and would certainly exclude the Sheffield School.

23. Harvard's experience with the elective system was hardly unusual—indeed, the other leading character in this chapter, Michigan, moved in exactly the same direction somewhat earlier—but it is particularly well documented. See especially Hawkins, *Between Harvard and America*, chs. 3 and 9.

24. History may seem to be missing here, but the reader will recall that it belonged, in aspiration and reputation if not in practice, more to the social sciences than the humanities in colleges between 1860 and 1900.

25. Hugh Hawkins suggests this; personal communication, February 26, 1990. The classic statement of these educational aims was a celebrated and much-quoted sentence from the influential Yale Report of 1828; the report is largely reprinted in Richard Hofstadter and Wilson Smith, eds., *American Higher Education: A Documentary History*, 2 vols. (Chicago, 1961), I, 275–91; the sentence in question is on p. 278.

26. Admirably analyzed in one of the finest of recent works in the history of higher education, Louise L. Stevenson, *Scholarly Means to Evangelical Ends: The New Haven Scholars and the Transformation of Higher Learning in America, 1830–1890* (Baltimore, 1986), esp. ch. 4. Stevenson also calls my attention to similar Christian versions of the liberal arts at other institutions (personal communication, June 4, 1990).

27. On the lability of the idea, see especially Bruce A. Kimball, *Orators and Philosophers: A History of the Idea of Liberal Education* (New York, 1986).

28. Psychology was commonly housed with philosophy in the same department until the twentieth century; but psychology courses (taught by William James) were distinguished from philosophy courses as early as 1875 at Harvard. Ralph Barton Perry, *The Thought and Character of William James* (Boston, 1935), I, 359–60. In contrast, at Michigan psychology was not taught as a separate subject prior to John Dewey's arrival in 1884.

29. On philosophy at Harvard in this period, see Bruce Kuklick, *The Rise of American Philosophy: Cambridge, Massachusetts, 1860–1930* (New Haven, 1977), pts. 1–3, as well as Perry, *William James*. There is nothing on Michigan (or, indeed, any other university) remotely comparable to Kuklick; but, besides the sources mentioned for Michigan's history, the work on John Dewey's early career, spent partly at Michigan, gives a useful picture.

30. *Calendar of the University of Michigan for 1886–87* (Ann Arbor, 1887), 51–52. I have omitted Dewey's psychology courses, also taught within the philosophy department. I take "speculative philosophy" to be metaphysics.

31. Absent a prosopography of philosophy professors—a desideratum for other disciplines, too—I rely on nothing more systematic than my impressions from biographical accounts. But these suspicions gain confidence from the closest thing to such a source for this issue: the collation by Bruce Kuklick of the reasons given for undertaking graduate study in philosophy by Harvard Ph.D. candidates in response to the department's request for such information post-1906. In the first five years (1907–1911), nineteen students mentioned religious problems or doubts, as compared to seven who gave other reasons for studying philosophy, and four whose motives could not be determined. The comparable figures for the next five years (1912–1916) are twelve, nine, and two. Kuklick, *Rise of American Philosophy*, 464–65. I see no reason why such concerns should have been less prominent in the late nineteenth century; if anything, the reverse.

32. I exclude Charles Peirce only because his truncated teaching career hardly qualifies him to be identified as primarily a college professor.

33. I owe this suggestion to David Hollinger (personal communication,

April 19, 1990), who cites George T. Ladd of Yale, Charles E. Garman of Amherst, George H. Howison of Berkeley, Jacob G. Schurman and James E. Creighton of Cornell, George S. Morris and Robert M. Wenley of Michigan, and George H. Palmer and Josiah Royce of Harvard.

34. On Palmer, see Kuklick, *Rise of American Philosophy*, ch. 12; on Garman, see Le Duc, *Piety and Intellect*, ch. 8, and George E. Peterson, *The New England College in the Age of the University* (Amherst, 1964), 134–36, 172–74. The quotation about Garman is from Palmer, quoted in Peterson, *New England College*, 173.

35. *Catalogue of the Officers and Students of the University of Michigan: 1854–55* (Ann Arbor, 1855), 33. (These catalogues, published annually under a variety of slightly differing titles, will henceforth be identified simply as UM, *Catalogue*, with the academic or calendar year as printed.) A freshman course in "English Language and Lit'ture" was part of the "Scientific Course" at Michigan from 1852 to 1853, Henry P. Tappan's first year as "chancellor" (president); but there is no reason to suspect that this involved anything more than the use of a few standard works as models of style. UM, *Catalogue* (1852–53), 24.

My utterly unsystematic survey of rhetoric and composition courses reveals *Paradise Lost* as the champion entry for parsing purposes. Is it possible that the poem owed its later prominence in the literary canon partly to its ubiquity in "pre-literary" college teaching?

36. Rudolph, *Curriculum*, 140. Matthew Boyd Hope lectured on "English literature" at Princeton in 1846–47; see Thomas Jefferson Wertenbaker, *Princeton, 1746–1896* (Princeton, 1946), 236. But, since the standard literature on the institutionalization of the subject does not recognize this precedent, I take Hope's lectures to have been either entirely ancillary to rhetoric or extracurricular. I am more generally puzzled as to the teaching of "belles lettres" referred to occasionally at still earlier periods; if this was the study of literature (as distinct, say, from training in writing), historians of the subject seem not yet to have noticed it.

Longfellow was teaching modern European literature at Harvard in the 1830s but does not appear to have dealt with English topics, except for some lectures on the Anglo-Saxon language. Simply because more information is available about the teaching of English than of foreign literatures (English being much more widely taught, as it still is), this chapter focuses on English literature. The very scattered information that I have indicates that the teaching of foreign literature did not significantly deviate from the patterns in English.

37. Rudolph, *Curriculum*, 134, 140; George Wilson Pierson, *Yale College: An Educational History* (New Haven, 1952), 299.

38. But not until 1868–69 did "English" appear as a distinct field of

study in the Harvard catalogue. Charles H. Grandgent, "The Modern Languages, 1869–1929," in Morison, *Harvard University*, 66–67. White added "the History of English Literature" and "the Masterpieces of our Literature" to his sophomore rhetoric classes at Michigan—apparently not *merely* as examples of style. UM, *Catalogue* (1858), 39. In 1861 White severed literature entirely from rhetoric, making it a distinct course for second-semester sophomores, and included a "weekly exercise" in the plays of Shakespeare. The plays studied were the histories along with four tragedies—*Lear, Hamlet, Macbeth*, and *Othello*—to be "critically examined" in connection with "Reed's English History." In the following year White added "the criticisms of Coleridge and Hazlitt" to Reed's work. Whereas only students in the "scientific course" had studied rhetoric, all Michigan undergraduates now studied literature. After 1863, however, when White switched to history (his real love), English literature virtually disappeared for a few years. "English Literature" did remain in the catalogue in 1864–65, as a senior elective taught by Erastus O. Haven, who doubled as president of the university and professor of rhetoric and English. But the catalogue described it as "a brief course of lectures on Logic and General Literature." UM, *Catalogue* (1861), 43–44; (1862), 39–40; (1864–65), 47.

39. The "Ballads" are only the greatest of Child's achievements. He produced as well an important edition of Spenser and a seminal essay in Chaucer studies; the best part of an entire generation of American philologists trained under him. It is a scandal to scholarship that Child lacks a biography (though the impenetrability of his handwriting may help to explain the absence). The closest thing is an engaging chapter in McMurtry, *English Language*, 65–110.

40. The biography is Howard Mumford Jones, *The Life of Moses Coit Tyler* (Ann Arbor, 1933).

41. Child seems from the beginning of his tenure as Boylston Professor of Rhetoric in 1851 to have met informally with students to discuss early English texts. Hawkins, *Between Harvard and America*, 11 n.20. But his official teaching was confined to the traditional routine of rhetoric and composition until after Lowell had opened the door for literature. In 1867, about the time that Child was gearing up English literature at Harvard, Moses Coit Tyler appeared at Michigan to fill the chair of Rhetoric and English Literature left vacant by President Haven two years earlier. From the first he apparently chafed more vocally than the long-suffering Child under the burden of freshman comp. But in his first years in Ann Arbor he seems to have assuaged these miseries only by resurrecting the second-term sophomore course in English literature, invented by White; see UM, *Catalogue* (1867–68), 48–49. This pattern continued through 1874–75.

42. Child's three electives prior to 1876 also included courses in the history of the English language and in Anglo-Saxon in addition to this literature course. Child created the distinct Shakespeare course when in 1876 Harvard finally relieved him of correcting freshman themes and made him its first professor of English literature. Grandgent, "Modern Languages," 66–67, 74–75, 80–81.

43. UM, *Calendar* (1874–75), 34; (1875–76), 37–38. (The title of the university's catalogue changed to *Calendar* in the 1870s and will henceforth be referred to as such.)

44. In 1878–79 the list comprised "Introductory" (offered in both terms), "Chaucer," "Shakespeare," and "Study of Masterpieces." UM, *Calendar* (1878–79), 32–33. It was the development of the elective system that opened these courses to all students.

45. It is important, especially for purposes of this chapter, to keep in mind the distinction between philology generally speaking (originating in classical philology with its Renaissance roots and particularly consequential in the nineteenth century in biblical criticism) and comparative philology properly speaking (the founding method of modern historical linguistics, with important nineteenth-century consequences in anthropology and evolutionary theory). My interest here obviously lies with the former rather than the latter.

Possibly the greatest current need in both European and Anglo-American intellectual history is for an imaginative comprehensive history of philology and its influence during the nineteenth century. The existing works on the subject, often worthy works of scholarship, are almost all narrowly conceived disciplinary histories. Hans Aarsleff's work on theories of language begins to break out of this mold—notably *The Study of Language in England, 1780–1860* (Minneapolis, 1983)—but is tangential to the main thrust of philology. The line to follow is more nearly that laid down in Thomas R. Trautmann, *Lewis Henry Morgan and the Invention of Kinship* (Berkeley, 1987).

46. Francis A. March, "Recollections of Language Teaching," *PMLA* 8 (1893), App. xx. There are obvious affinities between what I have called the philological mode of teaching and the controversial writings of E. D. Hirsch. The difference lies in March's and Child's assumptions that their students possessed a ready fund of information needed to read contemporary writings and Hirsch's assumption that his students lack one.

47. Robert Morss Lovett, *All Our Years* (New York, 1948), 37. Lovett's unflattering and largely uncomprehending description of Child's teaching, recorded decades later, gives some measure of how thoroughly philology was detested, stamped on, and finally suppressed by its methodological successors—for Lovett, in his day, was a prominent professor of English

literature and Child, in his, an admired and sought-after teacher. For Child
as teacher, see, e.g., Samuel A. Eliot, "Some Cambridge Pundits and
Pedagogues," *Proceedings of the Cambridge Historical Society* 26 (1941),
20.

48. Tyler to George H. Putnam, August 9, 1875, quoted in Jones, *Tyler*,
176. The method of Tyler's scholarship re-inforces this impression of his
teaching: Barrett Wendell, no philologist himself, characterized it as an
"unfalteringly conscientious" trek "through the boundless aridities of our
earlier literature." Wendell, memorial minute, *Proceedings of the Massachusetts Historical Society,* 2d ser., 14 (1900–1901), 393–394, quoted in
Shaw, *Encyclopedic Survey,* 547.

49. Philologists assumed that reading literature required no special
techniques: students could read Chaucer in the same way as George Eliot
or, for that matter, the *New York Times*. Nor did the text harbor latent or
unintended meanings: Chaucer and George Eliot were, at bottom, no more
mysterious than the *Times*. True, literature often contained symbolic or
allegorical levels of meaning rarely found in the newspapers; and early
literature courses doted on works laden with such meanings—*The Faerie
Queene, The Divine Comedy*. But such symbolism was neither mysterious,
unintended, nor hidden. The reader simply needed to learn the definitions
of the symbolic apparatus that the author had chosen to deploy. It was a
matter of knowledge, not insight, of fact, not interpretation.

Comment on the similarity between, and likely relationship of, these
views to Protestant biblical literalism is probably supererogatory.

50. March, *Method of Philological Study*, 8, cited in Graff, *Professing
Literature*, 38–39. The Hopkins instructor was Albert S. Cook, associate in
English from 1879 to 1881. The poet Sidney Lanier was lecturer in English
from 1879 until his death in 1881 but seems to have given only two series of
public lectures (at least one of which must have included modern literature,
for it was on the English novel) and "informal courses on Chaucer and
Shakespeare, seeking to awaken interest in their writings 'solely as works of
art.'" Hawkins, *Pioneer*, 164–66. Tyler, at Michigan, was unusual in bringing authors as modern as Burke, Wordsworth, and DeQuincey into the
curriculum and in allowing American literature any place. But even in Ann
Arbor the stress fell strongly on fourteenth- through early seventeenth-
century writers; and the American literature was not anything that today's
undergraduate would recognize, except perhaps from history courses, for it
seems to have included a high concentration of Puritan ministers and to
have stopped at the Revolution. UM, *Calendar*, (1875–76), 37–38; (1878–
79), 32–33. The *Calendar* gives no indication of the content of the American literature course, for which I rely on Tyler's books. As late as 1890,
although the English department at Michigan had expanded to five

members, instruction remained heavily concentrated on Shakespeare and earlier writers. UM, *Calendar* (1890–91), 52–54.

The overwhelming dominance of medieval and early modern literature in these first literature courses draws a sharp distinction between the use of literature for teaching rhetoric, on the one hand, and philological teaching of literature, on the other, *contra* Graff's efforts (*Professing Literature*, passim) to assimilate the two modes. Relatively recent works—Burke's, for instance—were quite commonly used to teach rhetoric, whereas it made little sense to offer Chaucer as a model of style to Victorian undergraduates. Philologists, unlike rhetoricians, did teach literature for its own sake.

51. It does seem that the line-by-line "linguistic analysis" inflicted on students at Lafayette College by Francis March made Stubby Child look methodologically broader than Northrop Frye. March, "Recollections," xx; also March, *Method of Philological Study of the English Language* (New York, 1879), 8, cited in Graff, *Professing Literature*, 38–39. (Graff makes this claim less equivocally. I say "it seems" because March's "Recollections" are not very specific, and I have been unable to lay hands on March's *Method*.) Branders Matthews reported an even less inspiring routine at Columbia circa 1870 under Charles Murray Nairne. Matthews, *These Many Years: Recollections of a New Yorker* (New York, 1917), 108–9. But it is hard to know what to make of such recollections, given the contempt of the next generation of professors for discarded philology.

The contempt seems to have been passed on to their intellectual progeny. See Graff, *Professing Literature*, which is riddled with it, an attitude that Graff manages to sustain by grouping the more obviously broad-gauged philologists, such as Lowell, with "generalists." Part of Graff's problem seems to be that, equipped with the dismissive prejudices of modern interpretive literary study, he does not make necessary discriminations but conflates all philology: comparative philology in linguistics courses is the same to him as the philological study of literature.

52. The dichotomy between generalist and specialist, between the professors of the genteel tradition devoted to culture and the professors of the new Ph.D. ideal devoted to research, is a very common one among historians who write about this period in American higher education. See, e.g., Laurence Veysey's perceptive essay, "The Plural Organized Worlds of the Humanities," in *The Organization of Knowledge in Modern America, 1860–1920*, ed. Alexandra Oleson and John Voss (Baltimore, 1979), 53–54. Without denying all validity to the distinction, I should nevertheless insist that it is much over-drawn, or, to be more precise, that there commonly co-existed in the same professor a high valuation of serious specialized research and an insistence on broad culture as the proper context for that research. Child is a perfect example. His friend Lowell, though never guilty

of serious research himself (despite his considerable erudition), was by no means hostile to the enterprise.

I believe that historians have sometimes confused complaints about pedantry or excessive narrowness in research (laments still heard today, after we have all presumably become convinced of the virtues of specialization) with a general hostility to research. Charles Eliot Norton, often cited as a genteel critic of the research ideal, did carp incessantly at academics whom he regarded as dry-as-dust pedants. Yet in other contexts Norton warmly praised tomes reporting highly detailed research that could not possibly have interested anyone beyond a small circle of scholars. He himself published both technical scholarship and general works intended for a cultured laity; even some of the latter reflected massive archival research. Veysey conveniently, if inadvertently, exemplifies this point about the co-existence of the culture ideal and the research ideal. He first cites (p. 54) Norton as a prominent "generalist" and then mentions (p. 89) the American School of Classical Studies at Athens—founded by Norton, though Veysey may have been unaware of this—as the first research institute in the humanities!

53. Horace Elisha Scudder, *James Russell Lowell: A Biography*, 2 vols. (Boston, 1901), I, 393–94. For a fuller account, see Barrett Wendell's memoir, "Mr. Lowell as a Teacher," in his *Stelligeri and Other Essays Concerning America* (New York, 1893), 205–17. It should be mentioned that Lowell's Dante classes met in the evenings at his home; presumably his other classes operated more formally.

54. Cf. Lowell's 1889 presidential address to the Modern Language Association: "Address," *PMLA* 5 (1890), 5–22. Graff's reading of this address is more than slightly strained (*Professing Literature*, 88). He regards it as an attack on philologically oriented teaching. In fact the address is a vindication of the study of modern languages and literatures as against the traditional primacy of classical studies. Toward the end Lowell does briefly address the relation in college teaching of modern languages and modern literature. Graff oddly interprets Lowell's plea at this point (p. 21) for the study of literature *as well as* language—and of language as a doorway to literature—as anti-philological. This makes sense only if one assumes that philology was *only* the narrowly construed study of language, opposed to the study of literature, rather than that philology was one approach to the study of literature as well as of language. The former assumption certainly was not Lowell's. In fact, in the passage Graff cites, Lowell was referring specifically to courses in "comparative philology," not to a philological approach to literature. Moreover, as far as I know there is no hint of skepticism on Lowell's part about Child's teaching, and Lowell was not a notably reticent man in his letters.

104 The Secularization of the Academy

55. "Imaginative writers" is my term. "Poets" was Lowell's; he meant it largely.

56. Lowell, "Address." Cf. his "Dante" and "Spenser," in *Literary Essays* (*Riverside Edition of the Writings of James Russell Lowell*), vol. 4 (Boston, 1897).

57. [Dwight C. Miner, ed.,] *A History of Columbia College on Morningside* (New York, 1954), 25; Pierson, *Yale College*, 298.

58. Arthur Richmond Marsh to Charles Eliot Norton, November 27, 1888, in Charles Eliot Norton Papers, Houghton Library, Harvard University.

59. Hiram Corson, *The Aims of Literary Study* (New York, 1901), 13.

60. I cannot forbear to record that, after having indited this simile, I learned that Logan Pearsall Smith, a Harvard student in this era, not only read devoutly "the works of Matthew Arnold" but "used to pore for hours" over "a little book of Rosicrucian doctrine." Smith, *Unforgotten Years* (Boston, 1939), 128. I cite this passage as a warning of the risks of loose-cannon prose: your wildest metaphors may turn literal on you.

61. See, e.g., Carl L. Johnson, *Professor Longfellow of Harvard* (Eugene, OR, 1944), 89.

62. R. Freeman Butts, *The College Charts Its Course: Historical Conceptions and Current Proposals* (New York, 1939), 141; Shaw, *Encyclopedic Survey*, 575–76; Rudolph, *Curriculum*, 140–43; Pierson, *Yale College*, passim.

63. E. W. Gurney to Norton, February 11, 1874, and C. W. Eliot to Norton, May 5, 1875, in Norton Papers. Norton's argument for giving art history a place in college studies was set forth at length in a letter to C. W. Eliot (January 15, 1874, in Norton Papers) intended for the eyes of the Harvard Corporation. There is some evidence that Eliot's desire to add Norton to his faculty owed less to his enthusiasm for putting art in the curriculum (though this was real) than to his enthusiasm for putting Norton specifically in the curriculum. See Gurney to Norton, January 14, 1874, in Norton Papers.

64. Howells to Norton, April 19, 1895, in Norton Papers.

65. Norton's art-historical scholarship was more considerable than now credited, but it is clear that his national reputation did not rest on it. As to his stature at Harvard, one sometimes reads that Norton's courses owed their enormous popularity to the fact that they were (in the local dialect) roaring guts—which they certainly were, apparently because Norton chose to lure football-obsessed philistines into the halls of "culture" by liberal dispensation of the gentleman's C. But even cursory reading of student comments, both contemporaneous and retrospective, makes clear that the influence and reputation of Norton's courses went far beyond this. The

student newspaper commented when Norton retired, "For years her [Harvard's] undergraduates have gained what is more important than Ancient and Medieval Art from his courses—an enlightened method of looking at the problems of life and an increased keenness of perception which could not be gained elsewhere." Harvard *Crimson*, February 18, 1898.

66. Lovett, *All Our Years*, 38.

67. Samuel Warren Davis to Norton, July 27, 1898, in Norton Papers.

68. Mary Elizabeth Blake (mother of two Harvard graduates) to Norton, June 1, 1898, in Norton Papers.

69. Garrison to Norton, December 30, 1895, in Norton Papers.

70. Ellery Sedgwick, *The Happy Profession* (Boston, 1946), 71. Sedgwick later became editor of the *Atlantic*.

71. Woodberry to Norton, July 17, 1886, in Norton Papers.

72. C. T. Copeland, "Norton in His Letters," *Harvard Bulletin*, October 29, 1913. This was the "Copey" of hundreds of repetitive Harvard tales.

73. Hart to Norton, March 4, 1898, in Norton Papers.

74. I mean "struggle to legitimate" in the senses both of wrestling with his own conscience in the 1860s and of wrestling with the Harvard Overseers in the 1870s. Some members of that body resisted the appointment of an unbelieving professor.

75. Norton to Nathan Haskell Dole, April 21, 1894, in Norton Papers.

76. [Norton,] *Report of the Committee on the Fine Arts* (October 1900), in *Reports of Visiting Committees of the Board of Overseers of Harvard College*, vols. 1–109, Harvard University Archives.

77. Norton to Leslie Stephen, December 20 23, 1897, in Stephen Papers, Berg Collection, New York Public Library. Norton published important translations of the *Vita Nuova* and the *Divine Comedy* and, through the students whom he trained formally and informally, effectively founded American academic Dante studies.

78. Norton to Ruskin, February 10, 1874, in Norton Papers.

79. Norton to Charles H. Moore, January 7, 1870, in Norton Papers.

80. Norton, "Lectures on Roman & Mediaeval Art 1894. Oct. 1894," in Norton Papers, Box 1.

81. Norton paraphrased in Constance Grosvenor Alexander, "An Evening in the Library of Charles Eliot Norton, 11 May 1905," typescript, 1942, in Norton Papers, MS Am 1088.7.

82. Norton, "The Culture of the Imagination," typescript lecture, 1899, in Norton Papers, Box 1.

83. Norton to Moore, January 7, 1870. A "truly liberal culture," Norton insisted to the Harvard Corporation in 1874, presupposed art in the curriculum—not art "from the purely aesthetic side," but art in its "relations to history and literature." Norton to Eliot, January 15, 1874.

84. Norton, "Lectures on Roman & Mediaeval Art."

85. Ibid.

86. Ibid.

87. Norton, "Culture of the Imagination."

88. The relation of the vagueness of this "religion" to its role in the curriculum gains plausibility from the fact that other late Victorians created much more specific doctrines of secularized religion. David Hollinger observes (personal communication, April 19, 1990) that, in contrast to teachers of the humanities, scientists and "science-advocates" in this period "managed to select from the Protestant heritage some fairly specific and consistent themes for perpetuation as 'the scientific spirit.'" This judgment is entirely consistent with my own; and it is particularly interesting to note that even Norton, *outside* of the classroom, advanced quite specific secular-religious teachings. See Turner, *Without God, Without Creed*, esp. chaps. 8–9, and, for Norton in particular, pp. 199, 212, 215, 235–38, 244, 252–54.

89. Eliot, "Cambridge Pundits and Pedagogues," 34.

90. *The Christian* (November 1908), clipping in Norton Papers, Box 6.

91. Although Curtius, citing H. Oppel (*Kanon*, 1937), says that the concept of a canon was introduced into philology in the eighteenth century by David Ruhnken, the definitions of *canon* and examples of its usage in the *Oxford English Dictionary* do not suggest that the word was used with respect to non-scriptural texts before the transformation in humanities teaching described herein. Ernst Robert Curtius, *European Literature and the Latin Middle Ages*, trans. Willard R. Trask (1948; Princeton, 1953), 256n.; *O.E.D*, s.v. "canon."

92. Such a sense of shared purpose—however vague—may go some way toward explaining a mystery alluded to by Laurence Veysey: how the humanities came to see an entity when in fact the term covers a congeries of unrelated subjects and approaches to knowledge, having far less in common methodologically than the natural or social sciences. Veysey, "Worlds of the Humanities," 56–57.

4

Faith and Learning in the Age of the University: The Academic Ministry of Daniel Coit Gilman

D. G. HART

American universities should be more than theistic; they may and should be avowedly Christian—not in a narrow or sectarian sense—but in the broad, open and inspiring sense of the Gospels.[1]   Daniel Coit Gilman, 1886

In 1901, at the age of seventy, Daniel Coit Gilman retired from the presidency of Johns Hopkins University, having successfully established the natural sciences and specialized research as permanent features of higher education in the United States. Although older institutions such as Harvard and new ones such as the University of Chicago had begun to produce more Ph.D.s than the Baltimore institution, Gilman's policies at Johns Hopkins set the pace and provided the model for many other universities. Rather than retiring to a life of travel, leisure, and writing, Gilman transferred his skills to the newly formed Carnegie Institution of Washington, D.C. By encouraging scientific research and sponsoring the publication of technical papers and books, this new agency, as Gilman understood it, would extend on a national scale what he had begun in Baltimore. Gilman's new position was a fitting climax to a career that before Hopkins had included stops at New Haven's Sheffield Scientific School and the University of California at Berkeley.[2]

107

One overlooked aspect of Gilman's career is another administrative post that he filled during his retirement. In 1903, having already served seven years as vice president, Gilman became president of the American Bible Society. Little evidence exists in his correspondence to indicate that this position required anything more than an address and attendance at annual meetings. Still, Gilman's presidential speech reveals his religious inclinations. Eschewing sectarianism and dogmatism, which bred "ecclesiastical differences and jealousies," Gilman praised the society for its "broad-minded and catholic" outlook. By using the Scriptures in "the conversion of barbarous peoples," the society had greatly assisted "in purifying and elevating human society." No matter how important science was to American higher education and to the improvement of society, Gilman could not shake the piety of his youth. Like his antebellum Protestant predecessors, he considered the Bible and religious experience still central to American culture and social reform.[3]

Gilman's conventional piety and his association with the American Bible Society are surprising, given the traditional image of American universities. Reading the so-called warfare between science and religion back into the revolution in higher education, students of American universities have generally interpreted the founding of institutions committed to scientific research as secular initiatives against the religious ethos of nineteenth-century American culture. Rejecting the antebellum college's dogmatic Christianity and confining classical education, according to many historians, university builders such as Gilman rallied under the banners of science and academic freedom and departed from older collegiate values. Laurence Veysey argued in the mid-1960s that the emergence of the university was one further step in the process of religious declension. "One more link with precise religious tradition had snapped," Veysey wrote; "another field had been urbanized and secularized." This perspective still persists in revisionist historiography, which has re-examined the levels of religious indoctrination and scientific inquiry at the old-time college. According to Louise Stevenson, who notes Yale's positive contribution to academic reform, such advocates of the modern university as Gilman and Andrew Dickson White "accepted and built upon" the antebellum college's "scholarly lessons while bracketing their teachers' religious ends." Meanwhile, David A. Hollinger argues that the university's ethic of science challenged Christian presuppositions once "cheerfully acknowledged by generations of scientists" and "fed the current of academic reform that resulted in the reorganization of American culture around universities devoted largely to research." Universities thus became the primary means by which science replaced religion as the source of cultural authority in the United States.[4]

Gilman's easy movement from Johns Hopkins University, a bastion of science, to the American Bible Society, a voluntary evangelical organization formed during the Second Great Awakening, suggests a different perspective on the emergence of American universities. As anomalous as it seems, Gilman's presidency of the American Bible Society was consistent with his aims as university president. Although his purpose at Hopkins had been to establish a place for scientific research, which older colleges neglected, Gilman always maintained that higher education and religion went hand in hand. Universities, he asserted, were by nature "conservative," and their dominant influence was "truly religious." "Without fear of contradiction," he asserted, "the influence of study is on the whole, favorable to the growth of spiritual life, to the development of uprightness, unselfishness, and faith."[5]

Gilman's attitude toward religion is hardly surprising since he was temperamentally as conservative as the university he envisioned. Still, his thoughts about the religious character of the university have generally been ignored. Instead, what has attracted the attention of some historians is the scientific ethos that university builders such as Gilman and Harvard's Charles W. Eliot promoted. Whether termed "intellectual gospel" or "scientific faith," this academic creed affirmed that the conduct of the scientific investigator, no matter what the discipline, was so morally demanding that it became religiously fulfilling. Tracing the intellectual gospel to nonreligious sources, historians have usually interpreted the academic faith of Gilman and his peers as an attempt to obscure from the religious public the secular consequences of the new learning. What this perspective misses, however, are the intellectual gospel's religious assumptions and intentions, which were rooted in older Protestant assumptions about higher education and the harmony of science and religion. Indeed, the defense of scientific investigation in ethical terms was of a piece with the moralistic and pragmatic character of American Protestantism and mirrored theological developments within New England Congregationalism. To be sure, Gilman's faith departed in some ways from that of antebellum college educators. But the intellectual gospel in the United States never approached the secularism of the British version represented by Thomas Henry Huxley's agnostic confession. Instead, academic reformers such as Gilman, Eliot, and Cornell's Andrew Dickson White believed that their institutions, while advancing knowledge, would also bolster an enlightened and non-sectarian Christian faith. Rather than inciting hostilities between scientists and theologians, America's leading universities would reassure believers that science encouraged religion, a message that Protestant leaders themselves eventually embraced and promoted.[6]

In examining Gilman's efforts and the ethos he helped to create at Johns Hopkins, a bastion of the intellectual gospel, this essay attempts not only to reexamine his career in the light of recent historiography but also to show that his faith, rather than being a public relations ploy to hoodwink the faithful, was rooted in antebellum ideas about religion and higher education. Nurtured on moral philosophy and natural theology while a student and instructor at Yale, Gilman drew on conventional conceptions of faith and learning in supervising the innovative Baltimore institution. Instead of leading a coup that saw the barricades of faith give way to free pursuit of truth, Gilman strove to baptize the new learning's commitment to research with the mist of traditional Protestant concerns. A century later his belief in the compatibility of religion and science may look naive. But Gilman's experience at Johns Hopkins reveals that the first generation of university builders, fully confident that their institutions would confirm Christian verities, are most intelligible when heard in the context of the old Protestant cultural consensus.[7]

Johns Hopkins University's revolutionary reputation has depended greatly on Gilman's decision to have Thomas Henry Huxley speak at the institution's opening. Huxley was well known for his debate over Darwinism in 1860 with England's Bishop Samuel Wilberforce, and his name was synonymous with agnosticism and infidelity. Had Gilman wanted to arouse ecclesiastical opposition, he could not have made a better selection. To make matters worse, Gilman and the university's trustees decided not to include prayer at the ceremonies. So Johns Hopkins began its first academic year with Huxley's advice on university education but without a petition for divine favor.[8]

Gilman's apparent disregard of religious etiquette incited some criticism, but far less than expected, given the presumed antipathy between science and theology. One perceptive Baltimore citizen noted that Huxley said little about the "science of morals" or "revealed religion." A New York minister thought it was "bad enough" to invite Huxley without God but added it "would have been absurd to ask them both." Still, he held out hope that the university could redeem itself. The sharpest rebuke came from the New York Presbyterian weekly the *Observer*, which opined that if the neglect of prayer was owing to "unchristian or materialistic sentiments of the authorities," then "God help them, and keep students away from the precincts of the young institution."[9]

Such warnings did not keep students away, however. In fact, by 1886 Gilman could boast that thirty-eight of Johns Hopkins's former students were clergymen. He also pointed out that four of the first seven faculty members "came from the families of gospel ministers" and another was a former fellow of Oriel College and "a man of quite unusual devoutness."[10]

The university failed to receive denominational sanctions in part because ministers were among its staunchest defenders. A Presbyterian minister in Baltimore explained to readers of the *Observer* that a "full and very evangelical" prayer had been offered at the university's inauguration. Indeed, Johns Hopkins opened officially on February 22, 1876, with Gilman's inauguration. On that occasion local well-wishers heard addresses by Charles W. Eliot and Gilman, sandwiched between a prayer and a benediction offered by the Reverend Alfred M. Randolph of Baltimore's Emmanuel Church (Episcopal). Gilman himself later explained that he had suggested a prayer before Huxley's address but trustees thought they should treat the occasion like any other public lecture. Such evidence may not seem sufficiently convincing to overturn the idea that Darwinism broke "the intellectual grip" of sectarianism on American education. But the meager criticism that Hopkins received from clerics and college presidents suggests that Gilman may have been closer to the truth when he declared, "Hostility to science by the religious part of the community has never been noteworthy."[11]

Attention to the religious implications of Gilman's encouragement of science has often obscured the appropriate context for evaluating the Baltimore university's significance. Rather than providing a home for infidel scientists, Hopkins, under Gilman's plan, reflected his frustration with the second-class status of science in American higher education. His policies in creating an institution in which science and research would flourish look less anti-religious when viewed from the perspective of his experiences at Berkeley and especially at Yale.[12]

Born in 1831 the son of a successful businessman, Gilman possessed a knack for management and assumed his duties at Johns Hopkins with rare administrative experience. For two decades he held a variety of academic posts, always with an eye to improving and systematizing American education. After graduating from Yale College in 1852, Gilman became a fund raiser and cheerleader for the college's Sheffield Scientific School. During this period he also worked as Yale's librarian, a job he held until 1865, and continually lobbied for increased funding to further the possibilities for research. In 1863 he also became Sheffield's professor of physical and political geography. Still, this was not enough for the energetic Gilman, who assumed responsibilities as secretary of Sheffield's governing board, superintendent (in effect though not in title) of New Haven's city schools, secretary of Connecticut's newly formed State Board of Education, and leading advocate of the Morrill land grant program. When Theodore Dwight Woolsey retired as president of Yale in 1870, Gilman was the leading candidate of college alumni who wanted a lay president. But the corporation hired Noah Porter, and Gilman headed west to preside over the University of California. Although Gilman rarely achieved depth or unity in his activities, his experience provided him with the necessary background for work as an administrator.[13]

To a large extent Gilman's experiences, first as a graduate student and then at Sheffield, shaped his aims as university president. By his own testimony, opportunities for advanced studies were "scanty." In 1852 and 1853 as a resident graduate he did some reading in German with Noah Porter at Yale and heard lectures by Louis Agassiz and Henry Wadsworth Longfellow at Harvard. But with no structured programs for advanced study, Gilman traveled to Europe, accompanied by his friend Andrew Dickson White, to study the school systems there. Duly impressed by Paris's Central School of Arts and Manufactures, Saxony's School of Miners, and the Royal Prussian Architectural Academy, Gilman returned to New Haven in 1855 to make his case for industrial education. Especially noteworthy to Gilman was that European industrial schools were "legitimate parts of the philosophical faculty." In the United States, however, scientific schools such as Sheffield and Harvard's Lawrence School labored under the image of inferior institutions whose pragmatic aims compromised a liberal education. To be sure, science and math had been part of liberal education. But traditional college aims were not tolerant of practicality. As industrialization created trades and professions that required technical skills, and as colleges enlarged their science offerings to meet this demand, a cleavage developed between scientific education and the liberal arts. Coming to maturity during the emergence of this split, Gilman set out to make scientific education, with its decidedly utilitarian purpose, a respectable partner in American higher education.[14]

After a rocky two-year interlude at the University of California, where state politics restricted his objectives and taught him the importance of independence from government funding, Gilman received the dazzling offer from Johns Hopkins's trustees to create a university from scratch. Gilman by no means had free rein in Hopkins's founding. Several of the trustees had well-formed ideas about higher education and the intent of their benefactor, and they exhibited remarkable patience and wisdom in their handling of such a novel situation. Still, the early character of the university shows the unmistakable hand of Gilman.[15]

The original vision that Gilman took to Baltimore was for a research-oriented graduate school. The university's first obligation would be to provide for "advanced special students" and to grant degrees "in one year or in ten years after their admission." This plan matched Gilman's own conception of a university. Structurally, a university was a place for advanced study, an institution distinct from college and professional schools. While Gilman hoped that universities would encourage newer academic disciplines in the natural sciences and modern languages, he looked upon the univer-

sity first as a home for scholars who conducted original investigation in all branches of knowledge and then as a place for graduate
students to pursue specialized learning through work in laboratories or seminars.[16]

Because of Gilman's stress on research and his use of German
phrasing, historians have assumed the influence of German models
on Johns Hopkins. To be sure, the rare opportunity of creating a
university gave Gilman freedom to import foreign ideas. He was not
an innovator, however, and stated repeatedly that "educational
institutions must be adapted to the civil, ecclesiastical, financial,
and social circumstances of this country." According to Hugh
Hawkins, the only aspect of Hopkins's original plan that reflected
European influence was the power it gave to faculty. Otherwise the
new university drew from existing American standards.[17]

In fact, the early Johns Hopkins bore the imprint of Yale's
Sheffield Scientific School. Scientific schools, like those created at
mid-century by Yale and Harvard, offered a three-year course of
instruction in subjects outside the classical curriculum, from the
applied sciences and political economy to modern languages and
some work in Greek and Latin. They allowed colleges to meet the
demand for vocational education by granting the B.Phil. or B.S.
They also helped conservative college administrators protect the
B.A., a mark of liberal education, from dilution. Significant especially for Gilman's plans at Hopkins were the ties between calls for a
university by professors at Sheffield and Yale's granting the first
American Ph.D. Rather than stepchildren of the colleges, scientific
schools in Gilman's view were the cutting edge of developments in
American higher education. For him, Sheffield heralded the recognition, which became a permanent feature at Hopkins, that the key
to progress was the "promotion of scientific research and education." Although Gilman associated progress primarily with physical
and applied sciences, he believed that scientific methods would also
benefit "scholars of the lamp" engaged in classical studies. "All
sciences," both literature and the study of nature, "are worthy of
promotion," he declared in his inaugural address, and "religion has
nothing to fear from science."[18]

The composition of Hopkins's faculty and students underscored
Gilman's interest in promoting science. The classicist Basil L. Gildersleeve was the first professor hired, but Gilman spent most of his

efforts persuading the mathematician James Joseph Sylvester, the physicist Henry Rowland, the chemist Ira Remsen, and the biologist Henry Newell Martin to join his fledgling university. Almost as an afterthought, Gilman hired Charles D'Urban Morris to teach Latin. Thus, the university's original faculty consisted of one mathematician, two classicists, and three scientists. Meanwhile, the interests and research of Hopkins's graduate students furthered the university's reputation. During the first ten years that the university granted the Ph.D. (1879 to 1888), of the 131 degrees conferred, 71 (54 percent) were in science (mathematics, biology, chemistry, and physics), 39 (30 percent) were in humanistic disciplines, (Latin, Greek, and modern languages), and 21 (16 percent) were in the social sciences (psychology and history/economics). Chemistry (twenty-four Ph.D.s) and biology (twenty-three Ph.D.s) were the most popular subjects of graduate study, in large part because Hopkins under Gilman provided for those disciplines better than other American institutions. Gilman did not intend to discourage humanistic learning, but his early decisions reflected his desire to put the study of nature on an equal footing with the study of antiquity and dispel the "somewhat justified belief that the scientific student is not as well trained as the graduate of the proper college."[19]

Even Gilman's few appointments in humanistic disciplines created the impression that the study of language could be justified only on the basis of science. Hopkins's classicist, Basil L. Gildersleeve, defended traditional learning forcefully, but his career reflected the growing appeal of scientific methods to humanistic scholars. His landmark studies of Justyn Martyr and Pindar only faintly resembled the classical learning of antebellum colleges. Indeed, his philological research characterized the study of languages at Hopkins. Dissertations with titles such as "The Anglo-Norman Vowel System," "The Infinitive of Xenophone," and "The Gerundial Construction in the Romance Languages" showed the lengths to which Gildersleeve's students tried to study literature scientifically.[20]

Nevertheless, undergraduate education at Hopkins balanced the institution's pioneering course in graduate studies. Initially, Gilman faced opposition from local Baltimoreans who believed that Mr. Hopkins's primary interest was in "education for the people and not sinecures for the learned." The need for local support forced university officials to include an undergraduate degree program. Once committed to offering a B.A., Hopkins's officials with surprising regularity showed their reliance on traditional notions about college education.[21]

Gilman's original plan to create a degree-granting institution for specialized research in no way implied hostility to the colleges. Rather, his notions about university education were predicated on the maintenance of collegiate ideals. As Laurence Veysey observes, Gilman's intention for university education was not to supplant colleges but rather to add on to them. For this reason, Gilman could sound every bit as stodgy as defenders of the old-time college. The aim of liberal education, he believed, was the development of character. Character could be formed only through discipline, or, in Gilman's own words, "submission, during . . . adolescence, to the precept, example, criticism and suggestion of those who have themselves been well trained." While Hopkins granted more freedom to undergraduates than older colleges did, Gilman stressed the importance of discipline. Human nature, "especially young human nature," he warned, "thinking less of preparation for the future, than of enjoyment for the present," was bound to select "with unerring instinct the courses which are likely to be most pleasant." "The young scholar must not recline upon a bed of roses if he would make progress," but must rather "have an orderly plan of study and be required to adhere to it." Consequently, Gilman insisted that universities depend on colleges and the traditional curriculum. Only with adequate discipline would students be "strong enough to walk alone" in the freedom of the university. To that end, Gilman restricted electives through Hopkins's "group system" of subject concentrations, had advisers closely monitor undergraduates, and required a core of courses complete with the time-honored senior course in Moral Philosophy, titled "Logic, Ethics, and Psychology."[22]

Gilman's major undergraduate innovation was to eliminate the Greek requirement for the B.A. Unlike other institutions, which offered the B.S. to graduates who studied science rather than Greek, Gilman made sure that all Hopkins graduates received the B.A. "No distinction is made between the scientific departments and what has elsewhere been called 'the college proper.'" This departure reflected Gilman's primary criticism of liberal arts colleges, namely, their inability to admit "that an education chiefly scientific was as good as an education chiefly classical." From his perspective, the conflict between literature and science, not the rivalry between religion and science, was the principal issue dividing educators.[23]

Gilman defended his reforms by distinguishing between the idea of liberal education "considered as an end to be aimed at" and "the constituent studies which may help us to reach that end." The mark of "a liberally educated man" was "a vigorous will, by which the downward tendencies of his nature are resisted, and the upward aspirations of his soul are sustained and developed." The subjects that the liberal course of training comprised were mathematics, which led to natural science, and language, which led to political and moral science. Stated in these terms, Gilman's notion of liberal education deviated little from the older ideals. Still, he wanted more than the old system in which classics constituted the core of liberal education. For Gilman the study of the physical world was equally valuable for imparting mental discipline. "A liberal education," he wrote, "requires an acquaintance with scientific methods, with the modes of inquiry, of observation, of comparison, of eliminating error and of ascertaining truth which are observed by modern investigators." Gilman saw no conflict, therefore, between his reforms and the aims of the old college. Liberal education, in his words, was "one of the most important heirlooms" of his generation, and his intent was always to be "on the side of the enlargement, the improvement, and the invigoration of all the intellectual powers of man."[24]

If Gilman upheld the goals of American colleges, he was no less mindful of their religious character. Indeed, Gilman recognized that sound religious instruction was integral to liberal education and rejected the inference that academic freedom permitted religious indifference or "that a college without religion is a university." Though Johns Hopkins was not affiliated with state or church, Gilman always affirmed its Christian identity. He even went so far as to state that the university had always "been conducted as a Christian institution, not as ecclesiastical or sectarian on the one hand, nor as without religious character on the other hand." The university was open to people of all creeds and nationalities, but,

Gilman said, Hopkins's "public utterances have been Christian and its teaching of ethics and philosophy have been Christian." He adamantly insisted that those who were unwilling to accept this policy could "cheerfully . . . seek a more congenial place for their education."[25]

One of Gilman's biographers, Abraham Flexner, overlooked such proclamations when he wrote that the Hopkins president as a young man had abandoned the Christian gospel to preach the "new educational gospel." Indeed, the prevailing image of Gilman, even if one takes his religious affirmations into consideration, is one of a public relations man who responded to anti-university pressures with Christian rhetoric. From the perspective of developments within New England Congregationalism, however, Gilman's choice of a career looks more like an extension rather than an abandonment of his Christian past.[26]

At the outset of his career Gilman had decided against the ministry. But his decision did not come without hesitation. Nor did it involve the renunciation of his liberal Congregationalist convictions. In 1854 Noah Porter, then Yale's professor of moral philosophy, encouraged Gilman to join the clergy. Gilman had confided to Porter that he wanted to preach on everyday affairs, much like Henry Ward Beecher, though not in the same style of "rough, crude and undignified forms of expression." Avoiding such doctrines as original sin and election, Gilman wanted to "urge the practical application of the Bible to common events and daily habits." As he said on more than one occasion, "I . . . abjure cant, and the technicalities of theology." These sentiments did not, however, prevent Gilman from studying theology in 1860 with Porter or from obtaining a license to preach from the Congregationalist New Haven Central Association, an accomplishment that required an hour-long examination "in all the Chief Doctrines." Gilman had an especially high regard for the controversial Hartford pastor Horace Bushnell, whom he called a "theological emancipator" and "the greatest" of Yale's theological graduates. Fearing the sort of opposition Bushnell encountered from "proper clergymen who are accustomed to preach upon abstractions," Gilman pursued academics.[27]

This choice was fully compatible with Gilman's conception of Christianity. The primary trouble he had with Protestant orthodoxy was its impracticality and abstraction. As a young man Gilman wrote, quoting the Epistle of Saint James, "Pure and undefiled Religion is to visit the fatherless and widows in their affliction and to keep himself unspotted in the world." This understanding of Christianity made his participation in the university movement a natural outlet for his faith. No matter what sectarian critics might say, Gilman was convinced that the university's goals were synonymous with Christianity: making students more virtuous and extending the benefits of learning to society. Natural science, for instance, pointed "steadily to the plan of a great designer," and psychology and history confirmed the idea "that righteousness exalteth a nation." Gilman also believed that "the two essentials of Christianity, on which hang all the law and the prophets—the love of God and the love of our neighbor" were "enforced and not weakened by the influence of universities." Furthermore, Gilman told the Evangelical Alliance in 1887 that universities were ultimately on the side of the gospel. When churches recognized "the value of advancing knowledge" and when universities affirmed "the truth of Christian doctrine" and "the beauty of Christian life," then humankind would acknowledge that "the beauty of poetry, the truth of science, the exactness of philosophy, and the faith which as Christians we hold most dear, are so many agencies by which the race is helped, or so many instrumentalities by which individuals are fitted for the world that is to come."[28]

Gilman's religious convictions paralleled developments within New England theology. Sometimes called the New Theology or Progressive Orthodoxy, this shift in religious thought, which many of its proponents traced to Horace Bushnell's innovations at midcentury, captured influential institutions in the 1880s such as Andover Seminary. The dominant theme of the movement, prefigured by Bushnell in *Nature and the Supernatural* (1858), was God's presence and activity in all aspects of culture. Stated positively, this idea seemed hardly different from New England orthodoxy, which also affirmed the need to make the world obedient to the gospel. Where the New Theology differed from traditional Protestantism was in its effort to move away from the older theology's sharp distinctions between God and humanity, grace and nature, and the church and society. For a younger generation of Congregationalists the concern was not so much to bring individuals into the kingdom as to show how grace infused all human activity. This theological outlook provided religious ballast for the remarkable outpouring of moralism and idealism in American thought between the Civil War and the Great Depression.[29]

Gilman was undoubtedly sympathetic to the New Theology. For him traditional Congregationalism was ill prepared to meet the intellectual and social changes of the late nineteenth century. What was needed was a faith that would extend Christian influence to all parts of society and demonstrate the compatibility of religion and science. His attraction to Bushnell is just one index of Gilman's theological disposition. Significantly, he also applauded the reforms in Andover Seminary's curriculum proposed by advocates of the New Theology. Writing for the church weekly, the *Congregationalist*, Gilman welcomed the addition of a fourth year devoted to psychology, biblical criticism, and scientific method. It compared, he said, with the improvements made in graduate education at Yale, Harvard, and Johns Hopkins. What Gilman found especially encouraging at Andover was the demise of sectarianism. "The most intelligent people of our day," he wrote, "are not much interested in the minor questions which in some historical epochs have been of great importance." "But there was never a time," he added, "when the foundations of belief were so much the subject of earnest thought and study." By harmonizing Christian truths with the results of modern science, Andover's changes promised the dawn of a "new era" in New England's religion.[30]

Gilman's religiosity informed his policies at Johns Hopkins. Two aspects of the old college's legacy were chapel and the senior course in Moral Philosophy. Although chapel was voluntary, Gilman revealed concern for students' religious life by suggesting it and by personally conducting the service for many years. The topics he chose for chapel reflected his desire to make Christianity practical and, as Hugh Hawkins observes, rank beside the homiletics of old-time college presidents. In "The Choice of a Vocation" he told undergraduates that a successful individual was one who acknowledged that God had given him powers to be employed "for the development of his own character, and for the good of his fellow man." Gilman advised students in "Bodily Discipline" to avoid "excess in any bodily gratification" because it would "impede moral activities." Not unlike his theological brethren at Andover who brushed aside traditional debates with little more than a shrug, Gilman refused to discuss ideas on original sin and election in "The Training of the Will." Of one thing he was certain: in order to assimilate the "human will to Divine," the freedom of the will had to be assumed "within certain limitations." Gilman also drew up a list of "Character Forming Books" for Sunday reading. Without giving titles he counseled that works in history should trace the "ethical progress" of the race, that biographies deal with "noble characters," and that poetry be "inspirational." Gilman also recommended books that had contributed to the "religious thought of Anglo-Saxon people." His list included Bunyan's *Pilgrim's Progress*, Butler's *Analogy*, Milton's *Paradise Lost*, and Paley's *Evidences*.[31]

With no philosopher on the original faculty, Hopkins's required course in Moral Philosophy, "Logic, Ethics, and Psychology" (LEP) got off to a shaky start. Gilman relied on graduate students for instruction in logic and ethics until 1884, when G. Stanley Hall, whose psychological studies were still under the umbrella of philosophy, was appointed. Under Hall's direction the course met for five hours a week throughout the whole year and steeped students in practicality. Logic stressed "practical drill" and "scientific reasoning." Psychology taught "practical applications" while avoiding "unsettled problems in the field." "Positive and Practical Ethics" covered such topics as "mental and physical regimen and hygiene," "social ethics," and "need of religious sentiments for the maturity and sanity of conscience." By 1886 Hall was teaching only the psychology section of the course, which met for ten weeks, and George Henry Emmott, a British instructor in law, took over Logic and Ethics, each of which was a twelve-week course. Under Emmott instruction in logic emphasized "the forms of thought," and ethics lectures gave "special reference to the Christian Theory of Morals." Finally, during the 1890s, under the steady hand of the newly appointed undergraduate dean, Edward Herrick Griffin, the LEP course achieved stability. Back to teaching five hours a week for one year, Griffin deviated little from Emmott's "short informal lectures" in logic, provided "the facts and laws of mental life" in psychology which would fit "one for wise self-government and effective influence," and taught ethics from a Christian perspective in order to form "a manly character." Although Griffin brought

order to philosophical instruction, Hopkins's philosophy department could hardly compete with those at Michigan, Chicago, or
Harvard, where some of its best philosophers had gone.[32]

Attributable in part to Gilman's emphasis on the natural sciences,
disruption in the philosophy department also stemmed from religious concerns at the university. Gilman had originally wanted the
Scotsman Robert Flint, professor of theology at Edinburgh, who
gained a reputation for orthodoxy after he devoted his Stone Lectures at Princeton Theological Seminary in 1880 to refuting agnosticism. When he turned down the university's initial offer, Gilman
contacted Egbert C. Smyth, president of the faculty at Andover
Seminary, to see if they could arrange a plan whereby Flint would
teach every other semester at Hopkins and Andover. Still unable to
secure Flint, Gilman hired the eclectic group of George Sylvester
Morris, a Hegelian idealist and philosopher of religion, Charles
Peirce, a founder of pragmatism, and G. Stanley Hall, a leader in
empirical psychology, all with the unlikely status of lecturer. Peirce
did not last long, partly because he never endeared himself to
Gilman. But the ensuing tussle between Hall and Morris, told ably
elsewhere, bears repeating because of the ironies that attended
Hall's eventual control of the department and Morris's departure
for Michigan. Of the two, Morris was the more conventional philosopher, and his *Philosophy and Christianity* (1883), a work designed to demonstrate the absoluteness of Christianity, was well
suited to Hopkins's needs for a philosopher who could refute materialism and agnosticism. In contrast, Hall's psychological studies
eventually broke off into a separate discipline. What finally won
Gilman over to Hall, however, was the latter's ability to clothe his
naturalist psychology in the garb of Christianity. Evidence of the
favorable impression Hall made on Gilman came in the president's
address at Hopkins's tenth anniversary. On that occasion Gilman
gladly quoted Hall's reassurance that the new psychology was
"Christian to its root and center" and was gradually reopening the
Bible "as man's great text-book in psychology." Some argue that
Gilman, faced with anti-evolution hostility, needed a good word
from the side of biology itself. The context for Gilman's quotation
of Hall, however, was not biology but rather the human soul as a
proper subject for academic study. Gilman's citation of Hall suggests that Hopkins's president could not resist the chance to place

a traditional subject such as philosophy on the sure footing of science.[33]

Hall's departure for Clark University in 1888 gave Gilman the opportunity to make a more conventional appointment in the person of Edward Herrick Griffin as professor of philosophy and dean. A graduate of Williams and Union Seminary (New York) and an ordained Congregationalist minister, Griffin had succeeded Mark Hopkins in 1872 as professor of moral philosophy at his undergraduate alma mater. His functions, according to Gilman, would be to act as "a moral and intellectual force among undergraduates," conduct morning prayers, and teach the LEP course. Known by students as "the gentle dean," Griffin represented the powerful hold that old-time college ideals had on American learning.[34]

The religious concerns of Gilman and the trustees also manifested themselves in affairs not directly related to moral philosophy. Gilman and the faculty encouraged student participation in the YMCA and regularly spoke at its weekly meetings. For instance, students heard Griffin on "The Influence of St. Paul upon the Development of Christianity," Gilman on "The Influence of Coleridge on Modern Christian Thought," Herbert Baxter Adams, professor of history, on "Old Testament History," and Richard T. Ely, professor of political economy, on "Christian Socialism." The study of languages made good Gilman's promise that science would assist all subjects, including religion. In its first years Hopkins offered advanced study in New Testament under Thomas Chalmers Murray and in Old Testament under Paul Haupt. This work was strictly academic, not devotional. But it did attract ministers interested in honing their exegetical skills and made Hopkins one of the only American universities outside Roman Catholic circles that offered a Ph.D. in biblical studies. While the application of scientific methods to the Bible passed without opposition, church history was another matter. When the Episcopal bishop of Maryland took exception to the textbook Herbert Baxter Adams had assigned to undergraduates for Early Church History, Gilman informed the professor that he had offended "a gentleman of high education & standing" and asked him to stop using the book at the college level. Gilman's desire to maintain the good will of the Christian community clearly outweighed the demands of academic freedom.[35]

To explain the conservatism of Johns Hopkins in the 1880s some have pointed to Gilman's concern for undergraduates. According to Hawkins, the hiring of Griffin, whom he calls the university's Mark Hopkins, was pivotal. Undergraduate concerns then began to dominate the founders' original stress on advanced scholarship and "the unique freedom which had penetrated even to the lowliest candidate for matriculation . . . departed." Indeed, Gilman had not wanted to accommodate undergraduates, and his gradual reliance on old college methods can be traced to the increase of students enrolled in the B.A. program. Had Gilman not been saddled with the burden of collegiate education, some historians imply, he would have been able to sever ties to the old college which encumbered Hopkins's innovative efforts.[36]

Gilman's ideas about universities, however, reveal that the evolution of his institution, rather than compromising the new learning, was rooted in old college ideals. The connection between new and old even went beyond Gilman's formal declarations predicating the freedom of the university on the discipline of the college. What bound university and college together was the idea that scientific research possessed ethical and moral qualities that made it religiously fulfilling and confirmed Christian truths. This notion explains Gilman's assertions about the Christian purpose of the university and his defense of the old-time college. More important, it reveals the source of Gilman's faith in modern learning and demonstrates the endurance of antebellum Protestant attitudes toward science. To be sure, in the late nineteenth century specific details in the relations between science, liberal education, and religion had shifted since the college era, and administrators such as Gilman usually left those details unspecified. Lacking a coherent principle for balancing the interests of the new and old learning did not, however, prevent university builders from finding ideological unity in their efforts. And the vision on which they consistently relied was the old college ideal of integrating faith and learning. Rather than a retrogression, then, the hiring of Griffin at Hopkins marked a continuity between America's antebellum colleges and new universities.

In his inaugural address at Hopkins, Gilman made clear that the university movement was rooted in American idealism. "It is a reaching out for a better state of society," he said; "it is a dim but indelible impression of the value of knowledge" and "a craving for intellectual and moral growth." The creation of universities implied "more intelligence, more happiness, more religion." From this vision Gilman never turned back. He told the Phi Beta Kappa Society at Harvard in 1886 that universities were not "harbingers of harm" because they were devoted to discovering truth as the ultimate object of "intellectual exertion" and "moral obligation." There was no better way "for securing intellectual and moral integrity," he said, than "to encourage those habits, those methods, and those pursuits which tend to establish truth." Finally, at the end of his career, in a 1903 address at the University of Chicago, Gilman once again invoked the inherently spiritual nature of universities. In the confidence that "science is the discoverer and interpreter of this divine order," universities had been founded "with the ardour of enthusiasm which has never been surpassed" as men of science devoted themselves to "searching and researching, hoping and believing, almost knowing, that every step of progress contributes to the welfare of humanity, to the physical, intellectual, moral, and social improvement of the race."[37]

Gilman's own confidence was rooted in the belief that scientific research required the kind of seriousness and zeal that made the scholar's vocation religious and ultimately sacred. Using one of the most common metaphors of the era, Gilman spoke of the comfort he took from the "fellowship of scholars" within the "temple of science." While admitting that he was only one of the "lay brethren," Gilman was convinced that there were "heroes and martyrs, prophets and apostles of learning" as surely as there were of religion. For him research possessed the emotional characteristics of religion. By making "more obvious the mystery of existence," science increased the scholar's sense of awe. "As 'knowledge' grows from more and more," Gilman wrote, "so 'more of reverence in us dwells.'" "Accurate, scientific, comprehensive knowledge" was also the "parent of wisdom and virtue." Science did not, however, permit sloth. The scientific spirit, according to Gilman, was "perpetually active," "questioning, doubting, verifying, sifting, testing, proving, . . . observing, weighing, measuring, [and] comparing." What made science most religious was its moral earnestness. "Love of truth" was so essential to science that any dishonesty deserved "a place in the penitentiary of science." "No love of ease, no dread of labor, no fear of consequences, no desire for wealth," Gilman averred, could "divert a band of well-chosen professors from uniting their forces in the prosecution of study."[38]

Gilman's heady rhetoric also reflected his belief that the aims of science and religion were one and that the university, which nurtured knowledge and faith, was a bastion of Protestant values. In an essay titled "The Responsibility of Educated Men" Gilman articulated the Christian character of American culture. "The Christian religion is the foundation of all law, of all literature, and to be hostile to the Christian religion is to be hostile to the country in which we live." Christianity, therefore, was the basis for the university's mission and for scientific discovery. Though a "fearless and determined investigator of nature," the university "carried on its work with quiet, reverent, and unobtrusive recognition of the immanence of divine power, . . . known to men by many names, revered by us in the words that we learned from our mothers' lips, Almighty God, the Father Everlasting." Gilman reminded Princeton students in 1898 that as "heirs of great possessions" they had numerous duties, the first of which was to spread "the good tidings of Christianity . . . with its pure and simple morality." What was true of universities was equally true of medical schools, at least at Johns Hopkins. Following Christ's command to the apostles to go and heal the sick, Gilman claimed that Hopkins's School of Medicine was "pervaded by the spirit which appeared upon the earth almost nineteen hundred years ago." For Gilman science had an even greater role in the spread of the gospel. In an unexpected reversal, Gilman maintained that the study of nature rather than the past provided the best religious instruction. For this reason Darwinism could not shake the academic confidence in the ultimate harmony of science and Christianity. Indeed, with the help of Herbert Spencer, the theory of evolution offered surer proof for God's existence than had Paley's *Natural Theology*. The progress of natural history provided evidence of God's providence and the superiority of Christian morals. In Gilman's own words, science revealed "the Creator and his laws," and biological evolution yielded "a sublimer and diviner doctrine of Providence." With confidence he asserted that the study of nature had "usurped the throne of human authority," "truth" had replaced "tradition," and scientists were finding "in an ancient Credo the best expression of their knowledge and their faith: 'I believe in God the Father Almighty, maker of Heaven and Earth, and of all things visible and invisible.'"[39]

Noticeably absent in Gilman's rendering of the Nicene Creed were affirmations concerning Christ's birth, death, and resurrection. That silence has prompted historians, who often have presumed animosity between religion and science, to observe that the intellectual gospel stemmed from non-religious sources and in fact enabled some intellectuals to abandon their faith. To explain the religious discourse of educators such as Gilman, students of American higher education have pursued three options. One common explanation suggests that such rhetoric was a public relations ruse. University builders such as Gilman stressed the religious purpose of science in order to gain support from a wary Christian public. Laurence Veysey stresses the psychological demands of scholarship. At a time when scholars were withdrawing from the concerns of the larger society, the task of investigation needed added devotion and zealotry. In perhaps the most sustained analysis of the intellectual gospel, David A. Hollinger points to the context of professionalization. In order to solidify their social standing, scientists in all disciplines appropriated the symbols churches had used to maintain their authority. But in addition to pacifying non-scientists, the intellectual gospel was "a means of self-comprehension." The rapid expansion of scientific practice in the late nineteenth century through industrialization, Darwinism, and the rise of universities prompted a large segment of American society to endow science with religious meaning.[40]

Without denying the value of these explanations, one must also pay attention to the Christian assumptions and intentions of the intellectual gospel's proponents and to their expectations that genuine continuity existed between scientific and Protestant imperatives. Undoubtedly Gilman's understanding of Christianity was not as orthodox as his predecessors' and may ultimately have contributed to the demise of traditional Protestantism in the academy. Still, his rhetoric was not merely a public relations device. No matter how selective his articulation of Christianity, Gilman drew on his faith not only when defending the university movement but also while speaking to sympathetic supporters and administering Hopkins's campus life. Indeed, the intellectual gospel mirrored

Gilman's own religious inclinations, reflected the general tenor of Victorian culture, and suggested the outlines of an emerging Progressive outlook.[41]

Gilman's faith was essentially moralistic. He relied on Christianity to supply the ethical framework and give meaningful direction to the emerging industrial and urban order. Writing in 1883 Gilman asserted, "Never was there a time when it was more important to uphold the essentials of religion, and to encourage the formation of right moral habits." Although sectarianism was harmful, university students needed "positive instruction in Christian morals, and their application to daily life and still more particularly to the dangers and opportunities of educated men." Despite its associations with infidelity, science, vaguely defined as the study of the natural world, was an essential article in this faith because, as Gilman reasoned, the character and benefits of Christianity and science were virtually indistinguishable. "There is no better way for securing intellectual and moral integrity," he affirmed, "than to encourage those habits, those methods, those pursuits which tend to establish truth." Likewise, Gilman told students during a chapel homily that the "end of investigation is to ascertain truth," and "truth leads to the good of man." Consequently, Gilman concluded that graduates of universities were the best men, committed to professional integrity, lovers of art and literature, useful and cooperative citizens, and attentive to public affairs. Not only did science instill virtues necessary for character, but it contributed to "the welfare of humanity, to the physical, intellectual, moral and social improvement of the race." For this reason, Gilman told the Civil Service League, it was quite natural that the leader of civil service reform was a geologist. Presaging the Progressive amalgamation of bureaucratic technique and religious ideology, Gilman asserted that science's "truth-seeking methods" always led to "righteousness in politics." He failed to make clear which was prior— whether Christianity was true because science supported it or whether science was true because it confirmed Christian truths. But such a distinction was unnecessary because for Gilman both true religion and science conformed to his belief in the certainty of moral truths and the axiomatic progress of human history.[42]

The intellectual gospel and its sibling the Social Gospel contributed a significant element to the Progressive ethos. The intellectual gospel differed from the social concerns of the churches only in its vigorous embrace of natural science. The Social Gospel offered a way to appropriate the emerging social sciences on Christian terms, whereas the intellectual gospel did the same for new discoveries about the natural world. To be sure, Gilman's language was an effective way of silencing the few religious conservatives who were critical of universities. But his rhetoric accurately reflected his own religious commitment to applying Christian morals to worldly affairs. If the practical implications of the intellectual gospel seemed to undermine the ideal of pure research, they were nonetheless responsible for forging links between the university and the Progressive movement. As Gilman's thought shows, the intellectual gospel made acceptable the apparent non sequitur that the reforms of objective scientific expertise would establish a Christian society. Because science and Christianity ultimately pointed in the same direction, Gilman saw no tension in defending universities as beacons of impartial investigation and true religion.[43]

Despite the fact that Gilman is often portrayed as an academic innovator, his reforms stemmed from the traditional synthesis of faith and science which he inherited from antebellum college ideals. Indeed, the intellectual gospel, rather than repudiating religious verities, perpetuated Protestant traditions. As a student at Yale, Gilman was steeped in the conventions of moral philosophy and natural theology. From Noah Porter, Yale's professor of moral philosophy, he learned the inherent unity and morality of all human knowledge. If human nature is capable of distinguishing between virtue and vice, the primary object of moral philosophy was to teach greater ethical responsibility. All other subjects of study were merely handmaids to this superior science. Thus, moral philosophy made ethics and personal duty the standard for truth and instilled the requisite religious principles necessary for maintaining a Christian republic. Gilman inherited the tradition of natural theology from the subject of one of his biographies, James Dwight Dana, Silliman Professor of Natural History at Yale and a leader in the formation of the Sheffield School. At older colleges scientists such as Dana assumed that their discoveries led to greater knowledge about God and his purposes in nature. Although certain findings might appear to foster infidelity, like their colleagues in moral philosophy scientists usually found a way to reconcile science with the Bible as well as Christianity's moral obligations.[44]

What stands out about moral philosophy and natural theology is the shared assumption that science, whether of morals or of the earth, would always confirm true religion and promote Christian civilization. The faith that science nurtured was not the dogmatic Protestantism usually associated with denominational colleges. Rather, the religious belief encouraged by moral philosophers and scientists mirrored the millennial faith that swept America during the revivals of the Second Great Awakening; it was optimistic, didactic, utilitarian, and moralistic. To avoid sectarianism, college educators and revivalists placed great weight on the moral demands of Christianity, which they believed provided the glue American society required. Charles G. Finney, the principal agent of the Second Great Awakening who concluded his career as professor of moral philosophy at Oberlin College, typified the assumption that Christianity and science worked toward moral ends. He counseled students to acquaint themselves with "works on anatomy, physiology, natural, mental and moral philosophy" that made evident "the structures and laws of the universe" because "all these things declare the wonderful works of God." Gilman's mentors at Yale were uneasy with Finney's excesses, but they were no less optimistic about the harmony and benefits of Christianity and science. For Dana science was the progressive discovery of the beneficent laws of a kind deity whose pursuit was "becoming a gentle and ready assistant . . . in the material progress of nations, as well as their moral and intellectual advancement." Speaking for philosophers, Noah Porter added that sociology, "so far as it can be a science, will in fact be perfected" as soon as "the capacities of Christian ethics to perfect society be tested and proved."[45]

The expectation that science would uphold Christianity continued to influence Gilman during his tenure at Johns Hopkins. Not only did he preserve many elements of the old-time college in his undergraduate policies, but he also conceived of the university as a place where science would vindicate belief in a benevolent God and a meaningful universe while shaping a righteous society. Gilman was undoubtedly less willing than Noah Porter to affirm the supernatural character of Christianity. For instance, Gilman would not affirm as Porter did, that "the supernatural and historical Christianity is the only Christianity which is worth defending." Gilman's faith was vague, and his God was sometimes little more than an immanent divine power. Moreover, he seemed more willing than his teachers to allow science to dictate how Christianity should be understood. Still, he shared Porter's conviction that Christianity, "when interpreted by enlightened judgment, . . . is not only friendly to the highest forms of culture, but is an essential condition of the same." Indeed, what made scientific revisions of Christianity possible were the assumptions, instilled at antebellum colleges, that God was the author of moral and natural law and that science, if it were true, had to reflect and contribute to the order and beneficence of the universe. Although Gilman stressed specialization and original research, the new science still taught the same old lessons. The scholar's investigation "into the manifestations of the Infinite," whether in society or the natural world, leads to the recognition of "a power not himself that makes for righteousness" and to the desire for "clearer glimpses of the Invisible." Science thus did not foster irreligion but rather encouraged scholars to listen "to the voice of faith and hope and prayer" from those who "have walked with God." The intellectual gospel, by encouraging reflection about moral and spiritual matters, was therefore compatible with liberal education and contributed to healing the breach between the study of nature and the classical curriculum.[46]

This "enlightened Christianity," as Gilman called it, also motivated Harvard's Charles W. Eliot and Cornell's Andrew Dickson White, two other prominent members of the university movement. Like Gilman, they insisted that the university, though opposed to sectarianism, could not function without Christian ideals. The type of Christianity Eliot favored was a non-denominational and non-creedal variety, prevalent in Unitarian circles, which leavened northeastern trinitarian Protestantism during the last third of the nineteenth century. Characteristically it championed moral and social concerns, and Eliot ensured that Harvard encouraged this spirituality through voluntary chapel and the YMCA. Although Eliot stressed utility more than research, he relied on the intellectual gospel for justification. During Gilman's inauguration at Hopkins, Eliot fittingly declared that universities, while non-denominational, still exerted "a strong moral and religious influence." Science brought scholars "on every hand face to face with inscrutable mystery and infinite power," thereby making "the whole work of the university . . . uplifting, refining, and spiritualizing." Eliot approved of the dominance of scientific methods, in all areas of study, including theology, but assured believers that science did not threaten true religion. It taught, instead, that the universe functioned according to harmonious and uniform laws or, in other words, that God pervaded the universe in such a way that "there is no separating God from nature, or religion from science, or things sacred from things secular." For this reason, Eliot encouraged the expansion of the Harvard Divinity School's curriculum to include social and natural sciences, reforms similar to those that Gilman had applauded at Andover. Eliot had learned the lessons of moral philosophy and natural theology at Harvard and believed that what united Christianity and science were their moral ends. Accordingly, for Eliot universities were "fountains of spiritual and moral power" which preserved the wisdom of the past, increased "the sum of knowledge," trained "leaders of the people," and "above all" taught "righteousness."[47]

Andrew Dickson White was less vocal than Gilman and Eliot in proclaiming the intellectual gospel but still showed dependence on it. Like Eliot's at Harvard, White's reforms at Cornell were designed to promote utility rather than research. Still, improving the stature of science was important to the changes at the new university. Like his peers, White saw little conflict between the essence of Christianity and the findings of science. His *History of the Warfare of Science with Theology* (1896) suggested hostility to religion, but the book was actually written from the perspective of the intellectual gospel. Science and religion, White thought, went "hand in hand" because science confirmed the religious truth "of 'a Power in the universe, not ourselves, which makes for righteousness,' and in the love of God and of our neighbor." Indeed, for White, American universities were committed to applying to society "the precepts and ideals of the blessed Founder of Christianity," and White encouraged at Cornell a non-denominational voluntary chapel program as well as an active YMCA chapter. Using a move characteristic of the intellectual gospel and liberal Protestantism, White premised such commitments on distinguishing religion from dogma, or "the simple religion of Jesus" from "primeval superstitions." Such a distinction not only "strengthened theistic ideals" but also "checked atheism." Less inclined to scholarly endeavors, White did not promote the religious and moral benefits of research the way that Gilman and Eliot did. Nonetheless, he readily acknowledged that science had improved "man's whole moral and religious nature" by liberating the race from "terror and fanaticism." Echoing moral philosophy's harmonizing impulse, he concluded that "the triumph of scientific thought has gradually done much to evolve in the world not only a theology but also a religious spirit more and more worthy of the goodness of God and the destiny of man."[48]

To be sure, such affirmations were often more sentimental than logical. But the rhetoric of these university presidents also bears a remarkable similarity to the arguments of antebellum college philosophers and scientists from whom they learned the tradition of harmonizing Christianity and science. Furthermore, the strong affinity between the intellectual and social gospels suggests that the university movement was an academic expression of the impulse within American Protestantism that sought to apply Christianity to public affairs. Indeed, the union of religious and academic ideals in the founding of the University of Chicago, almost two decades after the reforms at Johns Hopkins, Harvard, and Cornell, suggests that the Christian rhetoric of university presidents was no aberration. Gilman's thought reflected the traditional confidence in the ultimate harmony of science and religion and the trend within Protestantism to regard Christianity more as a code of ethics than as a system of doctrine.[49]

Instead of overturning the old college's system of discipline and piety in favor of specialization and science, the new university grafted the branch of modern learning onto the trunk of Protestant beliefs about God, humankind, and society. Gilman's efforts at Johns Hopkins reflected just how conservative American universities were initially. From the perspective of the late twentieth century his accommodation of science and religion may appear disingenuous. But in the context of Victorian culture Gilman's aspirations represent the perpetuation of older collegiate ideals while incorporating the new stress on science and its methods. By blessing modern learning with the benediction of Protestant moralism and idealism, Gilman continued the old college's function of integrating faith and learning. To be sure, Gilman's faith was more liberal than that of his predecessors, and his accommodation of science never quite

made room for its darker side. But that faith played a pivotal role in taming the harsher implications of science and harnessing the university to the emerging Progressive ethos.

Notes

I thankfully acknowledge the suggestions and criticisms offered by George M. Marsden, Bradley J. Longfield, Paul Kemeny, Kathryn Long, and Jeffrey Trexler.

1. Daniel Coit Gilman, *An Address Before the Phi Beta Kappa Society of Harvard University, July 1, 1886* (Baltimore, 1886), 33.

2. David Madsen, "Daniel Coit Gilman at the Carnegie Institution of Washington," *History of Education Quarterly* (hereafter *HEQ*) 9 (1969), 154–86; Nathan Reingold, "National Science Policy in a Private Foundation: The Carnegie Institution of Washington," in *The Organization of Knowledge in Modern America, 1860–1920*, ed. Alexandra Oleson and John Voss (Baltimore, 1979), 313–41; and Hugh Hawkins, *Pioneer: A History of the Johns Hopkins University, 1874–1889* (Baltimore, 1960), 15–20.

3. Daniel Coit Gilman, "Centennial of the British and Foreign Bible Society," *Annual Report: American Bible Society* 88 (1904), iv, xi, x. On Gilman's stint at the American Bible Society, see Fabian Franklin, *The Life of Daniel Coit Gilman* (New York, 1910), 268. On antebellum evangelicalism, see Timothy L. Smith, *Revivalism and Social Reform: American Protestantism on the Eve of the Civil War* (1957; reprint, Baltimore, 1980); Donald G. Mathews, "The Second Great Awakening as an Organizing Process, 1780–1830," *American Quarterly* (hereafter *AQ*) 21 (1969), 23–43; and Perry Miller, *The Life of the Mind in America: From the Revolution to the Civil War* (New York, 1965), chs. 1–3.

4. Laurence R. Veysey, *The Emergence of the American University* (Chicago, 1965), 55–56; Louise Stevenson, *Scholarly Means to Evangelical Ends: The New Haven Scholars and the Transformation of Higher Learning in America, 1830–1890* (Baltimore, 1986), 63; and David A. Hollinger, "Justification by Verification: The Scientific Challenge to the Moral Authority of Christianity in Modern America," in *Religion and Twentieth-Century American Intellectual Life*, ed. Michael J. Lacey (Cambridge, 1989), 135, 134. For assessments stressing the secular character of American universities, see Richard Hofstadter, "The Revolution in Higher Education," in *Paths of American Thought*, ed. Arthur M. Schlesinger, Jr. and Morton White (Boston, 1970), 269–90; Walter P. Metzger, *Academic Free-*

dom in the Age of the University (New York, 1955), chs. 1–3; Frederick Rudolph, *Curriculum: A History of the American Undergraduate Course of Study since 1636* (San Francisco, 1977), 107–9, 203; idem, *The American College and University: A History* (New York, 1962), chs. 13, 16; Lewis Perry, *Intellectual Life in America: A History* (New York, 1984), 289–94; Laurence R. Veysey, "The History of Education," in *The Promise of American History: Progress and Prospects*, ed. Stanley I. Kutler and Stanley N. Katz (Baltimore, 1982), 289; Hugh Hawkins, "Charles W. Eliot, University Reform, and Religious Faith in America, 1869–1909," *Journal of American History* (hereafter *JAH*) 51 (1964), 191–213; Mark A. Noll, "Christian Thinking and the Rise of the American University," *Christian Scholar's Review* 9 (1979), 3–16; William C. Ringenberg, *The Christian College: A History of Protestant Higher Education in America* (Grand Rapids, 1984), ch. 4; Winton U. Solberg, "The Conflict between Religion and Secularism at the University of Illinois, 1867–1894," *AQ* 18 (1966), 183–99. On recent revisions of the history of American higher education, see James Axtell, "The Death of the Liberal Arts College," *HEQ* 11 (1971), 339–52; Jurgen Herbst, "American College History: Re-Examination Underway," *HEQ* 14 (1974), 259–66; James McLachlan, "The American College in the Nineteenth Century: Toward a Reappraisal," *Teachers College Review* (hereafter *TCR*) 80 (1978), 287–306; and Douglas Sloan, "Harmony, Chaos, and Consensus: The American College Curriculum," *TCR* 73 (1971), 221–51. For an alternative perspective on the tensions between religion and science, see J. R. Moore, *The Post-Darwinian Controversies: A Study of the Protestant Struggle to Come to Terms with Darwin in Great Britain and America, 1870–1900* (Cambridge, 1979), 19–124; and the essays in *God and Nature: Historical Essays on the Encounter between Christianity and Science*, ed. David C. Lindberg and Ronald L. Numbers (Berkeley, 1986). On the authority of science and universities in American culture, see David A. Hollinger, "The Knower and the Artificer," *AQ* 39 (1987), 38–55; Jon Roberts, *Darwinism and the Divine in America: Protestant Intellectuals and Organic Evolution, 1859–1900* (Madison, 1988), xiv–xvi, 235–42; Thomas L. Haskell, *The Emergence of Professional Social Science: The American Social Science Association and the Nineteenth-Century Crisis of Authority* (Urbana, 1977); *The Authority of Experts: Studies in History and Theory*, ed. Thomas L. Haskell (Bloomington, 1984); Bruce Kuklick, *The Rise of American Philosophy, Cambridge, Massachusetts, 1860–1930* (New Haven, 1977); idem, *Churchmen and Philosophers: From Jonathan Edwards to John Dewey* (New Haven, 1985), ch. 13.

5. Daniel Coit Gilman, "The Utility of Universities," in *University Problems in the United States* (1898; reprint, New York, 1969), 56–57.

6. On Gilman's conservatism, see Hawkins, *Pioneer*, 67–71; and Veysey,

Emergence, 159–65. For representative explanations of the ethic of science, see Hollinger, "Justification by Verification"; and Veysey, *Emergence*, 133–58. It should be noted that Hollinger admits the intellectual gospel's appeal to liberal Protestants but concludes that in the end it legitimated a secular enterprise. In addition to Hollinger's discussion, see D. G. Hart, "'Doctor Fundamentalis': An Intellectual Biography of J. Gresham Machen, 1881–1937" (Ph.D. diss., Johns Hopkins University, 1988), ch. 5. For a comparison of Britain and America, see David A. Hollinger, "Inquiry and Uplift: Late Nineteenth-Century American Academics and the Moral Efficacy of Scientific Practice," in Haskell, *Authority of Experts*, 151–53; James R. Moore, "Crisis without Revolution: The Ideological Watershed in Victorian England," *Revue de Synthèse* 4 (1986), 53–78; and Fritz K. Ringer, *Education and Society in Modern Europe* (Cambridge, 1979), 250–51. On the religion of university presidents, see Hawkins, "Charles W. Eliot"; Glenn C. Altschuler, "From Religion to Ethics: Andrew D. White and the Dilemma of a Christian Rationalist," *Church History* (hereafter *CH*) 47 (1978), 308–24; Earl Hubert Brill, "Religion and the Rise of the University: A Study of the Secularization of American Higher Education, 1870–1910" (Ph.D. diss., American University, 1969); and Victor Roy Wilbee, "The Religious Dimensions of Three Presidencies in a State University: Presidents Tappan, Haven, and Angell at the University of Michigan" (Ph.D. diss., University of Michigan, 1967). Interestingly enough, neo-humanism and idealism also sustained the research ethos that emerged during the nineteenth century at German universities. On German higher education, see Charles E. McClelland, *State, Society, and University in Germany, 1700–1914* (Cambridge, 1980), chs. 4 and 5; and Fritz K. Ringer, *The Decline of the German Mandarins: The German Academic Community, 1890–1933* (Cambridge, 1969), 81–113.

7. Despite Johns Hopkins's importance to the university movement, little has been written on Gilman. The best study remains Hugh Hawkins's *Pioneer: A History of The Johns Hopkins University* (Baltimore, 1960). Nonetheless, Hawkins focuses appropriately on the institution and builds on the warfare between science and theology imagery.

8. On Huxley's address, see Hawkins, *Pioneer*, 69–70. Huxley's "Address on University Education" is reprinted in *Science and Education: Essays* (1898; reprint, New York, 1968), 235–61. For the event's importance in establishing Johns Hopkins's reputation, see Hawkins, *Pioneer*, 69–70; and Walter P. Metzger, *Academic Freedom in the Age of the University* (New York, 1955), 65. On Huxley's religious views, see Sheridan Gelley and Ann Loades, "Thomas Henry Huxley: The War between Science and Religion," *Journal of Religion* 61 (1981), 285–308; Moore, "Crisis without

Revolution," 69–75; and Bernard Lightman, *The Origins of Agnosticism: Victorian Unbelief and the Limits of Knowledge* (Baltimore, 1987), ch. 5.

9. *Baltimore American*, September 13, 1876; and S. S., "Johns Hopkins University and Prof. Huxley," *Observer*, September 21, 1876, quoted in Hawkins, *Pioneer*, 70, 71; Daniel Coit Gilman, "Reminiscences of Thirty Years in Baltimore," in *The Launching of a University and Other Papers: A Sheaf of Remembrances* (New York, 1906), 22–23, quoted the New York minister.

10. Gilman, "Reminiscences," 21–22. Figures on students come from *Johns Hopkins University Circulars* (hereafter *JHUC*) (1886), 79, which counted among the university's former students thirty-four attorneys and eighty-one physicians.

11. Daniel Coit Gilman, "Education in America, 1776–1876" (1876), 224; offprint in Gilman Papers. On Gilman's inaugural, see *Annual Report of the President of the Johns Hopkins University* (hereafter *AR*) 1 (1876), 3. For Gilman's account of the Huxley incident, see "Reminiscences," 20–23. The phrase "intellectual grip" comes from Hofstadter, "Revolution," 276. Accounts of the antipathy directed at universities by clergymen and denominational college officials are numerous. But the few citations of ecclesiastical opposition are disproportional to the warfare between religion and science thesis, suggesting that historians have often assumed rather than proved that the primary response of the churches to the changes in higher education was negative. See, for instance, Metzger, *Academic Freedom*, 58–63; Hawkins, *Pioneer*, 68–69; idem, *Between Harvard and America: The Educational Leadership of Charles W. Eliot* (New York, 1972), 120–24; Glenn C. Altschuler, *Andrew D. White—Educator, Historian, Diplomat* (Ithaca, 1979), 93–95; and Veysey, *Emergence*, 15–16. For a better account of the Protestant reception of Darwinsim, see Roberts, *Darwinism and the Divine*.

12. On Hopkins's significance, see Hawkins, *Pioneer*; Veysey, *Emergence*, 158–72; Francesco Cordasco, *Daniel Coit Gilman and the Protean Ph.D.: The Shaping of American Graduate Education* (Leiden, 1960); Richard J. Storr, *The Beginning of the Future: A Historical Approach to Graduate Education in the Arts and Sciences* (New York, 1973), ch. 4; Roger L. Geiger, *To Advance Knowledge: The Growth of American Research Universities, 1900–1914* (Oxford, 1986), ch. 1; and Edward Shils, "The Order of Learning in the United States: The Ascendancy of the University," in Oleson and Voss, *Organization of Knowledge*, 19–47.

13. Hawkins, *Pioneer*, 15–20; idem, "Charles W. Eliot, Daniel C. Gilman, and the Nurture of American Scholarship," *New England Quarterly* 39 (1966), 291–308; and Franklin, *Life*, ch. 2. On Sheffield, see Russell H.

Chittenden, *History of the Sheffield Scientific School of Yale University,
1846–1922* (New Haven, 1928). For the reforms Gilman desired at Yale, see
his "Proposed Change in the Corporation of Yale College," *Nation* 12 (May
25, 1871), 355–56.

14. Gilman, "Reminiscences," 8–9; idem, "Scientific Education the
Want of Connecticut" (1856), 2, offprint in Gilman Papers; idem. "Scientific Schools of Europe" (1861), 13, offprint in Gilman Papers. Interestingly
enough, Gilman, "Scientific Schools of Europe," 12, characterized Britain's
industrial education as "backward" compared to that of other Northern
European countries. McClelland, *State, Society, and University*, and
Ringer, *German Mandarins*, however, observe similar tensions between
classical and technical education in German universities.

On the study of science in antebellum colleges, see Stanely M. Guralnick, *Science and the Ante-Bellum American College* (Philadelphia, 1975);
and Sloan, "Harmony," 238–41. On the conflict between science and classics, the perceived inferiority of scientific training, and attempts to remedy
the situation, see Rudolph, *Curriculum*, ch. 3 and 103–9. For the role that
industrialization played in the rivalry between classical and scientific education, see Stanley M. Guralnick, "Sources of Misconception on the Role
of Science in the Nineteenth-Century College," *Isis* 65 (1974), 352–66;
Nicholas Hans, *New Trends in Education in the Eighteenth Century* (London, 1951), 209–12; Ringer, *Education and Society*; and the essays in *The
Transformation of Higher Learning, 1860–1930*, ed. Konrad H. Jarausch
(Chicago, 1983). On the rise of American scientific schools, also see David
F. Noble, *American by Design: Science, Technology, and the Rise of
Corporate Capitalism* (New York, 1977).

15. On Hopkins's trustees, see Hawkins, *Pioneer*, 3–14; and idem,
"George William Brown and His Influence on The Johns Hopkins University," *Maryland Historical Magazine* 52 (1957), 173–86. For a critique of
the focus on administrators, see Mark Beach, "President's-Eye-View of the
History of Higher Education," *HEQ* 12 (1972), 575–86.

16. Gilman to G. J. Brush, January 30, 1875, quoted in Veysey,
Emergence, 160. See also Gilman, "The Idea of the University," *North
American Review* 133 (October 1881), 353–67; and idem, "On the Growth
of American Colleges and Their Present Tendency to the Study of Science"
(1871), offprint in Gilman Papers. Hugh Hawkins, "University Identity:
The Teaching and Research Functions," in Oleson and Voss, *Organization
of Knowledge*, 285–312, puts Gilman's ideas in their context.

17. Daniel Coit Gilman, "Another Word on College Controversies,"
Nation 39 (July 17, 1884), 68; Hawkins, *Pioneer*, 37. On German influences
at Hopkins, see Veysey, *Emergence*, 160ff.; Cordasco, *Gilman*, 10–14;
S. Willis Rudy, "The Revolution in American Higher Education, 1865–

1900," *Harvard Educational Review* 21 (1951), 155–74; and Frederick Rudolph, *The American College and University* (New York, 1962), ch. 16. James Turner and Paul Bernard, "The Prussian Road to University? German Models and the University of Michigan, 1837–c.1895," *Rackham Reports* (1988–1989), 7–52, question German influences on American universities.

18. Daniel Coit Gilman, The Sheffield Scientific School of Yale University, New Haven," in *University Problems*, 124, 118; and "The Johns Hopkins University in Its Beginning," in *University Problems*, 18. Gilman's inaugural remarks should be compared to "Sheffield Scientific School," 132. The primary difference between Hopkins and Sheffield was the former's stress on theoretical as opposed to practical research. For the stress on pure research, see Gilman, "The Characteristics of a University," in *University Problems*, 87–89. For other connections between Hopkins and Sheffield, see Gilman, "Reminiscences," 3–5; Robert V. Bruce, *The Launching of Modern American Science, 1846–1876* (New York, 1987), 231, 239; Hawkins, *Pioneer*, 32, 37; and Nathan Reingold, "Graduate School and Doctoral Degree: European Models and American Realities," in *Scientific Colonialism: A Cross-Cultural Comparison*, ed. Nathan Reingold and Marc Rothenberg (Washington, DC, 1987), 129–50. Some of the early scientific work at Hopkins was still utilitarian; see Daniel Kevles, "The Physics, Mathematics, and Chemistry Communities: A Comparative Analysis," in Oleson and Voss, *Organization of Knowledge*, 139–150.

19. Hawkins, *Pioneer*, 32–3, ch. 3; *AR* (1878), 19. These figures come from *JHUC* 24 (1905), 73–77. On Hopkins's prominence in math and science during this period, see Kevles, "Physics, Mathematics, and Chemistry," 141–45; and Bruce, *Launching*, 335–38. Gilman relied on instructors, lecturers, and fellows for much of the undergraduate instruction.

20. On the place of languages at Hopkins and the rivalry with science, see Hawkins, *Pioneer*, 151–53, 255–56. On the conflict between liberal culture and philology in American learning, see Veysey, *Emergence*, 182–83; and idem, "The Plural Organized Worlds of the Humanities," in Oleson and Voss, *Organization of Knowledge*, 53–55. On Gildersleeve and his views, see *Basil Lanneau Gildersleeve: An American Classicist*, ed. Ward W. Briggs, Jr. and Herbert W. Benario (Baltimore, 1986); Hawkins, *Pioneer*, 50–52, 151; and Gildersleeve, "University Work in America," "Limits of Culture," and "Classics and Colleges," in *Essays and Studies*, (Baltimore, 1890), 3–123. Dissertation titles come from *AR* (1882), 52; *AR* (1884), 39; and *JHUC* (1881), 152. For Gilman's concerns about the tension between science and literature, see "A University Problem" (1883), offprint in Gilman Papers.

21. *Baltimore American*, February 2, 1875, quoted in Hawkins, *Pioneer*,

140		*The Secularization of the Academy*

23. On undergraduate instruction at Hopkins, see Charles H. Bishop, "Teaching at Johns Hopkins: The First Generation," *HEQ* 27 (1987), 499–515.

22. Daniel Coit Gilman, "Modern Education," *Cosmopolitan* 23 (1897), 36; idem, "Present Aspects," 537; *AR* (1882), 9; idem, "The Group System of College Studies in the Johns Hopkins University," *Andover Review* 5 (1886), 571; Veysey, *Emergence*, 160. See also Gilman, "The Shortening of the College Curriculum," *Educational Review* 1 (1891), 1–7. For Gilman's attitude toward the old colleges, see his remarks about Princeton, Yale, Harvard, and Cornell in "Four College Inaugurals" (1872), offprint in Gilman Papers. Hugh Hawkins, "The University-Builders Observe the Colleges," *HEQ* 11 (1971), 353–62, compares Gilman's views to those of other university presidents. Peter Dobkin Hall, *The Organization of American Culture, 1700–1900: Private Institutions, Elites, and the Origins of American Nationality* (New York, 1984), 249–61, argues for the traditional aims of the university movement.

23. *JHUC* (1883), 103; Gilman, "Present Aspects," 533.

24. Daniel Coit Gilman, "Is It Worthwhile to Uphold Any Longer the Idea of Liberal Education?" *Educational Review* 2 (1892), 110, 115, 118–9; idem, "Present Aspects," 536.

25. Daniel Coit Gilman, "The Characteristics of a University," in *University Problems*, 85; and untitled ms. (1876), Gilman Papers. For other affirmations, see Gilman, "The Johns Hopkins University in Its Beginning," 39; *AR* (1882), 11; and *AR* (1884), 60.

26. Flexner, *Daniel Coit Gilman: Creator of the American Type of University* (New York, 1946), 8.

27. Gilman, quoted in Franklin, *Life*, 29, 37, 29. Gilman's remark on Bushnell, whom he ranked "in genius" next to Jonathan Edwards, comes from "The Relations of Yale to Science and Letters," in *Launching*, 176.

28. Quoted in Franklin, *Life*, 29; "Characteristics," 96; "The Christian Resources of Our Country," in Evangelical Alliance, *U.S. Conference, Washington, D.C., 1887: National Perils and Opportunities* (New York, 1887), 283.

29. On theological developments in New England, see William R. Hutchison, *The Modernist Impulse in American Protestantism* (Cambridge, 1976), ch. 3; Kuklick, *Churchmen and Philosophers*, chs. 13–15; editors of "The Andover Review," *Progressive Orthodoxy: A Contribution to the Christian Interpretation of Christian Doctrines* (1892; reprint, New York, 1975). On the ties between liberal Protestantism and Progressivism, see Robert M. Crunden, *Ministers of Reform: The Progressives' Achievement in American Civilization, 1889–1920* (New York, 1982); Henry F. May, *The End of American Innocence: The First Years of Our Own Time, 1912–1917* (New York, 1959), 21–29, 115–16, 153–58; David B. Danbom, "*The World*

of Hope": Progressives and the Struggle for an Ethical Public Life (Philadelphia, 1987); John Higham, "Hanging Together: Divergent Unities in American History," *JAH* 61 (1974), 20–27; and Ferenc M. Szasz, "Protestantism and the Search for Stability: Liberal and Conservative Quests for a Christian America, 1875–1925," in *Building the Organizational Society*, ed. Jerry Israel (New York, 1972), 88–102.

30. Daniel Coit Gilman, "The Advanced Course at Andover," *Congregationalist*, September 12, 1880, 7–8, offprint in Gilman Papers.

31. Daniel Coit Gilman, "The Choice of a Vocation" (1884), "Bodily Discipline" (1889?), "The Training of the Will" (1889), and "Character Forming Books" (n.d.), all in Gilman Papers. Kuklick, *Churchmen and Philosophers*, 221–25, notes how little debate accompanied theological change at Andover.

32. Hawkins, *Pioneer*, 187, 201, 205, 252; *JHUC* (1884), 118; *JHUC* (1887), 114; and *JHUC* (1894), 101–2. Two of the philosophers Gilman let slip away were John Dewey and Josiah Royce.

33. Daniel Coit Gilman, "The Utility of Universities," in *University Problems*, 61; Gilman to Flint, April 27, 1881; Smyth to Gilman, August 25, November 8 and 11, 1881, and June 19, 1882; and James Carey Thomas to Gilman, June 7 and 14, 1881, Gilman Papers. On Flint, see Lightman, *Origins of Agnosticism*, 18–22. The best accounts of the changes in philosophy at Hopkins are Hawkins, *Pioneer*, ch. 11; and Max H. Fisch and Jackson I. Cope, "Peirce at the Johns Hopkins University," in *Studies in the Philosophy of Charles Sanders Peirce*, ed. Philip P. Wiener and Frederic H. Yound (Cambridge, 1952), 277–311, who argue, p. 285, for Gilman's need to soothe anti-evolution forces. On Morris, see R. M. Wenley, *The Life and Work of George Sylvester Morris* (New York, 1917). On Hall, see Dorothy Ross, *G. Stanley Hall: The Psychologist as Prophet* (Chicago, 1972). On developments in American philosophy and psychology, see Kuklick, *Rise of American Philosophy*, and Philip J. Pauly, "G. Stanley Hall and His Successors: A History of the First Half-Century of Psychology at Johns Hopkins," in *One Hundred Years of Psychological Research in America: G. Stanley Hall and the Johns Hopkins Tradition*, ed. Stewart H. Hulse and Bert F. Green, Jr.. (Baltimore, 1985), 21–51.

34. Quoted in Hawkins, *Pioneer*, 257. On these changes, see Hawkins, 204, 253–58; and Rudolph, *American Colleges*, 445–46. For Griffin's ideas on education, see his "College in the University," *Johns Hopkins Alumni Magazine* 1 (1912–13), 186–99; and Murray P. Brush, "To Edward Herrick Griffin, LL.D.," *Johns Hopkins Alumni Magazine* 4 (1914–15), 33–35.

35. Gilman, quoted in Hawkins, *Pioneer*, 176. On the YMCA, see *JHUC* (1892), 60; *JHUC* (1887), 65, 80; John C. French, *A History of the University Founded by Johns Hopkins* (Baltimore, 1946), 324–32; Hawkins,

Pioneer, 279; and "The Levering Hall at Homewood," *JHAM* 18 (1929–30), 14–27. On biblical studies at Hopkins, see Hawkins, *Pioneer*, 155–59. University divinity schools and seminaries primarily offered graduate programs in biblical studies which culminated in the Th.D. On the Adams incident, see Hawkins, *Pioneer*, 175–76, 313.

36. Hawkins, *Pioneer*, 257. Johns Hopkins granted four B.A.s in 1879, twenty-two in 1884, thirty-nine in 1889, and fifty in 1894. Figures come from W. Norman Brown, comp., *Johns Hopkins Half-Century Directory* (Baltimore, 1926), 446–48.

37. Daniel Coit Gilman, "Johns Hopkins University in Its Beginning," 12–13; idem, "Characteristics," 96–97; and idem, "Research," in *Launching*, 251.

38. Daniel Coit Gilman, "Sheffield Scientific School," 147; "Utility," 55; "Sheffield," 117; "Higher Education in the U.S.," *University Problems*, 309; "Remembrance," 147, 150; and "Utility," 55. For the prevalence of these sentiments in American learning, see Hollinger, "Justification."

39. Daniel Coit Gilman, "Responsibility of Educated Men" (n.d.), ms. in Gilman Papers; "Resignation: A Farewell Address after Twenty-Five Years' Service," in *Launching*, 131; "Books and Politics: An Address on the Completion of a New Library Building at Princeton University," in *Launching*, 217; "Presentation of Thorwaldsen's Statue of Christ in the Hopkins Hospital" (1896), offprint in Gilman Papers, 6; "Our National Schools," 28; "Christian Resources," 282; and "Research," 251. On Spencer's importance for the reception of Darwinism, see Jim Moore, "Herbert Spencer's Henchmen: The Evolution of Protestant Liberals in Late Nineteenth-Century America," in *Darwinism and Divinity: Essays on Evolution and Religious Belief*, ed. John R. Durant (Oxford, 1985), 76–100; and David N. Livingstone, *Darwin's Forgotten Defenders: The Encounter between Evangelical Theology and Evolutionary Thought* (Grand Rapids, 1987), 48–56.

40. Hollinger, "Inquiry and Uplift," 151. For the public relations argument, see Hollinger, "Justification;" Hawkins, *Pioneer*, 68–69, 175–76, 297–99; and Veysey, *Emergence*, 162–63. On psychological needs, see Veysey, *Emergence*, 158. For the context of professionalization, see Hollinger, "Justification;" idem, "Inquiry," 151–55; Burton Bledstein, *The Culture of Professionalism: The Middle Class and the Development of Higher Education* (New York, 1976); and George H. Daniels, *American Science in the Age of Jackson* (New York, 1968), who makes a similar argument for antebellum scientists. Hollinger, "Justification," also spells out the irreligious implications of the intellectual gospel. Arthur J. Engel, "The Development of the Academic Profession at Oxford, 1800–1854," in *The University in Society*, vol. 1, ed. Lawrence Stone (Princeton, 1975), 324–25,

argues that at Oxford the intellectual gospel originated as a way to counter the charge of utilitarianism; cf. Sheldon Rothblatt, *Tradition and Change in English Liberal Education* (London, 1976), 196–97, who traces it to a time when scientists saw that the quest for facts was never-ending and consequently needed greater legitimacy for their studies. On religious uncertainty in the Gilded Age, see Donald H. Meyer, "American Intellectuals and the Victorian Crisis of Faith," in *Victorian America*, ed. Daniel Walker Howe (Philadelphia, 1976), 59–80; and James Turner, *Without God, Without Creed: The Origins of Unbelief in America* (Baltimore, 1985), ch. 6.

41. Hawkins, *Pioneer*, 69, 297; Bruce, *Launching*, 337; and Veysey, *Emergence*, 164, stress Gilman's role as a public relations man for the university movement.

42. Daniel Coit Gilman, "Present Aspects," 539; "Sheffield Scientific School," 97; "Relation of Universities and Religion," ms. (n.d.), Gilman Papers; "Utility of Universities," 57; "Prospects of Science at the Beginning of the Twentieth Century" (1903), offprint in Gilman Papers, 36; and "Civil Service Reform," in *Launching*, 344, 345. On the Progressive synthesis of scientific management and religious ideals, see Higham, "Hanging Together," 24–25.

43. On the links between the Social Gospel and Progressivism, see the citations in note 29. For the early ties between Protestantism and the social sciences, see Haskell, *Emergence of Professional Social Science*; Mary Furner, *Advocacy and Objectivity: A Crisis in the Professionalization of American Social Science, 1865–1905* (Lexington, KY, 1975); Arthur J. Vidich and Stanford M. Lyman, *American Sociology: Worldly Rejections of Religion and Their Directions* (New Haven, 1985); and Dorothy Ross, "The Development of the Social Sciences," in Oleson and Voss, *Organization of Knowledge*, 109–21. For the importance of colleges and universities to Progressivism, see Hall, *Organization of American Culture*, 249–61; Stevenson, *Scholarly Means*, ch. 9; J. David Hoeveler, Jr., "The University and the Social Gospel: The Intellectual Origins of the 'Wisconsin Idea,'" *Wisconsin Magazine of History* (Summer 1976), 282–98; McLachlan, "American Colleges"; Steven J. Diner, *A City and Its Universities: Public Policy in Chicago, 1892–1919* (Chapel Hill, 1980); and George E. Peterson, *The New England College in the Age of the University* (Amherst, MA, 1964).

Hollinger, "Justification," 132–35, concedes that the intellectual gospel and the Social Gospel were twins. But because he stresses its secular implications Hollinger argues that the intellectual gospel encouraged knowledge and academic reform, thereby leaving religious concerns and social reform to the churches.

44. Daniel Coit Gilman, *The Life of James Dwight Dana* (New York,

1899). In his biography of Dana, p. 180, Gilman describes Dana's piety in terms similar to his own: "He was not a man who enjoyed cant phrases or who was eager to express his most sacred thoughts or display his emotions. Nor was he tenacious of denominational tenets, or inclined to philosophical and ecclesiastical discussions. . . . He was not only a man without guile,—he was a man of strong convictions, definite principles, and devout aspirations."

On moral philosophy, see D. H. Meyer, *The Instructed Conscience: The Shaping of the American National Ethic* (Philadelphia, 1972); Daniel Walker Howe, *The Unitarian Conscience: Harvard Moral Philosophy, 1805-1861* (Cambridge, MA, 1970); and Wilson Smith, *Professors and Public Ethics: Studies of Northern Moral Philosophers before the Civil War* (Ithaca, 1956). On the religious orientation of antebellum science, see Theodore Dwight Bozeman, *Protestants in an Age of Science: The Baconian Ideal and Antebellum American Religious Thought* (Chapel Hill, 1977); Herbert Hovenkamp, *Science and Religion in America, 1800-1860* (Philadelphia, 1978); Charles E. Rosenberg, *No Other Gods: On Science and American Social Thought* (Baltimore, 1976), 109-22, 137-44; Stanley M. Guralnick, "Geology and Religion before Darwin: The Case of Edward Hitchcock, Theologian and Geologist, 1793-1864," *Isis* 63 (1972), 529-43; Ronald L. Numbers, *Creation by Natural Law: Laplace's Nebular Hypothesis in American Thought* (Seattle, 1977); James R. Moore, "Geologists and Interpreters of Genesis in the Nineteenth Century," in *God and Nature*, ed. Lindberg and Numbers, 322-50; and Livingstone, *Darwin's Forgotten Defenders*.

45. Finney, *Oberlin Evangelist* 4 (August 17, 1842), 131, quoted in William G. McLoughlin, Jr., *Modern Revivalism: Charles Grandison Finney to Billy Graham* (New York, 1959), 120; James Dwight Dana, "Science and Scientific Schools," *American Journal of Education* 2 (1856), 156; Noah Porter, *Elements of Moral Science* (New York, 1884), 284. For connections between evangelicalism, moral philosophy, and science, see especially Meyer, *Instructed Conscience*, ch. 3; Guralnick, *Science*, 152-53; Smith, *Revivalism and Social Reform*; and Rosenberg, *No Other Gods*, 135-52. For the ties between revivalism and antebellum higher education, see James Findlay, "The SPCTEW and Western Colleges: Religion and Higher Education in Mid-Nineteenth Century America," *HEQ* 17 (1977), 31-62; and Timothy L. Smith, *Uncommon Schools: Christian Colleges and Social Idealism in Midwestern America, 1820-1950* (Indianapolis, 1978). For critical assessments of antebellum Protestant scholarship, see George M. Marsden, "The Collapse of American Evangelical Academia," in *Faith and Rationality: Reason and Belief in God*, ed. Alvin Plantinga and Nicholas Wolterstorff (Notre Dame, 1983), 219-64; and Noll, "Christian Thinking."

As much as scientists showed that their studies supported revealed truth, revivalists such as Finney also attempted to make the methods of revivalism scientific. On this aspect of revivalism, see Meyer, *Instructed Conscience*, 80–83, 93–95, 149–50; McLoughlin, *Modern Revivalism*, ch. 2; and Keith J. Hardman, *Charles Grandison Finney, 1792–1875: Revivalist and Reformer* (Syracuse, 1987), 198–211.

46. Noah Porter, *American Colleges and the American Public* (New Haven, 1870), 207; Daniel Coit Gilman, "The Rev. Maltbie D. Babcock, D.D." (1901), offprint in Gilman Papers, 2. For other expressions of the intellectual gospel at Johns Hopkins, see Hawkins, *Pioneer*, 293–315. On the continuing influence of moral philosophy in the Gilded Age, see James McLachlan, "American Colleges and the Transmission of Culture: The Case of the Mugwumps," in *The Hofstadter Aegis, A Memorial*, ed. Eric McKitrick and Stanley Elkins (New York, 1974), 184–206.

47. "Address at the Inauguration of Daniel C. Gilman," in *Educational Reform: Essays and Addresses* (New York, 1909), 43, 46; "What Place Should Religion Have in College?" quoted in Hawkins, *Between Harvard and America*, 130. On Unitarian influences on liberal Protestantism, see Hutchison, *Modernist Impulse*. On Harvard's moral philosophy, see Howe, *Unitarian Conscience*. For Eliot's religious policies while president, see Hawkins, *Between Harvard and America*, ch. 4.

48. Andrew Dickson White, *A History of the Warfare of Science with Theology*, vol. 1 (New York, 1896), xii; *Autobiography of Andrew White*, vol. 2 (New York, 1905), 533, 535; and *History of the Warfare*, I, 208; II, 95. For judicious assessments of White's history of science and theology, see Altschuler, *Andrew D. White*, ch. 12; and David C. Lindberg and Ronald L. Numbers, "Beyond War and Peace: A Reappraisal of the Encounter between Christianity and Science," *Church History* 55 (1986), 338–54. For White's religious policies at Cornell, see Altschuler, *Andrew D. White*, 80–81, 94–99; and White, *Autobiography*, II, 563–71. Interestingly, White, *Autobiography*, vol. 2, traced the evolution of his faith to the controversial Unitarian Theodore Parker, who distinguished between the transient and permanent in Christianity, and the popular Henry Ward Beecher, who domesticated the timeless-versus-temporary distinction.

49. On the University of Chicago, see Richard J. Storr, *A History of the University of Chicago: Harper's University, The Beginnings* (Chicago, 1966); and *The Idea of the University of Chicago: Selections from the Papers of the First Eight Chief Executives of the University of Chicago from 1891 to 1975*, ed. William Michael Murphy and D. J. R. Bruckner (Chicago, 1976), 1–77. For developments within Protestantism, see Hutchison, *Modernist Impulse*.

5

"For God, for Country, and for Yale": Yale, Religion, and Higher Education between the World Wars

BRADLEY J. LONGFIELD

> Yale then meets this first great test of a university, in that it trains its students in an atmosphere of Christian faith, and of high patriotism, and of broad democracy for leadership in our nation today.[1] Anson Phelps Stokes, 1927

In 1919 William Adams Brown, professor of systematic theology at Union Theological Seminary in New York and fellow of the Yale Corporation, accepted the position of acting provost at Yale. Although the institution had been transformed from a college to a university in the preceding years, its identity as a Christian school, at least as far as Brown was concerned, was still intact. Yale was, Brown maintained, a "Christian University."[2]

While most members of the Yale family at the time would probably have agreed with Brown's evaluation, the leadership of the university was no longer dominated by clerics, as it once had been. In 1899 Yale had selected its first lay president, Arthur Twining Hadley. Moreover, increasing belief that businessmen, not clergy, should oversee the business of the university had contributed to a dramatic decline in the ministerial representation on the Yale Corporation in the early twentieth century: ten clergymen sat on the corporation in 1899, but by 1921 this number had been reduced to four. Many alumni, convinced that a Christian school need not be run by ministers, supported this trend.[3]

The strength of the sentiment against clerical control, and thus the changing role of religion at Yale, was made crystal clear in 1920 and 1921 after Hadley announced his impending retirement. The Reverend Anson Phelps Stokes, an Episcopalian who had served as secretary of the Yale Corporation since 1899, was the obvious choice to replace him.[4] As secretary, however, Stokes had made enemies in the Yale family, including some who disapproved of his ecclesial ties and his enthusiastic support of Dwight Hall, the student Christian organization on campus.[5] Many alumni were hesitant to retreat from the advances of lay leadership by placing a minister, particularly Stokes, at the head of the school.[6] Although Yale was still generally seen as a Christian institution, this did not mean, as it had for nearly two hundred years prior to Hadley, that clergy would be favored as candidates to lead the university.

The strong opposition to Stokes allowed for consideration of numerous other candidates. Despite the resistance to Stokes on religious grounds, the renowned modernist Presbyterian minister and Yale graduate Henry Sloane Coffin soon came to the top of the list. When supporters of Stokes began to despair of his success, they turned to Coffin as an acceptable alternative, and by January 1921 Coffin appeared to have the inside track for the position. But those opposed to a minister-president were not to be denied. Even though corporation member William Howard Taft made a last-minute push for Coffin, the corporation opted to elect not simply a layman but one with no prior Yale connection at all, James Rowland Angell.[7]

Angell, born in 1869, was descended from New England stock, but had grown up in Michigan after his father was called to the presidency of the University of Michigan in 1871. Educated at Michigan, Harvard, and Halle, he counted John Dewey and William James among his most influential teachers. He taught at the University of Minnesota and then for twenty-six years at the University of Chicago, where he achieved fame in the field of psychology, before serving as acting president of the University of Chicago and president of the Carnegie Corporation. Angell's reputation as a scholar and administrator overcame concerns about his lack of a Yale degree and won him the position of president in 1921.[8]

His election not only confirmed Yale's move away from ecclesiastical influences, but also was widely viewed as a sign that Yale was becoming a truly national university.[9] Indeed, Angell's inaugural address dwelt primarily on the role of Yale as a national institution. "No thought has been so often brought to my notice by the alumni of Yale," he opened, "as their desire that she should somewhat enlarge her character as a national university." He continued:

> If Yale is to remain really national in her thought and feeling, she must keep in touch with the various currents of sentiment and opinion constantly flowing through the life of the people, and nothing can so fully assure this sympathetic contact as the presence in her midst of those who are among the finest representatives of the younger generation, from the various parts of the country.[10]

If Yale was to serve the nation, it needed not only to educate a national undergraduate student body, Angell argued, but also to provide top-notch graduate and professional training, "adjust . . . to the changing tides of life," and "push forward the boundaries of knowledge." Perhaps most important, it needed, in the wake of the war, to "set a new standard of excellence, a new ideal of service to mankind, a new conception of the devotion of trained intelligence to the essential needs of humanity." Out of loyalty "to country and to God," he concluded, it was the task of Yale's graduates to bring "back a distracted world to ways of sanity and peace."[11] While Yale still had a mission to serve God and country, the accent, in the years between the world wars, would fall more and more on the import of service to the nation.

Charles Foster Kent: Missionary to the State Universities

One way in which Yale came to the nation's service, in loyalty to country and to God, immediately after Angell's inauguration was through the activity of Charles Foster Kent, Woolsey Professor of Biblical Literature.[12] In 1921 Kent was given a leave of absence "to tour state universities as a good-will ambassador of Yale and an investigator of the status of religious education in state-supported institutions."[13] Kent, concerned that students at state universities lacked essential religious and moral guidance, proposed that schools of religion, funded by philanthropists, be founded as satellite institutions at those universities. Faculty would be drawn, he suggested, from professors in other areas of the university, from local religious leaders, and from the nation's religious elite, such as John R. Mott and Harry Emerson Fosdick.[14]

In order to further these plans, Kent (assisted by Anson Phelps Stokes) organized the Council of Schools of Religion in 1922.[15] The aims of the council included encouraging and facilitating the formation of schools of religion at state universities, instituting a national fellowship program to support promising graduate students in religion, and publishing bulletins addressing issues of religion in higher education. Kent himself wrote a number of booklets and oversaw the organization of the fellowship program, personally choosing the first nine 'Council Fellows' in 1923. Numerous Yale faculty—such as Luther A. Weigle, Henry B. Wright, Kenneth Scott Latourette, and John Clark Archer—sat on committees and commissions of the council.[16]

In 1923 Kent succeeded in persuading Marion Burton, president of the University of Michigan, to adopt his plan for a school of religion. Burton, a Congregationalist minister, held a theological degree and doctorate from Yale, and had served as president of Smith College and the University of Minnesota before going to Michigan in 1920.[17] Like Kent, Burton believed that religion, broadly conceived, had to hold a central place in higher education if universities were to complete their task of service to the nation. In an address to the Association of American Colleges he summarized:

> The thing that America needs more than anything else from American colleges and universities is the type of leader who understands that the first requisite of a public servant is not the desire to know what the people want, but the purpose to help the people want what they ought to have; and we will only produce that kind of leader when we get the inner reality for which I have been pleading, and send out a generation of students who understand religion in its largest terms, and know that we can only build a life with an inner reality which matches the stern ineradicable order of truth that life gives us.[18]

Despite the parade of eminent visiting scholars—such as Kirsopp Lake of Harvard and Shirley Jackson Case and Edgar Goodspeed of Chicago—that provided the faculty of the Michigan School of Religion for its first years, the untimely deaths of Burton and Kent left the school without guidance or support by the mid-1920s. In 1926 classes in the school were ended, and by the close of the decade the program was formally disbanded by its board.[19]

Nevertheless, Alexander Ruthven, installed as president at Michigan in 1929, brought a renewed concern for religion, and in 1934 inaugurated the position of counselor in religious education to supervise religious activities on campus.[20] Additionally, Ruthven in 1936 resurrected the idea of a formal program of instruction in religion at the university and oversaw the creation of an inter-departmental program of religion and ethics to prepare students "for intelligent spiritual and moral leadership in the modern world."[21] Given the problems of the depression and the rise of totalitarianism in Europe, the ideal of a religious basis for service to the nation looked more necessary than ever.

Michigan was not alone among state schools in its effort to buttress its curriculum with religious education. By the mid-1920s various programs offering courses for credit in religion could be found at the universities of Illinois, Iowa, Kansas, Missouri, and North Dakota, and Ohio State University.[22] At all of these schools, one key reason for addressing "moral and religious problems" was an effort to "turn out trained citizens with moral characters."[23] Devotion to God and country, though perhaps manifested in different ways, reigned as the ideal not simply at Yale and its sister schools but also at the public institutions west of the Appalachians.

Despite programs to address religion at state universities, largely spurred by Charles Foster Kent of Yale, the courses reached barely more than a handful of the student population. Kent's enthusiasm notwithstanding, the vast majority of students in the public universities were not in the market for courses in religion. In 1936, of almost 280,000 students in public universities, only slightly over 10,000 enrolled in religion courses.[24] Religion, at least as a matter of academic study, appears to have been a marginal concern of the student population.

Compulsory Chapel: The End of
Established Religion at Yale

The concern of Kent to further the integration of religion and higher education was soon mirrored by Yale's new president. In his 1924 annual report Angell acknowledged that "there is an undoubted confusion in the minds of many students regarding the relation of the spiritual and moral sides of their lives to religion." He contended that "the dissipation of this confusion may require a new approach in religious teaching, and the universities may well be called upon to take the lead." As a result, he announced that the university planned "to develop courses of study in the history and development of religion, in the Bible, and in Christian philosophy and ethics," and to establish a religious council to study the "problem of religious life" and make recommendations to the corporation, faculty, and students.[25]

Angell's concern over the religious confusion of the time was understandable. After all, the major denominations in the country, especially the Northern Presbyterians and Northern Baptists, were in the midst of a war between modernists, who sought to preserve the influence of the church in the culture by accommodating religious doctrine to the dominant ideas of the age, and fundamentalists, who sought to maintain a supernatural faith in the face of increasingly prevalent naturalistic views.[26] Coffin, a leading modernist in the Presbyterian church and Angell's one-time competitor for the Yale presidency, had been elected to the Yale Corporation in 1922 and had overseen a special committee of the corporation that resulted in the formation of the religious council that Angell announced.[27] Given the uproar in the major denominations, ferment on the college campuses could be expected.

Although Yale continued the courses in "the great living religions" and "biblical literature" that had been offered before the war, Dwight Hall, once one of the most prestigious organizations on campus, fell on hard times in the 1920s, and mandatory chapel came under heavier and heavier criticism.[28] Indeed, the fight over required chapel became the dominant symbol of the changing place of Christianity at Yale following the First World War.

Yale had long required its students to attend both Sunday worship and, with a certain number of excuses, a daily weekday assembly for prayers and announcements. Even though undergraduate feelings about these requirements fluctuated, every senior class from 1894 to 1909 voted in favor of preserving the chapel requirement. But in 1910 the seniors reversed their previous commitment to compulsory Sunday worship, and by 1915 they were on the verge of opposing the weekday assemblies. These requirements were dropped during the war, but the university, pressed by Anson Phelps Stokes and Charles Reynolds Brown, dean of the Divinity School, reinstituted compulsory worship in December 1918.[29]

Student sentiment against mandatory worship grew during the early 1920s, and in 1923 the senior class voted in favor of abolishing required Sunday and weekday worship by wide margins. While the corporation set up a committee to investigate the chapel issue, the *Yale Daily News*, under the chairmanship of Carlos Stoddard, began to pursue the issue with unflagging zeal, and in November 1925 sponsored a public debate and referendum on the question of mandatory chapel.[30]

In editorial after editorial the *Yale Daily* insisted that compulsory chapel had to go. The editors argued that they were not opposed to worship per se but to the element of compulsion and the damage this did to religious feeling. The chief motive for abolishing mandatory worship was to improve the religious tone of the chapel services. "There is one feature that distinguishes Yale services from others," one editorial read: "Compulsory attendance. Abolish this, and instead of being the worse than failures they now are, our services will be real, sincere gatherings, with an entirely new quality about them,—a religious quality."[31] Even if such rhetoric was as much political as genuine in feeling, the fact that this was the main argument against compulsion acknowledges the continuing sympathy for Christian influences among the powers of the university.

Some students, however, were not buying such arguments. They believed that Yale, as a Christian university, needed to maintain a formal institutional witness to its avowed commitments. Tradition, loyalty to Yale's heritage, the promotion of student unity, and the benefits of beginning each day in prayer all argued in favor of maintaining compulsory worship. No less important to some was the matter of Yale's distinctiveness. "Abolish chapel and Yale becomes but another Harvard, another Dartmouth," one student shuddered.[32]

But not even an appeal to Eli pride could redeem compulsory chapel in the eyes of most of the students, for when the *Yale Daily* poll was completed, 1,681 undergraduates had opposed compulsion and only 241 had supported the requirement.[33] In order to formalize this response, the *Yale Daily* sponsored a petition to the faculty opposing compulsory chapel; it was signed by 1,541 students.[34]

Many of the faculty, however, did not need the encouragement of the students to oppose compulsory worship. Whereas Dean Brown of the Divinity School argued for the "character-making" benefits of mandatory worship, he was, at least among the faculty who responded to the *Yale Daily* poll, in a decided minority.[35] Of the sixty-five Yale faculty who responded to the poll, forty-seven opposed compulsion and eighteen supported it.[36] Although the bulk of the Yale faculty had opted not to respond at all, this survey did not bode well for the continuation of mandatory chapel.

Yale alumni, not wanting to leave matters of such import in the hands of the students and faculty alone, also entered the fray. The editors of the *Yale Alumni Weekly*, who saw numerous problems with compulsory chapel, used the *Yale Daily* poll to call for a marked improvement in chapel or the discontinuance of the requirement. "There is hardly anything less desirable and more dangerous in the long run," the editors insisted in November, "than to force unwilling young men to religious service."[37] As the discussion continued, the *Alumni Weekly* pressed the matter. In the issue of February 5, 1926, the editors suggested that the university would be better served if it dropped compulsory chapel and revitalized the Church of Christ in Yale, thereby taking "one long step towards a higher spiritual level for the whole University, not Yale College alone."[38] The alumni thus joined in the chorus of those maintaining that Christianity would be better served by the disestablishment of religion on the campus rather than by mandatory chapel.

Later that month the recently retired editor of the *Yale Daily*, Carlos Stoddard, turned up the heat another notch when he told a roomful of alumni: "We *don't* get our sense of unity out of chapel. We don't even all meet at once now, and if we did have a building big enough it would merely be twice as much like a rabble army and not twice as much like the solidarity of . . . family prayers." Stoddard insisted that the true religious concerns of the college would be best served by abandoning compulsion. He continued, "If you believe that the Fear of the Lord is the Beginning of Wisdom, you might also remember that the End of Compulsion is the Beginning of Religion," and concluded:

> Once each Senior Class voted to keep chapel. Not so lately. I remind you that we who have been spokesmen are Seniors, and that our Class is about seven to one against it. We have nothing to gain personally. We *don't* think it would be a good thing for the other fellow, now that we're through. We know that it is not a good thing for anybody, and that it's a bad thing for many.[39]

The Yale faculty, convinced that this issue fell to their discretion and not to the corporation's, formed their own committee, which arrived at a compromise solution that, among other modifications, excused seniors from daily chapel. But when the faculty considered this report, they, now with the support of Dean Brown, voted to back the abolition of compulsory chapel altogether.[40] Coffin, among others, was astounded at this action of the faculty, but members of the corporation who sought to retain the requirement were in the minority, and the board voted to support the faculty's action.[41]

In voting to abolish required chapel, the corporation sought to lessen the blow and maintain the professed aim of the university to "uphold and propagate the Christian Protestant religion" by stating that in place of compulsory chapel,

> the University has taken measures to establish a strong undergraduate department of religion; to develop in every way the Church of Christ in Yale University, the official name of the College Church; to maintain and strengthen the various student religious organizations; and to call to the attention of the friends of the University the desirability of a suitable chapel building where voluntary services may be held.[42]

Angell seconded these concerns when, in announcing the new policy, he declared, "we are convinced that by these means a more wholesome and active religious life will come into being at Yale." "In the execution of this policy," he insisted, "the Corporation feels that the whole body of the Yale Alumni can confidently look to both the teaching staff and the students to carry Yale's Christian ideals forward out of the danger of indifference and into the richness of the traditions to which they are heirs."[43] Perhaps this was a case of making a virtue out of a necessity. Nonetheless, it appears that most parties involved in this decision were in fact seeking to inspire a more vigorous religious life on campus rather than to encourage secularization. The editors of the *Yale Daily*, at least, insisted that the abolition of compulsion "was not the admission of an 'unchristian' Yale, but of a Christian Yale."[44]

With the advent of a new academic year in 1926, the editors of the *Yale Daily* encouraged their peers to fulfill Angell's hope for a "more wholesome and active religious life" by attending daily chapel voluntarily. According to the editors, the very integrity of Yale was at stake. They put the case before the students:

> Yale without spiritual background, without religion in the daily
> life, without God—Yale in such a pagan and material atmosphere
> is as unimaginable as it would be unworthy of her sons to allow
> such a complete reversion of the fundamental principals [sic]
> upon which the University stands. . . . Are we going to be heretics
> to the traditions and ideals of the University?[45]

Unimaginable or not, most students failed to respond to the editors' appeal, opting instead to be, in the paper's words, "heretics." Given the student opposition to compulsory chapel, it is not surprising that attendance at daily services in the first year after the requirement was abolished ran between one hundred to two hundred students.[46]

Numerous factors, of course, contributed to the ending of formal religious exercises at Yale. In the years between the Civil War and the First World War, higher education in the United States had undergone a revolution. Whereas post-secondary education in the mid-nineteenth century had been largely in the hands of church-related colleges run by clergy presidents, by the 1920s the rise of the university had transformed the shape and nature of higher learning. Nineteenth-century colleges concentrated on the development of intellect and character under the umbrella of religion and moral philosophy, but the new universities stressed research, academic specialization, and a diverse curriculum. New private universities— such as Johns Hopkins, Stanford, and the University of Chicago— founded by industrial tycoons, the growth of state universities under the Morrill Act, and the transformation of former colleges—most notably Harvard—into centers of scientific research all worked to promote the ideal of the research university. Religious influences had accordingly been moved more and more from the center of the academic enterprise to its periphery.

Yale, of course, was not immune from these changes, and although it was more cautious in adopting the university model than was Harvard, it nevertheless moved with the times. Yale had granted the first American Ph.D. in 1861 and had changed its name from Yale College to Yale University in 1886.[47] The faculty, which numbered 64 in 1870, had swelled to 587 by the time Angell took office.[48] Under Hadley there was an increasing stress on research, and the number of non-Yale graduates on the faculty dramatically increased.[49] The percentage of faculty weaned on the old Yale concern for both moral and intellectual development gradually declined as an emphasis on research and specialization increased.[50] When the question of required chapel came to a vote in 1926, therefore, most of the faculty, recognizing the severe problems with the institution, and believing, in any event, that the school should be more concerned with matters of intellect than character, overwhelmingly voted to end the tradition.

In addition, during the preceding forty years the alumni had been gaining more and more influence over the school, and they exercised this newfound muscle in the battle over mandatory worship.[51] The alumni did not want to deny Yale's Christian heritage, but many believed that mandatory worship only harmed the cause of true Christianity. When the matter came to a head in 1926, alumni opposition to compulsion helped tip the balance in favor of disestablishment.

Finally, Yale's dual heritage as both a Christian and a public institution created an increasing tension that apparently could be resolved only through disestablishing religion. Although founded as a distinctly Christian institution, Yale had a mission to educate youth "for publick employment, both in church & civil state."[52] It had, as historian Brooks Kelley has noted, "never been wholly a private institution," and had always seen its duty as one to both church and nation.[53] But if Yale sought to maintain its service to the nation in a country becoming increasingly pluralistic, it could no longer insist on required religious observance. As the student body grew to reflect an increasingly pluralistic and secular nation, formal religious requirements came under heavier and heavier attack.

The administrators were thus placed in a dilemma by the university's twofold mission. Yale's Christian ideals could be preserved, but only if they were made non-binding. Yale, in seeking to admit the future leaders of America, could no longer pretend that its students would universally support the traditional religious exercises of the institution.

Angell understood that if Yale was to be a public university, its student body would necessarily reflect the religious tenor of the nation. He therefore placed the changes at Yale in a national context. Discussing the alteration in chapel requirements in 1931, he allowed, "The whole spirit of our time is compelling religion, both organized and individualistic, to reorient itself, and the colleges can by no means escape the repercussions of this situation in the world outside."[54] Likewise in 1934 he reported, "Our student body inevitably reflects the trends of opinion and practice in the world outside, where complete indifference to religion, colored at times with acrimonious hostility and ignorant contempt, is an altogether too common phenomenon."[55] As Robert Handy has shown, American mainline religion experienced a marked depression in the inter-war years, suffering a decline in worship attendance, Sunday school enrollment, new members, and missionary enthusiasm.[56] Schools such as Yale, which drew their clientele from the elite of the Protestant establishment, were, of course, affected by this mood and suffered a drop in religious vitality along with the churches.

Despite the need to alter the form of Yale's religious commitment, Angell did not dismiss Yale's religious mission. Rather, he perceived a "deep and serious concern among large and influential groups of students for the essential religious and ethical values in life" and personally sought to encourage religious values, broadly conceived, in his charges for the benefit of the nation.[57]

Although Angell frequently linked the preservation of religious principles with the upbuilding of the nation, his concern for God and democracy was revealed perhaps nowhere as well as in his baccalaureate sermon of 1936, titled "The Moral Crisis of Democracy." Against the backdrop of the depression and the growth of totalitarianism in Europe, he insisted that religion alone held the key to the nation's future. "It seems to me clear," he announced to the graduating class, "that only a moral and spiritual renaissance will serve definitely to turn the hands of progress forward once again." The religious revival he proposed was not a matter of "superstitions" or "outworn creeds" but rather "a vital reverence for the highest values in human life." With evangelical passion Angell strove to recruit missionaries for service to the nation:

> The old Yale Charter, as you well know, speaks of training youth for service in church and civil state. Both church and state need your help now as rarely before. . . . All this creates a matchless challenge to men willing to cast themselves unreservedly into the effort to build a saner and more generous world. The stakes are high, the risks are real, the instant reward may well be small. But to do one's full share in a great job like this, involving as it does the welfare of millions of people, and quite conceivably the fate of the nation, is a thing on which no spirited youth can turn his back.

No greater foundation for success in this great mission could be found, Angell declared, than the great commands of Jesus to love God and neighbor. "There are, to my knowledge," he argued, "no other principles of human conduct which sincerely accepted are so capable of transforming human society." "Reverently I commend them to you for today, and tomorrow, and for all the years to come," he concluded, "for what shall it profit a man to gain the whole world and lose his own soul?"[58]

Angell, in his own way, thus held together the dual traditions of Yale—devotion to God and nation—in an era when such a marriage was becoming increasingly difficult to maintain. The disestablishment of Christianity in the abolition of mandatory chapel was a clear admission that Christian piety could no longer be expected of Yale undergraduates, and that Yale, as a university, could no longer be in the business of mandating religious rituals. But Angell was still convinced that the teachings of Jesus provided the surest moral foundation for the nation and that Yale had an obligation to instill these priniciples in its young men. Even though Yale, along with all liberal Christians of the era, was broadening its conception of Christianity and though it was moving away from its traditional Christian practices, the Christian heritage continued to buttress Yale's mission to America.

Robert Maynard Hutchins
and William Adams Brown:
The Case for Theology in the University

In the same year that Angell was encouraging Yale's graduating
seniors to adopt the principles of Jesus in order to save the nation,
Robert Maynard Hutchins, Yale graduate, former secretary of the
Yale Corporation, former dean of Yale Law School, and now president of the University of Chicago, published the Stoors Lectures
that he had delivered at Yale in 1935 under the title *The Higher
Learning in America*.[59] These lectures, which condemned the fragmentation of American higher education and proposed metaphysics as a solution to the educational chaos, set off a debate in
university circles of national proportions and inspired Hutchins's
friend William Adams Brown to propose theology as the unifying
principle for university education.[60]

Hutchins opened his lectures to his Yale audience with the assertion
that the most "striking fact" about American higher education was its
utter confusion. He took American education to task for its service-
station mentality and suggested that the solution to the problems of
education lay in the "cultivation of the intellect." Citing Aquinas's
Summa Theologica, Hutchins insisted: "Education implies teaching.
Teaching implies knowledge. Knowledge is truth. The truth is everywhere the same. Hence education should be everywhere the same."
While acknowledging that theology had once provided coherence to
university education, Hutchins believed that it could no longer do the
trick in the modern world. He allowed:

> Theology is banned by law from some universities. It might as
> well be from the rest. Theology is based on revealed truth and on
> articles of faith. We are a faithless generation and take no stock in
> revelation. Theology implies orthodoxy and an orthodox church.
> We have neither. To look to theology to unify the modern univer-
> sity is futile and vain.[61]

But Greek thought was a different story, for the metaphysics of
Plato and Aristotle could provide unity without depending on
revelation. Inasmuch as "the aim of higher education is wisdom,"
and "wisdom is knowledge of principles and causes," metaphysics,

which "deals with the highest principles and causes," is the "highest wisdom." Since only theology or metaphysics could serve as a unifying principle, and since theology was out of the question, the future of the university rested on a return to metaphysics.[62]

Hutchins's proposals raised a storm of protest and numerous responses from across the nation, but one response from the Yale community in particular is noteworthy. In answer to Hutchins's lectures, William Adams Brown, former Yale fellow and former acting provost, delivered a series of lectures at Chicago published under the title *The Case for Theology in the University*.[63]

Cordially but firmly Brown criticized Hutchins for his contention that theology, inasmuch as it was based on "faith, or supernatural knowledge," could not unify the university. Rather, Brown insisted, theology, properly understood, could in fact "furnish a unifying philosophy of life which would bring meaning and consistency into our conception of education as a whole." If theology were viewed as "the philosophy of the Christian religion, or, in other words, the sum of the attempts to use the clue which Christian faith provides to bring unity and consistency into man's thought of the universe," then, Brown believed, it might well be able to give cohesion to higher education.[64]

Brown conceded that while metaphysics could "define the common assumptions which are necessary to any intelligible account of the universe," only theology offered "contact with a body of concrete facts which give it a specific subject matter" and "a tradition long and many-sided enough to furnish a point of contact with the variety of interests for which any university worthy of the name must make provision." Theology could take its place in the university only as a "philosophy among philosophies," but as such it could "serve as [an] organizing principle for the university because it can help men to differentiate between the things that are important and the things that are unimportant, and this both in the field of thought and in the field of practice." The task of the theologian in such a scheme would be "to vindicate man's faith that this is a meaningful world . . . and to show the consequences which follow for the life of today."[65]

While making theology the centerpiece of the university would be fairly easy at church-connected schools, Brown realized that at state schools and independent institutions—such as Yale, Harvard, and Chicago—there would be more difficulty. State schools, Brown allowed, could at least inform their students of religious answers to the large questions of life. Independent institutions, by contrast, with which Brown was much more familiar, could return theology to the center of the curriculum by way of "their own cultural tradition, which is that of historic Protestantism." The hope for such a return to Protestantism as a unifying factor, Brown suggested, lay in the developing ecumenical theology, "a theology . . . that shall be universal not only in the range of its interests but in the personnel which it is able to enlist in their pursuit." With the advent of an ecumenical theology, a theology concerned with all aspects of life free of distinctively denominational views, "a common platform" was being built on which the university could rest.[66]

The recovery of some sense of integrity to university education under the umbrella of theology was not, for Brown, merely an academic concern. Rather, the very survival of Western civilization hung in the balance. "If democratic civilization is to maintain itself," Brown insisted, "we must have a philosophy which is born of faith, a philosophy which is in fact, and which is not ashamed to call itself, religious—in other words, a theology." America was, Brown averred, grounded on a faith in God and a corresponding faith in the dignity of humanity, and it was "because the democratic countries have so largely lost their faith in the divine dignity and calling of man, that they are so ill-prepared to meet the attack of the new philosophies that are preaching their totalitarian gospel."[67] With the spread of totalitarianism in Europe, the recovery of the theological integrity of the university—and theology's faith in the value of human life—took on monumental urgency.

Here Brown admirably reflected the devotion of his alma mater to God and country and mirrored Angell's concern for the broadly Christian underpinnings of America. Higher education had to be based on theology—on a faith in God—if it was to provide a solid grounding for the upbuilding of democracy. Indeed, apart from such a faith, freedom itself, under the onslaught of atheistic, materialistic philosophies, might well vanish from the earth. To cement the point, Brown quoted Charles Seymour, newly installed president of Yale, who in his inaugural address proclaimed:

The duty of protecting freedom of thought and speech is the more compelling in these days when the liberal spirit in the world-at-large is in deadly peril. . . . I call on all members of the faculty, as members of a thinking body, freely to recognize the tremendous vitality and power of the teaching of Christ in our life-and-death struggle against the forces of selfish materialism. If we lose in that struggle, judging by present events abroad, scholarship as well as religion will disappear.

Only Christianity, with its belief in a rational God, a moral world, and the dignity of mankind, could "supply a religious basis for our democratic tradition" over against the communism and totalitarianism proclaimed by Marx and Lenin.[68] Only Christianity could provide the ultimate basis for the future of education and Western civilization.

Unless the university willingly engaged in a wholesale abdication of its responsibility, it would have to "give the principles which will help men to judge whether this or that particular calling is worth following, and . . . furnish them with tests by which to determine whether the type of character which is held up to them as an ideal is really excellent." Theology· could provide such principles and tests and thus give to the university a unifying principle. What the university needed therefore, was

a philosophical department that centers all its thinking about the living faiths that divide the allegiance of mankind and among these faiths gives the primary place to the Christian as the one which not only underlies our own cultural inheritance but which alone is able to furnish a rational foundation for the ideal of freedom to which the modern university is committed.

The change in philosophy, and the philosophy department, would also result in changes in the teaching of history, sociology, and the languages, and would finally result in a university that "realizes the central place which religion holds in human life." Inasmuch as theology addressed not any limited sphere of knowledge but "the nature of man, of the world, and of God," it could provide the polestar around which the university revolved.[69]

Brown, who had witnessed Yale's struggle to maintain its commitment to God and country since the close of the First World War, thereby proposed a solution to the dilemma of its being both a

Christian and a public school. Theology, understood not as a matter of doctrine but as "the philosophy of the Christian religion," which insisted on a moral, meaningful universe and the essential importance of personality, could not only provide the means to a unified university but also support the future of democracy. The Yale tradition of service to God and nation could redeem not just the nation's universities but the nation itself. In Charles Seymour, Yale's new president, Brown rightly saw an ally in his quest for the preservation of Christian higher education and democracy.

Charles Seymour and the Preservation of the Yale Tradition

With the inauguration of Charles Seymour in 1937, Yale installed a devoted Yale man with a deep respect for its traditions.[70] Seymour's rhetoric was more explicitly Christian than Angell's, and he, like his predecessor, looked to imbue Yale men with a devotion to God that would further their service to the nation.

As Brown had noted, Seymour, in his inaugural address, upheld Yale's commitment to Christianity as the foundation of civilization. "Never in the history of the world has the menace of materialism been more appalling nor the disastrous consequences of its triumph so obvious," Seymour warned the Yale family. He continued: "In the political, economic and social fields of endeavor it has produced and it will perpetuate suicidal strife. . . . If our historical studies have taught us anything it is that selfish materialism leads straight to the city of destruction." The menace of materialism could be successfully combatted only by the marriage of "clear intelligence" and "spiritual values," the consummation of which Yale should encourage. Seymour declared:

> Yale was dedicated to the upraising of spiritual leaders. We betray our trust if we fail to explore the various ways in which the youth who come to us may learn to appreciate spiritual values, whether by the example of our own lives or through the cogency of our philosophical arguments. The simple and direct way is through the maintenance and upbuilding of the Christian religion as a vital part of university life.[71]

Although Yale no longer required its students to participate in Christian worship, this was an adjustment in, not an abdication of, Yale's religious responsibility. Seymour was dedicated to the ideal of Yale as both a Christian and a national institution. As if to insist that these sentiments were not merely inaugural rhetoric, and yet realizing the problematic place of religion in the life of the university, he affirmed in his first annual report:

> Yale is historically a Christian institution. As I stated in my inaugural address, I believe that we fail in our educational mission if we permit the importance of spiritual factors to be overshadowed by intellectual paganism. It is not easy in this age to discover and to prosecute the processes by which religion shall assume its proper role in the life of the University. But it is necessary that we lose no chance of bringing to the student, whether in formal worship, in social relations, or in the classroom, a consciousness of religious realities.[72]

In a pluralistic culture Yale might not be able to require worship of its undergraduates; but it still had a mission to cultivate the moral leaders of the nation through the promotion of broad Christian values.

In an effort to further Yale's religious mission, the corporation arranged for a University Christian Conference in January and early February 1939.[73] The conference, organized by one hundred faculty and undergraduates, was designed to provide for "a widespread program of religious re-examination and re-emphasis, all to be carried on under the auspices of the Corporation."[74]

At the opening of the conference, President Seymour introduced the main speaker, George Buttrick, pastor of the Madison Avenue Presbyterian Church of New York and president of the Federal Council of Churches, with the claim, "Responsibility for the religious life of the students . . . is one which by our charter, our traditions, and our knowledge of history we cannot evade." Buttrick spoke on three successive nights, addressing "The Reality of God," "The Centrality of Christ," and "The Modern Meaning of the Cross." Throughout the month of February twenty student groups led by faculty members met weekly to address religious issues raised by the talks.[75]

Despite such efforts, Seymour was fighting an uphill battle. In

1938 the *Yale Literary Magazine* had averred that talking of "religion to the boys at Yale is as awkward as trying to impress your girl's kid brother with the dignity of love," and in 1941 an observer of Yale undergraduates reported in *Redbook* magazine that the typical Yale senior "is skeptical of emotional idealism, and . . . has very little interest whatever in organized religion. He never goes to church."[76]

The efforts of individuals such as Charles Foster Kent, James R. Angell, William Adams Brown, and Charles Seymour notwithstanding, maintaining Yale's commitment to God and nation in the inter-war years became more and more problematic. If disestablishing Christianity on the campus allowed Yale to maintain the rhetoric of its Christian tradition while becoming more pluralistic, this did not, as many had hoped, increase the vigor of Christian life in the university. Rather, students, faculty, and alumni, reflecting patterns in higher education and in American culture in general, were paying less and less attention to Christian beliefs and values.

Indeed, in an increasingly secular and pluralistic society, Yale, no matter what the commitment of the administration, could not count on a nationally representative student body and faculty to support Yale's Christian tradition. Yale's desire to maintain and enhance its position as a public institution, as a school that would serve the entire nation, conflicted with any desire to remain committed to the tradition of a particular faith and pulled it steadily away from its traditional Christian roots in the years after the First World War.

While those who had been raised inside the Yale tradition of devotion to nation and Christianity worked to keep the two streams together by broadening the definition of Christianity and abandoning required Christian rituals, those outside the tradition could see the inherent difficulties in trying to maintain such a position at all. In 1936 Morris Cohen, a Jew who had served as a visiting professor in the philosophy department, put the case this way:

> There is a certain duplicity about liberalism which shocks intellectually conscientious people. . . . This is the case with our Universities. They claim to stand for universal truth, but in the end they do not want to get away from certain sectarian and partisan

commitments. I have no objection to Yale University insisting that it is a white, Protestant organization and acting accordingly [as it used to in regard to compulsory chapel]; but it should make some effort at consistency.[77]

As long as an informal Protestant establishment still presided over the nation, Yale and other schools like it could maintain an informal Protestant ethos, straddling the camps of Christianity and the culture. By the 1960s, however, the earlier claims of Brown and Seymour that Yale was a "Christian University," would have a distinctly foreign ring. As America became a pluralistic country, Yale would drop its Christian pretensions and rhetoric completely in order to continue to educate the nation's leaders.

Notes

I gratefully acknowledge the criticisms of an earlier version of this essay by George M. Marsden, D. G. Hart, Diana Butler, Tony Jenkins, Paul Kemeny, Kathryn Long, and Jeffrey Trexler.

1. Anson Phelps Stokes, "Yale's Great Record and Her Present Need," *Yale Alumni Weekly* 36 (May 13, 1927), 930.

2. *Reports of the President, Acting Provost, and Secretary of Yale University and of the Deans and Directors of Its Several Schools and Departments for the Academic Year 1919-1920* (New Haven: By the University, 1920), 33, 74. See also William Adams Brown, *A Teacher and His Times: A Story of Two Worlds* (New York: Charles Scribner's Sons, 1940), 284-88.

3. George W. Pierson, *Yale: The University College, 1921-1937* (New Haven: Yale University Press, 1955), 548 n.5, 6-7.

4. Pierson, *Yale: 1921-1937*, 3-4.

5. Ibid., 5-6.

6. Ibid., 6-7.

7. Ibid., 10-12, 15.

8. Ibid., 16-19; James R. Angell, "James Rowland Angell," in *A History of Psychology in Autobiography*, vol. 3 (Worcester, MA: Clark University Press, 1936), 1-38.

9. Pierson, *Yale: 1921-1937*, 19. The *Harvard Alumni Bulletin* praised the selection of Angell, claiming Yale "has made herself free to select the best men the country can afford, to be her leaders; and in so doing has dedicated herself not to Yale, but to America." Quoted in Pierson, *Yale: 1921-1937*, 3.

10. James R. Angell, *American Education: Addresses and Articles* (New Haven: Yale University Press, 1937), 1, 3.

11. Ibid., 3–11.

12. Seymour A. Smith, *Religious Cooperation in State Universities: An Historical Sketch* (n.p.: University of Michigan, 1957), 25–26.

13. Marcus Bach, *Of Faith and Learning: The Story of the School of Religion at the State University of Iowa* (Iowa City: The School of Religion, 1952), 42; *Two Decades: The Story of the National Council on Religion in Higher Education (Founded by Charles Foster Kent), 1922–1941* (New York: National Council on Religion in Higher Education, 1941), 12–13. See also Patrick M. Malin, "The National Council on Religion in Higher Education," in *Liberal Learning and Religion*, ed. Amos N. Wilder (New York: Harper and Brothers, 1951), 324–34.

14. Bach, *Faith and Learning*, 44–45.

15. Ibid., 47; C. Grey Austin, *A Century of Religion at the University of Michigan* (n.p.; University of Michigan, 1957), 36; *The Origin, Organization, and Aims of the Council* (New Haven: Bulletin of the Council of Schools of Religion, n.d.), 6.

16. *Origin, Organization, and Aims*, 6–15; Charles F. Kent, *Filling the Gap in Modern Education* (n.p.: Bulletin of the National Council of Schools of Religion, n.d.), 12; *Two Decades*, 15.

17. Howard Peckham, *The Making of the University of Michigan* (Ann Arbor: University of Michigan Press, 1967), 138–39.

18. Marion L. Burton, untitled address, *Christian Education* 7 (March 1924), 305–6.

19. Austin, *Century of Religion*, 37–39.

20. Walter A. Donnelly, *The University of Michigan: An Encyclopedic Survey*, Pt. 9, *Student Life and Organization, Athletics* (Ann Arbor: University of Michigan Press, 1958), 1894, 1896.

21. Austin, *Century of Religion*, 41.

22. O. D. Foster, "Schools of Religion," *Christian Education* 7 (January 1924), 178–94; Hugh Hartshorne, Helen Sterns, and Willard Uphaus, *Standards and Trends in Religious Education* (New Haven: Yale University Press, 1933), 186–89. See also *Origin, Organization, and Aims*, 4.

23. Hartshorne, *Standards and Trends*, 188.

24. Clarence P. Shedd, *The Church Follows Its Students* (New Haven: Yale University Press, 1938), 131.

25. *Report of the President of Yale University for the Academic Year 1923–1924* (New Haven: By the University, 1924), 16–17.

26. On these controversies, see Bradley J. Longfield, *The Presbyterian Controversy: Fundamentalists, Modernists, and Moderates* (New York: Oxford University Press, 1991); and George M. Marsden, *Fundamentalism*

and American Culture: The Shaping of Twentieth-Century Evangelicalism, 1870–1925 (New York: Oxford University Press, 1980).

27. *Report of the President, 1923–1924*, 16–17; Reinhold Niebuhr, ed. *This Ministry: The Contribution of Henry Sloane Coffin* (New York: Charles Scribner's Sons, 1945), 103.

28. Ralph H. Gabriel, *Religion and Learning at Yale: The Church of Christ in the College and University, 1757–1957* (New Haven: Yale University Press, 1958), 223, 226.

29. Pierson, *Yale: 1921–1937*, 84–86.

30. Ibid., 86–89; Gabriel, *Religion and Learning*, 225–26; *Yale Daily News*, November 2–November 10, 1925.

31. *Yale Daily News*, November 5, 1925, 2.

32. *Yale Daily News*, November 3, 1925, 1, 2.

33. *Yale Daily News*, November 9, 1925, 1.

34. *Yale Daily News*, November 11, 1925, 1.

35. Pierson, *Yale: 1921–1937*, 86–89; *Yale Daily News*, November 6, 1925, 1–2.

36. *Yale Daily News*, November 10, 1925, 1.

37. *Yale Alumni Weekly*, 35 (November 13, 1925), 233.

38. *Yale Alumni Weekly*, 35 (February 5, 1926), 537.

39. *Yale Alumni Weekly*, 35 (February 26, 1926), 630–31.

40. Gabriel, *Religion and Learning*, 227–28; Pierson, *Yale: 1921–1937*, 92–93. See also *Yale Alumni Weekly*, 35 (March 12, 1926), 689; (March 19, 1926), 715; (May 14, 1926), 953–54.

41. Pierson, *Yale: 1921–1937*, 92–93. The corporation's action approved a trial period of voluntary services but compulsion was never resumed. Gabriel, *Religion and Learning*, 228.

42. Corporation Records, in Woodbridge Hall, Yale University, quoted in Gabriel, *Religion and Learning*, 228. The corporation's intentions were better than their actions, however, for it was another twenty years before Yale would create a department of religion. Ibid., 228.

43. *Yale Alumni Weekly*, 35 (May 14, 1926), 954; *Yale Daily News*, May 10, 1926, 1.

44. *Yale Daily News*, June 15, 1926, 2.

45. *Yale Alumni Weekly*, 36 (October 8, 1926), 69.

46. *Report of the President for the Academic Year 1926–1927* (New Haven: By the University, 1928), 14.

47. George W. Pierson, *Yale College, An Educational History: 1871–1921* (New Haven: Yale University Press, 1952), 52; Brooks M. Kelley, *Yale: A History* (New Haven: Yale University Press, 1974), 275.

48. Pierson, *Yale: 1871–1921*, 96; Kelley, *Yale*, 389.

49. Kelley, *Yale*, 328, 330; Pierson, *Yale: 1871–1921*, 37, 126, 287, 291, 300.

50. See, e.g., Pierson, *Yale: 1871–1921*, 37.

51. Kelley, *Yale*, 267–68, 355, 357; Pierson, *Yale: 1871–1921*, 385, 481.

52. Franklin R. Dexter, *Documentary History of Yale University* (New Haven, 1916), 21, quoted in Richard Hofstadter and C. DeWitt Hardy, *The Development and Scope of Higher Education in the United States* (New York: Columbia University Press, 1952), 4.

53. Kelley, *Yale*, 11. On the dilemma posed by this dual heritage see George M. Marsden, "The Soul of the American University: A Historical Overview," chapter 1 in this volume, esp. 25–28.

54. *Report of the President for the Academic Year 1930–1931* (New Haven, 1932), 13.

55. *Report of the President of Yale University for the Academic Year 1933–1934* (New Haven, 1934), 49.

56. Robert T. Handy, "The American Religious Depression, 1925–1935," *Church History* 29 (1960), 4–5.

57. *President's Report, 1933–1934*, 49.

58. Angell, *American Education*, 231–32, 242, 244–45.

59. See Harry S. Ashmore, *Unseasonable Truths: The Life of Robert Maynard Hutchins* (Boston: Little, Brown, 1989), esp. 160–61.

60. Ashmore, *Unseasonable Truths*, 161–64. See Robert M. Hutchins, *The Higher Learning in America* (New Haven: Yale University Press, 1936).

61. Hutchins, *Higher Learning*, 1, 6, 66–67, 97.

62. Ibid., 98–99.

63. Brown, *Teacher and His Times*, 273; William Adams Brown, *The Case for Theology in the University* (Chicago: University of Chicago Press, 1938).

64. Brown, *Case for Theology*, 3, 13–15.

65. Ibid., 48–51, 53, 83–84, 86–87.

66. Ibid., 87–90, 95, 99, 105.

67. Ibid., 77–78.

68. Ibid., 80–81, 112–15.

69. Ibid., 117–20, 123–24, 53–54.

70. Kelley, *Yale*, 393.

71. *New York Times*, October 9, 1937, 9.

72. *Report of the President of Yale University for the Academic Year 1937–1938* (New Haven, 1938), 33.

73. *Yale Alumni Magazine* 2 (December 9, 1938), 6; 2 (January 20, 1939), 3.

74. *Yale Alumni Magazine* 2 (January 20, 1939), 3.

75. *Yale Alumni Magazine* 2 (February 17, 1939), 4.

76. Quoted in *Yale Alumni Magazine* 2 (December 9, 1938), 6, and in *Yale Alumni Magazine* 4 (May 23, 1941), 5.

77. Quoted in Dan Oren, *Joining the Club: A History of Jews and Yale* (New Haven: Yale University Press, 1985), 123–24.

6

"The Survival of Recognizably Protestant Colleges": Reflections on Old-Line Protestantism, 1950–1990

ROBERT WOOD LYNN

The survival of recognizably Protestant colleges therefore seems to depend on the survival within the larger society of Protestant enclaves whose members believe passionately in a way of life radically different from that of the majority, and who are both willing and able to pay for a brand of higher education that embodies their vision. Such enclaves still exist, but they are few in number.[1]

Christopher Jencks and David Riesman, 1968

Over the last four decades David Riesman has served American higher education as one of its foremost observers and interpreters. Ever since the publication of *Constraint and Variety in American Education* in 1956, he has consistently offered the kind of sane, broad-gauged cultural commentary tht one could seldom find in other quarters. Not many other scholars can match his deft touch in offering portraits of single institutions or sectors of higher education.

One of Riesman's more intriguing sketches is a chapter in *The Academic Revolution* in which he and Christopher Jencks offer a view of "Protestant Denominations and Their Colleges." But that

170

portrait never aroused the attention it deserved as a provocative guess about the likely future of Protestant higher education in the last third of the twentieth century.

Despite Riesman's reputation as an opinion maker in American culture, the "old-line"[2] Protestant leaders in higher education largely ignored this dismal scenario for the prospects of their institutions. There were, of course, any number of people in that slice of Protestantism who would have rejected the interpretation, if pressed to respond. (Indeed, some of them, whose thought I will describe later, lavished considerable time on devising typologies of diverse yet "recognizably Protestant colleges.") I suspect that the lack of response reflected a deep discomfort with even the suggestion that serious Protestant education would someday be mostly confined to "cognitive minorities" (Peter Berger's term).

In 1990, however, the presidents of sixty-nine Presbyterian colleges and universities issued a manifesto that raised once again the specter of the possible disappearance of the "recognizably Protestant colleges," or at least those within the Presbyterian Church (USA). Unlike many of its predecessors, this statement is free of the usual practice of blaming the denomination for the troubles of the church-related college. "As church-related colleges and universities," they write, "we share in the responsibility for the declining emphasis on higher education [within the Presbyterian Church]. We do not seek to find fault or affix blame." The authors of the document then point to the pressing problems confronting both college and church. While the denomination struggles with "the demise of Protestant hegemony, the decline of mainline churches and the importance of denominationalism," its colleges "face incredibly difficult pressures in the years ahead (increasing competition from state universities for students and gifts; a critical press; price resistance from parents and students; unfavorable changes in federal policies including the U.S. tax code; a declining pool of high school graduates; and changing student populations)." After describing various historical shifts in recent decades, the presidents conclude by saying that "some of the developments we have observed may be irreversible. The Presbyterian Church could be close to the point where its involvement in higher education might be lost forever."[3]

Twenty years ago few informed observers would have equated the

fate of the church-related college with the sweep of a denomination's "involvement in higher education." Today that claim makes
more sense, particularly in light of the persistent shrinking of old-
line campus ministries programs on college and university campuses. F. Thomas Trotter, former staff member of the United Methodist Board of Higher Education and Ministry, is probably correct
when he notes that for all the "heroic work of the campus ministers
in the public-sector schools . . . , the future of Christian higher
education lies with the historic church colleges."[4]

And so the Presbyterian college presidents' conclusion merits
close inspection. That somber warning represents a new note in
pronouncements of this kind. While such statements in the past
have often included melodramatic exaggerations designed to
awaken church members to the colleges' need for money, this
candid assessment seems to embody a genuine worry about the
future of these institutions. What prompts this fear? Is there anything at work here beyond the predictable anxieties about money
and institutional survival? Whatever else may be on the minds of
these leaders, they also appear to be wrestling with the deeply
perplexing problems inherent in the relationship of old-line Protestantism to its colleges.

In this essay I explore some of those problems and the ways in
which a few prominent institutions have dealt with them since the
1950s. Several prefatory notes are in order before I begin to traverse
these four decades: (1) I have left to other interpreters the massively
difficult task of applying the large notion of secularization to the
topics under discussion.[5] That challenge exceeds the competence of
this "midnight" student of history, who has spent most of the last
thirty years in administration. And (2) I also note for the record
that my choice of institutions—especially my decision to focus on
the Presbyterian Church in the United States of America as a
representative old-line denomination and a foundation as a major
actor in this story—might well reflect some of my own personal
history.

The inquiry begins at mid-century. One old-line denomination—
the Presbyterian Church in the USA, or the Northern Presbyterian
church—is concerned about the survival of its affiliated colleges as
"recognizably Protestant" institutions.

Lowry's "Adventure"

In 1950 Howard Lowry, president of The College of Wooster, published a study on religion and education titled *The Mind's Adventure.*[6] Although volumes on that theme were hardly a novelty in those days, the arrival of Lowry's work created something of a stir in Northern Presbyterian circles. For the appearance of this book was an integral part of a larger effort intended to restore the inherited nineteenth-century Protestant ecology of educational institutions—the circle linking the Sunday school to the public school, the college, and the seminary.

During the 1940s the Presbyterian Board of Christian Education became the spearhead for renewing the denomination's power as an educational presence. The first step in this direction was the creation of the "Faith and Life" curriculum, a plan for rejuvenating the Sunday school and family instruction. Although its critics scoffed at it as amounting to little more than "Neo-Orthodoxy Goes to Kindergarten,"[7] this venture became a considerable success and soon produced enough surplus revenue for the denomination to work at strengthening all the other educational institutions around the Protestant circle. The renovation of Presbyterian efforts in youth ministry, campus ministry, and theological education proceeded apace in the 1950s. No less important was the denomination's unabashed advocacy of the cause of American public education and the need to maintain a working partnership between public schools and churches through released-time programs and similar arrangements.

But it was perhaps the denominational college that represented the toughest challenge of all for the reformers at the Board of Christian Education. Ever since the early years of the twentieth century, the denomination had tried intermittently to arrest the slow decline of its influence on its institutions of higher education. While a few of the stronger ones slipped away, many of the weaker ones remained behind. By the late 1940s the Presbyterian colleges were once again in varying states of fiscal trouble. The sudden postwar flood of income from the G.I. benefits extended to the returning veterans of the Second World War had slowed to a trickle. Even more significant, these institutions often reflected a tired and blurred vision of their own existence as Christian colleges. A quick review of their catalogues discloses a distressing reliance on bland bromides: Trinity University, for instance, declared that "education at its best is essentially Christian, cultural and useful",[8] meanwhile, the heart of Illinois College's position as a Christian institution was its "endeavor to hold before its students Christian ideals of life and conduct as essential to a complete personality."[9] Were such claims, the board asked, the best the Presbyterian schools could do by way of making a case for the distinctive character of Christian higher education?

E. Fay Campbell, head of the board's work in higher education, believed that Howard Lowry and The College of Wooster could lead the way. At mid-century the college's credentials as a Presbyterian institution were impeccable. Over half of the student body was Presbyterian, and about one-sixth of the male students went on to seminary in the early 1950s. (At that time Wooster alone supplied over one-third of the entering class at McCormick Theological Seminary in Chicago, while also sending large contingents of students to Princeton Seminary, Union Seminary, New York, and Yale Divinity School.) The administration and faculty took equal pride in the future lay church leaders among its students. All faculty members were required to be members of evangelical churches. In its life and commitments Wooster embodied the continuing presence of at least part of the old Protestant educational ecology in twentieth-century America.[10]

But in the eyes of the board in Philadelphia, the college's greatest asset was the person sitting in the president's office. Wooster had counted itself extraordinarily fortunate in 1944 to lure Howard Lowry, one of its own graduates, away from Princeton University, where he had carved out a comfortable life as a professor of English and a specialist in the thought of Matthew Arnold. In his first years at Wooster, Lowry quickly established a reputation, both on and off the campus, for his work as a reform-minded leader and as an eloquent interpreter of the meaning of liberal education.[11] Finally, Lowry did not make any secret of his own Christian convictions, or of the college's character as a Christian venture in higher education.[12] For all these reasons, therefore, the Wooster president seemed a natural choice for the task of writing a popular book that would set forth new standards for the Christian colleges, galvanize more support for these beleaguered institutions, and provide a theological response to the 1945 Harvard report, *General Education in a Free Society.*

Once Lowry agreed to take on this daunting assignment, Campbell gathered an advisory committee representative of the best talent he coud find, both inside and outside the Presbyterian fold. The group included professors from Yale and Princeton universities as well as the University of Chicago. The presidents of Lafayette and Occidental colleges (two schools in the Presbyterian tradition) served on the committee, along with nationally known pastors and some pivotal leaders in the denomination's bureaucracy. The heads of two of the three national agencies were among the Presbyterian power brokers on the committee's roster. In sum, here was a group that could help Lowry and Campbell make the most of what all agreed might be an enormously promising moment in American higher education. There were various signs suggesting the arrival of a new era: Merrimon Cuninggim's recently published book *The College Seeks Religion*,[13] the success of George F. Thomas (Lowry's old colleague from his Princeton days) in expanding the Department of Religion at Princeton University, and the post-war surge of interest in religion. Expectations ran high.

Lowry's eventual book, *The Mind's Adventure*, never lived up to those expectations, although it was, in retrospect, the most significant work about the church college produced with the full backing of an old-line denomination during the 1950s. The work suffered from the conflicting ambitions of its author and his advisers. Could any short, popular book, no matter how well written, do justice to the complex problems of religion in the modern university as well as to the future of the Christian college?

The diagnosis of the secular university and its ailments proved to be the most revealing part of *The Mind's Adventure*. Lowry and company were intent on refuting the Harvard report's contention that contemporary colleges and universities cannot resort to the belief

> generally shared by American colleges until less than a century ago: namely, the conviction that Christianity gives meaning and ultimate unity to all parts of the curriculum, indeed to the whole life of the college. . . . Some think it the Achilles' heel of democ-

racy that, by its very nature it cannot foster general agreement on ultimates, and perhaps must foster the contrary. But whatever one's views, religion is not now for most colleges a practicable source of intellectual unity.[14]

In other words, the Protestant era in American higher education was over. America at mid-century was intractably pluralistic. "Sectarian" colleges (whether Roman Catholic or Protestant) were free to appeal to the unifying power of their traditions, but that solution would no longer do for the whole enterprise of American higher education.

Lowry refused to concede that point or to retire gracefully to the margins of the academic enterprise along with the other "sectarians." Throughout his argument the Wooster president placed himself at the center, where he could speak on behalf of the deeper continuities of college and university life in this country. At the heart of that complex of traditions was the legacy of the "Hebraic-Christian tradition." "Religion" is therefore the source of integration and coherence in a liberal arts education. He never wavered from that conviction. Nor did he ever question, even for a moment, his own presuppositions about the decisive role that Protestants should play in the future of American education. Although Protestantism itself was in desperate need of renewal, the Protestant era in higher education could extend far into the coming decades.

From that vantage point Lowry attempted to mount a critique of the secular mentality pervading the universities and the independent colleges. But then a coincidence robbed him of the chance to be the chief critic of secularism. *The Mind's Adventure* presented a bill of complaints against the educational and intellectual shortcomings of "moral relativism," "naturalism" and the "cult of 'objectivity'" as the fruits of "humanism." But, unfortunately for Lowry and his backers, his book paled in comparison with another volume about some of the same matters. American readers who were seriously interested in pursuing the criticism of objectivity (the presumed conceit of those scholars who imagine themselves to be free of hidden presuppositions) could find more intellectual depth in the work of an Oxford philosopher whose book was released at just about the time Howard Lowry finished his manuscript. Sir Walter Moberly's reflections on *The Crisis in the University*[15] quickly became the standard reference for faculty and student Christians discussing the "university question," whether in this country or in the United Kingdom. And so the Presbyterians' bid to shape future thinking about American higher education was fated to failure almost from the outset.

The major success of *The Mind's Adventure* lay in Lowry's affectionate portrait of the Woosters scattered across the country, the church colleges "whose influence in American life is out of all proportion to their size."[16] (Interestingly enough, he felt quite comfortable in speaking of these institutions as "church" or "Christian" colleges; the phrase "church-related" did not figure in his analysis. That notion would become more popular in the next decade.)

Though limited in resources and scale, these schools have taken on the large and complex "task of trying to be true to their religious purpose and at the same time be genuine places of higher learning and free inquiry."[17] Lowry saw no contradiction between these twin imperatives, nor was he willing to settle for a diluted version of "their religious purposes" in order to make it easier to accommodate the requirements of "free inquiry." "The Christian college will be," he declared, "a community existing around a group of learners, both teachers and students, who confess Jesus Christ as their Saviour and Lord. They are engaged in a serious search for the knowledge of God and His universe and His demands upon human life."[18]

In his judgment this "serious search for the knowledge of God" did not lead to a unitary Christian worldview such that one could speak of a "Christian chemistry" or "Christian biology."[19] "Both the secular and the Christian scholar will deal with the same facts in his field; but the facts, once determined, will then begin to mean vastly different things to the *men* looking at them."[20] Consequently the crucial test for the Woosters of this world is the selection of faculty members whose Christian convictions, scholarly competence, and commitment to free inquiry equip them to lead others in that search for knowledge.

Such a college, Lowry believed, could appeal to the ablest Christians in the post-war generation of scholars coming out of graduate programs. But if the schools were to protect these gifted folk from the blandishments of wealthier independent colleges and universities, the church college presidents and the supporting denominations had to unearth new sources of major support. After warning his colleagues against seeking public funds or federal aid, he pinned his hopes on reaching the people in the pews. The appeal came in the form of a wistful thought that has doubtless figured in the midnight reveries of many a church college president: "Most Churches have never faced up to their educational task. In their membership they have wealth enough to put all of their colleges on a first-class basis, and to give them a really creative life."[21]

But the course of events in the 1950s did not confirm Lowry's hope, either for Wooster or for its counterparts. There was, for example, no relief in sight from the relentless problem of money. A year after the publication of *The Mind's Adventure*, the *Christian Century* noted that "the Northern Presbyterians, who have just distributed a special fund . . . to tide over their colleges which are in immediate difficulties, found only one in the whole number that did not need this emergency help. Church college balance sheets are a study in red ink."[22]

Moreover, the denomination's actual interest in these institutions was an issue subject to dispute. In 1951 and 1952 Fay Campbell sent out his staff members to find out how the Presbyterian schools were faring in the midst of this fiscal crisis. The visitor to Alma College wrote a report in which he concluded: "It looks like the Presbyterian Church in Michigan cares only enough about the college to keep it alive, but not enough to make it strong."[23] The reports from some of the other campuses were hardly more encouraging. In these circumstances enterprising college presidents hedged their bets. While continuing to work hard on the church circuit, they also kept alert for any possible help forthcoming from other quarters—local business leaders of other religious persuasions, corporations, and of course state and federal assistance.

All of these efforts helped the Presbyterian schools in their fight to survive in the 1950s. A few of them even made notable gains. Yet the pace of change in American higher education was so swift in the decade that the denomination's schools worked feverishly not to slip even farther behind in the academic procession. The increasing power of the state (at both the federal and state levels) in postsecondary education, the impressive growth of the modern research university—these were among the forces shaping a new context which neither Howard Lowry nor many of his contemporaries in the old-line Protestant colleges ever anticipated at the outset of the 1950s. His genteel musings about a Christian version of the Princeton University he had known in the early 1940s pointed to a vanishing past rather than the future breaking in upon his world.

The story seemed much the same in the other comparable churches. For a long time, throughout the first half of the twentieth century, old-line leaders had lived with a growing contradiction between implied claims for Protestantism's rightful place at the center of college and university life and its actual drift toward the margins of that enterprise. In the 1960s the churches would have to confront this contradiction and acknowledge the end of the Protestant era in American higher education.

The Danforth Years: 1960–1975

In the summer of 1961, the Commission of Higher Education of the National Council of Churches, along with representatives from the Council of Protestant Colleges and Universities, gathered at Conference Point, a site well known for many a memorable meeting of old-line Protestant leaders, on the shores of Lake Geneva in Wisconsin. The college presidents and church leaders attending the assembly would have ample reason to remember that occasion, for the speaker of the week was Merrimon Cuninggim.

Over the previous twenty years Cuninggim had enjoyed various vantage points from which to view Protestant efforts in higher education. In addition to writing his early work *The College Seeks Religion*, he had served as a professor of religion at Pomona College before becoming dean for nine eventful years at the Perkins School of Theology at Southern Methodist University. He came to the podium at Conference Point fresh from his first year as director of the Danforth Foundation, the one major American foundation unabashedly committed to supporting the work of old-line Protestants in higher education. Cuninggim's past experience in addition to his present assignment virtually guaranteed an attentive audience.

Thirty years later his Conference Point lectures, titled "The Protestant Stake in Higher Education," still merit attention as a docu-

ment that nicely captures the spirit of the Protestant establishment
in its waning days. By turns Cuninggim shocked and instructed,
cajoled and inspired his audience—always with élan, intelligence,
and confidence. Three points are particularly worthy of note.

First of all, these presentations helped confirm a shift in nomen-
clature. Earlier, old-line Protestants had used various terms—
church colleges, Christian colleges, or church-related colleges—in
interchangeable fashion. Merrimon Cuninggim clearly preferred
"church-related." Why? I suspect it offered a greater elasticity of
meaning and could therefore stretch over an increasingly broad
spectrum of institutions whose leaders, faculty, or constituencies
might find the other terms inappropriate, misleading, or possibly
even embarrassing.

Whatever reasons prompted his choice, the growing usage of this
phrase reflected the growing sense of *distance* between church and
college. In a passage that tells us much about what was happening
in old-line Protestant schools in the early 1960s, Cuninggim notes
that a college's responses to questions about its church-related
character "depend partly" on the identity of the questioner: "If it is
the denomination that is doing the asking, then the college's answer
is likely to be Yes. But if it is the general public, the Federal
Government, or some secular agency that is doing the asking, then
the college's answer may well be negative."[24] During the next
quarter of a century, that observation would become even more
illuminating as a way of understanding the shades of meaning
inherent in the notion of church relatedness.

Second, the speeches included his assessment of the "quality" of
the church-related colleges. In effect, he handed out a report card
on how the various institutions represented at Conference Point
measured up in comparison to other colleges and universities. For
the most part the grades ranged from fair to poor. The bleakest
comments came in his judgments about the failure of these schools
to embody the "intangible marks of the good college:" great teaching?—"fair"; encouragement of research?—"no better than poor";
the study of religion?—"poor."[25] "Things are so bad," he said, "that
we must ask, Do Protestants really believe in higher education? Do
Protestants belong in the college business?"[26]

To make his point even more vividly, he contrasted the current
state of the church-related colleges to the other two forms of

ministry in higher education. The seminaries seemed to be making progress in overcoming their former feebleness, and the campus ministry programs were exhibiting new vitality and promise. Meanwhile, the colleges constituted, in effect, the weakest link in that portion of the old Protestant circle of educational institutions.

That jeremiad-like recital of sins and failures was not, however his final word to the assembled throng. After reviewing the theological tradition of the Reformation and its implications for contemporary education, he then challenged the audience to renew Protestantism's cultural vocation as the standard-bearer, the "conscience" of American higher education.

Third, Cuninggim's description of the dictates of conscience embodied the deep confidence of his generation in the power of current Protestant theology to illumine vast areas of cultural activity. In his final lecture he outlined a "philosophy of education" that would apply to *all* efforts in higher education, whether in colleges or universities, private or public. Such a perspective would point toward a "belief in God as being the proper orientation and framework for education."[27] This "kind of lay theology" would strike "the great chords of radical monotheism. Its content, as I see it, is neither mere piety nor full, precise orthodoxy. It sees God as Creator, Judge and Redeemer; it sees man as creature, sinner and potential saint."[28] By way of summary, he declared: "All of this, as well as more of course, is contained in the mainstream current of the Hebrew-Christian tradition. . . . And this much, at least, constitutes the orientation that Protestants should insist upon for any adequate philosophy of education."[29]

Cuninggim anticipated that this brand of American "lay theology" (in the traditional terms of Christian theologians, a "natural theology") would worry both the "religionists" (translation: conservative Christians) and the "secularists." If the former would want to add to it their doctrines of "Christology" and "soteriology,"[30] the latter would subtract many of the affirmations contained therein. His response, in brief, was to advise the religionists (as well as his fellow old-line colleagues) to confine their insistence on Christological teachings to the church-related college and then to support the "general educational principles that Protestants as well as others may heartily accept and try to live by."[31] Meanwhile, the secularists would have to come to terms with the fact that "the university no more needs to be neutral about God than about democracy or morality or good manners."[32]

Who would lead the way toward a middle position between these extremes? At this point Cuninggim appealed to the assembled college presidents, the denominational and National Council dignitaries, as well as to their allies in campus ministry programs and theological seminaries. "The churches' efforts in higher education," he concluded, "can serve as forerunner for all the rest; they can go further and be more explicit about the fundamental premises. Protestant higher education can become the conscience for the totality of higher education."[33] This rousing finish said it all: the Protestant stake in higher education goes far beyond concern for just the renovation of the church-related institutions. That first step is necessary in order to move to the heart of the Protestant calling, the renewal of the standards of the whole American system of higher education.

This same blend of unsparing criticism and far-ranging vision marked all that Merrimon Cuninggim did on behalf of American colleges and universities during his remarkable tenure at the Danforth Foundation. He gathered a first-rate staff and helped create a powerful fellowship program for both promising and mature scholars. Out of that effort came a web of associations and friendships— still informally called the Danforth network—that continues to the present. If the foundation had made no contribution other than this one, the name Danforth would still figure prominently in any complete history of religion and higher education in the 1960s.

In its research program the foundation sponsored major parallel studies on two of the themes embedded in Cuninggim's Conference Point lectures. The first offered a comprehensive review of the types of church-related colleges,[34] while the second one comprised an inquiry into campus ministry. The latter study caught the public's fancy and quickly became known as *the* Danforth study.

In the course of the decade this inquiry turned into the most expensive, ambitious, and wide-ranging research project ever undertaken in this sector of Protestant church life. Its director was Kenneth W. Underwood, a young faculty member at Wesleyan University and a social ethicist trained at Yale Divinity School under Liston Pope and H. Richard Niebuhr. In turn, he recruited a corps of gifted graduate students who carried on their own research in different locales across the continent. The scope of the study kept expanding so that by the time its results were published in 1969,[35] Underwood and company were covering a vast array of issues that ranged well beyond any ordinary definition of the work of campus ministers. Underwood never lived to see his manuscript through the last stages of writing and editing. Perhaps his untimely death explains the shapeless character of the argument. In any event, the two volumes proved to be an anti-climactic disappointment to an audience that had been expecting a definitive piece of work.

The clue to understanding this mass of material lies in Underwood's conviction about the relation of church and university. While Merrimon Cuninggim had held out the hope that the churches might once again become the *independent* "conscience for the totality of higher education," the director of the Danforth study had come to believe devoutly in the churches' *dependency* on the university for instruction and guidance. After acknowledging "all the failures and illusions of scholars and students in sensing the political and social realities of our times," he went on to note that "the work going on in the university is the principal source of significant Christian education and action in the future."[36] Apart from that saving relationship, the Protestant churches will continue their decline toward social irrelevance. Cuninggim's position was similar—but with one important difference: the churches must maintain their links with the university system in order both to learn *from* and speak *to* that center of power. Underwood was not nearly so confident that American Protestantism, even the old-line denominations to which he owed personal allegiance, was able to do much more than learn from the university.

The considerable distance between Cuninggim in the early 1960s and Underwood near the end of the decade is an apt reminder of the long journey of many old-line Protestants in those years. At the beginning of that season of change, the "American Moberly," Alexander Miller of Stanford University, assumed that the "theological revival" made it possible for Protestants to address the university on its own territory. Thus he could write in 1960, "The university confronts a church which is confident, relatively unified, chastened by its own cultural failures, and consequently far less strident in its reaction to intellectual inquiry—obviously capable of articulating, out of a venerable heritage, a relevant contemporary word."[37]

Yet just a few years later that mood of confidence in old-line Protestantism had given way to an uncertainty about the future of theology. By 1964 the editor of *Christian Scholar*, a publication in the orbit of the National Council of Churches, was asking: "Whence the theological doldrums? Why is there so little intensive theological work being done today?"[38] "Neo-orthodoxy" was not so much a coherent school of thought as it was a convenient (and often misleading) label to apply to a congeries of diverse interests. But those various concerns—biblical theology and the like—now seemed stale and vulnerable to over-due criticism. Along with that important assessment of the work done in the "theological revival" came a flurry of experiments with a series of new theologies. Some of this activity offered promise for the future, but none of it could restore the sense of comfortable assurance that Cuninggim, Miller, and others had exhibited at the outset of the 1960s. In that respect, Underwood's embrace of the university as the "principal source of significant Christian education" belied the growing anxiety of old-line Protestantism about its ability to address American higher education in an intellectually responsible manner.

The mixed review of the Danforth study proved to be only one of several disappointments that the foundation staff experienced in the late 1960s and early 1970s. The most visible of these reversals occurred when the University Christian Movement, the latest embodiment of the national student Christian organization that had been so long dominated by old line Protestant groups, suddenly collapsed in 1969, despite the best efforts of a Danforth staff member, Robert Rankin, to help it survive the convulsive events of those years. The reverberations of that move would ricochet across the landscape of Protestant church life for years to come. In the words of Dorothy Bass: "The death of the American student Christian movement—so quickly, and after such a long period of growth—was a severe loss. With the exception of the Lutherans, denominational student organizations were not reconstituted."[39] Meanwhile, the campus ministry movement, though well nourished by Danforth help over the years, was also entering a period of retrenchment and adversity.

But the biggest blow of all came in the early 1970s, as the board of the Danforth Foundation decided to focus most of its attention and resources on its home city, St. Louis. Merrimon Cuninggim resigned his post as president in protest. Within the next several years the staff members who had helped create the programs of the 1960s scattered to take other jobs or to retire. Gradually the foundation retreated from the grant-making arena where it had once been so visible and imaginative. By the mid-1970s the Danforth years—at least as far as this story is concerned—had come to an end.

An Unraveling Fabric

The Danforth Foundation's move came at a time when old-line Protestantism could ill afford the loss of a lively national center that helped to link persons and institutions working on common concerns about religion and higher education. Once a reasonably effective clearinghouse for ideas in this field, the National Council of Churches was suffering from an eclipse of vision and a change in leadership. Likewise most of the denominational offices responsible for campus ministries and liaison with church-related colleges were battling the ravages of inflation and the slow erosion of their power as culture-shaping forces. (Indeed, Robert Wuthnow's provocative thesis about the "decline of denominationalism"[40] in these years could be amply documented in a study of these particular old-line Protestant agencies.)

Another feature of the older establishment in the middle third of the twentieth century was the indispensable services of graduate programs for preparing future leaders and scholars to work in this domain. By way of illustration, Yale Divinity School had long been the top "prep school" for campus ministers, college chaplains, and administrators, most of whom served old-line Protestant institutions. There were junior versions of Yale's program at other theological schools throughout the country. During the 1970s, however, these programs started disappearing from the seminary catalogues. Fittingly enough, the last stronghold of the old "Religion and Higher Education" training network to vanish was the grandparent institution; Yale ceased offering instruction along these lines in the late 1970s.

None of these trends, when considered one by one, seemed momentous at the time. But in retrospect, of course, one can discern the subtle dissolution of a pattern of relationships that formed a loose-knit fabric of institutions and individuals. The mid-century national coalition connecting the National Council, old-line denominational agencies, and various foundations (Hazen and Lilly as well as Danforth) with seminaries and church colleges was slowly unraveling.

Similar changes were affecting the larger educational ecology inherited from the nineteenth century. I will limit myself to two illustrations of other developments around the Protestant circle— the seminary and the church-related college.[41] Consider first the experiences of old-line theological schools, whether denominational or inter-denominational in orientation. In the 1970s seminary administrators started noticing a new problem. For years they had not worried unduly about recruitment of students since they could usually rely on the pipelines linking their schools to a predictable cluster of church-related colleges and other higher educational institutions where there were effective campus ministers. Then those pipelines started to run dry. McCormick Theological Seminary, to recall an earlier example, could no longer expect The College of Wooster to produce a hefty proportion of its entering class. Seminary administrators in the other old-line theological institutions reported the same trends. Since the 1970s a fair number of the so-called denominational schools have quietly shed their old identities and have become, in effect, ecumenical seminaries serving diverse constituencies in their own regions. Sometimes these institutions self-consciously embraced this transformation out of deep theological convictions. And then occasionally others simply drifted in this direction, prompted by "market imperatives" that lurked unacknowledged beneath the surface of talk about "service." In the latter instances, seminary representatives must be artful when supporters press them with questions about the school's tie to the sponsoring denomination. The answer given—as Cuninggim said years ago about church colleges in the same spot—depends partly on who is asking. But no matter how thoughtful the response, the percentage of seminary budgets forthcoming from hard-pressed denominations has plummeted in recent years.

Meanwhile, church college leaders in the 1970s faced these challenges, and even more. The new perplexities confronting the theological schools had haunted many Christian institutions of higher education for generations. From the early part of the nineteenth century, in fact, some schools were first community colleges, and then second denominational ventures in higher education.[42] Over the stretch of the last 150 years, the multiple efforts to adjudicate the claims of public service, confessional fidelity, and loyalty to church tradition, academic integrity, and institutional life has created a bewildering variety of relations between Protestant denominations and their colleges. By the mid-1970s the label "church-related" encompassed such a spectrum of schools that it was sometimes hard to explain the term to the public, or even to insiders within these institutions. That difficulty complicated the life of leaders who already bore the burden of raising new funds just to keep up with the rate of inflation. In addition, the old-line Protestants were slowly awakening to the presence of a new and largely unwelcome competitor in their midst—the fast-growing presence of evangelicals in higher education. The advent of the Christian College Consortium in 1971 and the Christian College Coalition in 1976 suggested to alert leaders within the orbit of the National Council of Churches (NCC) that they might soon be in a battle to define the purposes of Protestant higher education.

The publication of *Church-Related Higher Education* in 1978 appeared to be the opening salvo of old-line Protestants in that debate.[43] This book represented the culmination of several years of preparation and the results of a Wingspread conference. Although some of the participants in this ambitious project came from beyond the ranks of the old-line Protestant denominations, the final work clearly reflected the perspective of a veteran of earlier struggles over these issues. Now president of Salem College, Merrimon Cuninggim offered a broad—indeed a latitudinarian—definition of the notion of church relatedness, one that would do justice to the rich diversity of institutions invoking this designation. He suggested a way of placing markedly different schools along the stretch of a spectrum ranging from a college as conservative as a Lutheran Church–Missouri Synod institution, defined as an "Embodying College"—all the way over to Carleton College, which he described as a "Consonant College" in its relation to the United Church of Christ.[44] This visual image constituted, so to speak, a guide to understanding the pluralism of purposes and styles of church-related schools. Almost every one of these colleges could find its place on this map, or locate the general territory where it felt most at home. Cuninggim's assignment was to describe the varieties of terrain, not to make judgments about which place was the best one. That choice was the responsibility of the colleges. Whatever their final decision might be, the map offered reassuring evidence of the churches' presence in American higher education. In short, Merrimon Cuninggim seemed to entertain few doubts about the "survival of recognizably Protestant colleges."

The documents associated with this project represented a shrewd tactic designed to forestall the effort of any group that might equate one band of the spectrum with all of Christian higher education. Although the final report included a couple of unmistakable barbs aimed at the evangelicals, it also indirectly invited them to find their place on the map and thereby join in the ecumenical conversation. I know of no evidence confirming the success of that gambit.

Above all, the NCC-based sponsors of this project were intent on assisting the Protestant denominations then engaged in rethinking their responsibilities to the church-related colleges. In the mid-1970s, for instance, all the old-line churches were once again scrambling to find ways of matching their diminishing resources of funds and commitment with the rapidly expanding needs of the church colleges. In the blunt summary judgment of the editor of *Church-Related Higher Education*, "rising education costs, inflation, costs of government compliance, the tuition gap, or the competition of low-cost public institutions are a threat to the survival of church-related higher education."[45] (Note, if you will, how the power and encroaching presence of the state casts an increasing shadow over these "laundry-list" descriptions of problems.) Since the old-line denominations could offer little by way of direct fiscal aid, their main contribution would be restricted to suggestions about the nature of education and the relevance of Christian faith to that enterprise. What they discovered in the published results of this three-year project was help of a specific kind. The Cuninggim map could be enormously useful to those colleges and denominations that enjoyed such a strong sense of theological identity that they needed to learn the limits of their own position through exposure to other Christian options. It was of less help, however, in those instances where neither the college nor the denomination had a clear sense of its calling in higher education.

Most of the old-line churches in the 1970s were well aware of the considerable benefits of pluralism. But they had far greater difficulty in understanding their own vocation in this strange period. Consequently, their denominational pronouncements on this topic during the decade reflected a gnawing doubt about what, if anything, they could add to the mix of religious pluralism in higher education. Written in the leaden bureaucratic church prose of our time, their statements proclaimed fidelity to a great heritage and made many of the usual points found in earlier documents of this kind. Unfortunately, however, there were few genuine hints about the contours of a fresh perspective on the churches' work in higher education.

Probably the most revealing discoveries made in this decade-long search for clarity came out of the "field notes" of some of the investigators who talked with people on both ends of the denomination-college relation. One example will suffice. After retiring as president of Beloit College, Miller Upton helped the United Church of Christ as a consultant. He summed up the results of his findings:

> Within recent years I have heard questions such as, "Wouldn't it really be better if some of the colleges were allowed to fold?" or, "Do you mean to tell me that our young people could get a better education by going to one of our colleges instead of the University of Wisconsin?"
>
> On the other side of the ledger presidents, deans and faculty have indicated to me that the only reason for maintaining relationships with the Church was the hope for money and students that would not be available otherwise. Also, some will claim that while they see no value in the relationship now they are willing to continue it in deference to historical roots and traditions—provided the relationship remains passive and does not become too threatening.[46]

To be sure, that candid report from the field did not represent Upton's conclusions about the possibilities of the church-college tie, nor would such an account adequately reflect the full range of opinion in all the old-line denominations. Yet it does let us hear some of the hidden questions and ruling sentiments so often drowned out by the public utterances of those involved in this discussion.

The most illuminating *public* exchange of views on these matters did not come until late in the next decade. In the fall of 1988

Richard G. Hutcheson, Jr., a Presbyterian minister then serving as an associate of Richard John Neuhaus at the Center of Religion and Society, posted a thesis on the "bulletin board of American Protestantism" (John C. Bennett's fine description of the *Christian Century* in a former era). The article began with a story: "A minister of a mainline Protestant denomination, newly hired as a chaplain of a denominational college, met with a committee of the regional judicatory within whose bounds he would be working. 'Tell me,' a committee member asked him, 'is this college "church-related" or "Christian?"'"[47] Hutcheson offered more than anecdotes, however, as he explored the quandaries that this difficult question poses for contemporary old-line Protestants. Toward the end of the article he argued for an occasional church-related college that might "renew and emphasize the Christian dimension of higher education and enlist the support of the church in such an undertaking."[48] (His sketch of that sort of school bears a striking resemblance to Howard Lowry's portrait forty years earlier.)

His debating partner turned out to be F. Thomas Trotter, the Methodist executive who had done so much to stabilize and strengthen the work of the United Methodist Church in higher education in the 1970s and 1980s. Trotter's defense of the more or less official old-line position pivoted around a plea for recognizing the limits of what a church-related college could do in a time when the power of the federal government looms so large. As a result of court decisions and federal programs, he wrote, "the model of a church-related college eligible for aid is one which does not discriminate on the basis of religion in selecting students and faculty, does not require attendance at religious services, does not require courses in religion or theology that tend to indoctrinate or proselytize, and which has a strong commitment to the principles of academic freedom."[49] After noting that the churches contribute less than 1 percent of the operating costs of church schools, he asked, by implication, if any old-line denomination was now willing to pay that steep a price for independence. Is such a sacrifice necessary or even warranted, especially since the best of the current church-related colleges can play a creative role in higher education? For all the limits imposed by the state's presence, he appeared to be saying, these institutions can continue to be—in the phrase of Jencks and Riesman—"recognizably Protestant colleges."

In his rejoinder Hutcheson made it clear that he was not so optimistic about the shape of the future, unless the old-line denominations become far more intentional in developing at least a few institutions that would be "recognizably Protestant colleges" fifty years from now. "It is not necessary to leave the field to the non-church-related, often ultraconservative, and sometimes highly sectarian institutions that dominate the Christian College Coalition. There is a place for distinctively Christian higher education in mainline church-related colleges."[50]

And there the discussion rests, at least for the moment. I very much hope the debate continues within old-line circles in the years ahead. For all those interested in joining that argument, I would suggest one ground rule: all combatants must recognize the new cultural situation confronting old-line Protestantism near the beginning of the twenty-first century. The unraveling of the institutional fabric that bore the weight of Protestant efforts in education during the twentieth century now makes it impossible for any of us to turn the clock back to some alleged Golden Era (whether the heyday of the Lowries and Underwoods or even my favorite Protestant educator, William Rainey Harper). Only then will we be able to deal in a responsible way with the question about "the survival of recognizably Protestant colleges."

Notes

1. Christopher Jencks and David Riesman, *The Academic Revolution* (Garden City, NY: Doubleday, 1968), 330.

2. Along with other present-day commentators, I am perplexed about which of the usual shorthand adjectives—*mainstream, mainline,* or other such designations—to invoke when referring to the handful of denominations that have figured prominently in recent studies of mainstream Protestantism. That search goes on. In the meantime I will settle for the designation *old-line* as a way of pointing to the presence of seven denominations in the last half of the twentieth century—the Presbyterian Church (USA), the United Church of Christ, the Episcopal Church, the United Methodist Church, the American Baptist churches, the Evangelical Lutheran Church in America, and the Christian Church (Disciples of Christ). I have also drawn upon my own interpretation of *Between the*

Times: The Travail of the Protestant Establishment in America, 1900–1960, ed. William R. Hutchison (Cambridge: Cambridge University Press, 1989).

3. "A Statement of the Association of Presbyterian Colleges and Universities," March 25, 1990, 1, 2, 5, 6. For a more optimistic appraisal of the future of church-related colleges in another denomination, see Robert H. Conn with Michael Nickerson, *United Methodists and Their Colleges: Themes in the History of a College-Related Church* (Nashville: United Methodist Board of Higher Education and Ministry, 1989), 155f.

4. F. Thomas Trotter, "The College as the Church's Gift," *Christian Century* 105 (November 30, 1988), 1099.

5. If I had ventured along that line, I would have relied on Glenn T. Miller's essay "Protestants, Paideia, and Pioneers: Protestantism's First Great Cause," in *Caring for the Commonweal: Education for Religious and Public Life*, ed. Parker J. Palmer, Barbara G. Wheeler, and James W. Fowler (Macon, GA: Mercer University Press, 1991), 183–206. Miller opens up new ways of understanding the long-standing, intricate, and sometimes creative relation between Protestant education and the process of secularization.

6. Howard Lowry, *The Mind's Adventure* (Philadelphia: Westminster Press, 1950).

7. Edith Hunter, "Neo-Orthodoxy Goes to Kindergarten," *Religion in Life* 20 (1950–1951), 3–14.

8. Kenneth Reeves, "Survey Report on Expressions of Christian Influence, Trinity University" (unpublished document, 1952), 5, Historical Department of the Presbyterian Church (USA), Philadelphia.

9. Harold H. Viehman, "Survey Report on Expressions of Christian Influence, Illinois College" (unpublished document, 1952), 2, Historical Department of the Presbyterian Church (USA).

10. Kenneth Reeves and Harold H. Viehman, "Survey Report on Expressions of Christian Influence, The College of Wooster" (unpublished document, 1952), 15, 10, 2, Historical Department of the Presbyterian Church (USA).

11. For an example of his mastery of the art of convocation speeches and baccalaureate sermons, see Howard Lowry, *College Talks*, ed. James R. Blackwood (New York: Oxford University Press, 1969).

12. See Lowry's inaugural address, *Sketch for a Family Portrait: Wooster* (The College of Wooster, 1944), 16.

13. Merrimon Cuninggim, *The College Seeks Religion* (New Haven: Yale University Press, 1947).

14. Cited in Lowry, *The Mind's Adventure*, 53.

15. Sir Walter Moberly, *The Crisis in the University* (London: SCM Press, 1949).

16. Howard Lowry, *The Mind's Adventure*, 6.

17. Ibid., 6.

18. Ibid., 102–3.

19. Ibid., 104.

20. Ibid., 104.

21. Ibid., 123.

22. "Church Colleges in Trouble," *Christian Century* 65 (June 20, 1951), 733–34.

23. Kenneth Reeves, "Survey Report of Expressions of Religious Influence: Alma College" (unpublished document, 1952), 14, Historical Department of the Presbyterian Church (USA).

24. Merrimon Cuninggim, *The Protestant Stake in Higher Education* (New York: Council of Protestant Colleges and Universities, 1961), 3.

25. Ibid., 10, 11, 12.

26. Ibid., 31.

27. Ibid., 60.

28. Ibid., 60. The influence of his old teacher H. Richard Niebuhr is clearly visible in this summary of affirmations.

29. Ibid., 60.

30. Ibid., 60.

31. Ibid., 65.

32. Ibid., 63.

33. Ibid., 66.

34. Manning Patillo, Jr. and Donald M. Mackenzie, *Church-Sponsored Higher Education in the United States* (Washington, DC: American Council on Education, 1966).

35. Kenneth W. Underwood, *The Church, the University, and Social Policy: The Danforth Study of Campus Ministries*, 2 vols. (Middletown, CT: Wesleyan University Press, 1969).

36. Underwood, *The Church, the University, and Social Policy*, I, 201.

37. Alexander Miller, *Faith and Knowledge: Christian Faith and Higher Education in Twentieth-Century America* (New York: Association Press, 1960), 28.

38. Cited in Douglas Sloan, "The American Theological Renaissance and 'The Crisis in the University,' 1949–1969: A Case Study in the Faith-Knowledge Relationship," (unpublished ms., 1989), 48. When published, this extended essay will offer a fresh and important perspective on the matters discussed in this chapter.

39. Dorothy Bass, "Revolutions: Quiet and Otherwise: Protestants and

Higher Education during the 1960s," in Palmer, Wheeler, and Fowler, *Caring for the Commonweal*, 220. This essay is a valuable source of insight to any historian attempting to understand the relation of old-line Protestantism to higher education in the 1960s.

40. Robert Wuthnow, *The Restructuring of American Religion: Society and Faith since World War II* (Princeton: Princeton University Press, 1988), 71–99.

41. Some of the other possible examples include developments in youth work and campus ministry. In each instance the pace of change is different and stretches over varying lengths of time. Obviously the relation of the American public school system to this ecology began dissolving well before the beginning of the twentieth century in different regions of the country. The 1962 and 1963 Supreme Court decisions on prayer and Bible reading in public school classrooms confirmed what old-line Protestants had sometimes only grudgingly acknowledged in previous decades.

42. David B. Potts, "'College Enthusiasm!' as Public Response," *Harvard Educational Review* 47 (February 1977), 28–42.

43. *Church-Related Higher Education: Perceptions and Perspectives*, ed. Robert Rue Parsonage (Valley Forge, PA: Judson Press, 1978).

44. Merrimon Cuninggim, "Categories of Church-Relatedness," in Parsonage, *Church-Related Higher Education*, 34–39.

45. Robert Rue Parsonage, "An Overview of Current Denominational Policies and Studies in Higher Education," in Parsonage, *Church-Related Higher Education*, 284.

46. Miller Upton, "Why Bother?" *New Conversations* 6 (Spring 1981), 4.

47. Richard G. Hutcheson, Jr., "Are Church-Related Colleges also Christian Colleges?" *Christian Century* 105 (September 28, 1988), 838–841.

48. Hutcheson, "Are Church-Related Colleges also Christian Colleges?" 840.

49. F. Thomas Trotter, "The College as the Chruch's Gift," *Christian Century* 105 (November 30, 1988), 1098.

50. Richard G. Hutcheson's reply, *Christian Century* 105 (November 30, 1988), 1101.

7

American Learning and the Problem of Religious Studies

D. G. HART

Religious Studies, alas, is a political compromise, an Ellis Island for the "considerable company of migrants" who have had to leave their native intellectual homes for whatever reason and who have come to us for refuge. Indeed, our future lies in ruins![1]   Gerald James Larson, 1988

The 1960s was an important decade for American scholars who studied religion. Prospects for employment brightened considerably as public and private universities and colleges created undergraduate and graduate programs in religious studies. Becoming more self-conscious about their academic identity, professors who staffed these programs in 1964 founded the American Academy of Religion (AAR), an organization designed to promote scholarship and publication in religion. One index to the growing prominence of religious studies was the survey of humanistic scholarship commissioned by Princeton University's Council of the Humanities and funded by the Ford Foundation. Of the thirteen volumes in this series, two were devoted to religion: Clyde A. Holbrook's *Religion, A Humanistic Field* (1963), and *Religion* (1965), a summary of the various fields in religious studies, edited by Paul Ramsey.[2]

Despite such a strong showing, professors who taught religion were not readily welcomed by the academy. Although religious studies seemed to form a natural bond with other disciplines in the humanities, humanistic scholars were uncertain about this new field. Robert H. Knapp, who studied the background of humanistic scholars for the Princeton Council on the Humanities, gave no attention to the students of religion. His list of the humanistic disciplines included only literature, history, the arts, languages, and philosophy. Religious studies also escaped the attention of the historian John Higham, who used the Princeton series to assess the state of American humanistic scholarship. Higham focused on the schism between the social sciences and the humanities but failed to place the study of religion within the divisions of American learning. Equally important for defining the boundaries of the humanities was the creation in 1965 of the National Foundation on the Arts and the Humanities. During the congressional debates, many officials asserted that the humanities were concerned with values, broad culture, and excellence. But when the National Endowment for the Humanities specified those subjects it would fund, religion was absent.[3]

This discussion about the nature of the humanities was a fitting backdrop for the contemporaneous soul-searching experienced by American scholars of religion. Although religion had links to the humanities, many religion scholars thought such an identification undermined the scientific claims of their discipline. Perhaps the prime expression of these doubts came in a review of Holbrook's *Religion, A Humanistic Field* by John F. Wilson, a professor in Princeton University's highly regarded Department of Religion. Rather than welcoming the inclusion of religion in the humanities, Wilson took issue with what he described as Holbrook's "conventional defense" of the study of religion. What troubled Wilson was the "peculiar difficulty" noted by Richard Schlatter, the general editor of the Princeton series, in the foreword to Holbrook's book. "A considerable body of American scholars," Schlatter wrote, "are of the opinion that religious studies are no part of the humanities, no part of the liberal arts, not an objective scholarly discipline." The problem of objectivity also plagued humanistic scholars, but the pedigree for religious studies was so short that Wilson felt students of religion could not ignore such a charge. What Holbrook offered in Wilson's estimate, however, was the traditional rationale for including religion in higher education, namely, that the study of religion contributed to the "humanizing" and "liberalizing" mission of the liberal arts. In contrast, Wilson lobbied for a "phenomenological approach" to religious studies which shared the "empirical mood" of American scholarship and established the study of religion on a scientific basis. Nurtured as a humanistic discipline, the new field of religious studies seemed to need the steadying hand of the social sciences.[4]

These debates concerning the nature of the study of religion and the formation of the American Academy of Religion were a watershed in the history of religious studies in United States. Most historical treatments of the discipline focus on the shift from clerical to scientific explanations of religion, or from theology to religious studies. According to this view, a tradition of scholarship developed out of the Enlightenment which questioned the privileged position given to religion by universities dominated by theology. This tradition abandoned the notion that religious guidance or belief was necessary for the study of religion and insisted instead that religious phenomena could be explained in naturalistic categories as well as any other cultural artifact. To be sure, the scientific commitments of the AAR's leaders reflected the legacy of Enlightenment understandings of religion. Yet this account fails to explain why an approach to the study of religion that had been practiced by various scholars since the eighteenth century was not incorporated into American universities until the 1960s. As this essay seeks to demonstrate, much of the brooding experienced by American scholars of religion during the 1960s, as well as the relatively late acceptance of scientific methods within religious studies, stemmed from two important factors: first, the uncertain status of religion within American learning, and second, the ties between religious studies and the mainline Protestant churches.[5]

Despite the increasing reliance by religion scholars on the methods and assumptions of the social sciences, the study of religion has retained its identity within American learning as a humanistic discipline. Indeed, the tensions within religion departments generated by the rivalry between the humanities and social sciences reflect a deeper bewilderment in American higher education about how religion should be taught and studied. For almost a century the study of religion was an anomaly in the academy, unrecognized by learned societies and neglected within the curricula of most nonsectarian colleges and universities. Curricular reforms after the Second World War tried to address this imbalance by acknowledging the importance of religion. But the introduction of religion as a part of the general education curriculum did little to improve its academic respectability. The reconstitution of religious studies in the 1960s on a more scientific basis is an episode in this historic ambivalence about religion within American scholarship.[6]

The formation of the American Academy of Religion also marked a shift in the way religion was studied and taught at American colleges and universities. Although the rise of American universities diminished the churches' influence on higher education, Protestants devised a number of ways of maintaining an active presence at most public and private institutions. Limited to extra-curricular activities in the earlier part of the twentieth century, these efforts were encouraged by administrators and faculty. The fruit of these Protestant labors was a major role for church leaders in shaping the curriculum of religion departments, which began to flourish during the two decades after the Second World War. Most of the scholars who staffed these new departments had been trained and educated at the prominent old-line Protestant seminaries and divinity schools. The new methods of studying religion advocated by the AAR signaled the demise of this Protestant dominance as professors of religion became increasingly uncomfortable with their religious identification. Perhaps more significant for influencing current trends within religious studies than the university's historic ambivalence about religion was the control Protestants had exerted over religious instruction. By striving to make their discipline more scientific, religion scholars not only embraced the ideals of the academy but also freed themselves from the Protestant establishment.

The American Council of Learned Societies Devoted to Humanistic Studies did not list the American Academy of Religion as a constituent member until 1979. This late admittance of religion scholars did not necessarily reflect disrespect. Rather, it demonstrated the uncertain status of religion as an academic discipline. The ambiguities surrounding religious studies were the result of two key developments in American higher education. The first concerned the position and nature of religious instruction in antebellum colleges. The second was the schism that opened between the humanities and the social sciences in the twentieth century.[7]

Few historians of higher education, even recent revisionists, would deny that the old-time college was a stepchild of Protestant churches. Although some may debate how sectarian those institutions were, most agree that antebellum colleges were controlled largely by their ecclesiastical affiliations. Most college presidents, trustees, and faculty were ministers whose appointment depended on their beliefs. Students were required to attend daily chapel and worship services on Sundays. College campuses during this period witnessed numerous revivals which encouraged undergraduates to consider careers in the church. Revivalism, moreover, spawned a host of colleges throughout the Midwest.[8]

Despite pervasive Protestant influence, the antebellum college curriculum was not explicitly religious. To be sure, the classical curriculum gave many undergraduates the requisites for formal theological training. Still, the evolution of liberal education at American colleges between the seventeenth and nineteenth centuries virtually eliminated explicit instruction in the Bible and theology. While colonial colleges had combined the study of classics with Protestant divinity, the classical curriculum at antebellum colleges lost its pious hue as educators identified the liberal arts with good breeding and the training of gentlemen. The study of Greek and Latin, classical authors, and history outstripped study of the Bible and formal theology as the components of a liberal education.[9]

That religion was still prominent in the colleges was reflected by the required senior course in Moral Philosophy, which was usually taught by the college president. The capstone of the curriculum, Moral Philosophy attempted to integrate the entire course of study and to instill a common set of social values. The moral philosopher endeavored to show the essentially ethical character of humankind and the universe, and to prove that all study, if done properly, reinforced the truth of Christianity. Moral Philosophy offered little, if any, systematic instruction in theology or the Bible. Instead, the course applied Protestant morality to politics, economics, sociology, law, history, and aesthetics.[10]

To receive theological training in America, students had to attend seminaries or divinity schools. These institutions had their origins in the decline of Protestant divinity within the colleges. Because churches could no longer count on colleges to produce ministers, they established institutions specifically designed for training clergy. Princeton Theological Seminary, founded in 1812, provides a good example. Dissatisfied with the small number of ministers graduating from the College of New Jersey, Presbyterians established their first seminary adjacent to but separate from the undergraduate institution. Although Harvard and Yale made provisions that incorporated their divinity schools within the college administration, their plan paralleled Princeton's by making the theological curriculum independent of undergraduate instruction.[11]

The upshot of these developments was to remove serious study of religion from the liberal arts curriculum. Seminaries and divinity schools assumed the sole responsibility for biblical and theological studies, and these disciplines became the strict province of professional training for the ministry. Meanwhile, liberal education in the colleges lost its religious flavor and became identified with the classical curriculum. Protestant verities still pervaded college teaching but were included primarily to supply students with a moral outlook and to unify their education. Thus, while other disciplines within the undergraduate curriculum became more distinct and threatened to go their own way, the study of Bible and theology at colleges became more diffuse and lost its identity as an academic subject.[12]

Between 1870 and 1920, as universities fostered even greater specialization, the familiar three-fold division of subjects into natural sciences, social sciences, and humanities took shape. As many colleges and universities broke their ecclesiastical ties, the place of religion continued in the pattern established during the antebellum era. Moral Philosophy gradually disappeared, but students still heard about religion in a variety of other classes. Formal biblical or theological studies were rare. Seminaries and divinity schools continued to be the home of religious scholarship, and professors in these institutions formed their own learned societies such as the Society of Biblical Literature (1880) and the American Society of Church History (1888).[13]

In 1870 most educators still associated the humanities with the classical curriculum, but by 1900 it had expanded to include English, history, philosophy, modern languages, and the arts. This expansion was linked to the increasing prestige of science in higher education. From the perspective of professors who boasted of the practical benefits of higher education, the humanities were those subjects associated with the antiquated past. According to one scholar, the humanities were "something opposed to science and to the study of nature." They were "very desirable to possess, if you do not lose bread and butter by it." Though demeaning, this description was the obverse side of the justification that humanistic scholars had chosen. In the 1890s advocates of culture began to define the humanities as those subjects that were non-scientific in character and concerned with the past. By defining themselves in opposition to the natural sciences, humanistic scholars not only preserved their own identity but also reaffirmed their commitment to "civilization."[14]

Some educators recognized that the new definition of the humanities as culture studies included religion. Indeed, the historic importance of Greek and Latin to the training of ministers and the centrality of studying ancient texts for Protestant divinity made religion a natural ally of the humanities. A classics professor at the University of Texas held that religion was essential to the development of "culture-history" and so devoted much time in his courses to Roman and Greek mythology. While lamenting the state of liberal education, John Dewey in 1902 put Western Christianity alongside Greek and Roman civilization in his conception of traditional culture. One defender of the humanities during the First World War argued that students needed to know about the influence of Hebrew literature and civilization on the West through the Bible. Yet, despite the acknowledged affinities between the humanities and religion, the study of religion remained a distinct enterprise outside the emerging coalition of humanistic scholars. Instruction in philosophy, for instance, required little acquaintance with Christian theology, and the popularity of the Victorian literary canon left little room for the study of the English Bible as literature.[15]

Besides its apparent affinities with the humanities, religious studies in the early twentieth century also maintained loose connections with the emerging social sciences. In nineteenth-century colleges the subjects of psychology, anthropology, economics, sociology, and political science had been treated by moral philosophers as aspects of human behavior in a world ruled by God. As they began to forge distinct identities during the 1870s and 1880s, the social sciences retained their religious and moral orientation. Many of the prominent social scientists who worked to make their disciplines more scientific, such as the psychologist G. Stanley Hall and the economist Richard T. Ely, believed their research would vindicate the truth of Christianity and assist the moral improvement of society. One of the best expressions of the tie between the social sciences and Protestantism came from Albion Small, chairman of the sociology department at the University of Chicago. Unwilling to grant that social science was a substitute for religion, Small believed that it was "the holiest sacrament open to men." "The whole circumference of social science," he wrote, "is the indicated field for those 'works' without which the apostle of 'salvation by faith' declared that faith is dead." Still, such rhetoric did not ensure the formal study of religion in the undergraduate curriculum. Like humanistic scholars, social scientists assumed the importance of religious and moral concerns for their disciplines but rarely considered whether or how religion should be taught and studied.[16]

The place of religious studies in American higher education became even more problematic in the 1920s with the schism between the humanities and the social sciences. Just after the First World War the borders between the social sciences and humanities were still relatively fluid. One indication of the eclectic character of the study of humankind was the formation in 1919 of the American Council of Learned Societies Devoted to Humanistic Studies (ACLS). Originally this body embraced "the philological, archaeological, historical, moral, political and social sciences" and was designed to do for these disciplines what the National Research Council had begun to do for natural science. Rather than fostering intellectual cooperation, the ACLS actually drove the humanities and the social sciences into greater fragmentation.[17]

The impetus for this schism came primarily from social scientists. During the 1920s the disciplines of political science, economics, sociology, and related fields achieved remarkable growth and forged a common identity with the formation in 1923 of the Social Science Research Council (SSRC). Although many of the social sciences retained their membership in the ACLS, the SSRC provided funds and a sense of intellectual purpose, which undermined whatever appeal the ACLS once had. Leaders of the ACLS pleaded with the founder of the SSRC, Charles Merriam, not to divide the labor of the humanistic sciences. But Merriam thought the notion of humanistic sciences was anachronistic and so went ahead with his plans. The formation of the SSRC thus signaled the rise of a scientistic orientation within the social sciences which peaked during the 1930s. Believing that the methods used by the natural sciences were the only fruitful ones for the pursuit of knowledge, many social scientists moved to put the study of humanity on an objective footing. In the process, many academics came to regard the humanities as nonscientific subjects because of their preoccupation with values and abstractions that could not be quantified or measured. The efforts of some humanistic disciplines to become more realistic or empirical, such as the emphasis on logic in philosophy and the increased attention to structure in literary criticism, did little to overcome this perception.[18]

In the wake of the schism between the humanities and the social sciences, the study of religion became further isolated from the mainstream of American learning than it had been during the first three decades of the twentieth century. For instance, in Frederick Ogg's *Research in Humanistic and Social Sciences*, a 1928 survey funded by the ACLS, the Society of Biblical Literature was not mentioned. Ogg's catalogue did include the American Society of Church History, the American Catholic Historical Association, the American Jewish Historical Society, and the American Baptist Historical Society, but these associations received less attention that the Institute for Social and Religious Research and the Federal Council of Churches, two organizations that demonstrated religion's ties to the social sciences. The irony of Ogg's survey for the study of religion was that the majority of social scientists were becoming more hostile to historical alliances with the churches. Meanwhile, the common perception of religion as the basis for morality and social reform prevented religious scholarship from forming natural bonds with humanistic scholars, who increasingly justified their disciplines as necessary links to the past. As a result, the study of religion could not find a home in the academy. It was not sufficiently scientific for the social sciences and was to present-minded for the humanities.[19]

Although religion received little attention within the curriculum at most colleges and universities, Protestants concerned about higher education responded with a variety of extracurricular organizations designed to foster students' piety, and which formed the backbone for future developments in the academic study of religion. Precedents for such work dated back to the last decades of the nineteenth century when the Young Men's Christian Association, the Young Women's Christian Association, and the Student Volunteer Movement became prominent features of undergraduate life. Conducting Bible studies, sponsoring public lectures on religious subjects, and providing wholesome forms of sociability, these interdenominational Protestant associations were a principle source for religious training of college students. Another key component for religious instruction was chapel. Although major universities such as Harvard, Cornell, and Johns Hopkins made attendance at daily worship services voluntary, most institutions, from state universities to denominational colleges, continued to require chapel for undergraduates.[20]

By the turn of the century Protestants sensed that chapel and the YMCA were inadequate to meet the needs of the growing number of students attending non-sectarian colleges. They responded by founding university pastorates and Bible chairs. To ensure the religious well-being of students from their own denominations at large state and private universities, Presbyterians, Congregationalists, Baptists, Methodists, Lutherans, Episcopalians, and Disciples of Christ established churches in university towns and set up ecclesiastical boards to supervise these activities. University pastors not only conducted Sunday services and Bible studies but also were expected to participate in the life of the university and to encourage students to consider careers in the ministry. The Disciples of Christ led the way in founding Bible chairs at the universities of Michigan, Virginia, Texas, Kansas, and Missouri. The ministers who filled these posts provided students with instruction in the Bible either at churches or in denominational centers adjacent to campus. Even though these courses were not part of the curriculum, church leaders worked with university administrators to ensure that students could take them for credit. Eventually other Protestant denominations, as well as the Roman Catholics and the Jews, adopted the Bible chair model, especially at state universities, and courses in religion became a regular part of a university pastor's responsibilities.[21]

The Bible chair pattern fueled one of the most ambitious programs for religious instruction during the 1920s, at the University of Iowa's School of Religion. The Iowa school not only offered a wide variety of courses for credit to undergraduates but also became the first state university to offer a doctoral program in religion. Still, the school was staffed by clergy from the Protestant, Roman Catholic, and Jewish faiths, and its purpose resembled that of Bible chairs and university pastorates: "to create an active interest in the church" and "to create a natural expectancy for men to choose religious callings." Indeed, the foundation of the Iowa school in 1921 reflected the efforts of Yale Divinity School's Charles Foster Kent to establish schools of religion at public and private universities. Kent thought that by providing "laboratory" instruction by "scholarly specialists," these schools would give the next generation of church leaders an ecumenical vision designed to restore religion as a primary factor in American life. The administrators at Iowa eventually adopted a plan different from Kent's. Nonetheless, the Iowa school became the model for a number of Protestant organizations whose purpose was to enlarge the role of religion within American higher education. Despite these successes, religious scholarship was still ill defined, and religious instruction was rarely included in the undergraduate curriculum.[22]

Two organizations that built on Protestant extracurricular activities and began to give more credibility to the study of religion were the American Association of Colleges and the National Association of Biblical Instructors. These bodies were especially influential in establishing a consensus among educators that provided religious studies with a coherent framework.

Founded in 1915, the Association of American Colleges (AAC) traced its origins to the Council of Church Boards of Education and the efforts of a group of denominational college presidents who had met together at the National Educational Association convention of 1914. With the increasing prominence of state universities and mounting doubts about the future of small colleges, the AAC brought together presidents from "distinctive American Colleges" who would make clear "their distinctive mission" and "their permanent value" to the public. Although the AAC included many nondenominational colleges, its Protestant outlook could not be missed. At its first annual meeting, the first session's topic was "The Moral and Religious Phases of Education," and included papers by William Frasier McDowell, a bishop in the Methodist church, and Henry Churchill King, a prominent figure in the Social Gospel

movement and president of Oberlin College. The first president of
the AAC was Robert L. Kelly, previously the president of Earlham
College, a Quaker institution, and soon to become an important
player in Protestant higher education. Under his direction the AAC
became a platform for various university and college presidents to
voice concern about the disjointedness of American learning and to
prescribe religious instruction as a way to restore unity within the
undergraduate curriculum.[23]

The AAC also became a forum for discussions among Protestant
educators about liberal education. One of Kelly's motives in founding the AAC was to standardize and unify the mission and character
of American small-college education. Without developing such a
"national educational consciousness," Kelly warned, liberal colleges
would be overwhelmed by state universities. Kelly's outlook paid
dividends as AAC members took up the task of integrating the
college curriculum. Throughout the 1920s and 1930s college administrators introduced a variety of survey or orientation courses as a
way of restoring order to liberal arts education. These efforts came
to a head with the formation in 1942 of the AAC Commission on
Liberal Education. Despite the fact that its 1943 report on the
nature and responsibilities of liberal education failed to end debate,
the Commission on Liberal Education was indicative of a growing
desire among educators to give meaning and direction to American
higher education.[24]

The recognition of the need for unity within the college curriculum was important for the future of religious studies. No longer was
religion regarded as a diverse or sectarian subject. College administrators began to look to religion to supply integration. The AAC
report on liberal education stated that a "liberally educated person"
needed to be "*sensitive* to all the values that endow life with meaning and significance." This necessity required an acquaintance with
humankind's attempt to understand the meaning of life through
"art and literature, philosophy and religion." A similar report
issued by the ACLS in 1943 was no less explicit in affirming the role
of religion and morality in liberal education.[25]

The National Association of Biblical Instructors reinforced the
notion that religion was indispensable to liberal education and
helped to shape the content of much collegiate religious instruction.
Founded in 1909, the NABI was one of several Protestant organiza-

tions designed to promote and standardize religious instruction within ecclesiastical and educational institutions. Its specific domain was Bible instruction within secondary schools and church colleges. Although the NABI functioned as a professional organization for college instructors, its leaders made clear that the association was not a learned society. When its publication, the *Journal of Bible and Religion*, went to a quarterly format in 1937, the editor assured readers that the journal was concerned primarily with "*pedagogical* matters, teaching techniques and materials," not "technical scholarly work." [26]

To justify their precarious positions at colleges and universities, instructors in Bible and religion turned to the rhetoric of liberal education. Despite the boasts of NABI's leaders about the centrality of religion in American higher education, the rank and file knew better. Their courses were marginal to undergraduate curricula. But identifying the study of religion with the goals of humanistic subjects gave teachers of the Bible an acceptable and definite purpose. According to a Presbyterian teaching Bible at the University of Missouri, the study of Scripture was essential to the liberal curriculum because it involved mental discipline, it acquainted students with "the great fields of human thought," and it contributed to "an intelligent familiarity with modern citizenship." Several educators argued that religion was the remedy for the tendency of science to make undergraduate education atomistic. What students needed, observed one president of the NABI, was "a synthetic point of view," and the teacher of religion "is better prepared for this than the teacher of science." Although some debated whether the Bible or comparative religion should provide the core of religious education, both sides agreed that religious studies must be included for an education worthy of the name liberal. One advocate of the comparative religion approach wrote that colleges that integrated "the Christian tradition and the liberal arts tradition" were, from a "broad view of culture," "more complete" than ones that "merely stressed academic objectives." Meanwhile, a defender of a Bible-centered curriculum argued that Scripture preserved "the essential elements of our Christian faith and culture with which we should first of all be familiar in a so-called Christian nation." Perhaps the clearest sign of the direction in which the study of religion was headed was a 1935 survey of college courses in Bible and religion.

When questioned about the reasons for requiring religion courses, administrators and instructors repeatedly cited "cultural values," "orientation values," "character-building" and "the development of religious attitudes."[27]

Significantly, Protestant justifications for the study of religion overlapped with humanistic scholars' defense of their disciplines. Traditionally associated with "culture" or "higher civilization," the humanities were no longer defended on such elitist and antiquarian grounds. Instead, beginning around 1940 a spate of books appeared that referred to the humanities with what one historian has termed "an entirely new frequency and insistence." This newer conception of the humanities stressed their positive ethical and spiritual relevance to modern society. According to the president of the ACLS, the humanities dealt primarily with "the manifestations of man's spiritual existence." Other apologists agreed that the humanities were overwhelmingly concerned with "values." As a result, many educators began to speak of the "spiritual," "moral," and "humanizing" nature of humanistic studies.[28]

This defense of the humanities coincided with increased attention to general education. Notable expressions of these concerns were the reports of Harvard University in 1945, *General Education in a Free Society*, and the President's Commission on Higher Education in 1948, *Higher Education for American Democracy*. Both of these influential proposals subsumed older conceptions of the humanities and liberal education within general education. Lamenting that academic specialization had undermined the unity of higher education, both reports called for reforms that would advance human values and democratic citizenship. As other advocates of general education looked to science, methodology, and metaphysics for integration, the Harvard report and the President's Commission stressed that an acquaintance with the religious and humane values of Western culture would supply the desired unity. According to the President's Commission, general education should enable the student "to identify, interpret, select, and build into his own life those components of his cultural heritage that contribute richly to understanding and appreciation of the world in which he lives." Accepting the Western cultural heritage as the center of the curriculum, the Harvard report insisted that a necessary element of education was to perpetuate "a received idea of the good." For advocates of general education the humanities became indispensable. Indeed, the emergence of general education reforms greatly abetted the identification of the humanities with subjects that promoted humane, moral, spiritual and liberal ideals.[29]

Calls for unity in higher education provided Protestants concerned about the study of religion with added leverage. Generated by the crisis of the Second World War, many books and articles by mainline Protestant leaders appeared that picked up on the sense of upheaval within American universities. Echoing the concerns of the Harvard report and the President's Commission, these writers lamented the increasing fragmentation of knowledge and the secularization of learning. According to Henry P. Van Dusen, president of New York's Union Theological Seminary, specialization had contributed to "a bargain-counter theory of education," and secularization had undermined the "principle of coherence" and "instrument of cohesion" within American higher education. George A. Buttrick, a professor at Harvard Divinity School, observed that by stressing knowledge of facts and ignoring meaning and values, American education was "out of joint." Meanwhile, Albert C. Outler, whose essay "A Christian Context for Counseling" became necessary reading for Protestant educators, observed that "the traditional pattern of higher education in America is gravely deficient and must be reformed." Liberal education, he explained, had "failed to provide men with a unified vision of life or an integrative focus for human knowledge."[30]

Though dissatisfied, Protestants were not willing to abandon liberal education or its younger sibling, general education. Indeed, the solution to the problems of American higher education prescribed most often was religion. The study of religion, however, did not set aside traditional conceptions of education. Rather, many believed that religion assisted and completed the highest ideals of a liberal education. After surveying the faculty at various institutions, Outler concluded that an "intelligible and intellectually respectable" case could be made for including religion as a "crucial factor" in liberal education. Appealing to the goals of "trained intelligence" and "free inquiry," Yale's Robert L. Calhoun argued that Christianity, not "these newly god-intoxicated secularisms," went hand in hand with intellectual enterprise. C. P. Shedd, another student of religion in higher education, observed that the effort to join the insights of education and religion had always been a "central responsibility of liberal higher education" but was especially urgent in post-war society. For this reason he advocated instruction in *"the Hebrew-Christian faith"* in order to undergird "our American democracy with abiding foundations." John W. Nason, president of Swarthmore College, concurred that instruction in "the Hebraic-Christian tradition" would temper the prevailing secularism of American education and restore to liberal education its proper function of supplying "values" and "the ends of human life."[31]

Because Protestant concerns dovetailed with the shift toward relevance within humanistic disciplines, the study of religion began to be grouped with the humanities. At a time when many believed that the humanities supplied the "ideological basis for living in a democracy and fighting for it," the support from students of the Bible and Christian ethics could not be refused easily. Despite the dangers of indoctrination and evangelism, a 1943 report by the ACLS stated that the "liberal value" of religion was self-evident. Students needed to understand "what men have believed and approved of in moral and religious realms." The Stanford Conference on the Humanities gave further evidence that religion had come within the humanistic orbit. In debates about a proposed one-year general course, humanistic scholars barely batted an eye when the conference's administrators included religion. Meanwhile, a 1945 study of liberal education funded by the Rockefeller Foundation noted the increasing attention to religion in humanities courses. At Bennington College, according to this report, a course on "the Western Tradition in Literature and Philosophy" included readings in the Old and New Testaments, and an experimental course at Scripps College acquainted undergraduates with "Biblical and Hellenic literatures." Although humanistic scholars recognized the Bible as an important influence on Western literature, the new attention to religion also reflected the humanities' growing concern with moral and spiritual matters.[32]

The support that the study of religion gained from general education and humanities requirements explains in part the spread of religion departments after the war. Between 1945 and 1960 the number of undergraduate programs in religious studies increased almost 100 percent, rising from twenty to thirty-eight. Enrollment figures reveal that courses in religion attracted more students dur-

ing the post-war years than any other area of study. Total undergraduate enrollments in religion expanded most notably at private
non-sectarian institutions. Figures for graduate programs also increased dramatically. Between 1945 and 1960 sixteen institutions in
North America established programs that led to a doctorate in
religious studies (Ph.D. and Th.D.), an increase of approximately
60 percent. Meanwhile, the number of doctorates awarded during
the 1950s more than tripled the number granted during the 1940s.[33]

Even though Protestants concerned about higher education
benefited from the widespread interest in general education, they
were not always certain about the place of religious studies in the
liberal arts curriculum. A minority made the case that Christianity
had been a key factor in the history of the West and so deserved
attention on the grounds of cultural heritage. This attitude would
have aligned Protestants with the humanities, whose purpose had
been typically to preserve the traditions of the West. Nonetheless, a
number of anthologies published around 1950 indicated that advocates of religious studies had more in mind. Not content with
shaping a part of the curriculum, some Protestants wanted a religious perspective to be included in all subjects, thereby providing
the integration that liberal education demanded. The Hazen Foundation funded several volumes for the purpose of demonstrating
how the humanities, social sciences, and natural sciences could be
taught from a religious perspective. These publications revealed
that moral philosophy's ideals had not lost their grip on the Protestant mind. Consequently, the path of general education did not
necessarily lead to an alliance between religious studies and the
humanities.[34]

Still, the shape of the curriculum in most of the new departments
of religion solidified the identification of religious studies as a
humanistic discipline. Except for Roman Catholic and Jewish institutions, the offerings at most colleges and universities, whether
public, private, or church related, resembled the curriculum at
Protestant divinity schools and seminaries. Courses in the Old and
New Testaments, therefore, became the focal point of instruction,
while church history, systematic theology, and Christian ethics
filled out the typical religion department's program. To be sure,
faculty offered courses in comparative religion; but often non-
Christian religions were studied as partial expressions of the fuller

truth revealed in Christianity. Few educators questioned the Protestant orientation of the curriculum because these courses seemed to provide an understanding of important segments of Western civilization and American culture. These courses, moreover, relied on literary, historical, and philosophical methodologies, which gave religion and humanistic scholars a common orientation. Meanwhile, the appeal by both humanistic scholars and religious studies professors to the need for values and integration in liberal education made the study of religion and the humanities sympathetic if not willing academic bedfellows.[35]

The attention that religious studies received during the 1960s from the Princeton studies on humanistic scholarship came as little surprise. Although religious scholarship had not yet been recognized by America's learned societies, the decision to devote two volumes of the Princeton Council's series to religion reflected the recent resurgence of the subject within higher education. Indeed, the Princeton studies confirmed the Protestant and humanistic orientation of religion departments. The volume edited by Princeton University's Paul Ramsey, *Religion*, surveyed the dominant fields within religious scholarship and consisted of chapters corresponding to the seminary curriculum. The section on the history of religions, a relatively recent addition to theological education, was the only mention of non-Western religions. Meanwhile, Holbrook's reasoning in *Religion, A Humanistic Field* summed up almost three decades of American Protestant thought about religion and higher education. The crucial issue was whether religious scholarship was a "liberalizing and humanizing area of instruction and scholarship." Although this was a complex question, Holbrook believed that religious studies were most fruitfully conducted in a humanistic context because the study of religion made "available to the present the worthy embodiments of man's creativity."[36]

A small irony attended the appearance of Holbrook's book, however. As a respected member of the National Association of Biblical Instructors and professor of religion at Oberlin College, Holbrook played an influential role on the NABI Self-Study Committee whose task was to make the study of religion more academically respectable. To this end Holbrook lobbied to reconstitute the NABI as the American Academy of Religion, a learned society that would be more pluralistic, more scholarly, and more representative of scholars in North America. When the AAR finally gained membership in the ACLS in 1979, it accomplished the goal that Holbrook and many other religion professors had established. Still, academic respectability came with a price. As the AAR grew in stature, religion scholars sought to establish their field on empirical and scientific grounds. In the process the study of religion diverged from Holbrook's ideal of a humanistic discipline.[37]

An important reason for changing the name of the National Association of Biblical Instructors concerned the final term in the title. For many members the word *instructor* suggested "some sort of junior status" and a "primary emphasis on teaching as opposed to scholarship and research." The switch to the word *academy* in the new title, therefore, designated the academic ambitions and insecurity of religion professors. This term suggested "a society of learned men united to advance art or science." The American Academy of Religion signaled a growing effort to establish the boundaries and to refine the methods of the discipline. To be religious was no longer as important for professors of religion as methodological sophistication and academic achievement.[38]

The name change of the professional organization of religion scholars did not settle the issue of advocacy or indoctrination, however. One traditional aspect of religious instruction had been concern for the student's personal faith. To be sure, the proliferation of religion departments in public universities raised the issue of the separation of church and state and forced religion professors to consider whether their instruction constituted an establishment of religion. But this problem did not raise the question of indoctrination as forcefully as did the alliance between religion and humanistic learning. Many professors in religious studies were ardent advocates of raising scholarly standards but still appealed to the rationale of making students more humane, religious, and moral. While admitting that indoctrination was intolerable, Holbrook, for instance, did not want to exclude from religious studies "speaking to the question of the truth value of religion or theology." Others within the profession, however, insisted that the humanistic orientation merely perpetuated the Protestant dominance of religion departments. In order to be truly objective and scientific, religion scholars would have to be more inclusive in their subject matter and more critically objective in their teaching and research.[39]

Claude Welch's 1971 report *Graduate Education in Religion: A Critical Appraisal* attempted to resolve the questions debated by AAR members during the 1960s. Sponsored and administered by the ACLS, Welch's study helped to legitimate the discipline within American higher education. Welch's own standing as president of the AAR during 1970 gave the report credibility within the field of religious studies. Designed to survey the study of religion in North American colleges, universities, and seminaries, the Welch report drew the most attention for the recommendations it made. It marked a clear defeat for the older humanistic and Protestant orientation of religious studies and called for increased methodological sophistication within the profession.[40]

For Welch, religious studies needed to move away from the dominance of literary and linguistic approaches to a "plurality of methods." In particular, he believed that the field had been dominated by attention to "scriptural texts" and "*normative* ideas." What the field needed instead were anthropological, sociological, and phenomenological studies that dealt "with the actual ways in which people act and believe." Welch also urged that more attention be given to religious traditions other than Judaism and Christianity. "The time has come," he wrote, "when the parochialism of restricting religious studies to a single tradition can no longer be afforded." For scholars stifled by the Protestant dominance of religion departments, Welch's proposals came as a breath of fresh air.[41]

Had Welch stopped with prescriptions for revising the methods and content of religious studies, Protestants might have been able to absorb the changes and maintain control. Instead, the report distinguished between theological education at seminaries and religious studies within the university and suggested that for the study of religion to fulfill its academic responsibilities, it would have to give up its ecclesiastical connections. Welch believed that his distinction was "irenic" and hoped that seminaries and religion departments would continue to cooperate in some fashion. Still, professors within seminaries and university divinity schools came out looking second rate. Welch evaluated the various graduate programs in religious studies and concluded that most seminaries, except for those connected to well-respected universities, were either "marginal" or "inadequate." Quite naturally, Welch based his ratings on the ability of an institution to prepare scholars for academic careers. The report gave the impression, however, that scholars involved in the training of ministers and who studied the traditional theological subjects were inferior. The Welch study significantly undermined Protestant hegemony within religious education and made the academy rather than the church the primary orientation of religious studies.[42]

Graduate Education in Religion was indicative of the newer developments within religious studies. The programs at leading universities and the major works in religious scholarship lost their Protestant orientation, made room for other religious traditions, and relied on the methods of other disciplines. One index to this shift was the publication in 1970 of a study edited by two Princeton University professors, John F. Wilson and Paul Ramsey.[43] Five years earlier, as Ramsey's volume in the Princeton Council on the Humanities series indicated, the dominant fields in religious studies mirrored the Protestant theological curriculum. By the time of the 1970 volume, however, the field had expanded to include biblical studies, Christian theology, Catholic studies, Jewish studies, sociology of religion, comparative religious ethics, religion and literature, and religion and art.

During the 1970s religious studies continued to expand. Contributions to the *Journal of the American Academy of Religion* reflected the pluralistic and at times incoherent character of the field. Presidential addresses before the AAR ranged from a mildly liberal Protestant critique of the hidden agenda of humanistic psychology and a standard summary of developments in the field of theology and literature to such innovative studies as "Cargo Cults as Cultural Historical Phenomenon" and "Institutions as Symbols of Death." Articles that dealt with explicitly Christian subjects continued to outnumber contributions on other religions. For instance, the combined categories of biblical studies, history of Christianity, and theology accounted for seventy-six articles, compared to forty-three for Asian religions and twenty-four for Judaica. Still, essays on Christian topics accounted for only 19 percent of the total number of published articles. Moreover, biblical studies (thirty-seven articles) received less attention than religion and the arts (forty-eight). Perhaps even more revealing of changes within religious studies during the 1970s were the subjects of manuscripts submitted to the *Journal of the American Academy of Religion*. Whereas yearly submissions in such subjects as Old Testament, New Testament, ethics, and Judaica rarely climbed into double digits, the journal received on the average thirty-five manuscripts a year in the philosophy of religion and twenty-one on Asian religions.[44]

Surprisingly, few articles appeared on religion and the social sciences during the 1970s, even though religion scholars increasingly turned to methodological considerations and found anthropology, sociology, and psychology the most fruitful. The demise of the Protestant theological curriculum brought with it a loss of coherence within religious studies. To restore unity, students of religion gave increasing consideration to the methods of their discipline. The focus on theoretical issues explains to a large extent the wider use of the history-of-religions approach. The English equivalent for *Religionswissenschaft*, the history of religions, originated in nineteenth-century European scholarship. The explicit intention of this method was to develop a scientific way of studying religion that accounted for the diversity of religious experience. Relying heavily on the social sciences, the history of religions enabled scholars to regard religion as an enduring feature of society, culture, and personality. Indeed, the lure of this method was the frequent claim that it explained all religious phenomena scientifically. In the context of the 1960s and 1970s, the history of religions offered professors of religion a method that justified their presence within the university and a means by which to study non-Western religions, thereby making their discipline more scientific and less Protestant.[45]

The history of religions by no means excluded other approaches to the study of religion. The AAR continued to serve as a forum for a variety of approaches within religious studies. Some scholars resisted the influence of the social sciences by arguing for continued use of philosophical, historical, and literary methods in the study of religion. Meanwhile, the curriculum within religion departments was slower to reflect the changes in the profession. Most continued to offer courses in traditional subjects while adding some courses in the newer approaches. Theologians were especially critical of the dominance of comparative approaches and worked out a variety of methods by which to theologize within the university. Still, for religious scholars seeking a theoretical framework compatible with the scientific ideals of the academy, the history of religions appeared to be the best alternative.[46]

The dramatic transformation of religious studies since the Second World War looks like another chapter in the story of the professionalization of higher learning. In most accounts of this process, a group committed to a specific task establishes an organization to set qualifications, adopts a code of ethics stressing public service, and creates and supervises training facilities that reinforce the organization's standards of expertise. Laurence Veysey has argued convincingly that the specialization of academic disciplines does not fit the typical model of professionalization. Rather than being created from scratch, many fields of learning emerged from an already existing cultivated elite with its own professional outlook. Under the spell of scientific research and specialization, younger scholars rejected as amateurish the older style of academics. In order to supervise and encourage their own disciplines, scholars committed to the new models of learning established professional associations, encouraged publication through their own journals, and took control of graduate education.[47]

The newer form of religious studies that began to take shape with the founding of the American Academy of Religion, although it had taken a longer time to gain admittance into the university, repeated the same patterns through which other disciplines passed in the late nineteenth century. Like other fields of learning, the newer form of religious studies emerged from an existing professional outlook dominated by the old-line Protestant churches. Instruction in Bible and religion before the 1960s often benefited from research conducted at seminaries and divinity schools, but the perspective of the National Association of Biblical Instructors remained one of cultivated generalism. The study of religion, according to this view, was considered an important part of a humanistic education and basic to American ideals of freedom and democracy. As religious studies became a part of the university, scholars in this field shifted their loyalties from the church to the academy. Advanced research, rather than the social role of religion, became the norm for the discipline. One difference from the social sciences and humanities was that while professionalization broke down general fields of learning into various specialties with their own departments, religious studies often served as the clearinghouse for a multitude of scholars whose only common interest was religion in some vague sense.

What is especially interesting to observe about the transformation of religious studies is the motive behind the switch to an academic orientation. Here a comparison with the history of the social sciences in the United States is illuminating. Like the study of religion, the social sciences emerged from a field of learning dominated largely by the clergy. In order to break with the traditional religious orientation of their labors, social scientists, as students of religion did years later, set out to give their disciplines a firmer academic foundation. Thus, during the 1880s social scientists embraced the ideal of the research-oriented scholar and identified with the newly formed universities. A significant factor in this shift, according to many historians, was the sense of cultural crisis generated by industrialization and urbanization. A major result of that crisis was the shift of cultural authority away "from the moral advice of the clergy to the expert advice of the university social scientists." A concatenation of sociocultural forces at work during the late nineteenth century, not a direct confrontation between reason and revelation, broke the cultural power of the churches and established the moral authority of the university.[48]

As in the social sciences, the changes within religious studies in the twentieth century have depended as much on cultural factors as on the dictates of objective scholarship. Indeed, the academic study of religion demonstrated both the remarkable persistence and the failings of mainline Protestantism. Like the social sciences during the late nineteenth century, religious studies became a growing concern in colleges and universities owing in large part to the cultural crisis generated by the two world wars. Science and technology seemed to be more of a threat than a solution to social ills, and educators took steps to ensure that undergraduates received a proper training in values and morality. Proponents of religious studies, which often meant the ethos of liberal Protestantism, made common cause with humanistic scholars and resurrected the philosophical idealism of the old genteel tradition under the label of general education. Apparently a marginal force within American culture during the 1920s and 1930s, after the Second World War liberal Protestantism revealed its continuing strength and influence through the rise of departments of religion.[49]

By the 1960s, however, the synthesis of the so-called pan-Protestant establishment would not hold. To explain the demise of Protestantism by pointing to the rise of pluralism as a positive cultural value borders on triviality. Still, forces were at work in American society that undermined consensus. Beginning with the return of American troops from the Orient after the war, a widespread fascination with Eastern cultures emerged. At the popular level this interest fostered the penetration of Oriental art, literature, cuisine, martial arts, and religions into American culture. Within American scholarship this interest sparked the growth of area studies and foreign language programs, particularly in Asian studies but also generally in non-Western studies. Meanwhile, anti–Vietnam War protests and the civil rights movement subjected Western religion and American values to much criticism, especially on college campuses, the recent home of religion scholars. Unable to assume the superiority of Christian ideals, students of religion were forced to derive a more objective basis for their presence in higher learning. The best alternative was the scientistic orientation provided by the history of religions and the social sciences. Students of religion did not face this problem alone. Humanistic scholars, who had resisted the dominant conception of the pursuit of knowledge either in the name of tradition or in the rhetoric of humanizing studies, also scrambled to ground their disciplines in a scientific basis. Religious studies thus broke with its Protestant heritage, but not because of an inherent antipathy between religion and learning. Rather, the formation of the American Academy of Religion signaled a reaction against the humanistic and liberal Protestant orientation of religious studies during the 1940s and 1950s.[50]

The discipline of religious studies continues to be shaped by its past. In a 1985 ACLS report on the humanities, the AAR celebrated its diversity as a "quantum leap" beyond the "halcyon humanistic days of the colonial college" and the "cultural isolation of the independent seminary." The study of religion had progressed from "nineteenth century WASP theology" to recover the religious visions of blacks, Chicanos, Orientals, Hasidic Jews, Oglala Sioux, and Pure Land Buddhists. Not quite so optimistic, a participant in a colloquium on the state of graduate religious studies observed that the field has "no identifiable frame of discourse," that the discipline is an "in-house concoction," and that there is no "cogent legitimation or authority" for the academic study of religion. To be sure, some might argue that the phenomenology of religion, cultural anthropology, the history of religions, or the sociology of religion supplies religious studies with adequate coherence. Yet the lack of consensus is apparent to both the discipline's detractors and its well-wishers and reflects as much the historical tension between religion and learning in American education as it does the intellectual ferment within contemporary academic circles concerning methodology, the authority of a canon of texts, and boundaries between disciplines. Consequently, as some members of the profession call for increased attention to the discipline's roots in intellectual developments since the Enlightenment, American scholars of religion might do well to reflect on the particular way that the recent history of their discipline has shaped their studies.[51]

Notes

I thankfully acknowledge the suggestions and criticisms offered by George M. Marsden, Bradley Longfield, Paul Kemeny, Kathryn Long, and Jeffrey Trexler.

1. Gerald James Larson, "An Introduction to the Santa Barbara Colloquy: Some Unresolved Questions," *Soundings* 71 (1988), 194.

2. Between 1961 and 1970 twenty-seven graduate programs were established, three more than in the previous three decades combined (five in the 1930s; eight in the 1940s, and eleven in the 1950s; before 1930 only twenty-one programs existed). Of the ninety-six programs in four-year public institutions that existed in 1970, sixty-one had been founded in the 1960s. Moreover, undergraduate enrollments in religion at private liberal arts colleges and public institutions increased at a faster rate than the growth of the student body. Enrollments in graduate programs doubled between 1959 and 1969, a rate of expansion second only to that in anthropology. These figures come from *Graduate Education in Religion: A Critical Appraisal*, ed. Claude Welch (Missoula MT, 1971), 178, 230–35.

The other volumes in the Princeton series (all Englewood Cliffs, NJ) were Eric R. Wolf, *Anthropology* (1964); James S. Ackerman and Rhys Carpenter, *Art and Archaeology* (1963); Wen Fong, *Chinese Painting*

(1964); Eric A. Havelock, *Classics* (1963); Felix Gilbert, John Higham, and Leonard Krieger, *History* (1965); William Haas and Karl D. Uitti, *Linguistics* (1964); David Daiches and Howard E. Hugo, *Literature* (1964); Walter Sutton, *Modern American Criticism* (1963); Frank L. Harrison, Mantle Hood, and Claude V. Palisca, *Musicology* (1964); Robert H. Knapp, *The Origins of American Humanistic Scholars* (1964); and Roderick M. Chisholm et al., *Philosophy* (1964).

3. Knapp, *Origins*; Higham, "The Schism in American Scholarship," in *Writing American History: Essays in Modern Scholarship* (Bloomington, 1970), 3–24. According to Knapp, p. 2, the return to liberal education by private colleges and Ivy League universities in the twentieth century involved an abandonment of the humanities' "prior alliance with religious concerns."

4. John F. Wilson, "Mr. Holbrook and the Humanities," *Journal of Bible and Religion* (hereafter *JBR*) 32 (1964), 253, 260; Schlatter, "Foreword" to Clyde A. Holbrook, *Religion, A Humanistic Field* (Englewood Cliffs, NJ, 1963), ix. For Holbrook's response to Wilson, see his "Mr. Schlatter's Dilemma Re-Examined," *JBR* 32 (1964), 262–65.

5. On the history of the study of religion, see Robert Michaelsen, *The Study of Religion in American Universities* (New Haven, 1965); John F. Wilson, "Introduction: The Background and Present Context of the Study of Religion in Colleges and Universities," in *The Study of Religion in Colleges and Universities*, ed. Paul Ramsey and John F. Wilson (Princeton, 1970), 3–22; Joseph M. Kitagawa, "Humanistic and Theological History of Religions with Special Reference to the North American Scene," *Numen* 27 (1980), 198–221; Charles H. Long, "The Study of Religion in the United States of America: Its Past and Its Future," *Religious Studies and Theology* 5 (1985), 30–44; J. Samuel Preus, *Explaining Religion: Criticism and Theory from Bodin to Freud* (New Haven, 1987); William R. Darrow, "The Harvard Way in the Study of Religion," *Harvard Theological Review* 81 (1988), 215–34; Harold E. Remus, E. Stanley Lusby, and Linda M. Tober, "Religion as an Academic Discipline," in *Encyclopedia of American Religious Experience: Studies of Traditions and Movements*, vol. 3, ed. Charles H. Lippy and Peter W. Williams (New York, 1988), 1653–69; Murray G. Murphy, "On the Scientific Study of Religion in the United States, 1870–1980," in *Religion and Twentieth-Century American Intellectual Life*, ed. Michael J. Lacey (Cambridge, 1989), 136–71; and Grant Wacker, "A Plural World: The Protestant Awakening to World Religions," in *Between the Times: The Travail of the Protestant Establishment in America, 1900–1960*, ed. William R. Hutchison (Cambridge, 1989), 268–75.

6. By 1975 the National Endowment for the Humanities recognized ethics and comparative religion as part of the humanities. See *NEH Pro-*

gram Announcement (Washington, DC, 1975), 1. For other examples of the connections between religious studies and the humanities, see *The Humanities: A Selective Guide to Information Sources,* ed. A. Robert Rogers (Littleton, 1974), chs. 6–8; American Council of Learned Societies, *A Report to the Congress of the United States on "The State of the Humanities"* (New York, 1985), 1–16.

7. *ACLS Newsletter* 31 (1979), inside cover. For a brief history of the AAR, see Leo J. O'Donovan, "Coming and Going: The Agenda of an Anniversary," *Journal of the American Academy of Religion* (hereafter *JAAR*) 53 (1985), 557–65.

8. On sectarianism at antebellum colleges, see Stanley M. Guralnick, "Sources of Misconception on the Role of Science in the Nineteenth-Century American College," *Isis* 65 (1974), 352–66; James McLachlan, "The American College in the Nineteenth Century: Towards a Reappraisal," *Teachers College Record* (hereafter *TCR*) 80 (1978), 287–306; Douglas Sloan, "Harmony, Chaos, and Consensus: The American College Curriculum," *TCR* 73 (1971), 221–51; and James Axtell, "The Death of the Liberal Arts College," *History of Education Quarterly* (hereafter *HEQ*) 11 (1971), 339–52. On Protestant influence on nineteenth-century colleges, see Richard Hofstadter and Walter P. Metzger, *The Development of Academic Freedom in the United States* (New York, 1955); Laurence R. Veysey, *The Emergence of the American University* (Chicago, 1965), ch. 1; Sloan, "Harmony," 227–32; James F. Findlay, "The SPCTEW and Western Colleges: Religion and Higher Education in Mid-Nineteenth-Century America," *HEQ* 17 (1977), 31–62; and Timothy L. Smith, *Uncommon Schools: Christian Colleges and Social Idealism in Mid-Western America, 1820–1950* (Indianapolis, 1978).

9. On the colonial colleges' curriculum, see Bruce A. Kimball, *Orators and Philosophers: A History of the Idea of Liberal Education* (New York, 1986), 103–13, 133–41; Mark A. Noll, *Princeton and the Republic, 1768–1822* (Princeton, 1989), 20–21, 35–36, 100–102; Norman Fiering, *Moral Philosophy at Seventeenth-Century Harvard: A Discipline in Transition* (Chapel Hill, 1981), 22–42; and Roland H. Bainton, *Yale and the Ministry* (New York, 1957), ch. 4.

10. On nineteenth-century moral philosophy, see D. H. Meyer, *The Instructed Conscience: The Shaping of the American National Ethic* (Philadelphia, 1972); Wilson Smith, *Professors and Public Ethics: Studies of Moral Philosophers before the Civil War* (Ithaca, 1956); Daniel Walker Howe, *The Unitarian Conscience: Harvard Moral Philosophy, 1805–1861* (Cambridge, MA, 1970); and Douglas Sloan, "The Teaching of Ethics," in *Education and Values,* ed. Douglas Sloan (New York, 1980), 192–200.

11. On Princeton, see Mark A. Noll, "The Founding of Princeton Theo-

logical Seminary," *Westminster Theological Journal* 42 (1979), 72–110. On Yale, see Bainton, *Yale and the Ministry*, 79–81. And on Harvard, see Conrad Wright, "The Early Period, (1811–40)," in *The Harvard Divinity School: Its Place in Harvard University and in American Culture*, ed. George Huntston Williams (Boston, 1954), 28–36. On the rise of seminaries in the early nineteenth century, see Natalie A. Naylor, "The Theological Seminary in the Configuration of American Higher Education," *HEQ* 17 (1977), 17–30; Frank Dixon McCloy, "The Founding of Protestant Theological Seminaries in the United States of America, 1784–1840" (Ph.D. diss., Harvard University, 1959); and William Warren Sweet, "The Rise of Theological Schools in America," *Church History* 6 (1937), 260–73.

12. On academic specialization during the early nineteenth century, see the essays in *The Pursuit of Knowledge in the Early American Republic: American Scientific and Learned Societies from Colonial Times to the Civil War*, ed. Alexandra Oleson and Sanborn C. Brown (Baltimore, 1976); Sloan, "Teaching of Ethics," 195; and Frederick Rudolph, *Curriculum: A History of the American Undergraduate Course of Study since 1636* (San Francisco, 1977), 107–9.

13. On theological education in the late nineteenth century, see Glenn Miller and Robert Lynn, "Christian Theological Education," in *Encyclopedia of American Religious Experience: Studies of Traditions and Movements*, vol. 3, 1638–44. On the Society of Biblical Literature, see Ernest W. Saunders, *Searching the Scriptures: A History of the Society of Biblical Literature, 1880–1980* (Chico, CA, 1982); and on the American Society of Church History, see Henry W. Bowden, "The First Century: Institutional Development and Ideas about the Profession," in *A Century of Church History: The Legacy of Philip Schaff*, ed. Henry W. Bowden (Carbondale, IL, 1988), 294–332. Exceptions were the Oriental Seminary at Johns Hopkins, which provided a home for Old Testament scholarship, and Catholic universities and colleges, which encouraged biblical and theological scholarship.

14. Felix E. Schelling, *Humanities Gone and to Come* (Philadelphia, 1902), 3–4, and J. Irving Manatt, "The Future of Greek Studies," *Leader* (March 1903), 195, quoted in Laurence Veysey, "Plural Organized Worlds of the Humanities," in *The Organization of Knowledge in Modern America, 1860–1920*, ed. Alexandra Oleson and John Voss (Baltimore, 1979), 55. For these developments, see Veysey, 55–57; idem, *The Emergence of the American University* (Chicago, 1965), ch. 4; and Bruce Kuklick, "The Emergence of the Humanities," *South Atlantic Quarterly* 89 (1990), 195–206.

15. Thomas Fitz-Hugh, *The Philosophy of the Humanities* (Chicago, 1898); Dewey, *The Educational Situation* (Chicago, 1902), 82ff; William

224 *The Secularization of the Academy*

Nielson, "The Inaugural Address of the President of Smith College," *School and Society* 8 (1918), 63. On instruction in philosophy, see Mary Whiton Calkins, *The Persistent Problems of Philosophy*, rev. ed. (New York, 1917). In Frank G. Hubbard's survey of American colleges and universities, "The Undergraduate Curriculum in English Literature," *PMLA* 23 (1908), 258, only six institutions offered courses in the English Bible. For further examples of the affinity between religion and the humanities, see R. M. Wenley, "Transition of What?" *Educational Review* 33 (1907), 447; William Douglas Mackenzie, "The Place of Greek and Latin in the Preparation for the Ministry," and A. J. Nock, "The Value to the Clergyman of Training in the Classics," in *Latin and Greek in American Education: With Symposia on the Value of Humanistic Studies*, ed. Francis W. Kelsey (New York, 1911), 154–70, 171–78; and *The Value of the Classics*, ed. Andrew F. West (Princeton, 1917), 253–56.

16. Albion Small, *The Meaning of Social Science* (Chicago, 1910), 275, 277. On the transition from moral philosophy to social sciences, see Dorothy Ross, "The Development of the Social Sciences," in Oleson and Voss, *The Organization of Knowledge*, 109–21; Mary Furner, *Advocacy and Objectivity: A Crisis in the Professionalization of American Social Science, 1865–1905* (Lexington, KY, 1975); Thomas L. Haskell, *The Emergence of Professional Social Science: The American Social Science Association and the Nineteenth-Century Crisis of Authority* (Urbana, 1977); Arthur J. Vidich and Stanford M. Lyman, *American Sociology: Worldly Rejections of Religion and Their Directions* (New Haven, 1985); and three articles by Gladys Bryson, "The Emergence of Social Sciences from Moral Philosophy," *International Journal of Ethics* 42 (1932), 304–23; "The Comparable Interests of the Old Moral Philosophy and the Modern Social Sciences," *Social Forces* 2 (1932), 19–27; and "Sociology Considered as Moral Philosophy," *Sociological Review* 24 (1932), 26–36.

17. Waldo G. Leland, *ACLS Bulletin* (1920), 2. On these developments, see Higham, "Schism," 16–20; and Veysey, "Plural Organized Worlds," 56–57.

18. Higham, "Schism," 17–18. See also Edward A. Purcell, Jr., *The Crisis of Democratic Theory* (Lexington, KY, 1973). For evidence of the growing self-consciousness of the social sciences, see Frederick Ogg, *Research in Humanistic and Social Sciences* (New York, 1928), 3–4, n.2. Ogg believed that the humanities still included the social sciences, or for that matter any discipline concerned with the study of humanity. But he was forced to differentiate linguistics, literature, and archaeology from "economics, political science, and kindred disciplines." He blamed this division on social scientists who limited the humanities "to the older 'cultural studies' having to do chiefly with languages, arts, and letters." For developments in philosophy and literature, see Bruce Kuklick, *The Rise of Ameri-*

can Philosophy, Cambridge, Massachusetts, 1860–1930 (Cambridge, MA, 1977), ch. 28 and 29; Elizabeth Flowler and Murray G. Murphy, *A History of Philosophy in America*, vol. 2 (New York, 1977), ch. 15; David Daiches, *English Literature* (Englewood Cliffs, NJ, 1964), ch. 5; and Kermit Vanderbilt, *American Literature and the Academy: The Roots, Growth, and Maturity of a Profession* (Philadelphia, 1986), ch. 19, 20, 26.

19. Ogg, *Research*, 136–38, 229–31, 252. According to Ogg, the Institute for Social and Religious Research applied "scientific methods of research to the socio-religious field" (p. 229), while the Federal Council of Churches of Christ in America used $42,000 of its budget to conduct research in the "religious and ethical aspects of economic, industrial, international, and community problems" (p. 252). See also Waldo G. Leland, "Recent Trends in the Humanities," *Science* 79 (1934), 281–82; A. Lawrence Lowell, *At War with Academic Traditions in America* (Cambridge, 1934), 105; and C. J. Ducasse, "Are the Humanities Worth Their Keep?" *American Scholar* 6 (1937), 460–70.

20. On the YMCA, see Clarence Prouty Shedd, *The Church Follows Its Students* (New Haven, 1938); idem, *Two Centuries of Student Christian Movements* (New York, 1934); Howard Hopkins, *History of the YMCA in North America* (New York, 1951); and Committee on the War and the Religious Outlook, *The Teaching Work of the Church* (New York, 1923), ch. 10 and 11. Even the allegedly godless institutions Johns Hopkins University and Cornell University welcomed the YMCA. See John C. French, *A History of the University Founded by Johns Hopkins* (Baltimore, 1946), 324–32; and Richard Henry Edwards, *Cooperative Religion at Cornell University: The Story of United Religious Work at Cornell University, 1919–1939* (Ithaca, 1939). On chapel, see Seymour A. Smith, *The American College Chaplaincy* (New York, 1954); Merrimon Cuninggim, *The College Seeks Religion* (New Haven, 1947), ch. 9; Edward W. Blakeman, *The Administration of Religion in Universities and Colleges: Personnel* (Ann Arbor, 1942); and Henry T. Claus, "The Problem of College Chapel," *Educational Review* 46 (1913), 177–87.

21. Shedd, *Church Follows*, 62ff.; idem, *Religion in the State University* (Haddam, CT, 1946); Robert Michaelsen, *The Study of Religion in American Universities* (New Haven, 1965), 106–8; Blakeman, *Administration*, 10–21; *Teaching Work of the Church*, ch. 11; Paul M. Limbert, *Denominational Policies in the Support and Supervision of Higher Education* (New York, 1929); and Dorothy C. Bass, "Ministry on the Margin: Protestants and Education," in Hutchison, *Between the Times*, 57–61. Related to the work of university pastors were the Wesley, Westminster, and Wayland Foundations, established by Methodists, Presbyterians, and Baptists, respectively, as on-campus student associations. See Shedd, *Church Follows*,

53ff.; *Teaching Work of the Church*, 261–64; James Chamberlain Baker, *The First Wesley Foundation: An Adventure in Christian Higher Education* (Nashville, 1960); and Blakeman, *Administration of Religion*.

22. Marcus Bach, *Of Faith and Learning: The Story of Religion at the State University of Iowa* (Iowa City, 1952), 52, 42–49; and M. Willard Lampe, *The Story of an Idea* (Iowa City, 1958). See also O. D. Foster, "Schools of Religion at State Universities" *Christian Education* (hereafter *CE*) 5 (1922), 183–93; Robert L. Kelly, "Schools of Religion," *Religious Education* (hereafter *RE*) 22 (1927), 603–6; C. Grey Austin, *A Century of Religion at the University of Michigan: A Case Study in Religion and the State University* (Ann Arbor, 1957), 24, and ch. 5; and Seymour A. Smith, *Religious Cooperation in State Universities: An Historical Sketch* (Ann Arbor, 1957). On plans for a school of religion at Yale, see Bainton, *Yale and the Ministry*, 209, 211; Anson Phelps Stokes, "University Schools of Religion," *Religious Education* 9 (1914) 323–35; and Benjamin W. Bacon, *The Yale University School of Religion* (New Haven, 1914). Important organizations that became outlets for Protestants concerned about higher education were the Religious Education Association, the Edward W. Hazen Foundation, and the Council for Religion in Higher Education. For the history of these associations, see Herman E. Wornom "The Religious Education Association" in *Religious Education: A Comprehensive Survey*, ed. Marvin J. Taylor (Nashville, 1960), 359–70; Patrick Murphy Malin, "The National Council on Religion in Higher Education," and Thornton W. Merriam, "Religion in Higher Education through the Past Twenty-five Years," in *Liberal Learning and Religion*, ed. Amos N. Wilder (New York, 1951), 324–34, 3–25; and Stephen A. Schmidt, *A History of the Religious Education Association* (Birmingham, AL, 1983).

23. Robert L. Kelly, "The Place and Function of the Proposed Association," William Frasier McDowell, "The Christian Ideal of Education," and Henry Churchill King, "The Methods of Its Attainment," *Association of American Colleges Bulletin* (hereafter AACB) 1 (1915), 39–43, 15–28, 28–39. On Kelly and the AAC, see Hugh Hawkins, "Problems in Categorization and Generalization in the History of American Higher Education: An Approach through Institutional Associations" *History of Higher Education Annual* 5 (1985), 47ff. In addition to serving as president of the Church Council of Boards of Education, Kelly also played a major role in the accreditation of Protestant seminaries. See Kelly, *Theological Education in America, A Study of One Hundred Sixty-One Theological Schools in the United States and Canada* (New York, 1924); and David Blaine Cable, "The Development of the Accrediting Function of the American Association of Theological Schools, 1918–1939" (Ph.D. diss., University of Pittsburgh, 1970), 11–12, 40–46.

24. On the efforts of the AAC and the changing meaning of liberal education between the world wars, see Robert Lincoln Kelly, "The Liberal College and Human Values," *AACB* 16 (1930), 340–46; Harold W. Dodds, "The Place of Religion in the Curriculum and on the Campus," *AACB* 21 (1935), 476–77; Meta Glass, "The Contribution of the Humanities," *AACB* 23 (1937), 55–63; William Ernest Hocking, "Philosophy and Religion in Undergraduate Education," *AACB* 23 (1937), 45–54; John W. Nason, "The Nature and Content of a Liberal Education," *AACB* 27 (1941), 53–61; Committee on the Re-Statement of the Nature and Aims of Liberal Education to the Commission on Liberal Education of the Association of American Colleges, "The Post-War Responsibilities of Liberal Education," *AACB* 29 (1943), 275–99; and Kimball, *Orators and Philosophers*, 191–204. For a similar and contemporaneous effort by the ACLS, see Theodore M. Greene et al., *Liberal Education Re-Examined, Its Role in a Democracy* (New York, 1943).

25. "The Post War Responsibilities of Liberal Education," *AACB* 29 (1943), 285–86; Greene, *Liberal Education*, 66–69.

26. "Editorial," *JBR* 6 (1938), 88. For the history of NABI, see Elmer W. K. Mould, "The National Association of Biblical Instructors: An Historical Account," *JBR* 18 (1950), 11–29.

27. Samuel R. Braden, "The Place of the Bible in a Liberal Education of Today," *CE* 4 (1922–23), 211; I. R. Beiler, "Some Implications of Our Teaching Aims," *CE* 14 (1931), 638; Bernard Eugene Meland, "The Study of Religion in a Liberal Arts College," *JBR* 5 (1937), 63; Laura H. Wild, "The Bible the Foundation of a Course in Religion," *JBR* 5 (1937), 168; and Gould Wickey and Ruth A. Eckhart, "A National Survey of Courses in Bible and Religion in American Universities and Colleges," *CE* 20 (1936–37), 32–5. See also Ernest F. Johnson, "College Courses in Religion," *JBR* 10 (1942), 147–50, 183; Robert W. McEwen, "A Study of Objectives Published in College Catalogs," *JBR* 10 (1942), 152–53; Carl E. Purinton, "Objectives of Teachers of Bible and Religion in Liberal Arts Colleges," *JBR* 10 (1942), 153–55; Edgar M. McKown, "Methods and Materials in Teaching the Message of Jesus," *JBR* 10 (1942), 155–58; Charles F. Nesbitt, "The Bible in the Curriculum," *CE* 21 (1937–38), 69–75; William J. Davidson, "Conserving Religious Education in the Academic Curriculum," *CE* 18 (1934–35), 294–304; Gould Wickey, "Christian Education—Whither?" *CE* 15 (1931–32), 335–45; Charles D. Mathews, "A Curriculum for a Department of Religion," *JBR* 4 (1936), 89–92; Beatrice Allard Brooks, "The Place of the Study of Religion in the Liberal Arts Curriculum in the Light of Recent Theories of the Higher Learning," *JBR* 6 (1938), 187–94; Lloyd V. Moore, "A College Program for the Teaching of Religion," *CE* 21 (1937–38), 83–91; Walter G. Clippinger, "The Liberal Arts College—

Whence? Where? Whither?" *CE* 18 (1934–35), 277–87; and Muriel S. Curtis, "Why and How I Teach Religious Education in College," *JBR* 7 (1939), 125–32.

For evidence of the marginal status of religion courses, see Charles Foster Kent, "The Undergraduate Courses in Religion at the Tax-Supported Colleges and Universities of America," *Bulletin of the National Council on Religion in Higher Education* (hereafter *BNCRHE*) 4 (1923) 3–34; Lura Beam, "Classroom Instruction in Religion in Two Hundred and Fifty Colleges," *CE* 8 (1925), 211–64; Willard E. Uphause and M. Teague Hipps, "Undergraduate Courses in Religion at Denominational and Independent Colleges and Universities of America," *BNCRHE* 6 (1924), 5–94; Theron Charlton McGee, *Religious Education in Certain Evangelical Colleges—A Study in Status and Tendencies* (Philadelphia, 1928); and Hugh Hartshorne, Helen R. Stearns, and Willard E. Uphaus, *Standards and Trends in Religious Education* (New Haven, 1933). Although surveys indicated a great number of courses offered, they also showed that enrollments were small and that the study of religion, which was often conducted in many different departments, had little coherence.

28. Veysey, "Plural Organized," 57; Leland, "Recent Trends," 281; and Higham, "Schism," 21.

29. "Higher Education for American Democracy," in *Education for Democracy: the Debate over the Report of the President's Commission on Higher Education*, ed. Gail Kennedy (Boston, 1952), 24; Paul H. Buch et al., *General Education in a Free Society: Report of the Harvard Committee* (Cambridge, MA, 1945), 47. For background on the issues these reports addressed, see Sloan, "Teaching of Ethics," 240ff.; Kimball, *Orators and Philosophers*, 190–200, 233–34; Higham, "Schism," 17–18; Laurence Veysey, "Stability and Experiment in the American Undergraduate Curriculum," in *Content and Context*, ed. Carl Kaysen (New York, 1973), 1–63; Russell Thomas, *The Search for a Common Learning: General Education, 1800–1960* (New York, 1962), ch. 4; Daniel Bell, *The Reforming of General Education: The Columbia College Experience in Its National Setting* (New York, 1966); Earl J. McGrath, *General Education and the Plight of Modern Man* (Indianapolis, 1975); and Daniel Catlin, Jr., *Liberal Education at Yale: The Yale College Course of Study, 1945–1978* (Washington, DC, 1982).

30. Van Dusen, *God in Education: A Tract for the Times* (New York, 1951), 47, 52; Buttrick, *Faith and Education* (New York, 1952), 9; Outler, "Colleges, Faculties, and Religion," *Educational Record* 30 (1949), 45, 46. See also Stewart Grant Cole, *Liberal Education in a Democracy* (New York, 1940); George F. Thomas, *Religion in an Age of Secularism* (Princeton, NJ, 1940); Arnold S. Nash, *The University in the Modern World: An*

Essay in the Philosophy of University Education (New York, 1949); Howard Lowry, *The Mind's Adventure: Religion and Higher Education* (Philadelphia, 1949); Nevin Cowger Harner, *Religion's Place in General Education* (Richmond, 1949); Walter Moberly, *Crisis in the University* (London, 1951); Bernard Meland, *Higher Education and the Human Spirit* (Chicago, 1953); and, for a later expression, Alexander Miller, *Faith and Learning: Christian Faith and Higher Education in Twentieth-Century America* (New York, 1960). For evangelical sentiments, see Frank E. Gaebelein, *Christian Education in a Democracy* (New York, 1951); Edwin H. Rian, *Christianity and American Education* (San Antonio, 1949); and Bernard Ramm, *The Christian College in the Twentieth Century* (Grand Rapids, 1963).

31. Outler, "Colleges," 57; Robert L. Calhoun, "The Place of Religion in Higher Education," in *Religion and the Modern World* (Philadelphia, 1941), 70–71; Shedd, *Proposals for Religion in Postwar Higher Education* (Haddam, CT, 1946), 10, 19; John W. Nason, "Religion in Higher Education: The Program of Faculty Consultations," *Educational Record* 27 (1946), 426.

32. John W. Dodds, "Realities in Time of Crisis," *AACB* 29 (1943), 359; Greene, *Liberal Education*, 66; Stanford Conference on the Humanities, *Elementary Courses in the Humanities* (Stanford, 1945), 111; and Fred B. Millett, *The Rebirth of Liberal Education* (New York, 1945), 26, 45. For other examples of the convergence of religion and the humanities, see Hocking, "Philosophy and Religion," 45–54; John W. Nason, "The Nature and Content of a Liberal Education," *AACB* 27 (1941), 53–61; Robert Lowry Calhoun, "Theology and the Humanities," in *The Meaning of the Humanities*, ed. Theodore Meyer Greene (Princeton, 1938), 119–50; Jacques Maritain, *Education at the Crossroads* (New Haven, 1943), 71–75; William A. Nielson, "The Future of the Humanities," *Harper's Magazine* 186 (1943), 388–91; and Harold B. Dunkel, *General Education in the Humanities* (Washington, DC, 1947). For evidence that religion was not considered a part of the humanities during the 1930s, see two surveys of courses, Patricia Beesley, *The Revival of the Humanities in American Education* (New York, 1940), and Edward Safford Jones, "Comprehensive Examinations in the Humanities," *AACB* 23 (1937), 209–313.

33. Figures come from Welch, *Graduate Education in Religion*, 230–35.

34. The anthologies subsidized by the Hazen Foundation were *College Reading and Religion: A Survey of College Reading Materials Sponsored by the Edward W. Hazen Foundation and the Committee on Religion and Education of the American Council on Education* (New Haven, 1948); *Liberal Learning and Religion*, ed. Amos N. Wilder (New York, 1951); *The Teaching of Religion in American Higher Education*, ed. Christian Gauss (New York, 1951); *College Teaching and Christian Values*, ed. Paul M.

Limbert (New York, 1951); and *Religious Perspectives in College Teaching*, ed. Hoxie N. Fairchild (New York, 1952). For a fairly common expression of the mainline Protestant philosophy of education, see Cuninggim, *College Seeks Religion*, 142–52.

35. For examples of religion programs, see Cuninggim, *College Seeks Religion*, ch. 13; Michaelsen, *The Study of Religion*; and *Religious Studies in Public Universities*, ed. Milton D. McLean (Carbondale, IL, 1967). For examples of Protestant perspectives on instruction in other religions, see Mary Francis Thelen, "The Biblical Instructor and Comparative Religion," *JBR* 20 (1952), 71–76; and Joachim Wach, "General Revelation and the Religions of the World," *JBR* 22 (1954), 83–93. For the continuing appeal of liberal education to religious studies professors, see Robert M. Montgomery, "The Religion Instructor as Learner," *JBR* 26 (1958), 99–106; Arthur C. Wickenden, "Rightly Dividing the Word of Truth," *JBR* 24 (1956), 3–9; and J. Allen Easley, "Appreciation of the Bible as Literature and Religion," *JBR* 18 (1950), 96–98.

36. Holbrook, *Religion*, 51, 41. Joseph C. Kiger's *American Learned Societies* (Washington, DC, 1963), a history of learned societies, did not mention any of the professional associations in the field of religious studies.

37. Dwight Beck et al., "Report of the NABI Self-Study Committee," *JBR* 32 (1964), 200–201. See also Holbrook, "Why an Academy of Religion?" *JBR* 32 (1964), 98–105.

38. Beck et al., "Report of the NABI Self-Study Committee," 200. See also "Editorial Preface," *JBR* 29 (1961), 277–79.

39. Clyde A. Holbrook, "Mr. Schlatter's Dilemma Re-Examined," *JBR* 32 (1964), 264. For more discussion of this issue, see Robert S. Michaelsen, "Religion as an Academic Discipline," *Liberal Education* 47 (1961), 72–83; Wilson, "Mr. Holbrook and the Humanities"; Jacob Neusner, "Do Others Face this Problem?" *Bulletin of the American Academy of Religion* (hereafter *BAAR* 4 (1967), 17–19; Victor Nuovo, "A Response to Prof. Neusner," *BAAR* 4 (1967), 3–4; Ross Jackson, "A Response to Dr. Neusner," *BAAR* 4 (1967), 5–6; William A. Beardslee, "The Undergraduate Professor of Religion: Stabilizer or Prophet?" *BAAR* 4 (1967), 7–10; Henry O. Thompson, "On the Personal Dimension of Academic Religion," *BAAR* 4 (1967), 7–8; Roy W. Battenhouse, "A Strategy and Some Tactics for Teaching in Religion," and Stephen T. Cary, "The Study of Religion as an Academic Discipline," in *Religious Studies in Public Universities*, ed. Milton D. McLean (Carbondale, IL, 1967), 29–34, 35–44; Van A. Harvey, "Reflections on the Teaching of Religion in America," *Journal of the American Academy of Religion* (hereafter *JAAR*) 38 (1970), 17–29; Wilson, "Introduction: The Background and Present Context"; and Robert S. Mi-

chaelsen, "The Engaged Observer: Portrait of a Professor of Religion," *JAAR* 40 (1972), 419-24.

40. Welch, *Graduate Education in Religion*. On the need for the report, see Claude Welch, "Reflections on the Academic Study of Religion: Patterns, Problems, and Prospects," *ACLS Newsletter* 19 (October 1968), 1-8. Welch also composed a report for the Association of American Colleges. See *Religion in the Undergraduate Curriculum: An Analysis and Interpretation*, ed. Claude Welch (Washington, DC, 1972).

41. Welch, *Graduate Education in Religion*, 24, 25, 24. For reactions to the report among religion scholars, see William A. Clebsch, "Is Mr. Welch Itching Where He Ain't Scratching?" *Bulletin of the Council for the Study of Religion* (hereafter *BCSR*) 3 (1972), 4-7; Samuel Sandmel, "The Welch Survey: One Man's Opinion," *BCSR* 3 (1972), 8-12; John F. Wilson "Where Do We Go? Reflections on the ACLS Appraisal of Graduate Education in Religion," *BCSR* 3 (1972), 13-16; and Robert Michaelsen, "The Future of Graduate Studies in Religion," *BCSR* 3 (1972), 17 20.

42. Welch, *Graduate Education in Religion*, 94-95. For reactions from the seminary world, see Paul L. Bechtold, Arthur R. McKay, and William E. Hull, "Some Implications of the ACLS Study for Education in the Theological Seminaries," *Theological Education* 8 (1972), 83-120.

43. *The Study of Religion in Colleges and Universities*, ed. John F. Wilson and Paul Ramsey (Princeton, 1970).

44. J. Wesley Robb, "The Hidden Philosophical Agenda: A Commentary on Humanistic Psychology," 37 *JAAR* (1969), 3-14; John C. Meagher, "Pictures at an Exhibition: Reflections on Exegesis and Theology," 47 *JAAR* (1979), 3-20; Charles H. Long, "Cargo Cults as Cultural Historical Phenomenon," 42 *JAAR* (1974), 403-14; and William F. May, "Institutions as Symbols of Death," 44 *JAAR* (1976), 211-23. For figures on the publishing trends of the AAR during the 1970s, see Ray L. Hart, "*JAAR* in the Seventies: Unconcluding Unscientific Postface," 47 *JAAR* (1979), 513-16.

45. For the growing reliance on the history of religions in American religious studies, see Kitagawa, "Humanistic and Theological History of Religions"; idem, "The History of Religions in America," in *The History of Religions: Essays in Methodology*, ed. Mircea Eliade and Joseph M. Kitagawa (Chicago, 1959), 1-30; idem, "The History of Religions (*Religionswissenschaft*) Then and Now," in *The History of Religions: Retrospect and Prospect* (New York, 1985), 121-44; Darrow, "The Harvard Way"; John F. Wilson, *Research Guide to Religious Studies* (Washington, DC, 1982), 17-19, 101-3; Grant Wacker, "Liberal Protestants and the Challenge of World Religions, 1890-1960" (ms., 1986), 20-28; Eric J. Sharpe, *Comparative Religion, A History* (London, 1975); Remus, Lusby,

Tober, "Religion as an Academic Discipline," 1664–69; Kathryn O. Alexander, "Religious Studies in American Higher Education since Schempp: A Bibliographical Essay," *Soundings* 71 (1988), 389–412; *Contemporary Approaches to the Study of Religion*, 2 vols., ed. Frank Whaling (Berlin, 1983 and 1985); and *Methodological Issues in Religious Studies*, ed. Robert D. Baird (Chico, CA, 1975). For examples of ambitious claims on behalf of the history of religions, see Philip H. Ashby, "The History of Religions," in Ramsey, *Religion*, 1–50; and H. P. Sullivan, "The History of Religions: Some Problems and Prospects," in Ramsey and Wilson, *The Study of Religion in Colleges and Universities*, 246–80.

46. For an argument on behalf of diversity and humanistic methods, see John F. Wilson, "Developing the Study of Religion in America," *Journal of General Education* 20 (1968), 190–208. For arguments in support of theology in the university, see George A. Lindbeck, *University Divinity Schools: A Report on Ecclesiastically Independent Theological Education* (New York, 1976); and "Religious Studies/Theological Studies: The St. Louis Project," *JAAR* 52 (1984), 727–57. For a balanced perspective on the benefits and liabilities of the social sciences in the study of religion, see Mark A. Noll, "'And the Lion Shall Lie Down with the Lamb': The Social Sciences and Religious History," *Fides et Historia* 20 (1988), 5–30. Ironically, the AAR was not as methodologically precise as social scientists wanted it to be. As a result, social scientists who studied religion went their own way in 1969 by pulling their Society for the Scientific Study of Religion out of the Council for the Study of Religion, an organization which had included the AAR and the Society of Biblical Literature. For background on the division, see John H. Schultz, "Editorial," *BCSR* 1 (1970), 2; Robert N. Bellah, "Confessions of a Former Establishment Fundamentalist," *BCSR* 1 (1970), 3–6; and James E. Dittes, "Confessing Away the Soul with the Sins, or: The Risks of Uncle Tomism among the Humanists. A Reply to Robert Bellah," *BCSR* 1 (1970), 22–5.

47. Veysey, "Plural Organized Worlds," 57–62; idem, "Higher Education as a Profession: Changes and Continuities," in *The Professions in American History*, ed. Nathan O. Hatch (Notre Dame, 1988), 15–32; and Bruce Kuklick, "The Professionalization of the Humanities," in *Applying the Humanities*, ed. Daniel Callahan, Arthur L. Caplan, and Bruce Jennings (New York, 1985), 41–54. For standard accounts of professionalization, see Furner, *Advocacy*; Robert A. McGaughey, "Transformation of American Academic Life: Harvard University, 1821–1892," *Perspectives in American History* 8 (1974), 237–332; Haskell, *Emergence*; and Burton J. Bledstein, *The Culture of Professionalism: The Middle Class and the Development of Higher Education in America* (New York, 1976). See also Samuel Haber, "The Professions and Higher Education in America: A Historical View," in

Higher Education and the Labor Market, ed. Margaret S. Gordon (New York, 1974), 237–80; and the essays in Oleson and Voss, *Organization of Knowledge*.

48. Ross, "Development of the Social Sciences," 121. See also Furner, *Advocacy*; and Haskell, *Emergence*.

49. On the cultural crisis generated by the two world wars, see Higham, "Schism." On the alliance of religious studies with philosophical idealism, see Wilson, "Mr. Holbrook and the Humanities."

50. Wacker, "Liberal Protestantism," 21ff.; Kitagawa, "Humanistic and Theological History of Religions," 209–12; Lyman H. Legters, "The Place of Religion in Foreign Area Studies," *JAAR* 35 (1967), 159–64; Lewis Perry, *Intellectual Life in America: A History* (New York, 1984), ch. 8; Sydney Ahlstrom, "The Radical Turn in Theology and Ethics: Why It Occurred in the 1960s," *Annals of the American Academy of Political and Social Science* 387 (1970), 1–13.

51. "American Academy of Religion," in *A Report to the Congress of the United States on "The State of the Humanities" and the Reauthorization of the National Endowment for the Humanities by the American Council of Learned Societies* (New York, 1985), 3–4; Larson, "An Introduction," 194. On the current disarray within the humanities, see ACLS report, viii–xii. For proposals calling for more reflection about the history of the field, see Larson, "An Introduction," 256; Eric J. Sharpe, "Religious Studies, the Humanities, and the History of Ideas," *Soundings* 71 (1988), 258; and Philip E. Hammond, "The Relationship between Method and Theory," *Soundings* 71 (1988), 372. On the variety of models within the field, see Remus, Lusby, and Tober, "Religion as an Academic Discipline," 1664–68.

8

American Catholic Higher Education, 1940–1990: The Ideological Context

PHILIP GLEASON

> When I look back now at the Catholic colleges and seminaries
> I knew in the late 1930s, they appear so strange and different
> that I am almost tempted to believe that they existed on
> another planet.[1]   Theodore M. Hesburgh, c.s.c., 1984

Catholic higher education has changed so much over the past half-century that it is impossible to cover the whole subject in a brief essay. Hence this chapter will focus on the ideological dimension— that is, on the underlying religious and cultural assumptions that shaped the general outlook of Catholic educators. Some attention will also be given to social and institutional factors that influenced the development of Catholic colleges and universities. But focusing primarily on shifts in overall outlook is, I believe, the best way to impose order on the story of Catholic higher education since the Second World War.

The Situation in 1940

There were on the eve of the war almost two hundred American Catholic colleges and universities, with a total enrollment of just under 162,000.[2] Despite an awareness of weaknesses at the graduate level and in scholarship generally, the morale of Catholic educators was high. Indeed, their outlook could be called triumphal, for they believed that a mighty Catholic intellectual and cultural revival was under way and that it was being carried forward on the tide of history itself.

On the negative side, their triumphalism rested on the conviction that the modern world was in crisis because it had turned its back on God. Intellectual and moral relativism, the breakdown of family life, economic collapse, totalitarianism, war—these were the results of "secularism," that is, disregard of God and of divine law in private and public life. On the positive side, what was sometimes called the Catholic Renaissance embodied two beliefs: that the truth of the Catholic religion constituted the sovereign remedy for the ills of the modern world, and that contemporary Catholic thinkers were propounding those truths with ever greater effect. The Thomistic revival, as personified in Jacques Maritain and Etienne Gilson, was central to the whole movement; the English convert and historian Christopher Dawson was also very influential, especially in formulating the goal of the Catholic Revival in terms of a revitalized Christian culture.[3]

"Catholic Action," which Pope Pius XI defined as the participation of the laity in the apostolate of the hierarchy, reached the United States in full force in the 1930s. It furnished a new rallying cry and a new programmatic basis for systematic efforts to overcome secularism and create a truly Catholic culture in its place. The liturgical movement and the theology of the Mystical Body of Christ, which took hold about the same time as Catholic Action, blended beautifully with it, furnishing, along with Thomism, the spiritual underpinning of the Catholic Revival.[4] The note of affectively intense spirituality, which permeated the work of the major literary figures of the revival and, indeed, the whole movement, was expressed most succinctly by Leon Bloy: "There is only one sadness; not to be saints."[5]

This self-consciously counter-cultural outlook dominated the mental world of Catholic educators on the eve of the Second World War and persisted well into the post-war era. How did it express itself in practice? First and foremost in the amount of classroom time devoted to Scholastic philosophy and the emphasis placed on its study as the unifying and integrating element in the curriculum.

In the early 1930s requirements in philosophy ranged from twelve to fourteen hours (the average in forty-one women's colleges surveyed) to twenty-four hours, which was proposed as the minimum for non-majors by a leading Thomist; as late as the mid-sixties, Georgetown still required all arts and sciences students to take eighteen hours of philosophy.[6] After the late 1930s theology challenged philosophy's prerogative as the integrating study, but the respective curricular roles of the two disciplines remained murky, not least because both were included under the rubric of Thomism.[7]

In the mid-thirties Catholics hailed Robert M. Hutchins and Mortimer J. Adler as allies in the effort to make metaphysics the integrating element in undergraduate education. For his part, Hutchins challenged Catholic educators to live up to their own heritage, a challenge that inspired Samuel Knox Wilson, s.J., president of Loyola University (Chicago), to begin publication of a newsletter serving the college and university department of the National Catholic Educational Association (NCEA).[8]

Apart from philosophy and theology, the curricular impact of the revival mentality was most clearly visible in courses focusing specifically on the Catholic Literary Revival, which had been introduced in twenty-five institutions by 1939.[9] Courses on marriage and the family were likewise multiplying rapidly. They too were intimately related to the revival, since re-establishing the family on a truly Christian basis was perhaps the most fundamental element in the battle against secularism. Indeed, the Catholic large-family ethos, which continued strongly through the 1950s, affected more Catholic collegians, and affected them more profoundly, than any other aspect of the Catholic Revival outlook.[10] Closely related were the crusades against indecency on the screen and in literature. Although not centered in the colleges, and despite the discomfiture they caused Catholic intellectuals by mid-century, the Legion of Decency and the drive against "smut" on the newsstands enlisted the energies of an active minority and helped shape the moral sensibility of Catholic collegians for a quarter-century.[11]

Both the American Catholic Sociological Society (established 1938) and the Catholic Economic Association (1941) strove to translate *Quadragesimo Anno*'s corporative features into terms that Americans could understand, but "Catholic social teaching" was probably more talked about than actually taught in a systematic way. Apostolically oriented faculty and students, however, threw themselves into various movements aimed at building a better social order, and many of the "Catholic labor schools" that burgeoned in the late thirties and forties had some sort of connection with Catholic colleges and universities. The most successful adult-education program—Chicago's Sheil School of Social Studies (established 1943)—drew heavily on personnel from the seminaries and colleges of the area.[12]

In addition to the sociologists' and economists' associations already mentioned, a number of other Catholic professional societies, newly formed for the most part, took their place in the ranks of "organized Catholic intelligence."[13] The Catholic Renascence Society (1940), the very namesake of the revival, made explicit the relation between these societies and the cultural resurgence of the Catholic church. Revivalist intellectual militance animated, in greater or lesser degree, the NCEA (1904), the American Catholic Historical Association (1919), the American Catholic Philosophical Association (1926), the Catholic Anthropological Conference (1926), the Catholic Book Club (1928), the Catholic Poetry Society (1931), the Catholic Biblical Association (1936), the Catholic Theatre Conference (1937), the Catholic Art Association (1937), the Canon Law Society (1939), the Catholic Theological Society of America (1946), and the American Catholic Psychological Association (1947). Academics constituted the backbone of membership in most of these organizations, many of which began publishing specialized journals within a year or so of their foundation. In addition, *Orate Fratres* (1926) and *Liturgical Arts* (1931) publicized the liturgical renewal; *Thought* (1926) and the *Review of Politics* (1939) provided scholarly commentary over a wide range of issues; the *Thomist* (1939) and *Theological Studies* (1940), published by the Dominicans and the Jesuits, respectively, represented new levels of professionalism in philosophy and theology.

Different from the professional academic bodies, but equally permeated by the spirit of the Catholic Revival, were a number of action-oriented movements. The best known of these, Dorothy Day's Catholic Worker movement (1933), awakened the apostolic zeal of many Catholic collegians (and faculty members), drawing them into active participation in the CW or other "social-action" causes. The Catholic Interracial Council (1934) likewise won a small but influential following in the colleges; wartime attention to improving race relations fostered its growth, and in the post-war era Catholic Actionists across the board were sensitized to the "sin of segregation."[14]

Two national organizations of Catholic high school and college students—the Catholic Students' Mission Crusade and the Sodality of the Blessed Virgin Mary—threw themselves into Catholic Action (CA for short), including the cause of racial justice. The Sodality was especially important. Its Jesuit sponsorship linked it to the program of the most influential Catholic teaching order; its dynamic director, Daniel A. Lord, S.J., built up a vast organization (thirteen thousand units at its peak) and invested it with his own enthusiasm. Besides its national Summer Schools of Catholic Action, the Sodality spun off a city-wide network in Chicago known as CISCA (Chicago Inter-Student Catholic Action). By 1940 CISCA enrolled some three thousand members, about a third of whom were said to be "true blue" CA activists. Two of the giants of post-war Catholic liberalism—*Commonweal* editors John Cogley and James O'Gara—began their journalistic careers on CISCA's bi-weekly *Today* (established 1945).[15]

In addition to CISCA and the Sheil School, CA in Chicago included two Catholic Worker centers, Bishop Sheil's CYO (Catholic Youth Organization), a chapter of the Association of Catholic Trade Unionists, a Catholic Labor Alliance, and the first home of the Grail, a Catholic women's movement originally founded in Holland.[16] The spirit of these movements penetrated deeply into Catholic schools and colleges, and Monsignor Reynold J. Hillenbrand, rector of the archdiocesan seminary, played a key role in introducing another one that was primarily centered in institutions of higher education. This was "specialized Catholic Action" or "Jocism," pioneered by Belgium's Canon Joseph Cardijn and known in the United States as Young Christian Workers (YCW) and Young Christian Students (YCS). As a result of co-operation between Hillenbrand and Louis J. Putz, C.S.C., of the University of Notre Dame, YCW/YCS established a foothold on the eve of the Second World War, inspiring an elite of CA "militants" who carried the Catholic campaign against secularism into the post-war years.[17]

Post-War Cross-Currents

The war reinforced the Catholic Revival and at the same time set off countervailing forces that worked against it, or at least in tension with it.[18]

By way of reinforcement, the war confirmed the Catholic diagnosis that Western culture was in crisis—was indeed threatened with destruction.[19] The revelation it provided of the depths of human depravity and of the demonic power of evil made religion intellectually respectable once again. Protestant neo-orthodoxy as expounded by Reinhold Niebuhr enjoyed the greatest éclat, but Catholic thinkers such as Jacques Maritain (who resided at Princeton from 1948 to 1961) were also taken seriously; Maritain's refugee compatriot and fellow Thomist Ives Simon moved from Notre Dame to the University of Chicago. The Jesuit John Courtney Murray's invitation to serve as visiting professor at Yale in 1951–52 marked a breakthrough, for he was the first American Catholic theologian to be so honored. On a more popular level, a broadly based "revival of religion" arose in the immediate post-war years and persisted into the mid-fifties.

Accompanying the religious revival was a more general rehabilitation of traditional ideas in various areas of life. There was, for example, a widespread reawakening of interest in the liberal arts, and a corresponding reaction against "progressive education," of which the Harvard report on general education and Arthur Bestor's *Educational Wastelands* (1953) were, perhaps, the most widely known manifestations.

Catholics endorsed these developments enthusiastically. John J. Cavanaugh, c.s.c., the president of Notre Dame, personally taught a Great Books group that eventuated into a new curricular structure in the university (the General Program of Liberal Education); his successor as president, Theodore M. Hesburgh, c.s.c., inaugurated a major curricular self-study intended to integrate the undergraduate liberal arts program around the study of philosophy and theology. Other widely noted curricular experiments were undertaken at St. Xavier College in Chicago and Manhattan College in New York, while the Catholic University of America sponsored a series of summer workshops on curricular integration.[20]

These workshops, and most other Catholic theorizing on the subject, stressed the unifying role of neoscholastic philosophy and theology. But Christopher Dawson, who entered the discussion in the early fifties, argued that the core of Catholic collegiate education should be integrated around study of the culture inspired by the Christian religion. Despite his eminence and the interest aroused by Dawson's suggestions, they had little effect in practical terms: only St. Mary's College in Indiana introduced a two-year "Program in Christian Culture" as an optional undergraduate major.[21]

In political and social thought, Russell Kirk's book *The Conservative Mind* (1953) heralded the appearance of what was called the New Conservatism. It was institutionalized at the level of rough-and-tumble journalism by the *National Review*, founded in 1955 by William F. Buckley, a Catholic who established himself as conservative *infant terrible* with *God and Man at Yale* (1951), an exposé of secular liberalism. Cold War anti-communism of course put American Catholics on the right side of the fence politically. "In the era of security clearances," as Daniel P. Moynihan's witticism had it, "to be an Irish Catholic became *prima facie* evidence of loyalty. Harvard men were to be checked; Fordham men would do the checking."[22]

Reinforced by these culture-wide developments, the Catholic critique of secularism reached its high tide in the late forties, with formal statements by the American hierarchy and the commentaries they occasioned. The closely related Catholic family-life drive, which likewise continued to expand, embraced everything from hierarchically sponsored programs through expanded academic offerings to the virulently anti-modern large-family ethos of the Catholic radicals associated with *Integrity* magazine. The most popular new movements were the Cana Conference and the Christian Family Movement, the latter being a continuation for married couples of Jocist-inspired Catholic Action.[23]

But, as we used to learn in high school physics, to every action there is an equal and opposite reaction. The Catholic intellectual and cultural revival was no exception. Its very strength eventually set off a strong backlash among Protestants and secular liberals, who were grievously offended by what came across to them as arrogance and aggressiveness on the part of Catholics.[24] This reaction had already begun before the war, owing especially to Father Charles E. Coughlin's anti-Semitism and Catholic support for Franco in the Spanish Civil War. It continued to fester below the surface during the early forties, but could not express itself freely because of the need for national unity in wartime. When that restraint was lifted, the stage was set for an eruption of anti-Catholic feeling.

Protestants and liberals had many complaints, but the school question, church and state, the use of pressure tactics on birth control and other moral issues, and Catholic "authoritarianism" headed the list. The prospect of federal aid to education, and the question whether parochial schools would be eligible for it, set off fierce polemics that coincided with and were intensified by a series of Supreme Court rulings on the question of church and state as it relates to education. One by product of the *Everson* decision in 1947 was the founding of the POAU (Protestants and Other Americans United for Separation of Church and State), which, although it later came to be regarded as an extremist anti-Catholic group, included highly respectable leaders of mainstream Protestantism among its charter members.

The alleged divisiveness of Catholic schools drew criticism from leading establishment figures such as James B. Conant, the former president of Harvard, and Paul Blanshard spoke for the liberal intelligentsia in portraying "Catholic power" as a threat to "American freedom." Senator Joseph R. McCarthy's irresponsible charges of communist subversion came shortly after Blanshard's blast against Catholic authoritarianism. The fact that McCarthy was himself a Catholic and had strong Catholic support made it natural to add McCarthyism to the list of grievances liberals held against Catholics for their political behavior.

Catholics, of course, rejected the charges brought by their critics, interpreting them as expressions of old-fashioned religious bigotry. But at the same time they were concerned to remove any legitimate grounds for complaint. For this reason—and also because their wartime experiences had engendered among them a deeper appreciation for American liberalism (meaning primarily freedom, tolerance, and pluralism)—Catholics began to search for ways to accommodate the teachings of the church to the American situation in a more positive way.

The most obvious, and by far the most important, example of the more accommodating approach was John Courtney Murray's reformulation of the Catholic teaching on church and state.[25] Although Murray also reacted to "the new nativism" with vigorous polemics, it is noteworthy that he took up the church-state project when the anti-Catholic backlash was in full flood. He was working at a high level of abstraction, to be sure, but his irenic approach to religious freedom encouraged a more favorable assessment of democratic liberalism all along the line. The same is true of two books by Jacques Maritain—*Man and the State* (1951) and *Reflections on America* (1957)—both of which were generous in their praise of the American experiment. A like spirit manifested itself in the post-war outpouring of Catholic historical scholarship which interpreted the ecclesiastical controversies of the 1880s and 1890s in terms very favorable to the liberal "Americanists." And the new appreciation for American-style liberalism affected other Catholic academics as much as it did historians.

As had long been true, post-war changes in the larger world of American higher education—for example, upgraded standards in respect to teacher-training programs—affected Catholic institutions in ways that brought them into closer contact with non-Catholic educators.[26] Among students in Catholic colleges and universities, a positive desire to expand their horizons and cooperate with their non-Catholic counterparts expressed itself in enthusiastic Catholic participation in the National Student Association, which came into being (with a strong assist from YCS militants) in 1947. The same enthusiasm produced a high-quality (albeit short-lived) publication called *Concord*, which was put out at Notre Dame under YCS auspices but was dedicated to serving the international student movement on a non-sectarian basis.[27]

The leading organ of the new Catholic liberalism was the weekly magazine *Commonweal*, which was widely read in the Catholic academic community. Although it rejected what Murray called "the new nativism" of Paul Blanshard and championed neoscholastic natural law as the guiding principle in social and political matters, *Commonweal* also denounced McCarthyism, deprecated Catholic pressure-group tactics, and deplored Legion of Decency philistinism. Most pertinent in this context, it spearheaded the campaign against "Catholic separatism" and the "siege mentality." What

Catholics ought to do, in the view of *Commonweal*'s editors, was break out of their "ghetto" of self-imposed isolation, accept the reality of American pluralism, and plunge into "the mainstream" by cooperating with non-Catholics of good will in the effort to build a better society.[28]

The mainstream policy, as one may call it, implied a strategy at odds with the older ideal of creating a distinctively Catholic culture and converting others to it. No one seemed to realize that at the time—or, if they did, they refrained from calling attention to the point. The proponents of the new approach were, however, overtly critical of Catholic "ghetto organizations," that is, the specialized scholarly and professional associations set up in part to help create a Catholic culture. The problem was that these organizations had the practical effect of cutting Catholics off from their professional peers. Indeed, some were unkind enough to imply that their func tion was to provide a protective cocoon for persons too timid to venture into the "real world" of "big-time" scholarship. Eventually, even parochial schools, which were expanding at a fantastic pace and which most Catholics defended passionately, came in for criticism from "*Commonweal* Catholics" because they reinforced separatism and because of their allegedly low academic quality.

The self-criticism and rejection of earlier modes of thinking that were implicit in this anti-ghettoism erupted in volcanic fashion after the publication in 1955 of Monsignor John Tracy Ellis's famous critique of American Catholic intellectual life.[29] This episode, which had particular relevance for institutions of higher education, well illustrates the cross-currents affecting American Catholics at mid-century. On the one hand, Ellis was unsparing in his indictment of Catholic failures in the realm of ideas, culture, and influence on American society; and despite the many other contributing factors, he laid most of the blame for the mediocre performance of Catholic scholars on their "self-imposed ghetto mentality." On the other hand, his address was originally delivered before a typical "ghetto" organization (the Catholic Commission on Intellectual and Cultural Affairs); and, far from calling on his fellow religionists to abandon their distinctive intellectual position, Ellis exhorted them to present it more effectively.

The overwhelming weight of Ellis's message was, however, critical, and its effect was all in that direction: self-criticism and a "search for excellence" along the model of Harvard or Berkeley became the order of the day in the late 1950s.[30] The self-critical mood coincided with and reinforced the efforts to upgrade their graduate programs that many Catholic institutions had undertaken in the post-war era. But expansion of graduate work, along with the overall growth of enrollments, required Catholic universities to hire more lay faculty members, many of whom had received their training in leading secular universities; this trend, of course, continued through the higher education boom of the 1960s. Even though most of these new faculty members were Catholics, they belonged to a more socially assimilated post-war generation and had imbibed more of the atmosphere of secular higher education than earlier cohorts of Catholic academics.[31] Understandably enough, they thought it more important to improve Catholic scholarship than to align their intellectual interests with a distinctively Catholic viewpoint, or to concern themselves with how their findings might be integrated into an overall synthesis.[32]

It is clear in retrospect that by 1960 the mentality of the Catholic Renaissance had sunk below the intellectual horizon of Catholic higher education. At the same time, the appearance of "two men named John"—Pope John XXIII and John F. Kennedy—gave promise of the dawn of a new era in American Catholicism. But despite the self-criticism of the fifties, Catholic academics did not suspect that the coming decade would witness a wholesale rejection of the assumptions that had dominated their thinking since the early thirties.

The New Era:
Early Sixties to the Present

The seismic upheaval that shook American Catholicism in the 1960s resulted, as I see it, from the coming together of three streams of influence.[33] First, indigenous processes of change of the sort discussed in the preceding section not only prepared the ground for further change but also continued to make themselves felt with increasing force in the 1960s. The upward mobility, social assimilation, and political acceptance that made Catholics more and more like their non-Catholic neighbors inevitably called into question the need for a distinctively Catholic viewpoint on marriage, on education, and on practically everything else.[34]

Second, there was the influence of new European approaches to philosophy and theology. These began to filter onto the American Catholic scene after the Second World War, but their impact was vastly enhanced by the Second Vatican Council, which served as an extended crash course in the new theology, not only for the American bishops who took part in it but also for those who followed events from afar.[35] Moreover, the new conciliar-inspired outlook fitted beautifully with the general thrust of the first stream of influence mentioned earlier. The importance of this congruence between indigenous American and overseas influences has not, in my opinion, been sufficiently appreciated in discussions of the Catholic upheaval of the sixties.

Only a moment's reflection is required to bring out the depth of resonance that existed between conciliar and American themes— between collegiality and self-government; between people-of-God ecclesiology and democratic equality; between ecumenism and pluralistic tolerance; between the church's new respect for personal conscience and American individualism; between the council's pastoral orientation and our national predilection for the practical; between the concern for social justice and American social activism; between the church's opening to the modern world and American this-worldliness. The council, in other words, summoned American Catholics to move in the direction in which they were already going. By so doing it provided a new spiritual warrant for assimilation to American cultural norms.

The third stream of influence was more of a raging flood. I am referring, of course, to the social, political, and cultural upheaval that shook American society in the sixties as a result of the racial crisis, the Vietnam War and opposition to it, New Left radicalism, campus violence, the rise of the counter-culture, the sexual revolution, and women's liberation. This cultural maelstrom affected American Catholics by reinforcing and accelerating the two streams of influence already mentioned, while at the same time cutting across them and working at cross-purposes. It had the latter effect by virtue of the denunciation of America ("AmeriKKKa" to the most extreme of the radicals) that accompanied the upheaval. Although this anti-Americanism was largely rhetorical, it nevertheless complicates the picture I have sketched of an easy congruence between the several forces interacting on American Catholics in the sixties. But if it complicates the picture for us in retrospect, it did so in spades for people at the time. This anti-Americanism thus added immensely to the bewilderment, confusion, and sense of impending revolution (or breakdown) that characterized the period.

Despite this complication, the culture-wide eruption of the late sixties did indeed reinforce the two previously discussed streams of influence. It did so by virtue of the anti-traditional, anti-authoritarian—often, indeed, antinomian—spirit that permeated its various manifestations. Coming hard on the heels of a council that called hitherto accepted attitudes, beliefs, practices, and institutions into question, the cultural earthquake of the late sixties could not help exacerbating the Catholic crisis. On the one hand, Catholics heard it said that their church was corrupt and its leaders bankrupt. On the other, they heard that their country was a racist, imperialist monster, its leaders war criminals. The rhetoric of revolutionary politics merged with that of religious prophecy. Gestures of ritual sacrifice accompanied political dissent. Everything became intermingled, confounded, chaotic. The overall effect, however, was to discredit the past and lend plausibility to millennial projections for the future.[36]

The effects of this confluence of forces on Catholic higher education were manifold and profound. We have as yet nothing like a comprehensive view of what happened. The sketchy remarks that follow are based more on my impressions as participant-observer than on a systematic review of the evidence, for I have not researched this period in detail. With that caveat, let me outline events in schematic fashion.

The first stage, the early sixties, was dominated by a continuation of the themes of self-criticism and search for excellence that had emerged in the fifties. The optimism inspired by Pope John XXIII's call for *aggiornamento*, and the enthusiasm generated by Kennedy's presidential panache, lent new impetus to these indigenous developments. The opening of the council intensified the demands for freedom in the church, the need for which was dramatized for American Catholic academics by the repressive activities of Archbishop Egidio Vagnozzi as Apostolic Delegate. Vagnozzi's chief target was biblical scholarship, which did not directly affect the majority of institutions or faculty members since biblical studies were carried on almost exclusively by priests teaching in seminaries. But the council validated the biblical turn in theology, and the closer connections forged between priestly training and university studies later in the decade brought the sensitive issues associated with biblical interpretation more directly into the mainstream of Catholic higher education. Before that happened, however, the conciliar emphases on religious freedom and lay autonomy raised issues of academic freedom that were new for American Catholics. A great outcry followed the Catholic University of America's refusal to allow Hans Küng, John Courtney Murray, s.j., Gustave Weigel, s.j., and Godfrey Diekmann, o.s.b., to lecture in 1963. And the uproar set off by the firing of some thirty professors by St. John's University in 1965 can serve as the transitional point into the next phase of my expository scheme.[37]

In this second and far more feverish stage, which extended to 1970 or so, academic freedom issues multiplied and became more deeply entangled with conflicts over the scope of papal and episcopal authority and the limits (if any) of theological dissent. This was especially the case as a result of the reaction against *Humanae Vitae* in 1968. But by that time the culture-wide crisis was nearing its climax; the Catholic Left had embarked on its campaign of draft-board actions; and the importation of direct-action tactics to college campuses created scenes of turmoil never before witnessed in American higher education. In these circumstances academic freedom—which now seemed to some an elitist imposition designed to serve the power structure—receded rapidly from the forefront of live issues. True, it was a central problem for Catholic administrators newly embarked on a series of conferences, among themselves and with Rome, on how to combine the autonomy proper to a university with preservation of an institution's Catholic character.[38] Attempts to define the latter, however, revealed that Catholic educators—including those in the key area of theology—were no longer certain what constituted the distinctively *Catholic* curricular or programmatic elements in Catholic higher education.[39]

Thus we arrive at the famous "identity crisis." To get a closer view of the organizational and operational changes that accompanied its emergence, let us look briefly at a study of shifts in the religious orientation of the Catholic colleges and universities in New York

State between 1962 and 1972.[40] The author, Edward F. Maloney, s.j., found that the boards of trustees of the twenty-five institutions he studied had been to a greater or lesser extent laicized, a movement weakening the control exercised by sponsoring religious communities. The declining proportion of priests, brothers, and sisters as faculty members and administrators, and their replacement by lay persons (including many non-Catholics), contributed to the same effect; these changes, along with growing demands for a meaningful faculty role in governance, gave institutions much more autonomy vis-à-vis external religious authorities.

Maloney also reported that non-Catholic representation in student bodies had increased by 11 percent; that wholesale curricular revisions eliminated, or drastically reduced, course requirements in philosophy and theology; that more schools had become co-educational; that disciplinary regulation of student life was much less stringent than in the past; and that the atmosphere on the campuses had changed in many subtle ways, one symptom being a decline of student interest in strictly religious extracurricular organizations, which was accompanied by increased student sensitivity to social problems.

The catalogues of most of the institutions Maloney surveyed no longer stated their religious objectives in clear-cut terms, and in some cases remained entirely silent about them. The presidents he talked to confessed "an inability to articulate properly their religious objectives today, even though they want[ed] the college to have a strong religious orientation." Maloney concluded his summary by predicting that within a few years only about a fifth of the schools he had studied would still be calling themselves Catholic. His own recommendation was that Catholic colleges in New York emphasize values and "declare themselves as ecumenical colleges."[41]

The fact that state aid—the so-called Bundy money—was made available in New York to private colleges and universities that could demonstrate their non-sectarian character no doubt reinforced the movement toward secularization in that state.[42] But aside from the incentive this provided to modify the language of catalogues and drop the Catholic label, everything Maloney said of Catholic institutions in New York applied equally to other parts of the country.

The changes that overwhelmed Catholic higher education in this second phase of the new era can legitimately be called revolutionary when we view them against the background of the Catholic Revival mentality that had prevailed thirty years earlier. Clear-cut transitions are less easy to discern in the period that followed phase two.

Developments set in motion at that time have, of course, continued to make themselves felt. This is true, for example, of the decline in religious personnel, the enhancement of institutional autonomy, the appointment of more non-Catholics to faculties and administrative posts, and the deepening concern over the preservation of an institution's Catholic identity. The decline in vocations and continuing resignations from the religious life, along with the trend toward co-education, had the most severe impact on Catholic colleges for women, and these suffered the heaviest attrition.[43] Although the prospect of continuing decline in religious personnel and in financial support from sponsoring religious communities was not reassuring, the situation had stabilized by the early eighties. In fact, enrollment at Catholic women's colleges grew faster between 1978 and 1982 than in all Catholic institutions taken together. Much of the increase resulted from enrollments in part-time non-traditional programs, which Catholic women's colleges have developed very imaginatively.[44]

Non-traditional programs illustrate the kinds of practical adjustments Catholic institutions have made in response to the new situation created by the changes of the sixties. But what of responses in the ideological realm, that is, efforts to deal with the Catholic identity issue as such?

In one sense the amount of explicit attention devoted to the subject is in itself a significant response, for what it indicates is the recognition that something formerly taken for granted now has to be addressed as a problem requiring self-conscious and systematic attention.[45] Numerous essays by individuals, committee reports in various institutions, and self-studies undertaken by religious communities, as well as the regular contacts initiated in the 1970s between Catholic educators and a committee of American bishops, along with more irregular interaction with Vatican officials, all represent efforts to clarify the notion of Catholic identity and to define what it means in practical terms.[46]

In more substantive terms, efforts to define the religious character of Catholic institutions of higher learning take both a progressive or liberal direction and a traditional or conservative direction.

The two orientations are not directly opposed to each other, but tensions exist between them.

The progressive answer to the challenge is peace-and-justice education. This effort to specify the distinguishing mark of Catholic higher education is clearly related to the emphases of Vatican II, the social concerns of the sixties, and the emergence of liberation theology. Even before the 1971 Synod of Bishops declared endeavors for social justice "constitutive . . . to the preaching of the Gospel," curricular innovations such as Notre Dame's Program in Non-Violence and Manhattan College's peace studies major had been initiated. Over the next few years the Jesuits' strong institutional commitment to "the preferential option for the poor" involved the most influential of the teaching orders deeply in this work. In 1975 the Association of Catholic Colleges and Universities appointed a Task Force on Education for Justice and Peace, and during the eighties, peace-and-justice programs, curricular and co-curricular, multiplied rapidly in Catholic institutions large and small.[47]

Although systematically promoted by leaders who are simultaneously concerned about the identity issue, peace-and-justice programs were not put forward primarily as a solution to that problem. On the contrary, their promoters are sincerely convinced that this is what Catholic colleges and universities should be doing because of the intrinsic nature of their religious commitments. But specifying the programmatic implications of those commitments along peace-and-justice lines would, if widely enough accepted, in fact constitute a solution to the Catholic identity problem. And to say, as Peter Henriot, s.j., has said, that launching into peace-and-justice work would amount to a "second founding" for Catholic colleges suggests that its advocates are not unaware of this dimension and regard it as at least a desirable by-product of their program.[48]

The conservative approach to the identity problem stresses reaffirmation of traditional Catholic teachings.[49] Obviously this orientation comprises a wide range of positions from moderate to extreme, just as the progressive orientation does. In general, however, the conservative approach reflects the belief that things have gone too far, that the religious identity of Catholic institutions has been attenuated to the point of disappearance. It can legitimately be associated with what has been called the restorationist campaign pursued by Cardinal Joseph Ratzinger, with the support of Pope John Paul II. The case of Father Charles Curran's removal from the theological faculty at the Catholic University of America, and the issuance of Vatican guidelines for Catholic institutions of higher education, supply striking evidence of official ecclesiastical support for this conservative tendency.[50] Manifestations at the grass-roots level include the creation of institutions such as St. Thomas Aquinas College (California), Christendom College (Virginia), and the University of Dallas; the formation of groups such as the Fellowship of Catholic Scholars; and the emergence of neoconservative voices (for example, Michael Novak, Richard John Neuhaus, Alasdair MacIntyre) among Catholic intellectuals. And one frequently hears that today's undergraduates—for whom post-conciliar liberalism represents the conventional wisdom—respond eagerly to traditional orthodoxy.

Although this sketch of tendencies on the contemporary scene is impressionistic, it is quite clear that Catholic colleges and universities have yet to solve their identity problem. From the viewpoint of one who matured during the later stages of the Catholic Renaissance, what seems most grievously lacking today is consensus, not just about the content of religious faith but about the kind of difference—if any—religious faith ought to make in the intellectual work carried on by a Catholic institution of higher education. The old Catholic understanding of that issue has been transformed by the changes outlined in this chapter. In searching for new answers, Catholics might take heart from the realization that, as the volume of which this essay is a part suggests, they are not the only ones for whom such questions are meaningful.

Notes

1. Foreword by Theodore M. Hesburgh, c.s.c., in Paul A. Fitzgerald, s.j., *The Governance of Jesuit Colleges in the United States, 1920–1970* (Notre Dame, 1984), ix.

2. These figures, which are taken from the biennial survey of the National Catholic Welfare Conference, break down as follows: colleges for women, 116, with 47,838 students; men's colleges, 52, with 32,685 students; universities, men's and co-educational, 25, with 81,363 students.

3. See James Hitchcock, "Postmortem on a Rebirth," *American Scholar* 49 (Spring 1980), 211–25; William M. Halsey, *The Survival of American Innocence: Catholicism in an Era of Disillusionment, 1920–1940* (Notre Dame, 1980); and Arnold J. Sparr, *To Promote, Defend, and Redeem: The Catholic Literary Revival and the Cultural Transformation of American Catholicism, 1920–1960* (Westport, CT, 1990).

4. On the connections between Mystical Body theology, liturgical renewal, Catholic Action, and building a Catholic culture, see Gerald Ellard, "Catholic Cult and Culture," *Catholic Mind* 32 (February 8, 1934), 41–53; John Fitzsimons and Paul McGuire, eds., *Restoring All Things: A Guide to Catholic Action* (New York, 1938), 233; Mary Perkins, ed., *The Sacramental Way* (New York, 1948), 325. Ellard, a leading liturgist, reported in 1940 that emphasis on the Mystical Body had "come to the fore so rapidly in late years that we can all sympathize with the good soul who wearied her friends with a sudden enthusiasm for the 'mythical' body of Christ." Gerard Ellard, *Men at Work at Worship* (New York, 1940), 39.

5. Dolores Elise Brien, "Catholic Revival Revisited," *Commonweal* 106 (December 21, 1979), 714–16, emphasizes the search for sanctity; see also Joseph P. Chinnici, *Living Stones: The History and Structure of Catholic Spiritual Life in the United States* (New York, 1989), pts. 4 and 5. The quotation about sanctity is the concluding line of Leon Bloy, *The Woman Who Was Poor* (New York, 1939).

6. Sister Mary Thomas Aquinas, "Philosophy in Catholic Colleges for Women," *National Catholic Educational Association Bulletin* [hereafter *NCEAB*] 28 (November 1931), 144–52; ten years later a fifth of ninety-one women's colleges responding to a survey required eighteen or more credit hours of philosophy, and 71 percent required "the equivalent of two or more years of philosophy taken three times a week." See Sister M. Redempta Prose, *The Liberal Arts Ideal in Catholic Colleges for Women in the United States* (Washington, D.C., 1943), 54–59. For the ideal proposed in the early thirties, see Gerald B. Phelan, "The Sequence of Courses in Philosophy in the Undergraduate Department in Catholic Colleges," *NCEAB* 29 (November 1932), 102–8; for the situation at Georgetown, see Georgetown University Archives, file for Department of Philosophy, 1964ff. Apropos of the religious purpose served by philosophy, Phelan observed that teaching it was intended to guide the student in "the right way of thinking" about the truths necessary to attain salvation. See also Philip Gleason, "Neoscholasticism as Preconciliar Ideology," *U.S. Catholic Historian* 7 (Fall 1988), 401–11.

7. See Philip Gleason, *Keeping the Faith: American Catholicism Past and Present* (Notre Dame, 1987), 143–49. Describing his own earlier study

of philosophy, Daniel A. Lord, s.j., wrote in his autobiography: "The thing that struck me . . . [about philosophy] was the amazing unity and consistency of what I was learning. Philosophy . . . seemed more and more the structural steel of life's edifice. It was the blueprint of human existence. It laid out a clear road map for man's progress. I liked the fact that what religion had taught, philosophy strongly affirmed. It was good to find the Supreme Being and the soul and immortality and free will searched out by Plato and Aristotle and Socrates as they were taken for granted by the clear-minded Christ." Lord, *Played by Ear* (Chicago, 1956), 212–13.

8. Hutchins's critical remarks were delivered before the NCEA's Midwest Unit and printed by Wilson in his trial balloon issue (vol. 0, May 1937) of *College Newsletter*, a publication that continued to appear until the mid-1970s.

9. A survey presented to the Franciscan Educational Conference in 1940 reported 25 courses offered on the Catholic Literary Revival, 22 on modern Catholic writers, 20 on Dante in translation, 14 on Newman, and a wide scattering of others in topics such as the French Catholic revival, Francis Thompson, and so on. *Franciscan Educational Conference* 22 (1940), 397–98. See also Sparr, *To Promote, Defend, and Redeem*, 101–4.

10. See Jeffrey M. Burns, *American Catholics and the Family Crisis, 1930–1962: The Ideological and Organizational Response* (New York, 1988).

11. See Paul W. Facey, *The Legion of Decency: A Sociological Analysis of the Emergence and Development of a Social Pressure Group* (New York, 1974), and Harold C. Gardiner, *Catholic Viewpoint on Censorship* (Garden City, NY, 1958).

12. David J. O'Brien, *American Catholics and Social Reform: The New Deal Years* (New York, 1968), and Neil Betten, *Catholic Activism and the Industrial Worker* (Gainesville, FL, 1976), are helpful, but there is no comprehensive study of Catholic labor schools.

13. For a general treatment of Catholic academic societies, see David L. Salvaterra, *American Catholicism and the Intellectual Life, 1880–1950* (New York, 1988), ch. 5; for a detailed study of one such, the Catholic Biblical Association, see Gerald P. Fogarty, *American Catholic Biblical Scholarship* (San Francisco, 1989), chs. 11 and 12.

14. See Thomas J. Harte, *Catholic Organizations Promoting Negro-White Race Relations in the United States* (Washington, DC, 1947), esp. ch. 5; Richard J. Roche, *Catholic Colleges and the Negro Student* (Washington, DC, 1948); Martin A. Zielinski, "Working for Interracial Justice: The Catholic Interracial Council of New York, 1934–1964," *U.S. Catholic Historian* 7 (Spring-Summer 1988), 233–60; George H. Dunne, "The Sin of Segregation," *Commonweal* 42 (September 21, 1945), 542–45.

15. For Lord and the Sodality, see his autobiography, *Played by Ear*, and Sparr, *To Promote, Defend, and Redeem*, ch. 3; for CISCA, Edward R. Kantowicz, *Corporation Sole: Cardinal Mundelein and Chicago Catholicism* (Notre Dame, 1983), 280–81; Robert A. Senser, "Screwballs Extraordinary," *Catholic Digest* 5 (December 1940), 50–53; John Cogley, *A Canterbury Tale* (New York, 1976), 38. The first president of CISCA, Robert A. Hartnett, went on to become a Jesuit and an editor of *America*.

16. See Francis J. Sicius, *The Word Made Flesh: The Chicago Catholic Worker and the Emergence of Lay Activism in the Church* (Lanham, MD, 1990); Alden V. Brown, *The Grail Movement and American Catholicism, 1940–1975* (Notre Dame, 1989), ch. 2; Kantowicz, *Corporation Sole*, ch. 13; Dennis J. Geaney, "The Chicago Story," *Chicago Studies* 2 (Winter 1963), 287–300; and Andrew M. Greeley, *The Catholic Experience* (Garden City, NY, 1967), ch. 8. A forthcoming study by the Reverend Steven A. Avella of Cardinal Stritch College in Milwaukee sets these movements in the context of Chicago Catholicism in the 1940s and 1950s.

17. See Dennis M. Robb, "Specialized Catholic Action in the United States, 1936–1949" (Ph.D. diss., University of Minnesota, 1972).

18. For a discussion of post-1945 Catholic higher education that stresses its academic and intellectual weaknesses, see William P. Leahy, "Jesuits, Catholics, and Higher Education in Twentieth-Century America" (Ph.D. diss., Stanford University, 1986), ch. 5.

19. Thus the papers given at the tenth-anniversary meeting of the Catholic Renascence Society were published under the title *The Catholic Renascence in a Disintegrating World*, ed. Norman Weyand (Chicago, 1951).

20. The proceedings of the workshops, edited by Roy J. Deferrari, were published by the CUA press. The most relevant of the series were *The Philosophy of Catholic Higher Education* (1948); *Integration in Catholic Colleges and Universities* (1950); *Discipline and Integration in the Catholic College* (1951); *The Curriculum of the Catholic College* (*Integration and Concentration*) (1952); and *Theology, Philosophy, and History as Integrating Disciplines* (1953). Of related interest are Leo R. Ward, *Blueprint for a Catholic University* (St. Louis, 1949), and William F. Cunningham, *General Education and the Liberal College* (St. Louis, 1953), the latter of which grew out of an abortive effort by the NCEA to produce a consensus statement on liberal arts education.

21. For curricular proposals and a description of the St. Mary's College program, see Christopher Dawson, *The Crisis of Western Education* (New York, 1961), 207–46.

22. Nathan Glazer and Daniel P. Moynihan, *Beyond the Melting Pot* (Cambridge, MA, 1963), 271; Donald F. Crosby, *God, Church, and Flag:*

Senator Joseph R. McCarthy and the Catholic Church, 1950–1957 (Chapel Hill, 1978).

23. See Burns, *American Catholics and the Family Crisis*.

24. For the literature on which the discussion that follows is based, see my article "Pluralism, Democracy, and Catholicism in the Era of World War II," *Review of Politics* 49 (Spring 1987), 208–30.

25. See Donald E. Pelotte, *John Courtney Murray: Theologian in Conflict* (New York, 1976), esp. chs. 1–2; and Gerald P. Fogarty, *The Vatican and the American Hierarchy from 1870 to 1965* (paperback ed., Wilmington, DE, 1985), chs. 14–15.

26. For example, the formation of the American Association of Colleges of Teacher Education in 1948 prompted Catholic educators to pay closer attention to the activities of the National Education Association, and contributed to the movement that led to the Sisters' Formation Conference in the 1950s. See *College Newsletter* [hereafter *CL*] 14 (December 1950), 5; *CL* 14 (May 1951), 2; *CL* 15 (December 1951), 1; *CL* 16 (May 1953), 6; and, for a general study, M. Patrice Noterman, "An Interpretive History of the Sister Formation Conference, 1954–1964" (Ph.D. diss., Loyola University, Chicago, 1988). For the *College Newsletter*, see note 7.

27. *Concord* appeared as a monthly (during the academic year only) between October 1947 and December 1949. It contains much information on NSA; see also Philip G. Altbach, *Student Politics in America: A Historical Analysis* (New York, 1974), 122ff.

28. See the volume of essays from *Commonweal* titled *Catholicism in America* (New York, 1953), and, for a general study, Rodger Van Allen, *The Commonweal and American Catholicism* (Philadelphia, 1974).

29. Ellis, "American Catholics and the Intellectual Life," *Thought* 30 (Autumn 1955), 351–88. For discussion, see Gleason, *Keeping the Faith*, 71ff., and John Whitney Evans, "American Catholics and the Intellectual Life: Thirty Years Later," in *Studies in Catholic History in Honor of John Tracy Ellis*, ed. Nelson H. Minnich et al. (Wilmington, DE, 1985), 366–91.

30. Items that could be called post-Ellis fallout were reported in *CL* 19 (March 1956), 3; *CL* 19 (May 1956), 1–6; *CL* 20 (October 1956); for the search for excellence, see *CL* 22 (May 1959), 4. The expansion of facilities (which was primarily a response to the pressure of numbers, but not unrelated to the search for excellence) was regularly reported in *CL*; see, for example, *CL* 23 (November 1959), 15–19.

31. See John D. Donovan, *The Academic Man in the Catholic College* (New York, 1964), esp. 83, 193ff. This book, incidentally, was commissioned by the CCICA as part of that body's post-Ellis follow-up. Of interest as indicative of a more professional concern for the needs of laypersons in

Catholic institutions is the detailed discussion of "Fringe Benefits and Faculty Personnel Matters," *CL* 22 (June 1959), 1, 7–10.

32. For interesting perspectives on the processes of change among Catholic sociologists, see the articles in the fiftieth anniversary issue of *Sociological Analysis* 50 (1989), especially the contributions of Loretta M. Morris, Peter Kivisto, Paul Reiss, and Thomas Imse.

33. For fuller discussion, and citation of the literature on which the interpretation that follows is based, see Gleason, *Keeping the Faith*, chs. 3–4, 7–9. See also David O'Brien, *Public Catholicism* (New York, 1989), 232–34, for the same three-fold identification of forces.

34. Consider the following series, all published by Hanover House (Garden City, NY): John LaFarge, *Catholic Viewpoint on Race Relations* (1956); John L. Thomas, *Catholic Viewpoint on Marriage and the Family* (1958); Harold Gardiner, *Catholic Viewpoint on Censorship* (1958); Neil McCluskey, *Catholic Viewpoint on Education* (1958); Anthony F. Zimmerman, *Catholic Viewpoint on Overpopulation* (1961); and Jerome G. Kerwin, *Catholic Viewpoint on Church and State* (1961).

35. See Thomas F. O'Dea, *The Catholic Crisis* (Boston, 1968), which stresses the importance of the council's Pastoral Constitution on the Church in the Modern World, *Gaudium et Spes*.

36. This adopts, without direct quotation, some language from Gleason, *Keeping the Faith*, 88–89. For the activities of the "Catholic Left" in the anti-war movement, see Charles A. Meconis, *With Clumsy Grace: The American Catholic Left, 1961–1975* (New York, 1979), which notes the importance of CW and YCS influences on many of the leaders of the movement.

37. Pelotte, *Murray*, 81; Daniel Callahan, *The New Church: Essays in Catholic Reform* (New York, 1966), esp. ch. 11; Fogarty, *Biblical Scholarship*, chs. 13–14; Joseph Scimecca and Roland Damiano, *Crisis at St. John's* (New York, 1967); Edward Manier and John Houck, eds. *Academic Freedom and the Catholic University* (Notre Dame, 1967).

38. For the early stages of this development, see Neil G. McCluskey, ed., *The Catholic University: A Modern Appraisal* (Notre Dame, 1970), esp. 1–28, 336–65; for later developments, see the discussion by Ann Ida Gannon, cited at note 46.

39. A late-1960s faculty report on academic freedom at the University of Dayton, a Catholic institution, declared that the university should be secularized, "for to be secularized means to come of age, to come into the time and forms of the city of man today." At about the same time, the faculty of religious education at the Catholic University of America abandoned the systematic presentation of Catholic teaching, adopting instead a history-of-religions approach that stressed "man's search for meaning." At

Marquette University the theology program was reformed to reflect the "fragmentation" that actually existed since "hypothesis" had come to replace "synthesis" for Catholic theologians. For the first two items, see Gleason, *Keeping the Faith*, 244 n. 39, 150; for the third, Patrick W. Carey, "Theology at Marquette University: A History" (offset first draft, 1987), 34–35.

40. Edward F. Maloney, "A Study of the Religious Orientation of the Catholic Colleges and Universities in New York State from 1962 to 1972" (Ph.D. diss., New York University, 1973).

41. Quotations are from the abstract of Maloney's study which is bound with the dissertation as published by University Microfilms International.

42. In 1968 state financial aid for private colleges and universities was recommended by a special commission chaired by McGeorge Bundy; it became available to institutions that could meet the requirements for non-sectarianism the following year. See Maureen Manion, "The Impact of State Aid on Sectarian Higher Education: The Case of New York State," *Review of Politics* 48 (Spring 1986), 264–88.

43. According to Alice Gallin, o.s.u., executive director of the ACCU, there were 136 Catholic women's colleges in 1962, and only 44 in 1990. But, as Gallin points out, these figures give a misleading impression of the extent of attrition for several reasons. For one thing, the 1962 figure included about 50 schools that were so-called Sister Formation Colleges, which admitted only religious sisters as students. Moreover, the 1990 figure leaves out 66 colleges originally founded as Catholic women's colleges that have become co-educational. See Gallin, "The Role of Women in Catholic Higher Education since Vatican II," an unpublished paper given at a conference on Vatican II and the Post-Conciliar Church in Washington, DC, September 29, 1990.

44. For nontraditional programs, see Mary Daniel O'Keeffe, "Factors Affecting the Growth of Adult Degree Programs in Catholic Women's Colleges" (Ph.D. diss., Boston College, 1984).

45. An important study, which stresses the significance of the shifting character and outlook of the faculty at Marquette University, is Gregory F. Lucey, "The Meaning and Maintenance of Catholic as a Distinctive Characteristic of American Catholic Higher Education: A Case Study" (Ph.D. diss., University of Wisconsin-Madison, 1978).

46. Regular meetings between representatives of Catholic colleges and a committee of bishops began in 1974; six years later the American hierarchy issued a pastoral letter on Catholic higher education, for which see *Origins* 10 (November 27, 1980). Interaction with Roman officials is traced in Ann Ida Gannon, "Some Aspects of Catholic Higher Education since Vatican II," *CCICA Annual, 1987*, 11–32; for the most recent Vatican statement,

see "*Ex Corde Ecclesiae*: Apostolic Constitution on Catholic Universities," *Origins* 20 (October 4, 1990).

47. See *Occasional Papers on Catholic Higher Education* 4 (Winter 1978); *Current Issues in Catholic Higher Education* 1 (Winter 1981); David M. Johnson, ed., *Justice and Peace Education* (Maryknoll, NY, 1986); and Joseph A. Tetlow, "The Jesuits' Mission in Higher Education: Perspectives and Contexts," *Studies in the Spirituality of Jesuits* 15-16 (November 1983, January 1984), esp. 52ff., 60, 63, 75. At a 1985 conference at Fordham, the formation of a new-style "ghetto organization," the "Catholic Association of Scholars in Peace and Justice," was discussed. See *ACCU Update* 12 (June 30, 1985).

48. For Henriot's statement, see *ACCU Update* 8 (June 30, 1981). Citing this statement, the ACCU's Alice Gallin observed that justice was central to Catholics' new self-understanding and that it had relevance to Catholic colleges and universities; see *Current Issues in Catholic Higher Education* 2 (Summer 1981), 2.

49. For an early example, see George A. Kelly, ed., *Why Should the Catholic University Survive?* (New York, 1973); for a more recent critique of Catholic educators' resistance to oversight from the Vatican, see K. D. Whitehead, *Catholic Colleges and Federal Funding* (San Francisco, 1988).

50. Both of these episodes are discussed, and the relevant sources cited, in C. Joseph Nuesse, *The Catholic University of America: A Centennial History* (Washington, DC, 1990), 412-16. See note 46 for citation to the most recent papal document.

9

The Secularization
of British Universities since
the Mid-Nineteenth Century

DAVID BEBBINGTON

[T]he Bible has entered deeply into the British mind and into
the accepted values and attitudes of the older British universities. In modern times both have fallen away from this tradition.[1]   Sir Walter Moberly, 1949

In the middle years of the nineteenth century Christianity was an
integral part of the universities of Britain. Their religious dimension
was acknowledged by friend and foe. John Henry Newman, in
lovingly portraying for Roman Catholics the ideal of a university
education he had assimilated as an Anglican at Oxford, declared in
1852, "Religious Truth is not only a portion, but a condition of
general knowledge."[2] A less kindly Dissenting critic had dismissed
Oxford three years earlier as an "antique, gothicized, politico-
religious Establishment."[3] The universities were regarded as
branches of the established churches of England and Scotland.

In 1850 at Oxford all heads of house except one were in the
Anglican ministry; virtually all tutors were clergymen; and about 80
percent of undergraduates were intending to pursue a clerical career.[4] Students had to subscribe to the Thirty-Nine Articles of the
Church of England on admission to the university; they took an
obligatory test in the Greek New Testament and attended compulsory college chapel. Cambridge, the other ancient university of England, insisted that undergraduates study Paley's *Evidences of*

Christianity, made conformity to the Church of England a condition of the granting of any degree, and similarly expected attendance at college chapel. St. David's College, Lampeter, a small
Welsh institution that had been founded in 1827 and had awarded
degrees from 1852, was an exclusively Anglican body. So was the
University of Durham, another tiny institution created in 1831 by
the dean and chapter of the city's cathedral. King's College, London
(founded in 1828), imposed no Anglican tests but required attendance at daily chapel and a weekly divinity lecture.

Students at Scotland's five universities—two in Aberdeen and
one each in Edinburgh, Glasgow, and St. Andrews—were under
less strict supervision than their English counterparts, since they
lived at home or in lodgings. All professors, however, were supposed to subscribe to the Westminster Confession, the doctrinal
standard of the Church of Scotland, and at Aberdeen in the 1850s
between 40 and 48 percent of the graduates intended to enter the
ministry.[5] Universities, as they had been since the Middle Ages,
were Christian institutions, supplying the churches with their
clergy. Higher education was bound up with religion.

There was one exception to the general rule. University College,
London, had been established in 1826 by a mixed group represent-
ing the secular interests of the Utilitarians and the aspirations of the
religious Dissenters. By imitating the non-residential policy of the
Scottish universities, the college circumvented the vexed question
of religious instruction. None was provided, as it was expected that
such instruction would be arranged by guardians. The cry went up
that the college was godless. Since degrees were badges of a Christian education, Oxford contended, Parliament should refuse the
college the power to confer them. The controversy was settled in
1836 only by a curious compromise under which University College
provided the instruction and a shadow University of London gave
the degrees.[6] There was no question of the college's teaching theology.

Many Dissenters, excluded from the ancient universities, were
drawn to this secular institution. Others attended the theological
colleges of their denominations for their post-school education even
if they were intending to enter a lay career rather than the ministry.[7]
The Methodists, Congregationalists, Baptists, and Unitarians each
possessed several colleges by the middle of the century. These

bodies were the nearest equivalent of the bulk of the 516 colleges established in the United States before the Civil War.[8] In principle, had their lay training side developed, the Nonconformist colleges might have grown, like many of their American cousins, into recognized universities. The colleges, however, never aimed so high. They were content to give basic non-theological courses to men who sometimes went on to take degrees elsewhere. The university sector remained a separate and superior world. Apart from University College, London, the sector was controlled at mid-century by the established churches.

The religious profession of the ancient English universities nevertheless seemed hollow to their critics. The colleges of which the universities were composed might claim to exercise a salutary discipline over their undergraduates, but in reality, according to a Dissenting journal in 1851, a student was at total liberty. "His time is his garden," the journal went on, "to which his will is the gardener; and none but he claims any interest in the virtues or the vices which he shall choose to plant there."[9] Religious instruction was normally rudimentary. Twenty years later an undergraduate at Trinity College, Cambridge, declared that he received no distinctive training except Paley's *Evidences* (which was treated as a memory test) and university sermons (where attendance was not in practice enforced), and the two often conflicted.[10] No additional theological study was required of ordinands in the mid-nineteenth century. An arts degree from Oxford or Cambridge was considered sufficient professional qualification. Although worship in college chapel was enforced for disciplinary reasons, there was rarely any preaching. Services that were not compulsory were thinly attended.

The Christian enthusiasms of youth ran in non-official channels. In 1848 there was created a Cambridge Prayer Union to encourage private prayer among students. In 1857 David Livingstone, the pioneer missionary and explorer of Africa, addressed a packed audience in the Cambridge Senate House, and as a direct result a Cambridge University Church Missionary Union was established the following year. From 1862 a Daily Prayer Meeting was held in Cambridge.[11] Such evangelical organizations, always stronger at Cambridge than Oxford, were complemented by high church bodies: the Confraternity of the Holy Trinity (1857) and the Universities Mission to Central Africa (1859).[12] The strength of religion lay in its voluntary dimension. The outward forms of Christian practice might provide vessels into which popular undergraduate piety could be poured, but there was plenty of scope for criticizing the spiritual tone of Oxford and Cambridge. The universities, even on their religious side, seemed ripe for reform.

Demands for reform were becoming loud by 1850. Although they enjoyed great prestige, the ancient English universities were small and exclusive, the training ground of the landed elite and its spiritual advisers. The university sector as a whole was exiguous. It was calculated in the 1860s that there was only one university place for every 5,800 in the English population. Although Scotland did much better, with one place for every 1,000 in the population, the same social groups there were calling for changes in a similar direction.[13] Essentially the middle classes, benefiting from the fruits of industrialization, wanted to recreate the universities in their image. Practical training was required. In the thriving Yorkshire metropolis of Leeds there was demand for "instruction in those sciences which are applicable to the Industrial Arts, especially those which may be classed under Engineering, Manufacturing, Agriculture, Mining and Metallurgy . . . designed for the use of persons who will afterwards be engaged in those trades as foremen, managers or employers; and also for the training of teachers of technical science."[14]

There was even more call for general intellectual training. In the 1850s it was settled that in future the civil service would be recruited on the basis of competitive examinations, not personal patronage. Meritocracy was in the air. More families wanted their sons to have a chance of achieving high public posts. A university education, especially at Oxford or Cambridge, was also desired because it conferred (as it was put in 1869) a "certain social status, which is of some practical value."[15] A degree was the best passport to the elite. Consequently there was pressure for changes in the curriculum and, where there were restrictions on entry, for their abolition. New civic colleges were set up in centers of industry, the first being Owens College, Manchester, in 1851. Higher education had to adapt and grow.

How was the religious tone of the universities affected by subsequent change? The period from 1850 to 1920 can usefully be considered first.

The fresh momentum in demand for higher education gathered force in circumstances of religious pluralism. The churchgoers of England and Wales, as the religious census of 1851 revealed, were divided roughly equally into Anglicans and Nonconformists, who were themselves fragmented into a variety of denominations. Although Roman Catholics were as yet few, their numbers had recently been augmented by immigrants from Ireland and looked likely to increase further. Scotland, though overwhelmingly Presbyterian, was divided between the Church of Scotland, the Free Church, and the United Presbyterians. In such a setting any form of education was problematic. The established churches considered themselves entitled to a monopoly, at least of publicly supported education; others insisted, by contrast, on having a fair share of influence over the rising generation. Political battles about the provision and funding of elementary schools were fought and re-fought during the reign of Victoria. Religion was therefore an issue that threatened to engulf in controversy any new institutions of higher education. It is no wonder that the founders of the civic colleges and universities imposed religious neutrality on their creations. John Owens, who had been a Congregationalist until a squabble over a pew induced him to worship in a parish church, directed that at his new college in Manchester "nothing will be introduced in the matter or mode of education in reference to any theological subject which shall be reasonably offensive to the conscience of any student."[16] It was agreed that, in the spirit of the will, there should be no religious instruction given by the professors, even of a voluntary kind. Likewise the trust deed of Firth College (1879), the nucleus of the University of Sheffield, prohibited religious tests; and the charter of University College, Liverpool (1881), went further by banning gifts for religious purposes.[17]

The storms that could blow up on these perilous seas are well illustrated in the early years of the University College of Wales, Aberystwyth. Knowing that denominational loyalties were particularly strong in Wales, the founding committee declared the institution non-sectarian. The first principal, a Calvinistic Methodist minister, however, held a voluntary daily service at which he read from the Book of Common Prayer of the Church of England. There was an outburst of passionate resentment. One indignant newspaper correspondent denounced the "poisonous Catholic teachings" at the college. It seemed that the flow of private subscriptions on which the college wholly relied might dry up.[18] Religion was a divisive issue. Dedicated Christian men were eager to drop it in order to ensure the welfare of higher education. Secularization was given a powerful impetus on entirely pragmatic grounds.

Some, however, wished to reduce the religious distinctiveness of the universities on grounds of principle. The privileged position of the established churches in the existing institutions aroused the ire of excluded religious groups. In Scotland the obligation of new professors to indicate their adherence to the standards of the established church before their local presbytery was strictly enforced in the wake of the setting up of the rival Free Church in 1843. There was widespread dissatisfaction. As a result, from 1853 all professors except theologians were no longer expected to appear before a presbytery, but instead had to declare that they would teach nothing opposed to the doctrine of the Church of Scotland. In 1889 this vestigial declaration was abolished.[19]

In England the Nonconformists took up with passion the issue of their effective exclusion from the ancient universities. From the 1840s most Congregationalists and Baptists saw their right to admission as no less than a deduction from the gospel. Any form of Christianity, they held, was professed by the free choice of the believer. It was wrong that human rules should attempt to sway free choice by holding out advantages to one denomination rather than another. Those holding any creed or none should be equally at liberty to enjoy the benefits of civil society. This socio-political philosophy, drawing heavily on American example, was asserted as Voluntaryism. It dictated that higher education should be available on the basis of aptitude alone.[20] Its bête noire was the religious test. For many years Unitarians had been inveighing against the idea that intellectual inquiry should be fettered by tests of orthodoxy. Now Nonconformists professing evangelical sentiments joined them in their stand. Their demand for the abolition of religious tests was voiced by the Liberation Society, the pressure group aiming for the disestablishment of the Church of England that was at its peak in the 1860s and 1870s. Its overriding aim was to achieve religious equality within the state at large. One corollary was that, as a Nonconformist put it in 1875, the best hope for the future of the universities lay *"in their secularisation."*[21] Once more the interests of religion were undermined not by its opponents but by some of its most zealous advocates.

The Nonconformist case was endorsed by many liberal intellectuals, most of them Anglicans. Especially within the universities themselves, it was part of the rising spirit of the age to condemn religious exclusiveness. Freedom was in the air. "Protection did no more good to religion," remarked a former Oxford professor of political economy in 1880, "than it did to trade."[22] Religious tests seemed manifestly unfair. Most seriously for academic reformers they restricted the pool from which qualified scholars could be drawn. Educational efficiency demanded the termination of the privileges of the Church of England. That should not disturb Churchmen, according to one of the liberal Anglican academics, because at present the tests had the function of excluding a portion of the population from the ministrations of the Church.[23]

The crucial recruit to the cause of removing religious restrictions at the universities was W. E. Gladstone, Member of Parliament for the University of Oxford from 1847 to 1865 and Liberal prime minister from 1868. Although deeply Anglican and deeply Oxonian, Gladstone was willing to undertake legislation so that the more obvious anomalies of the ancient universities could be pruned away. In 1854 he steered a bill through the House of Commons that made religious tests at Oxford optional for the B.A. (a measure abolishing B.A. tests at Cambridge altogether was carried two years later), and in 1871 he ended all university tests except for those relating to clerical fellowships in colleges. The cause enjoyed solid support among Liberal M.P.s. Despite resistance from clerical traditionalists and many Conservatives, the trend of political opinion was clearly in favor of opening the universities to all. Other legislation was carried abolishing religious restrictions at the Scottish universities (1858, 1889), London (1898), and Durham (1908). The state was a powerful engine of secularization.

The effects of legislation were profound. Together with associated royal commissions, the acts of Parliament speeded the process of professionalization in the universities. Whereas early nineteenth-century Oxford and Cambridge college fellows had been mostly unmarried clergymen who would soon move on to more permanent positions in the Church of England, by the end of the century they were generally married laymen pursuing a career as scholars and teachers. Of Oxford dons in residence between 1813 and 1830, 53 percent had a future career exclusively in the Church and only 13 percent had one in a university; of those in residence between 1881 and 1900, 13 percent had a Church career ahead of them and 57 percent a university career.[24] The crucial stage was the work of a royal commission appointed in 1877 which removed the restriction of most college fellowships to celibate Anglican clergy. Once they were permitted to marry, far more junior fellows chose to pursue an academic career. Oxford remained disproportionately blessed with clergy. In 1903 one fellow of Lincoln College wagered another that they would see at least fifteen clerics in the relatively short distance between the Banbury Road cemetery and the college: he won, for they saw eighteen.[25] Yet their numbers had declined so that by 1900 there were 213 lay and only 68 clerical fellows.[26] Ordination was no longer the normal preparation for academic life.

Consequently, the colleges of the ancient English universities no longer seemed adequate for the task of preparing candidates for ordination. If they were not controlled by clergy, they were hardly the right place for clerical formation. Furthermore, the colleges had been infiltrated by non-Anglicans. Compulsory attendance at chapel could no longer be the universal rule. An existing trend for ordinands to proceed from university to separate seminaries was therefore accentuated in the 1870s.[27] Oxford and Cambridge no longer provided the basic training for the clergy of the Church of England. It is true that the same trend toward clerical professionalization led to the establishment of undergraduate courses in theology at Oxford in 1869 and Cambridge in 1874. These measures could be regarded as a reversal of the secularization of the curriculum. Yet in a broader perspective they are themselves a symptom of the advance of the secular. The steps were taken because the arts course was no longer thought to be impregnated with Christian values. The staff, the students, and the curriculum at the ancient English universities were all becoming formally less religious.

Secularization in Britain was rarely the result of proclaimed hostility to religion. In France, where Roman Catholic higher education did not exist between the Revolution and 1875, and in Italy, where theology faculties were abolished in 1877, Positivism flourished as an anti-Catholic ideology. In Britain there were only occasional incidents in which a similar animus surfaced. At University College, London, in 1866, for instance, James Martineau, a well-qualified Unitarian divine, was not appointed to the chair of the philosophy of mind because of opposition to a minister of religion concerted by George Grote, a militant Utilitarian.[28] The rise of agnosticism among intellectuals in the so-called Victorian crisis of faith from the late 1860s was in the main mild and tentative rather than brash and polemical. Thus, when in 1869 the Cambridge philosopher Henry Sidgwick resigned his Trinity College fellowship in order, as an agnostic, to be free from "dogmatic obligations," the gesture was an act of personal sacrifice rather than an assault on institutional religion.[29] An exception must be made, however, for T. H. Huxley, a leading biologist and the coiner of the term *agnostic*, who took an active interest in the development of university education in the later nineteenth century. He denounced tests and opposed theology in the name of "scientific methods of inquiry."[30]

It was partly in response to such pitting of science against religion that divinity at the new universities, from its introduction at Manchester in 1904 onwards, took the form of "scientific theology." The subject was taught and examined un-dogmatically, as a type of phenomenology, with regard (it was said at the time) "to facts not opinions."[31] Even the discipline concerned with religion was ceasing to make a religious profession. Yet this pedagogic development was more a result of the changing intellectual atmosphere than of any campaign against doctrinal teaching. The man who defended scientific theology as a triumph of fact over opinion was the historian T. F. Tout, himself a devout Anglican. Battle lines were far less sharply drawn in British higher education than in many Continental countries. Major institutional changes affected the welfare of religion in the universities of Britain in the period up to 1920. The changes, however, consisted of gradual modifications called for by professing Christians rather than any sharp discontinuity achieved by militant secularists.

In the period of equal length between 1920 and 1990 there have been fewer institutional alterations affecting religion. It has largely been left to the free play of social forces to determine the direction and pace of secularization. Because twentieth-century society has seen a decline of religion, so have the universities. Because the young and the educated are usually in the vanguard of change, the transformation in universities has been drastic. Yet because university students have been disproportionately drawn from the higher social classes, where churchgoing for long remained customary, the sharpest fall was delayed until well after the Second World War. Figures gathered for students at the University of Sheffield are revealing. In 1961, 94 percent reported some religious upbringing; in 1972, 88 percent; in 1985, 51 percent.[32] The collapse in the religion of the home occurred in the lifetime of those who were students in 1985, that is, in the preceding twenty years. Family background helped sustain undergraduate religiosity long into the twentieth century.

At the university, however, religious practice was frequently laid aside. It was reported in 1932 that on average only 12.2 percent of students at a Cambridge college attended the main weekly chapel service, which was now wholly voluntary. From 1959 to 1963 average attendance at an Oxford college chapel was 5 to 10 percent of all residents.[33] At Christ's College, Cambridge, in 1973 an informal survey showed that 38 percent of undergraduates called themselves Christians, but 52.4 percent were agnostics, atheists, or humanists.[34] As the Church of England Board of Education ruefully commented in its submission to the Robbins Committee on Higher Education in 1961, "Lack of beliefs is the conformity of today."[35] Yet the process was to go much further, as successive surveys of Sheffield students illustrate. In 1961, 73 percent claimed to hold religious belief; in 1972, 53 percent; in 1985, 38 percent. Statistics for churchgoing among the same students reveal a similar pattern. In 1961, 46 percent said they attended church; in 1972, 25 percent; and in 1985, 15 percent. Church membership fared no better. In 1961, 38 percent were active church members; in 1972, 16 percent; in 1985, 9 percent.[36] Religion was a decaying force in the universities of the later twentieth century.

Apart from trends in society at large, what factors were responsible? The state no longer intervened to determine the balance of the religious and the secular in the universities. With the more prosperous middle classes enjoying access and most religious barriers a thing of the past, political pressure for the remodeling of higher education had vanished. From 1919 to 1989, furthermore, the universities were buffered from the state by the Universities Grants Committee (UGC). Consisting chiefly of academics, the committee disbursed the public moneys allocated to the universities according to its own free choice. Direct political manipulation of the content of higher education was ruled out. Yet the state did play a major part in marginalizing religion within the universities. Its role as their paymaster steadily increased. By 1935 about one-third of university funds came from public taxation; after 1946 the proportion was more than half; by 1970 it was over 90 percent. Through increased public funding there was a huge growth in the number of university students, from 51,000 in 1935 to 113,000 in 1961. A course leading to a degree was ceasing to be the privilege of an elite. Whereas in 1937 there were only twenty-one universities, by 1965 there were fifty-two.[37]

Governments, civil servants, and the Universities Grants Committee all wished to ensure that their investment in the future was well placed. The Second World War revealed the power of technology to transform the world. Accordingly, the preference of those who allocated funds was the development of science and technology. Of 268 building projects authorized by the UGC between 1957 and 1962, 91 were devoted to these areas. In 1957 ten existing institutions were designated Colleges of Advanced Technology, and all in due course achieved university status.[38] Humane studies where ultimate questions of a religious kind could be raised were not neglected, but they received a smaller share of the cake. Theology attracted little public financial support. The balance of studies was altered in favor of disciplines where religion counted for less.

The vicissitudes of theology well illustrate the decline of the religious presence in universities. Its study was resisted at many of the newer institutions. At Birmingham, a university created in 1900 to boost the commercial fortunes of the city, a chair of theology was not set up until 1940.[39] The University of Reading never introduced the subject (although an element of religious studies was eventually provided for those intending to become teachers), since, as a leading opponent alleged, it was an "easy subject."[40] At other twentieth-century foundations, including Keele and the Open University (designed for learning at a distance), the growth of theology or religious studies was stunted at an early stage.[41] Religious studies could itself be a symptom of secularization. In the 1960s the job advertisement for the first chair of religious studies at Lancaster, a department that was to achieve considerable size and prestige, aroused a furor by inviting applications from candidates "of any faith or none."[42] Where theology was still taught, its tendency was to become less dogmatic and more descriptive.

The Scottish universities nevertheless remained bastions of the older approach. In the wake of the fusion of the United Free Church with the Church of Scotland in 1929, the enlarged national church was given an equal share with the universities in the membership of the appointments boards for divinity chairs. In 1989, of the fifteen divinity professors in Scottish universities, eleven were ministers of the Church of Scotland and three were ministers of other denominations.[43] Yet even there the secular corrosive was at work. At New College, Edinburgh, the largest divinity faculty in Scotland, there was only slow attrition up to the late 1960s. At that time the numbers of students taking theology were similar to the figures for the 1930s. The change was that the university had tripled in size over the intervening period, so the proportion of theologians had fallen. In 1966 about two-thirds of the undergraduates in the theology faculty were candidates for the Church of Scotland ministry, a ratio unchanged since the 1930s. By 1980, however, the position was reversed; now, though some undergraduates intended to serve in other denominations, two-thirds were *not* candidates for the ministry of the Church of Scotland. From 1971 religious studies somewhat in the Lancaster mold was available within the faculty alongside theology.[44] Similar trends may be discerned elsewhere in Britain. Theology was still attracting students, but it was doing so by catering to non-professionals with a more generalist approach. Ex cathedra pronouncements on religious questions were no longer to be expected from professors of divinity. The discipline of theology had traditionally given fiber to the Christian presence in higher education. The sapping of the discipline necessarily meant the weakening of the presence.

Secularism as an ideology had some role in minimizing the place of religion in the universities—greater than in the nineteenth century, but nevertheless only a minor one. From 1909 to 1932 there existed at Cambridge a body called the Heretics, membership of which entailed "the rejection of all appeal to Authority in the discussion of religious questions."[45] It was at this body that the philosopher Bertrand Russell made his celebrated quip about the Ten Commandments being like an examination paper in which only six need be attempted.[46] A Cambridge Humanist Society was set up in 1955. Its Oxford equivalent, established four years later, claimed one thousand members by 1964.[47] A handful of individuals of this persuasion made stands against what they regarded as the lingering relics of superstition. G. H. Hardy, a zealous atheist who was appointed to a Cambridge chair of mathematics in 1931, submitted only with great reluctance to making his Trinity College fellowship declaration in chapel.[48] A more public controversy sprang up surrounding the foundation of Churchill College, Cambridge, as a national memorial to Sir Winston Churchill in the 1960s. There was a powerful current of opinion that in a secular age there should be no college chapel. One of the fellows, the geneticist Francis Crick, resigned in protest against the proposal. In the end, as a compromise the chapel was privately funded, built on land leased by the college to a separate trust and situated in a remote corner of the grounds.[49]

Far more powerful than outright hostility to religion, however, was a diffuse assumption that its claims had been discredited. The logical positivism propagated from 1936 by A. J. Ayer, a philosopher successively at Oxford and London, reinforced this view. Unbelief drew much greater strength, however, from the scientism associated with T. H. Huxley in a previous generation. There had arisen, wrote the vice chancellor of Birmingham in 1930, a "subconscious assumption that the 'old theology' had been torpedoed by science."[50] Insofar as ideology played its part in undermining belief, an exaggerated regard for science was the most subversive force.

It must not be supposed that secularization has made unimpeded progress since 1920. On the contrary, factors have existed to retard its advance. One is the dominance of Oxford and Cambridge as the oldest, the wealthiest, and the most academically prestigious institutions within the British education system. Their example has been pervasive throughout the university world, and they have retained much of their ancient religious profession. At Oxford the theology faculty, where certain chairs are still restricted to Anglican clergymen, is alleged to be the largest in the world; at Cambridge up to the 1970s one professor of theology, C. F. D. Moule, began his lectures with prayer. University sermons, albeit thinly attended, continue. The separate colleges maintain daily worship in their chapels, say grace before dinner, and employ chaplains. The universities and their colleges alike remain involved in the intricate maze of Church of England patronage. "The Vice-Chancellor gives notice," ran an advertisement in the *Cambridge University Reporter* in 1973, "that presentation to the vacant benefice of Brantham, in the Diocese of St. Edmundsbury and Ipswich, devolves on the University. Candidature is restricted to graduates of Emmanuel College, Cambridge, who are *either* the kin of Sir Wolstan Dixie *or* who have been educated for one year at Market Bosworth School."[51] The royal charter of Fitzwilliam College, Cambridge, granted in 1966, still provided that its object should be to advance "education, religion, learning and research."[52]

Newer universities have habitually recruited staff from Oxford and Cambridge. For them it was natural for Christianity to have a presence in a place of higher learning. Likewise the general public, whose awareness of universities up to the student riots of the 1960s was confined primarily to the annual boat race between Oxford and Cambridge and the equally popular broadcast Christmas carol service from King's College, Cambridge, expected religion to be institutionalized in every university. Gifts were received to complete the facilities of modern universities—an Anglican hostel at Sheffield in 1912, an Anglican center at Reading in 1926, a theology department at Leeds in 1932.[53] Hostels were usually designed to fill the place occupied by colleges at the ancient universities. Chaplains, sometimes (as at six of the eight Scottish universities and Keele) paid by the university, were appointed, and chaplaincy centers followed. If the substance of the establishment of religion in the ancient universities had been swept away in the nineteenth century, enough survived to bequeath a legacy to the whole university system in the twentieth.

The other factor tending to sacralize rather than secularize the universities has been the existence of substantial voluntary religious organizations. Many have declined in recent years, but they are still far from negligible. In 1961, 15 percent of Sheffield students belonged to a student religious group; in 1972, 9 percent; and in 1985, 6 percent.[54] The largest such body was for many years, up to its collapse in the 1960s, the Student Christian Movement (SCM), Protestant but inter-denominational, cerebral but popular. Its supporters among university staff, stimulated by the crisis of war, thrashed out issues of Christian academic responsibility in discussions during the 1940s that led to the influential work by Sir Walter Moberly, *The Crisis in the University* (1949).[55] The conservative Evangelical equivalent, the Inter-Varsity Fellowship (IVF), now the Universities and Colleges Christian Fellowship, gradually gathered strength until by the 1970s it supported Christian Unions which were frequently the largest student organizations in the various universities. Missions promoted by SCM or IVF regularly drew thousands.

Equally there was an upsurge of the Roman Catholic presence. Ever since in 1895 the Vatican had lifted the ban on the faithful attending non-Catholic places of higher education, there had been a growing Catholic population. The Oxford Catholic chaplaincy served 125 in 1926, 230 in 1938, 456 in 1947, and 770 in 1963.[56] There were Catholic halls of residence at four universities by 1961, Newman Societies at many more, and chaplains at all of them.[57] The Nonconformists likewise sustained denominational student societies wherever they could. Their theological colleges, by the 1920s all transferred to university cities, provided rallying points for their members. The Church of England also promoted societies, usually reflecting one strand in that variegated body. Jews had their own organizations. By the 1980s, when their numbers for the first time permitted it, so did Muslims. Normally university authorities welcomed student religious organizations, only occasionally (as at Leeds in the 1920s)[58] fearing their divisive influence in the community. Whatever the official attitude, religion remained a vital force among a minority of students.

By the middle of the twentieth century the universities were nevertheless essentially secular bodies. Nobody was better placed to diagnose their mood than Sir Walter Moberly, the chairman of the Universities Grants Committee as well as an SCM supporter. "In the assumptions governing syllabus and academic method," declared Moberly in 1949, "the universities of to-day are, implicitly, if unintentionally, hostile to the Christian faith."[59] Moberly was risking exaggeration in order to make the point that in practice ultimate issues raising questions about God were ruled out of debate in British higher education. Rather than being actively anti-Christian, as Moberly explains elsewhere, universities had become pluralistic. There were residual marks of their earlier Christian purpose, especially in the old universities of England and Scotland, and these traces were not to be eliminated in subsequent years. Yet there was an element of truth in Moberly's suggestion of hostility to Christianity, for there was a widespread sense that traditional religion had been superseded. Universities in the period after the Second World War could properly be called post-Christian institutions.[60] This was an enormous contrast with their mid–nineteenth-century role as trainers of clergy and upholders of orthodoxy.

The transformation had come about in two phases. In the period 1850 to 1920 pressure from Nonconformists outside the universities and liberals within led to the ending of the virtual monopoly of the established churches in higher education. Secularization was achieved through the state as a result of deliberate policies pursued by professing Christians. In the period 1920 to 1990, by contrast, there were few demands for further dismantling of the religious apparatus in higher education. What happened was that secularization in society at large, reinforced by the side-effects of public policy and the ideology of scientism, further diminished the Christian presence in universities. The state did not interfere directly. Secularization was not consciously willed, except by a handful of people. Although there were religious counter-currents, the advance of the secular was inexorable. The post-Christian universities of Britain reflected a post-Christian nation.

Notes

1. Sir Walter Moberly, *The Crisis in the University* (London: S.C.M., 1949), 25.

2. J. H. Newman, *The Idea of a University*, ed. I. T. Ker (Oxford: Clarendon Press, 1976), 71.

3. "The Dissenters: Their Grievances and Their Policy," *Eclectic Review*, n.s., 25 (May 1849), 645.

4. A. J. Engel, *From Clergyman to Don: The Rise of the Academic Profession in Nineteenth-Century Oxford* (Oxford: Clarendon Press, 1983), 177.

5. R. D. Anderson, *Education and Opportunity in Victorian Scotland* (Oxford: Clarendon Press, 1983), 78.

6. H. H. Bellot, *University College London, 1826–1926* (London: University of London Press, 1929), chs. 2, 7.

7. E. A. Payne, "The Development of Nonconformist Theological Education in the Nineteenth Century, with Special Reference to Regent's Park

College," in *Studies in History and Religion*, ed. E. A. Payne (London: Lutterworth Press, 1942), 241.

8. Richard Hofstadter, *Academic Freedom in the Age of the College* (New York: Columbia University Press, 1961), 211.

9. "The University Commission," *Eclectic Review*, n.s., 1 (June 1851), 705.

10. *Cambridge Chronicle*, December 10, 1870, 7.

11. J. C. Pollock, *A Cambridge Movement* (London: John Murray), ch. 2.

12. V. H. H. Green, *Religion at Oxford and Cambridge* (London: S.C.M.), 321–22.

13. T. C. Smout, *A Century of the Scottish People, 1830–1950* (London: Collins, 1986), 216.

14. Inaugural prospectus of Yorkshire College, Leeds, 1872, quoted by A. J. Taylor, "County College and Civic University: An Introductory Essay," in *Studies in the History of a University, 1874–1974*, ed. P. H. J. H. Gosden and A. J. Taylor (Leeds: E. J. Arnold and Son, 1975), 2.

15. Neville Goodman, *How we may best avail Ourselves of the Universities of Cambridge and Oxford for the Education of our Ministers* (Cambridge, 1869), 4.

16. H. B. Charlton, *Portrait of a University, 1851–1951* (Manchester: Manchester University Press, 1951), 26.

17. A. W. Chapman, *The Story of a Modern University: A History of the University of Sheffield* (London: Oxford University Press, 1955), 22. Thomas Kelly, *For Advancement of Learning: The University of Liverpool, 1881–1981* (Liverpool: Liverpool University Press, 1981), 53.

18. E. L. Ellis, *The University College of Wales, Aberystwyth, 1872–1972* (Cardiff: University of Wales Press, 1972), 38–39.

19. Anderson, *Education and Opportunity*, 53.

20. D. W. Bebbington, "The Dissenting Idea of a University: Oxford and Cambridge in Nonconformist Thought in the Nineteenth Century," University of Cambridge Hulsean Prize Essay, 1973, ch. 3.

21. "The Future of the English Universities," *British Quarterly Review* 62 (July 1875), 109.

22. J. E. Thorold Rogers, quoted by Lewis Campbell, *On the Nationalisation of the Old English Universities* (London: Chapman and Hall, 1901), 214.

23. G. C. Brodrick, quoted in *The Abolition of Religious Tests at the Universities of Oxford and Cambridge* (London, 1866), 22.

24. Engel, *From Clergyman to Don*, 286.

25. Green, *Religion at Oxford and Cambridge*, 332–33.

26. W. G. Addison, "Academic Reform at Balliol, 1854–1882," *Church Quarterly Review* 153 (1952), 91.

27. Alan Haig, *The Victorian Clergy* (London: Croom Helm, 1984), ch. 2.

28. Bellot, *University College*, 340–41.

29. Green, *Religion at Oxford and Cambridge*, 303–4.

30. Leonard Huxley, *Life and Letters of Thomas Henry Huxley*, vol. 2 (London: Macmillan, 1900), 310.

31. T. F. Tout, "The Study of Ecclesiastical History in Its Relation to the Faculties of Arts and Theology in the University of Manchester," in *Inaugural Lectures Delivered by Members of the Faculty of Theology during Its First Session, 1904–5*, ed. A. S. Peake (Manchester: Manchester University Press, 1905), 19.

32. *LandMARC* (New Year 1987).

33. Green, *Religion at Oxford and Cambridge*, 351, 363n.

34. *Stop Press* (the Cambridge student newspaper), March 9, 1973, 3.

35. *Higher Education: Evidence: Part I*, vol. A (London: H.M.S.O., 1963), Cmnd. 2154–VI, 76.

36. *LandMARC* (New Year 1987).

37. John Carswell, *Government and the Universities in Britain: Programme and Performance, 1960–1980* (Cambridge: Cambridge University Press, 1985), 3, 11, 14, 55. Sydney Caine, "British Universities, 1900–1970," in *University Independence: The Main Questions*, ed. J. H. M. Scott (London: Rex Collings, 1971), 14.

38. Carswell, *Government and the Universities*, 20.

39. E. W. Vincent and Percival Hinton, *The University of Birmingham: Its History and Significance* (Birmingham: Cornish Brothers, 1947), 101.

40. J. C. Holt, *The University of Reading: The First Fifty Years* (Reading: Reading University Press, 1977), 82, 254n.

41. Sir James Mountford, *Keele: An Historical Critique* (London: Routledge and Kegan Paul, 1972), 173. John Ferguson, *The Open University from Within* (London: University of London Press, 1975), 34–35.

42. Christopher Driver, *The Exploding University* (London: Hodder and Stoughton, 1971), 181–82.

43. *The Church of Scotland Year Book, 1989* (Edinburgh: St. Andrew Press), 304.

44. Hugh Watt, *New College, Edinburgh: A Centenary History* (Edinburgh: Oliver and Boyd, 1946), 275. More recent figures for New College have kindly been supplied by D. F. Wright, dean of the Faculty of Divinity.

45. P. S. Florence, "The Cambridge Heretics (1909–1932)," in *The Humanist Outlook*, ed. A. J. Ayer (London: Pemberton, 1968), 228.

46. T. E. B. Howarth, *Cambridge between the Two Wars* (London: Collins, 1978), 52.

47. Green, *Religion at Oxford and Cambridge*, 358.

48. Howarth, *Cambridge between the Two Wars*, 173.

49. Green, *Religion at Oxford and Cambridge*, 366. *The White Book, 1987* (Cambridge: Churchill College), 4. I am grateful to Richard Shaw for this point.

50. Sir Charles Grant Robertson, "Religion in the Modern Universities," in *The Life of a Modern University*, ed. Hugh Martin (London: S.C.M., 1930), 74.

51. *Cambridge University Reporter*, May 9, 1973, 865.

52. *Charter and Statutes of Fitzwilliam College in the University of Cambridge* (Cambridge: University Printing House, 1973), 12.

53. Chapman, *Modern University*, 238. Holt, *University of Reading*, 81. W. B. Stephens, "The Curriculum," in Gosden and Taylor, *Studies in the History of a University*, 283.

54. *LandMARC* (New Year 1987).

55. J. D. McCaughey, *Christian Obedience in the University: Studies in the Life of the Student Christian Movement of Great Britain and Ireland, 1930–1950* (London: S.C.M., 1958), ch. 4.

56. Green, *Religion at Oxford and Cambridge*, 356.

57. *Higher Education: Evidence: Part One*, vol. D (London: H.M.S.O., 1963), Cmnd. 2154–IX, 1349, 1351.

58. P. H. J. H. Gosden, "The Student Body," in Gosden and Taylor, *Studies in the History of a University*, 74.

59. Moberly, *Crisis in the University*, 27.

60. D. M. Paton, *Religion in the University* (London: S.C.M., 1946), 27.

10

Protestant Colleges in Canada: Past and Future

G. A. RAWLYK

I have no quarrel with learning—wise doctors have their place—But the scalpel of the scholar cannot dissect God's grace.[1]   J. W. Bengough, 1895

Virtually every serious student of the contemporary North American world of higher education has recognized that the universities, as George Marsden has bluntly observed, "are morally bankrupt as culture-shaping institutions."[2] Despite the standard hollow moral platitudes offered by countless university administrators, the essential justification for the university is its technological usefulness and its crucial hegemonic role in the shaping of the consumer and the therapeutic culture. The contemporary university has thus become a convenient center "for a collection of technical disciplines— disconnected except by some common methodologies and goals."[3] And as the twentieth century blurs into the twenty-first, the humanities and the social sciences, to an ever greater extent, merely exist as concessions to an increasingly distant and seemingly irrelevant past. The true Canadian academic "Centers of Excellence" are pristinely pure in their commitment to technological and scientific relevance and to so-called progress. And at the core of this powerful secular value system is the belief that the only valid authority is that created by the high priests of technology and science and their multi-national masters.

Most North American religious leaders appear to have supinely accepted this post-Christian analysis of reality. Whether on the right or the left of the religious spectrum, they have enthusiastically embraced what T. J. Jackson Lears has referred to as "a therapeutic world view."[4] And in the process they have admitted, either explicitly or implicitly, that Christianity has virtually nothing to offer the world of higher education. For those on the left, religion, broadly defined, merely teaches that the essential goal of the humanities and social sciences in higher education is to encourage tolerance and diversity. For those on the right, "secular humanism" is a far more pernicious evil than technology and science, and they are therefore determined to ensure that their brand of higher education is either Bible centered or else technologically pure.

Few North American scholars in the 1990s, I am sure, would want to use Karl Marx to try to buttress a historical argument. Yet in the late nineteenth century Marx was able to see with a flash of prophetic insight the essential contours of "modern bourgeois society." For Marx, such a society "has conjured up such gigantic means of production and of exchange that it became in the process like the sorcerer who is no longer able to control the powers of the subterranean which he has called up by his spells." Marx went on:

> Constant revolutionizing of production, uninterrupted disturbance of all social relations, everlasting uncertainty and agitation, distinguish the bourgeois epoch from all earlier ones. All fixed, fast-frozen relations, with their train of ancient and venerable prejudices and opinions, are swept away, all new-found ones become antiquated before they can ossify. All that is solid melts into air, all that is holy is profane.[5]

Marx for many had laid bare the essential nature of life in modernizing society, and he had intuitively realized what had happened to the nineteenth-century North American Protestant evangelical consensus. The "holy" had in a profound sense become "profane," and all that was "solid" had melted into a mush of nothingness.

Few, if any, Canadian Protestant academics in the late nineteenth century and the early twentieth would have—or, more accurately, could have—accepted the validity of Marx's analysis concerning the possible symbiotic relationship between the emerging modern, bourgeois society and the swift decline of traditional

Christianity. Yet a powerful argument may be put forward that the evangelical Protestant consensus of the nineteenth century was destroyed not from outside by the twin forces of Darwinism and biblical scholarship but rather from within by the insidious influences of consumerism and its "culture of gratification."[6]

North American academics were quick to jettison traditional Christian values. Having lost their collective faith in past verities, they gradually abandoned their attempt to balance piety and scholarship and instead wedded themselves to so-called objective modernity. Those who were not an essential part of the new technological society found themselves increasingly marginalized in the humanities and social sciences. Here many would be content to mouth the shibboleths of moral relativism and individualism; they would be brain workers, increasingly irrelevant, increasingly bitter, and increasingly powerless. But a few would try to spit into the wind of progress and to resonate with Jacques Ellul that "beyond Jesus, beyond him there is nothing—nothing but lies."[7]

In a very real sense, from an orthodox Christian perspective Ellul's lament is particularly relevant with respect to the realm of higher education. Committed Christian teachers, teaching in a committed Christian environment, were remarkably successful throughout most of the nineteenth century. And they continue to be remarkably successful, in the fullest sense of that word, wherever they teach in the late twentieth century. A renaissance of Christian higher education in Canada may be seen on the distant horizon largely because so much of contemporary secular learning and teaching has proved bankrupt. Greed and growth may provide short-term satisfaction, but in the long run they can only produce bitter despair and a sense of hopelessness.

The apex of nineteenth-century Canadian Protestant higher learning, which attempted to balance the new scholarship and the old evangelical pietism, probably stretched from the 1840s to the 1890s. By the 1920s, however, most Protestant denominational colleges had virtually abandoned their commitment to nineteenth-century evangelicalism and had instead become the enthusiastic proponents of secular learning. Some of the salient features of this fascinating transformation may be seen in the evolution of what is now McMaster University from its official founding in 1887 until

1923, when H. P. Whidden was appointed the eighth chancellor of the Baptist institution.[8]

I have chosen McMaster as a case study not because it was the most important or most influential Canadian Protestant denominational institution at the turn of the century, but simply because I know something about McMaster and because I am a Baptist who is still concerned about the possible relevance of Christian higher education in contemporary Canada. Before getting to McMaster, however, I believe that some comments about its Maritime sister institution, Acadia, may be of some relevance.

From the very beginning of Acadia College in 1838, Maritime Baptists, in their perception of Christian higher education, revealed what Barry Moody has perceptively and accurately described as "a breadth of vision and a breadth of mind remarkably free of fear or narrow prejudice, sectarian or otherwise."[9] Though committed to a traditional New Light evangelicalism, a remarkable mix of conversionism, biblicism, activism, and what may be called crucicentrism, they were eager to locate their denomination, as the nineteenth century unfolded, within the mainstream of contemporary scholarship. Nineteenth-century Maritime Baptist leaders believed, perhaps naively, that they could quite easily reconcile their evangelical traditions with modern "science" and "Art," which had, according to a leading nineteenth-century Baptist scientist and Acadia professor, Isaac Chipman, "raised the human mind from a fearful depth of degradation."[10]

If any one nineteenth-century Maritime Baptist leader personified the accommodationist spirit, it was J. M. Cramp. Cramp may be regarded as the quintessential nineteenth-century Anglo–Nova Scotian Calvinist New Light Baptist. He was born in Ramsgate, England, in 1796, and died in Wolfville, Nova Scotia, in 1881. A prolific author, a distinguished Baptist minister, and a gifted newspaper editor, he was principal of the Montreal Baptist Seminary from 1844 to 1848 and president of Acadia College from 1851 to 1853 and again from 1855 to 1869. Cramp was, as far as his biographer Robert Wilson is concerned, "a key figure for Maritime Baptists." "On one level," Wilson has observed, Cramp was "one of their most important leaders and a shaper of the history of the denomination." On yet "another level, the fact that a scholar of his standing would devote the last thirty years of his life to education and scholarship at Acadia added immeasurably to the stature of the College and the denomination."[11]

Students at Acadia College, as was also the case of other nineteenth-century Protestant colleges in Canada, expected to have their evangelical faith strengthened while studying, and they also expected their unconverted student associates to be converted. After the end of the Second Great Awakening in the 1840s, a widespread religious revival that had swept through much of North America for almost four decades, there was a significant shift in evangelical circles from "personal to bureaucratic evangelism."[12] Denominational colleges were seen not only as instruments for channeling this so-called bureaucratic evangelism but also as the organizational means available to achieve the much-coveted respectability.

At Acadia College in 1855 Cramp played a key role in shaping the "extensive revival of religion in Wolfville largely among the students."[13] Over seventy students were baptized in the Gespereaux River. According to one revival participant:

> Rev. Dr. Cramp . . . having had but little experience in [Maritime] revivals . . . gave the special services over to the students, assuring us always of his sympathies and prayers. This wonderful movement on "the Hill" became so all engrossing that the regular class-work of the College was, for a time, partially suspended. . . . During this revival, nearly all the students of the Academy and College submitted to Christ, and the blessed influence extended to the Village. Acadia College has been highly favoured in having had many revivals among her students during her history, but this great work was one of the most remarkable of these gracious visitations.[14]

"These gracious visitations" obviously were not limited to Baptist institutions of higher learning. At approximately the same time, at Mount Allison, the Methodist counterpart to Acadia, Phoebe Palmer, the remarkable American holiness preacher, was coaxing into existence yet another of her revivals. "At no place have we seen the Lord more signally displayed than at Sackville," it was observed. "Over fifty" Mount Allison students were converted, and many others "received the more enlarged baptism of the Holy

Spirit."[15] And who sent the invitation to Palmer and her husband, and who organized the revival meetings at Mount Allison? Charles Allison, the founder of the institution, had orchestrated the entire visit.

A little more than a decade after the 1855 Acadia revival, Cramp emphasized yet again his belief in the efficacy of scientific progress, which to him and to other Maritime Baptists was intimately "united with the most powerful energies of Christianity."[16] Darwin's ideas were not anti-Christian shibboleths designed by the devil to destroy the essentials of Christianity. Rather, Darwinism, together with all true learning, was viewed by Cramp as the means whereby "the pains of perplexity and doubt . . . speculations, and guesses" were being replaced by the Almighty with "glorious occasions to our knowledge" which were shaping the modern "world of light and purity."[17]

For President Cramp of Acadia, and for virtually every other key administrator of the various Protestant denominational colleges in nineteenth-century Canada, institutions of higher learning existed for two major reasons. First, they were there to convert non-believers and to strengthen the faith and spirituality of the believing students. Second, the colleges, through committed Christian teachers, communicated relevant knowledge to the students and to society, but always within the context of forming and strengthening faith.

Senator William McMaster, one of Canada's most influential entrepreneurs in the 1870s and 1880s and a leading Reform politician and active Baptist, was determined to build a Baptist institution of higher learning in Toronto. He and his Baptist friends were not really interested in creating a "theological institute," a kind of "Bible college." Rather, they wanted to join the Canadian Protestant establishment, and to share in the glow of its respectability, by building their own proper university.[18]

If one uses a Gramsci-like lens to view unfolding events in the late nineteenth century in the Canadian Protestant community in general and the Central Canadian Baptist community in particular, what emerges is to some a disconcerting reality. McMaster and his Baptist business associates may be seen as creators of a new stratum of intellectuals whose central role is perceived to be "to win over the traditional strata to support . . . the new social, economic order."

For Gramsci, in new societies such as that of Canada in the late nineteenth century, the new group of intellectuals, broadly defined, were expected to "fuse together in a single national crucible with a unitary culture the different forms of culture imprinted by immigrants of differing national origins."[19]

It was also Gramsci's contention that the new class of university-trained leaders, including, of course, the religious leaders, are locked into a kind of integrative symbiotic relationship with a new social order thrown up by the fundamental changes affecting every aspect of economic production. The so-called intellectual-priest thus functions at two levels, which "correspond on the one hand to the function of 'hegemony' which the dominant group exercises throughout society and on the other hand to that of 'direct domination'—a command exercised through the state. . . . The functions in question are precisely organizational and connective. The intellectuals are the dominant group 'deputies' exercising the subaltern functions of social hegemony and political government."[20]

The essential ideology of the new social order, it may be argued, was North American consumer culture, which contained at its core the antithesis of evangelical orthodoxy. Gradually this narcissistic gospel of intense "therapeutic self-realization," buttressed by liberal individualism and the belief in the fundamental goodness of economic growth and technological development, destroyed what to some were the essentials of true Christianity.[21]

Because of the tremendous political pressure exerted by McMaster and his friends, as well as their denominational influence, on March 15, 1887, a bill was finally introduced at Queen's Park uniting the Toronto Baptist College (established in 1880) and Woodstock College (which had been founded in 1857 at the Canadian Literary Institute) and incorporating them as McMaster University. On April 22, 1887, the act of incorporation became law, and exactly five months later Senator McMaster died, leaving close to $1 million to his university. "The monumental irony of the situation," McMaster University's historian, Charles Johnston, has noted, "struck even the most insensitive." For "at one stroke, the university that McMaster had promoted was instantly financed but at the cost of his vigour, direction, and inspiration."[22]

It is evident from the 1887 act of incorporation that, while McMaster University was to be a Christian institution, only its seminary was to be explicitly Baptist. There was, it seems clear, to be no theological litmus test for McMaster students, but all university teachers and officials were to be evangelical Christians, and the theology faculty members were to be evangelical Baptists, broadly defined, who could be subjected by the board of governors to some kind of "test as to religious belief." Taking everything into account, the act in many respects was quite progressive in tone and content, but so much, of course, depended on what was meant in the act by the phrases "Christian school of learning" and "Evangelical Christian Church."[23] The underlying assumption of the act, however, was crystal clear. Students at McMaster would be educated by evangelical Christian teachers in a Christian environment so that they would "be thoroughly equipped with all the resources of the best and most liberal culture to enable them to meet the polished shafts of a refined and subtle infidelity."[24]

The third chancellor of McMaster University, the Reverend O. C. S. Wallace, enunciated in his inaugural address in 1895 what he must have realized was the prevailing rationale for Christian higher education. He was widely regarded as a staunch defender of the evangelical status quo, but he was also known as someone very concerned about preparing his "students for the challenges of life in the outer world."[25] Though a pious traditionalist in one sense, Wallace, very much an accommodating Maritime Baptist, was also as his later career would show, determined to make Christianity relevant for modern society. He was not opposed, therefore, to a shift in Protestant theology from a preoccupation with "salvation in the next world to therapeutic self-realization in this one."[26] But this still would take place only gradually during Wallace's ten-year sojourn at McMaster.

As far as Wallace was concerned, in 1895 McMaster University existed "for the teaching rather than the pursuit of truth." "Much of the educational work of the present day," he went on,

> is a menace to all that is holiest in faith and loftiest in morality because it is moulded in form and determined in spirit by the contrary of that principle. . . . We are not denying that there is truth to pursue, but we do most confidently and solemnly affirm that there is truth to teach. However vast may be the domain of the unexplored and the unknown, it is yet true that something is known [and is] ours by the . . . attestation of the ages [or by the

unequivocal revelation of God . . . Before such truths as have
been abundantly proven or clearly revealed we dare not take the
attitude of the . . . doubter and the agnostic. . . . It is our aim to
send forth . . . scholars whose opinions of truth and whose principles of conduct shall not be . . . a source and occasion of irreligion in the communities in which they live.[27]

Some of Wallace's friends, however, did not accept the new
chancellor's point of view. One of them informed him:

When once that spirit—that "a university exists for the teaching
rather than the pursuit of truth"—has laid hold of an institution
its zenith has been reached. Like the perfectionists in character no
advance is believed possible, no advance will be made . . . every
truth that is not brought home to the individual conscience and
judgment and there accepted as truth on its own merits is, to a
student, a worse than useless incumbrance. . . . I believe in the
scientific method, the method that is used in all good schools at
the present day . . . and which the sentence quoted opposes.
There is a wide difference between the scientific search for truth
and the agnostic search for ignorance.[28]

By the time of his resignation in 1905, Wallace had moved quite a
distance in the direction of his friend's position of encouraging "the
scientific search for truth" in order to make McMaster into a
"good" modern university.[29]

In his journey toward accommodation, the Nova Scotia–born
educator was encouraged by some of his board members, as well as
some of his faculty, especially those who were scientists. But Wallace, it should be stressed, would never abandon his commitment to
the paramountcy of the evangelical New Light tradition.

Wallace's successor as chancellor was A. C. McKay, who for
years had been the key administrative factotum at McMaster. He
played an important role in keeping McMaster a separate educational institution by leading the fight against federation with the
University of Toronto. Federation, of course, would have produced
a radically different McMaster. McKay was enthusiastically committed to the "scientific search for truth," and he seemed amazingly
indifferent to the growing theological civil war between so-called
liberals and fundamentalists being fought in the Ontario and
Quebec Baptist Convention and his own theology faculty.

What came to be known as the "Matthews Controversy" reached a crisis point in 1908 and 1909. The critics of I. G. Matthews—the Chicago-trained Old Testament scholar—argued that he was a pernicious modernist determined to destroy the orthodox faith of his theological students. To counter the growing fundamentalist movement in the convention, McKay saw the need for McMaster's senate to emphasize the institution's theological orthodoxy—but without abandoning his belief in the efficacy of science and modern scholarship. An investigating committee submitted its report to the senate on May 29, 1909, declaring Matthews innocent of the charges of unorthodoxy. Although he accepted many of the "results of critical scholarship," he nevertheless "held firmly to the inspiration and supernatural character of the Old and New Testaments." Then the senate boldly declared:

> McMaster stands for freedom, for progress, for investigation. It must welcome truth from whatever quarter, and never be guilty of binding the spirit of free enquiry. As a Christian school of learning under Baptist auspices, it stands for the fullest and freest investigation, not only in the scientific realm but also in the realm of Biblical scholarship. Holding fast their historic position on the personal freedom and responsibility of the individual, refusing to bind or be bound by any human creed, rejecting the authority of tradition and taking their stand on the word of God alone as the supreme and all-sufficient rule of faith and practice, the Baptists have ever been ready to accord to all students of the Sacred Scriptures the largest possible measure of freedom consistent with loyalty to the fundamentals of the Christian faith.[30]

At the December 2, 1909, senate meeting it was agreed that "while complete freedom should be accorded in the investigation and discussion of facts, no theory should be taught in [the] University which fails to give [its] proper place to supernatural revelation . . . or which would impair in any way the supreme authority of the Lord Jesus Christ."[31]

When the Matthews controversy was brought to the floor of the convention in October 1910, the senate position was endorsed by a large majority. A leader in the movement to prevent a convention denunciation of McMaster and Matthews was the Reverend T. T. Shields, the minister of Jarvis Street Baptist Church and a leading fundamentalist in the convention. Shields probably did not want to alienate some of his key church members who were keen supporters of Matthews and McKay.

The senate response to the controversy is important in at least two ways with respect to Baptists and Christian higher education in central Canada. First, McMaster's senate and also the convention explicitly endorsed the key role of higher education in bringing about human "progress"—bourgeois progress and consumerism. Second, it was emphatically agreed that accommodation was indeed possible between the evangelical consensus and the new scholarship. And, moreover, it was contended that McMaster University had a special role in bringing about this accommodation which, for some, was merely the articulation of a British-oriented liberal evangelical point of view.

By 1911, however, a beleaguered McKay had come to the realization that he was "not born to be in the midst of theological controversy."[32] He therefore resigned as chancellor to become principal of a new technical high school in Toronto. Many Baptists were genuinely sorry to see McKay leave McMaster. Others were not, feeling that he was too soft on modernism and liberalism. They looked for someone a little more spiritual, a little more pious, a little more evangelical to replace him. They saw such a person in Abraham Lincoln McCrimmon.

McCrimmon was born in 1865 on a farm a mile north of Delhi in western Ontario. He graduated from the University of Toronto in 1890 as gold medalist in logic and philosophy. As a student at the University of Toronto, he excelled not only in his studies but also in athletics. A fine pitcher, he once "struck out twelve men consecutively," and it was said "that he was one of the first exponents in Ontario of the curve ball."[33] When he graduated, therefore, McCrimmon had to choose between Christian service and a career in professional baseball. He gladly chose the former. In 1892 he became classics master at Woodstock College, and five years later he became its principal. While at Woodstock, McCrimmon showed that he "possessed one of the finest intellects among the educational leaders of America."[34] As a preacher and platform speaker, the former baseball star began to "rank with the most polished and forceful orators in the country."[35] He was widely perceived as an "intensely religious and ever zealous" Baptist, who always "sought to convey the message of God in clear and convincing language."[36]

Until his death in 1935, McCrimmon regarded himself as an un-reconstructed Baptist evangelical; an advocate of "soul-liberty," he always "made the necessity of regeneration . . . the centre of my message to a lost world."[37] Moreover, throughout his teaching career he regarded, as he once put it, "my relationship to my students" as a "sacred relationship." It was based on mutual confidence and respect and "spiritual power."[38]

During the 1903–4 academic year, McCrimmon pursued graduate studies at the University of Chicago. On his return to Woodstock, he was appointed, while still principal of Woodstock College, to a lectureship in political economy at McMaster University. In 1906 he was persuaded to leave Woodstock and join the faculty of McMaster as a full-time professor, occupying the chair of economics, education, and sociology.

In 1893, the year after he began teaching at Woodstock, McCrimmon published a very brief description of his philosophy of Christian education. As far as the twenty-eight-year-old McCrimmon was concerned, "the Highest Type of Human Character is Therefore the Christian Character. The Ideal For the Christian [and for Christian Education] is Jesus Christ, As Revealed in the Word of God. . . . Here we have combined the absolute surrender of individuality and its most intense assertion."[39] Eight years later McCrimmon developed his educational ideas at much greater length at another Baptist institution of higher learning when he spoke at Brandon College, on October 1, 1901, on the topic "Christian Education."[40] According to McCrimmon, "While it is the inalienable right of every man to have an education, it is the doubly emphasized responsibility for the Christian whose heart should be tender to God's teaching and whose will should be ready and anxious to do his work." Moreover, only Christian education molded the youthful mind in the image of Christ. The Woodstock principal then went on to assert that at the core of Christian education was the person of Christ:

> Our starting point is that we hold our connection with Christ as the supreme element in our lives. Identification with Him brings salvation to our souls. Identification with Him means that His thoughts are our thoughts and His work is our work. If we rear a structure whether of personal attainment or of objective work,

which has not the purpose of Christ in it, it means that the work perishes. Not every education will do. We desire not knowledge alone but that knowledge rightly articulated to the work of Christ.

For McCrimmon, true "Christian Education" had to—as he expressed it simply—"Honour the Body" and "the Intellect." Christian education was concerned not only with the minds of students but also with "the condition of the body." McCrimmon's Christian school was definitely not "some sort of goody-goody establishment where intellectual powers are at a discount." Rather, "the greatest intellects of this world are the intellects of Christian men. . . . It is only the Christian who has the proper motive to instigate him to the fullest development of the mind. It is the Christian alone who is in touch with the fountain of truth. In this age as in the preceding ones, the Christian teacher is the only safe one." For McCrimmon, "daily intercourse with Christian teachers" was the most "potent influence" for making students good moral citizens—even those who refused to become Christians.

Yet there was more to Christian education, of course, than the mere development of individual strengths within an evangelical environment. As far as McCrimmon was concerned, "the Christian college not only teaches how to develop the life but also instructs how to give that life for the benefit of mankind." He concluded his address on a powerful nationalistic note:

> When we view the opportunity before us our hearts warm with enthusiasm and inspiration. The desire to serve our country and our God, comes with ever increasing power. We are Canadians and we wish to see in Canada the highest type of manhood. Let us do our best to cultivate its people to nobility of character and purity of life. Let us grow them large because they are capable of such growth. Let us catch the sentiments of Dean Stanley when he said, "The heroes of mankind are the mountains, the highlands of the moral world. They diversify the monotony. They furnish the water shed of its history." The highest, holiest manhood must ever be our ideal.

For McCrimmon, Baptist education had a special role to play in creating Canadian "moral giants"—men and women who would tower over their contemporaries and be as "Cities upon the Hill" pointing in the direction of the New Jerusalem.

As chancellor of McMaster from 1911 to 1922, McCrimmon attempted to implement what he called his "missionary conception" of higher education. He often would refer to the evangelical Baptist "view of Christian Education which has led many of the men who have joined the staff of our colleges to leave even the pastorate that they might weave their Christian influence into the lives of developing young men and women destined in different callings in life."[41] For McCrimmon, "the Christian college is the natural and inevitable complement to the Christian home, the church and the Sunday school. The state schools are worthy of all praise as they direct students to the truth, but after all any truth is unrelated truth, is truth without its meaning for life, until it is centred in Christ, the Son of God and the God of truth."[42]

For Baptists, however, just any Christian college would not do. It would have to be a Baptist institution because of what McCrimmon felt was the crucial significance of the denominational "matrix" in Christian education.[43] He stressed the fact that "our mission in education is with the adolescent in the uncertain years of his youth when he is trying out his tentatives, striving in this direction and that, criticizing his social and religious relations, seeking his ideals, discovering his life-work." It was therefore incumbent on the Ontario and Quebec Baptist Convention to thrust

> Christ at the centre of [McMaster] life . . . so that His creative personality may organize and direct the developing powers, that to accomplish this purpose there are required Christian teachers, Christian conditions, continuous action of these personalities and conditions, and freedom to exercise such influences; that to furnish this continuous exercise of Christian influence, there must be adequate control so that there may be as great a guarantee as possible respecting the character of the teachers and the conditions; that as a Baptist determination we must act consistently with our principles, or not act at all.[44]

For McCrimmon, these "principles" were obviously contained in McMaster University's 1887 act of incorporation.

He proudly described in 1920 the McMaster he had helped shape into what he called a leading "Christian University in this Canada of ours."[45] At McMaster, the unique Baptist blend of pietism, soul liberty, and missionary outreach had greatly influenced each student "every day." The university, moreover,

> furnishes him with Christian teachers chosen because they are members of evangelical churches; it indoctrinates him with the principles of scholarship and civilization efficiently; it furnishes him with an atmosphere in which it is the natural and customary procedure to attend Church service; it gives the student a broad course of liberal culture in which to find himself and his sphere of work and at the same time gives an introduction to specialization . . . there is no thought too strenuous for its activity, no freedom too great for its chastened democracy; it is conducive to the cohesiveness and solidarity of our denomination and renders it a more effective fighting unit in the church militant; it furnishes . . . Christian leaders . . . it turns the thoughts of its Arts students to the ministry to keep them within calling distance; . . . it complements from a religious standpoint and under religious influences, the home, the church and the Sunday school, and at the same time complements from the educational standpoint the other universities of Canada.[46]

McMaster, in theory and in practice, according to McCrimmon, was emphatically not an introverted, morbidly introspective, defensive Baptist Bible College. Rather, it was a small Christian university, open to new scholarship, concerned with the preservation of Christian truth, but always within the context of "liberal culture." It obviously offered the best of both worlds—orthodox evangelicalism on the one hand and "strenuous thought" and specialization on the other. McCrimmon sincerely believed that he could energize McMaster with the potent mix of orthodoxy and innovation. Instead of energizing the institution, however, and using it to strengthen the convention, in the 1920s McCrimmon saw his beloved McMaster University help precipitate a furious denominational civil war, from which the convention has still not yet fully recovered.

The First World War threatened to destroy McCrimmon's McMaster even before T. T. Shields endeavored to accomplish this end in the 1920s. Despite a myriad of external and internal problems, McCrimmon successfully steered his institution through the war years. In the process his already fragile health suffered, and he found himself without the necessary physical and mental strength to deal constructively and energetically with the renewed and even more bitter fundamentalist-modernist controversy that engulfed the convention at McMaster during the years immediately following the end of hostilities. McCrimmon in 1920 felt compelled to inform his dean of arts that "owing to the persistent character of my sleeplessness and the fiendish delight it takes in making me super-nervous over the most trivial matters it was best that no further University correspondence should be sent to me."[47] The chancellor was immobilized. In 1921 the senate began to look for a replace-ment, and the next year Howard Primrose Whidden was named the new chancellor.

McCrimmon's illness may have had both physiological and psy-chological roots. He saw his idealized McMaster being transformed before his very eyes; the small "Christian university" intent on making good, pious Baptists was being transformed by the forces of change unleashed by the war into an increasingly secular institution of higher learning. Science and the social sciences were replacing Christian orthodoxy as the primary molders of student minds. McCrimmon found himself increasingly isolated. His conservative theology pushed him in the direction of fundamentalists such as T. T. Shields—people he instinctively disliked because of their spir-itual hubris, their violent language, and their vociferous alienation from Canadian cultural norms. At the same time, McCrimmon's deep concern about education and learning pushed him toward those liberal Christians who were increasingly committed to intel-lectual accommodation at the expense of orthodoxy. It is not surprising that McCrimmon was immobilized in 1920 and 1921, incapable of providing leadership and direction to his much-troubled convention and university.

On his retirement from the chancellorship, McCrimmon returned to teaching at McMaster. He was president of the Baptist Conven-tion of Ontario and Quebec for three terms between 1921 and 1932, and he also served as vice president of the Baptist World Alliance. Up to his death in 1935, McCrimmon was still teaching at McMas-ter—now located in Hamilton—where he had seen his small Baptist institution transformed into a largely secular university and an academic outpost of the new industrial order.[48]

Abraham Lincoln McCrimmon's obituary in the *Canadian Baptist* on April 25, 1935, captured the man as well as any contemporary analysis. According to the *Canadian Baptist*,

> the deep secret of his life was found in Christ. That was the centre he sought for himself and to that centre he sought to lead others. . . . He rejoiced in the intimations and certainties of immortality. How he loved in his classroom discussions to speak of the lines that went out into the unseen. His faith in his Saviour was as simple and humble as that of a child. In that faith he lived nobly, he laboured fruitfully, and he died triumphantly.

Such an obituary could never have been written about H. P. Whidden when he died in 1952. In fact, when his successor, G. P. Gilmour, wrote Whidden's official "tribute," there was a remarkable absence of any references to spiritual and religious gifts and attributes. After discussing briefly Whidden's successful defense at McMaster during the turbulent 1920s, Gilmour maintained:

> Graduates remember Howard Primrose Whidden chiefly as a man of striking appearance, unusual dignity and broad educational outlook. A goodly number of them remember him as a helpful personal friend, for he had a gift for friendship and became the confidant and adviser of many. . . . His staff knew him as a man who chose men and women with care, who inspired faith in the work of a small university, and who guided them more by gentle hints and wise suggestions than by orders or interference.[49]

Whidden was born in Antigonish, Nova Scotia, in 1870; after graduating from Acadia University in 1891, he studied theology at McMaster, where he received his B.D. degree in 1894. He did further graduate work at the University of Chicago and then served as a Baptist minister in Morden, Manitoba, and Galt, Ontario. In 1900 he was appointed professor of English and biblical literature at Brandon College. Three years later he accepted a call to the prestigious Northern Baptist Convention Church in Dayton, Ohio, where he served for almost nine years before returning in 1912 to Brandon as its president. He left Brandon in 1923 for McMaster. It should also be noted that he served as a Union member of Parliament from 1917 to 1921.

Whidden, as the *Winnipeg Tribune* correctly observed on June

28, 1939, was very "cool" and "suave" and handled pressure extremely well. "No matter how sharply he differed" from his critics, "one never saw him ruffled to the point of sarcasm and unkindness in debate."[50] He was, without question, a consummate academic politician. A close friend and president of the University of Western Ontario, W. Sherwood Fox, once wrote that Whidden had, since his early Brandon days, "revealed a natural flair for administration and the handling of people."[51] As far as Fox was concerned in 1941, Whidden had been chosen as McMaster's chancellor in 1922 because of his administrative gifts and not because of his spirituality. In fact, the evidence suggests that Whidden had definitely moved from a conservative evangelical position in the late 1890s to a liberal Christian position in the 1920s, far beyond McCrimmon's conservative evangelicalism.

A persistent and persuasive advocate of modernity and progress, and a man closely associated with the Ontario business elite, an active Mason, and a committed Conservative in politics, Whidden was perceived by many members of McMaster's board of governors—many of whom were key members of the Canadian business elite—as just the man to lead the university out of the dark forests of theological backwardness into the North American mainstream of success and respectability. He was in so many ways the perfect "organic intellectual," determined to win the support of the traditional Canadian Baptists in what Gramsci has called "the new social, economic order." McCrimmon, who had tried to walk the knife edge between the nineteenth century and the twentieth by finding his theological bearings in a distant past had failed to solve McMaster's problems. Moreover, he was profoundly suspicious of various aspects of capitalism and consumerism. Perhaps, Whidden thought, he could influence McMaster positively, not by looking backward but forward, his vision unencumbered either by embarrassing evangelical outcroppings or by seemingly outmoded rural values.

Whidden's insensitivity to the fundamentalist criticism of McMaster's apparent move to modernism in the 1920s undoubtedly played a key role in bringing about the bitter split in the convention. Whidden, of course, was not responsible for the split. A myriad of complex forces merged in the mid-1920s to bring it about.[52] Yet he could have done more to placate the fundamentalists—but probably not enough. Perhaps only the replacement of Whidden by Shields would have persuaded the followers of Shields to remain in the convention.

As might have been expected, Whidden said little and wrote little about Christian higher education. Evidently he was far more interested in actually getting things done at McMaster than in talking about what might be done. He was always the pragmatic Nova Scotian, far more concerned with present realities than with spinning theories off into the imagination.

In his inaugural address, given in November 1923, Chancellor Whidden clearly revealed how his philosophy of education differed from that of his predecessor. It was a very brief address, and one of the few available statements that Whidden ever published about education.[53] There were only eleven brief paragraphs in Whidden's speech.[54] The first seven dealt with his predecessors, McVicar, Rand, Wallace, McKay, and McCrimmon. He also made passing mention of the "fine Christian idealism" and "rugged confidence" of Senator William McMaster. Then Whidden very briefly discussed what he referred to as "Certain Essentials of Liberal Education." The word *Christian* or the word *Christ* was not mentioned even once in the body of the new chancellor's speech. It was Whidden's contention that

> the chief business of the smaller university is to furnish a liberal education. If, as Kant said, "Man's greatest concern is to know how he shall properly fill his place in the universe and understand what he must be in order to be a man," then education is, as Galsworthy recently said, the sacred concern, indeed the only hope of the nation. *Liberal education should seek to relate the individual to his universe.* I refer more especially to the universe of things. Think of all that nature has in store for those who are willing to learn the simple yet sublime laws of nature.

It is noteworthy that Whidden underscored only one sentence in the first section of his speech: "*Liberal education should seek to relate the individual to the universe.*" No mention was made of McMaster's motto, "In Christ All Things Consist." No mention, moreover, was made of "Truth" being "centered in Christ." And Whidden was strangely silent about any special aspect of Christian education, either narrowly or broadly defined.

After discussing generally the rise of "the great newer sciences . . . Physics . . . Chemistry, Biology and Geology," Whidden suddenly declared, "Through these four the modern world has largely become what it is." He then went on:

> As a result of the application of scientific knowledge the stellar spaces have been measured and brought near, the subtle forces hidden in air and earth and sea have been harnessed and made to serve man's need. The whole development and structure of material things in past ages is brought within our ken; the life of plant and animal is so much better understood that human life is conserved in previously unthought of ways. In connection with all this there has gone on steadily an emancipation of the mind of man with regard to the dominance of the material.

Thus, for Whidden the "newer sciences"—not the Bible, not Christ, not fundamentalism—had brought about the modern "emancipation of the mind." Scientific knowledge and not evangelical orthodoxy—and not even experiential Christianity—had led to true freedom, the "emancipation of the mind."

Even though he did not expect that the "newer sciences" would produce great specialists at McMaster, Whidden nevertheless hoped that they would produce intelligent students aware of the basic rudiments of "modern scientific" life. But, building a bridge in his argument to other areas of the university, Whidden agreed with John Tyndall, the English scientist, that "it is not through science, nor through literature that human nature is made whole, but through a fusion of both." He developed this argument a little further:

> We see then how natural it is to urge that in a truly liberal educational programme recognition be given to the study of universal things in human life. *The mind of youth must be brought into sympathetic acquaintance with the best there is in the experience of man.* There is still need for the classics as well as for modern language and literature. If the coming leaders of thought and action are to know the best that has been thought or said in other days, the old humanities must not be thrown to the discard.

So in the second part of his inaugural address Whidden underlined one other sentence, a sentence he must have regarded as being especially heavy with meaning. "*The mind of youth*," he stressed "*must be brought into sympathetic acquaintance with the best there is in the experience of man*." Whidden had thrown his knowledge net over the entire "experience of man," not only a tiny section of it, and had urged all of his teachers to bring their students "into sympathetic acquaintance" with the best there was in the "experience of man."

McMaster's sixth chancellor then concluded his address with a call for a greater interest in and awareness of the "New Humanities." The historical, social, and political sciences, he asserted, "must be more vitally understood and set forth if we are rightly to orient the student into his world of citizenship."

By the 1920s virtually every Canadian Protestant institution of higher learning had evolved in the McMaster manner (most of them, however, had moved at a far more accelerated rate), even its sister Baptist university in Nova Scotia. Moreover, by the 1920s all the mainline Protestant seminaries had abandoned the nineteenth-century conservative evangelical consensus and replaced it with an accommodating liberalism. Being a committed Christian in the inter-war years provided little advantage, it should be stressed, for the applicant for a teaching position at, for example, Acadia, Mount Allison, McMaster, Brandon, or Victoria University.

The secularization of Protestant higher education in Canada was accompanied, it should be noted, by the extraordinary growth of the Bible school movement.[55] It is sometimes forgotten that in the period after the First World War there were, in per capita terms, far more Canadians in Bible schools in Canada then there were Americans in American Bible schools. In a sense, Bible schools in Canada became the new institutions of higher learning for the besieged fundamentalists and conservative evangelicals. And they continue to perform this role in the latter part of the twentieth century as they themselves try to find an acceptable location in the North American academic mainstream. The transformation of many of the Bible colleges into accredited academic institutions is a fascinating development and one that certainly demands serious study.

Paralleling the Bible school transformation have been the attempts at Trinity Western University in British Columbia, Redeemer College in Ancaster-Hamilton, and St. Stephen University in New Brunswick to emulate the American evangelical college example.

Trinity Western, by any number of criteria, has been a remarkable success, and Redeemer continues to amaze even its most caustic and pessimistic critics.[56] St. Stephen, by contrast, largely because of the absence of any denominational base and because of its failure to understand the culture of New Brunswick, has been an embarrassing failure. During the 1988–89 academic year, for example, there were only four full-time students at St. Stephen and five faculty members. (Some—including Stephen Leacock—might say that here indeed was the ideal Christian university.)

These attempts to create Wheatons and Calvins north of the forty-ninth parallel, as well as the transformation of the Bible schools, have not, of course, been the only efforts on the part of Protestants in recent years to organize a counter-offensive in the areas of Christian higher education. The affiliated church college approach of the University of Waterloo, Laurentian University, and the universities of Manitoba, Regina, Saskatchewan, and Alberta was more than an attempt to build on institutional structures from the nineteenth century. It was a reflection of a growing conviction, in a variety of denominations, that learning, teaching, and scholarship in a Christian environment was both essential and possible. The affiliated college approach, of course, has been both a success and a failure—a success for Mennonites, Lutherans, and Christian Reformed, and an embarrassing failure for Anglicans and the United Church.

Despite the fact that, by a variety of indicators, Canada is more secularized than the United States, in recent years church-related colleges have made a remarkable recovery, especially in the Canadian West. Christian higher education in Canada may, in fact, be entering the first phase of an extended renaissance. This so-called Great Reversal may be traced to a number of complex forces coming together in the post-1970 period. First, a variety of Canadian denominations, notably Christian Reformed, Lutheran, and Mennonite, have become increasingly concerned about providing a Christian-based undergraduate education for their younger members and adherents. Disenchanted with what they see in the large, impersonal secular institutions, leaders of these and other denominations have looked to the Canadian past and to the United States for their inspiration.

Second, such denominational colleges have been encouraged by provincial governmental funding policies. For example, in Alberta and Manitoba church-supported and church-controlled colleges receive from the state 50 percent of the Basic Income Unit for undergraduates. In Saskatchewan the percentage is 70 percent. This kind of financing, of course, is a real source of encouragement to advocates of denominational colleges.

Third, some evidence suggests that a few of the larger Canadian universities want to surrender more and more of their undergraduate teaching responsibilities in the humanities and social sciences to the burgeoning denominational colleges. Desiring to be centers of technological and graduate excellence, these larger universities are eager to brush the crumbs from their table in the direction of the denominational colleges. And these colleges are not afraid to pick up these crumbs eagerly, realizing that by carefully controlling new appointments—only those who accept the doctrinal position of the college need apply—they are able to receive considerable state funding for denominational purposes. As the provincial governments confront the thorny problem of increased funding for the universities, they may also turn to the denominational colleges to help them save money. In the process, existing governments may be winning badly needed political support from a variety of Protestant denominations.

Despite the shrill lamentations of the prophets of academic doom, to which I add my own, there are still these hopeful signs. Although rates of religious practice may be higher in the United States, Canadian society may be more open to encouraging genuine religious pluralism.

Notes

1. J. W. Bengough, *Motley: Verses Grave and Gay* (Toronto, 1895), 166.

2. See George M. Marsden's unpublished paper "The Soul of the American University," presented at the Cape Cod Seminar in American Evangelical Studies, July 8, 1989, 1.

3. Ibid.

4. T. J. Jackson Lears, *No Place of Grace: Antimodernism and the Transformation of American Culture, 1880–1920* (New York, 1981), xvii.

5. Karl Marx and Friedrich Engels, *The Communist Manifesto* (New York, 1964), 63.

6. D. W. Frank, *Less Than Conquerors: How Evangelicals Entered the Twentieth Century* (Grand Rapids, 1986), 222.

7. Quoted ibid., 277.

8. For a more detailed analysis of this transformation process, see my "A. L. McCrimmon, H. O. Whidden, T. T. Shields, Christian Higher Education, and McMaster University," in *Canadian Baptists and Christian Higher Education*, ed. G. A. Rawlyk (Kingston, 1988), 31–62, 118–22.

9. See his "Breadth of Vision, Breadth of Mind: The Baptists and Acadia College," in Rawlyk, *Canadian Baptists*, 28.

10. Quoted in Moody, "Breadth of Vision," 25.

11. R. S. Wilson, "John Mocket Cramp as a Church Historian," in *An Abiding Conviction: Maritime Baptists and Their World*, ed. R. S. Wilson (Hantsport, 1988), 148.

12. C. D. Johnson, *Islands of Holiness: Rural Religion in Upstate New York, 1790–1860* (Ithaca, 1989), 155.

13. I. Wallace, *Autobiographical Sketch with Reminiscences of Revival Work* (Halifax, 1903), 16.

14. Ibid., 16–17.

15. P. Palmer, *Promises of the Father* (Boston, 1859), 301–7.

16. *Christian Messenger* (Halifax), May 8, 1867.

17. Ibid.

18. See Rawlyk, "A. L. McCrimmon," 31–34.

19. See Antonio Gramsci, *Selections from the Prison Notebooks* (New York, 1971). This quotation is from Paul Craven, *"An Impartial Umpire": Industrial Relations and the Canadian State, 1900–1911* (Toronto, 1981), 15.

20. Quoted in Craven, *"An Impartial Umpire,"* 16.

21. See Frank, *Less Than Conquerors*, 222–23.

22. Charles Johnston, *McMaster University: The Toronto Years*, vol. 1 (Toronto, 1976), 40.

23. N. W. Rowell to H. P. Whidden, May 30, 1928, Whidden Papers, Canadian Baptist Archives, McMaster University, Hamilton (hereafter cited as CBA).

24. *Baptist Year Book* (1883), 75.

25. See Johnston, *McMaster University*, I, 73.

26. R. W. Fox and T. J. Jackson Lears, eds., *The Culture of Consumption* (New York, 1983), xiii.

27. *McMaster University Monthly* 5 (1895), 100–105.

28. T. P. Hall to Wallace, December 17, 1895, Wallace Papers, CBA. The quotation is to be found in Johnston, *McMaster University*, I, 72.

29. See Johnston, *McMaster University*, I, 70–84.

30. Minutes of McMaster University Senate, May 29, 1909, Senate Papers, CBA.

31. Ibid., December 2, 1909.

32. W. S. M. McLay to McKay, May 17, 1911, McLay Papers, CBA.

33. *Simcoe Reformer*, April 15, 1935.

34. Ibid.

35. Ibid.

36. Ibid.

37. "Baptists Facing the Future," n.d., McCrimmon Papers, CBA.

38. Ibid.

39. *McMaster University Monthly* (February 1893).

40. All quotations in McCrimmon Papers, CBA.

41. See A. L. McCrimmon, *The Educational Policy of the Baptists of Ontario and Quebec* (Toronto, 1920), 9.

42. Ibid., 21.

43. Ibid., 22.

44. Ibid., 25.

45. Ibid., 31.

46. Ibid., 26.

47. *McMaster University Alumni News*, May 4, 1935.

48. For McCrimmon's critique of the new McMaster, see his essay "The Preservation of the Christian Character and of the Denominational Control of McMaster University" (1930), in the McCrimmon Papers, CBA.

49. *McMaster University Alumni News*, May 23, 1952.

50. *Canadian Baptist*, April 15, 1952.

51. Fox to the McMaster University Alumni Office, June 1, 1941, CBA.

52. See W. E. Ellis, "Social and Religious Factors in the Fundamentalist Modernist Schisms among Baptists in North America, 1895–1935" (Ph.D. diss., University of Pittsburgh, 1974).

53. Whidden, "What Is a Liberal Education?" *Canadian Journal of Religious Thought*, 1 (1924), is obviously a boiled-down version of his 1923 address.

54. All quotations in *Canadian Baptist*, November 22, 1923.

55. See J. Stackhouse, "Proclaiming the Word: Canadian Evangelicalism since World War I" (Ph.D. diss., University of Chicago, 1988), 55–116.

56. See ibid., 195–206.

11

Christianity and the University in America: A Bibliographical Essay

D. G. HART

Since the founding of the History of Education Society and its journal, the *History of Education Quarterly*, in 1960, the history of American higher education has grown in scope and sophistication. Once primarily the domain of retired professors reminiscing about developments at their local campuses, the history of colleges and universities has become almost as complex as the subject it examines. No longer content with institutional histories, biographies of university presidents, or chronicles of their administrations' accomplishments, historians of higher education have turned to student populations, alumni, academic disciplines, curriculum, the social function of undergraduate education, and the status of the faculty. Yet, for all this intricacy the study of religion and higher education remains remarkably simple. It is still bound to a perception that traces the weakening if not the actual subversion of Protestant churches' cultural authority to the rise of universities and the specialized scientific research they fostered. Of course, not all historians accepted this view. Still, the perception of American higher educational history as moving from sectarian and pious colleges to enlightened and secular universities, what James Axtell called "Whig historiography" in "The Death of the Liberal Arts College," *History of Education Quarterly* 10 (1971) 339–52, was the common understanding presented not only in introductory lectures and textbooks but also in learned journals.

The failure of educational historians to weave religion into the tapestry of higher education stems in part from bad timing. The history of American universities took a substantial leap forward during the 1950s and 1960s with the publication of four works: Richard Hofstadter and Walter P. Metzger, *The Development of Academic Freedom in the United States* (New York: Columbia University Press, 1955); John S. Brubach and Willis Rudy, *Higher Education in Transition* (New York: Harper and Row, 1976); Frederick Rudolph, *The American College and University* (New York: Knopf, 1962); and Laurence Veysey, *The Emergence of the American University* (Chicago: University of Chicago Press, 1965). These studies treated education properly as part of intellectual history and consequently gave considerable attention to the late nineteenth-century shift from a religious to a scientific orientation in academic circles with the rise of universities. The subsequent application of social history to higher education, however, froze in place the warfare-between-religion-and-science imagery established by Hofstadter and Metzger. As historians of colleges and universities featured the social function of higher education over the topics taught or discoveries made by academics, the place of religion in American universities received little if any examination.

Of course, the conventional view of American higher education was ripe for revision. The most fruitful area of study was the antebellum college. Historians of higher education, who sought to overturn the notion that the era of the denominational college was a time of "great retrogression," did so in a variety of ways. For instance, David Allmendinger, *Paupers and Scholars* (New York: St. Martin's, 1975), and Colin Burke, *American Collegiate Populations* (New York: New York University Press, 1982), showed that colleges were neither as elitist and exclusive as commonly thought, nor was their decline in numbers as severe as many have supposed. Wilson Smith, "Apologia pro Alma Mater: The College as Community in Ante-Bellum America," in *The Hofstadter Aegis, A Memorial*, ed. Eric McKitrick and Stanley Elkins (New York: Knopf, 1974), 125–53, surveyed college reminiscences to argue that most graduates perceived their education in a positive light, and that Henry Adams's complaints about poor teaching and student unhappiness were the exception. Marilyn Tobias, *Old Dartmouth on Trial* (New York: New York University Press, 1982), demonstrated the powerful effect of alumni concerns and pressures in transforming the scholarly aspirations of an institution. Meanwhile, Stanley Guralnick, *Science and the Ante-Bellum College* (Philadelphia: American Philosophical Society, 1975); Frederick Rudolph, *Curriculum: A History of the American Undergraduate Course of Study since 1636* (San Francisco: Jossey-Bass, 1977); and Louise Stevenson, *Scholarly Means to Evangelical Ends* (Baltimore: Johns Hopkins University Press, 1986), put to rest the idea that the old classical curriculum resembled "a prison guarding a subject population." It should be noted that this revisionist history has its detractors. One of the most sustained critiques comes in Bruce A. Kimball's *Orators and Philosophers* (New York: Teachers College Press, 1986), appendix I.

Still, challenges to received wisdom focused on antebellum colleges and failed to apply revisionist insights to the university. Indeed, most revisionist accounts have read the university and its curriculum, ideals, and sophistication back into the antebellum colleges, thereby leaving the conventional image of the university intact. This is especially true in the area of religion, where Guralnick, Stevenson, Rudolph, and others have soft-pedaled the religious influence on the colleges in order to find greater continuity between college and university education. Just as the importance of scientific research in universities resulted in the demise of religious authority, the argument goes, so the teaching of science at the antebellum colleges meant a slackening of religious zeal.

Educational historians have been hard-pressed to look at the rise of universities from a perspective other than the warfare perspective because of the prevalence of older interpretations of the impact of Darwinism. This aspect of the historiography is readily understandable in older works such as Hofstadter and Metzger, *Development of Academic Freedom*; Veysey, *Emergence of the American University*; Hugh Hawkins, *Pioneer: A History of The Johns Hopkins University* (Baltimore: Johns Hopkins University Press, 1960); Winton U. Solberg, *The University of Illinois, 1867–1894: An Intellectual and Cultural History* (Urbana: University of Illinois Press, 1968); and J. Richard Storr, *Harper's University: The Beginnings: A History of the University of Chicago* (Chicago: University of Chicago Press, 1966). These histories, of course, did not reflect the efforts, for instance, of James R. Moore, *The Post-Darwinian Controversies* (New York: Cambridge University Press, 1979), and Jon H. Roberts, *Darwinism and the Divine in America* (Madison: University of Wisconsin Press, 1988), which show how late nineteenth-century Protestants accommodated evolution with relative ease. Still, more recent works, such as Stevenson, *Scholarly Means to Evangelical Ends*; David Hollinger, "Justification by Verification: The Scientific Challenge to the Moral Authority of Christianity in Modern America," in *Religion and Twentieth-Century American Intellectual Life*, ed. Michael J. Lacey (Cambridge: Cambridge University Press, 1989), 116–34; and William C. Ringenberg, *The Christian College: A History of Protestant Higher Education in America* (Grand Rapids: Eerdmans, 1984), continue to cite Darwinian controversies as the context for the struggles that American universities and their scholars encountered and for the demise of religion in the academy. Aside from George Marsden, "The Collapse of American Evangelical Academia," in *Faith and Rationality*, ed. Alvin Plantinga and Nicholas Wolterstorff (Notre Dame: University of Notre Dame Press, 1983), 219–64, and Mark A. Noll, "Christian Thinking and the Rise of the American University," *Christian Scholar's Review* 9 (1979), 3–16, who consider the legacy of evangelical moral philosophy, historians have rarely looked beyond Darwinism to understand the effects of science on religion's demise within the university.

Because of the widespread impression of hostility between religion and the modern academy, little work has been done on the role of religion in American universities. Exceptions to this observation are David J. Hoeveler, Jr., "The University and the Social Gospel: The Intellectual Origins of the Wisconsin Idea," *Wisconsin Magazine of History* 59 (1976), 282–98; James Tunstead Burtchaell, "The Decline and Fall of the Christian College," *First Things* 12 (April 1991), 17–29, and 13 (May 1991), 30–38; Robert S. Shepard, *God's People in the Ivory Tower: Religion in the Early American University* (Brooklyn: Carlson Publishing, 1991); and Edward Schaffer, "The Protestant Ideology of the American University: Past and Future Prospects," *Educational Theory* 40 (1990), 19–34. Still, a number of works have been written on educational and intellectual topics that shed light on Christianity and the university.

Several institutional histories are valuable for exploring the impact of university methods and ideals on older religious commitments. They include Hugh Hawkins, *Pioneer*; Stevenson, *Scholarly Means to Evangelical Ends*; Samuel Eliot Morison, *Three Centuries of Harvard* (Cambridge, MA: Harvard University Press, 1936); Solberg, *The University of Illinois*; idem, "The Catholic Presence at the University of Illinois," *The Catholic Historical Review* 76 (1990), 765–812; Morris Bishop, *A History of Cornell* (Ithaca: Cornell University Press, 1962); Ralph Henry Gabriel, *Religion and Learning at Yale* (New Haven: Yale University Press, 1958); Storr, *Harper's University*; and James M. Turner and Paul Bernard, "The Prussian Road to University? German Models and the University of Michigan," *Rackham Reports* (1988–1989), 6–52.

Biographical studies of important educators provide further access to religious tensions within academic institutions. Among the most useful are Hugh Hawkins, *Between Harvard and America: The Educational Leadership of Charles W. Eliot* (New York: Oxford University Press, 1972); John Mulder, *Woodrow Wilson* (Princeton: Princeton University Press, 1978); Glenn C. Altschuler, *Andrew D. White* (Ithaca: Cornell University Press, 1979); Harry S. Ashmore, *Unseasonable Truths: The Life of Robert Maynard Hutchins* (Boston: Little, Brown, 1989); James P. Wind, *The Bible and the University: The Messianic Vision of William Rainey Harper* (Atlanta: Scholars Press, 1987) and Paul C. Kemeny, "President Francis Landey Patton, Princeton University, and Faculty Ferment," *American Presbyterians* 69 (1991), 111–21.

An especially fruitful area of study has been the history of academic disciplines, which also reveals the way disciplinary debates bore upon the place of Christianity in the university. Histories of the social sciences have stressed religious impulses in the origins of these disciplines. Among the important works are Mary O. Furner, *Advocacy and Objectivity* (Lexington: University of Kentucky Press, 1975); Thomas L. Haskell, *The Emergence of Professional Social Science* (Urbana: University of Illinois Press, 1977); Arthur J. Vidich and Stanford M. Lyman, *American Sociology* (New Haven: Yale University Press, 1985); and Dorothy Ross, *The Origins of American Social Science* (Cambridge: Cambridge University Press, 1991). For developments in philosophy, Bruce Kuklick, *Rise of American Philosophy* (Cambridge: Cambridge University Press,

1977), and Daniel J. Wilson, *Science, Community, and the Transformation of American Philosophy, 1860–1930* (Chicago: University of Chicago Press, 1990), provide important insights. In addition, Kermit Vanderbilt, *American Literature and the Academy* (Philadelphia: University of Pennsylvania Press, 1986), and Peter Novick, *That Noble Dream* (New York: Cambridge University Press, 1988), illustrate the way academic ideals shape the teaching and study of literature and history, respectively. Of related interest are works on the specialization and professionalization of learning such as Burton J. Bledstein, *The Culture of Professionalism* (New York: W. W. Norton, 1978); Alexandra Oleson and John Voss, eds., *The Organization of Knowledge in Modern America* (Baltimore: Johns Hopkins University Press, 1979); Thomas L. Haskell, ed., *The Authority of Experts* (Bloomington: Indiana University Press, 1984); and Laurence Veysey, "Higher Education as a Profession: Changes and Continuities," in *The Professions in American History*, ed. Nathan O. Hatch (Notre Dame: University of Notre Dame Press, 1988), 15–32. The impact of these changes on the undergraduate curriculum at American universities is discussed in Rudolph's *Curriculum*; Laurence Veysey, "Stability and Experiment in the American Undergraduate Curriculum," in *Content and Context*, ed. Carl Kaysen (New York: McGraw-Hill, 1973), 1–64; and Douglas Sloan, "The Teaching of Ethics in the American Undergraduate Curriculum, 1876–1976," in *Education and Values*, ed. Douglas Sloan (New York: Teachers College Press, 1980), 191–254.

A critical theme in intellectual history is the shift in the orientation of American learned discourse from the church to the academy. Works that make this point well are Bruce Kuklick, *Churchmen and Philosophers* (New Haven: Yale University Press, 1985); Thomas Bender, *New York Intellectuals* (New York: Alfred A. Knopf, 1987); and Lewis Perry, *Intellectual Life in America* (New York: Franklin Watts, 1984).

A related issue to the topic of Christianity and the university concerns the nature of academic freedom. Despite the implicit antagonism between faith and learning assumed in Metzger and Hofstadter, *Academic Freedom*, most cases involving the abridgement of academic freedom at American universities have resulted from controversies over political and economic views. In addition to the work of Metzger and Hofstadter, Carol S. Gruber, *Mars and*

Minerva (Baton Rouge: Louisiana State University Press, 1975), and Ellen W. Schrecker, *No Ivory Tower* (New York: Oxford University Press, 1986), are worthwhile for tracing the effects of politics on the academy. Little has been written on religion and academic freedom. But the essays in Edward Manier and John W. Houck, eds., *Academic Freedom and the Catholic University* (Notre Dame: University of Notre Dame Press, 1967), furnish one place to begin.

The most fruitful and least studied topic that illuminates the interplay between the Christian and the university is the teaching and study of religion at both university divinity schools and religion departments. Robert Michaelsen, *The Study of Religion in American Universities* (New Haven: Yale University Press, 1965); John F. Wilson's introduction to *The Study of Religion in Colleges and Universities*, ed. John F. Wilson and Paul Ramsey (Princeton: Princeton University Press, 1970); Harold E. Remus, E. Stanley Lusby, and Linda M. Tober, "Religion as an Academic Discipline," in *Encyclopedia of American Religious Experience*, vol. 3, ed. Charles H. Lippy and Peter W. Williams (New York: Scribners, 1988), 1653–69; and Murray G. Murphy, "On the Scientific Study of Religion in the United States, 1870–1980," in Lacey, *Religion and Twentieth-Century American Intellectual Life*, 136–71, are instructive but do not explore the subject in great detail.

Index

311